SAVING THE EARTH

SAVING THE EARTH

A Citizen's Guide to Environmental Action

by

WILL STEGER
and
JON BOWERMASTER

Illustrations by Mike Mikos

A Byron Preiss Book

ALFRED A. KNOPF
New York

THIS IS A BORZOI BOOK
PUBLISHED BY ALFRED A. KNOPF, INC.

Copyright © 1990 by Byron Preiss Visual Publications, Inc.
Text copyright © 1990 by Byron Preiss Visual Publications,
Inc., Will Steger, and Jon Bowermaster.

All rights reserved under International and Pan-American Copyright
Conventions. Published in the United States by Alfred A. Knopf, Inc.,
New York, and simultaneously in Canada by Random House of Canada
Limited, Toronto. Distributed by Random House, Inc., New York.

Library of Congress Cataloging-in-Publication Data
Steger, Will.
Saving the earth.
1. Environmental protection—Citizen participation.
I. Bowermaster, Jon, 1954-   . II. Title.
TD171.7.S74   1990   363.7'0525   89-43366
ISBN 0-679-73026-5
Manufactured in the United States of America
First Edition

Produced by Byron Preiss Visual Publications, Inc.
Associate Editor: Megan Miller
Photo Editor: Patty Delahanty
Front cover photograph by Geoff Spear
Front cover design by Chip Kidd

Diagrams by Isaac Victor Kerlow

This book is sold with the understanding that the storyboard illustrations
only may be reproduced by community groups, individuals, and institutions
on a not-for-profit educational basis without payment or special permission,
provided said individuals or institutions include the credit: "From *Saving the
Earth* © 1990 Byron Preiss Visual Publications, Inc. Illustrations by Mike
Mikos," and forward a copy of the publication in which they are used to
Byron Preiss Visual Publications, Inc., 24 West 25th Street, New York,
NY 10010. Said permission does not apply to any photograph or any other
illustration in this book whatsoever.

Grateful acknowledgment is given to Wendell Berry for his permission to
reprint an excerpt from his commencement speech, "Word and Flesh,"
delivered at the College of the Atlantic in Bar Harbor, Maine in June 1989.

For future generations,
in hope the Earth will remain a comfortable,
safe environment for all humankind,
for centuries to come.

CONTENTS

THE ATMOSPHERE

THE LAND

CONTENTS

THE WATER

THE PEOPLE

CONSULTANTS

ENVIRONMENTAL EDITORIAL CONSULTANT
Joyce E. Rosenthal
Assistant Director
Council on the Environment of New York City

RESEARCH CONSULTANTS

INFORM, Inc.
New York, New York

Natural Resources Defense Council
New York, New York

Pollution Probe Foundation
Toronto, Ontario

SPECIAL CONSULTANTS
Dorene Bolze
National Audubon Society

James S. Cannon
INFORM, Inc.

Maarten De Kadt
INFORM, Inc.

David Doniger
Natural Resources Defense Council

Mark H. Dorfman
INFORM, Inc.

Joe Kane
Rainforest Action Network

Bruce Manheim
Environmental Defense Fund

Nina Sankovitch
Natural Resources Defense Council

Jonathan Scott
Clean Water Action

Dianne Sherman
Zero Population Growth

Lisa Speer
Natural Resources Defense Council

Mark Trexler
World Resources Institute

PREFACE

This book is the result of a long search for a guidebook that proved nonexistent,
a book that provided lucid, understandable explanations of the causes, effects,
and solutions to the fast-growing environmental ills that face the world today. Witnessing the
effects of pollution on Antarctica made the urgency of the task even more apparent.

We have assembled *Saving the Earth* as a resource of information, text, diagrams, photos, illustrations,
lists, bibliographies, and advice. The text offers, in layman's terms, a short history of each type of pollution,
its causes and effects, and suggests solutions that are within the reach of individuals, communities, corporations,
and governments. The storyboards that end each chapter serve as a visual guide to the text, illustrating
the problem in diagrams and pictures. Concluding each chapter are specific recommendations that
individuals and governments can follow in helping to slow environmental degradation. If you want to learn
more about the chapter's topic, there are lists of both books and articles to read and groups to contact for
more information. A general list of environmental organizations, along with explanations
of each group's concerns and specializations, concludes the book.

We could not address *every* single environmental problem. As a result, drift-net fishing, the desertification
of millions of acres of arable land, sustainable agriculture, and nuclear testing and weapons production are
not discussed at length. That is not to suggest that they are "lesser" evils. We chose to concentrate on
the most public problems, with the hope that individuals *can* make a difference in solving them.

As for individuals who helped smooth this project into print, we'd like to thank again the experts who
advised us on each chapter—Joyce Rosenthal, who read the book from start to finish and offered wise
counsel, and Mia Fienemann and her associates at INFORM, Inc.; Cathy Dold at NRDC; Jonathan Segal, Ida
Giragossian, and Andy Hughes at Alfred A. Knopf; Stuart Krichevsky; Cathy deMoll and the Trans-Antarctica
Expedition office; Mike Mikos and his assistants, Aric Liljegren and Mike Mantas; Cathy Saypol; Patty
Delahanty and everyone else at Byron Preiss Visual Publications, most importantly Megan Miller.

—W.S., J.B.

INTRODUCTION

By Will Steger

By the time I stepped off the plane onto the ice of Antarctica in July 1989, I had already thought many times of my first trip to Alaska 26 years before. I was 19 and had come to kayak the Yukon with a boyhood friend. Alaska then was a true frontier, unexploited by man or enterprise. It is twice the size of Texas, and much of it was unexplored. We spent that summer hiking, paddling, and climbing the natural wonders of the majestic state. We surprised feeding bears, trailed packs of wolves, caught 30-pound trout, and saw the remnants of the cabins built in the 1890s by speculators who had come north in search of gold. We took away a unique perspective on America's last great wilderness.

It was an exciting, occasionally sobering adventure, yet I was enthralled by the place and the people. Most of the native Alaskans we encountered lived there simply because they loved their state and the wilderness. They were filled with a spirit I've rarely experienced since—drawn to the land by a desire to know it better. Their lives were full and challenging; for all the hardship there were sizable rewards. Most were homesteading, making do by fishing and barter. They were driven, it seemed, by a constant sense of wonderment. Their spirit, combined with the daily challenge of coping with the often brutal elements, so captured me that I almost stayed.

Despite bouts of loneliness and fear, I couldn't wait to return. I had discovered a kind of excitement that only that kind of wilderness can engender. The very next summer—accompanied by Ole Olson, a friend since grade school—I kayaked the Mackenzie River system, a 3,000-mile journey from the Canadian Rockies, across Alaska to the Arctic Ocean. On that trip we rarely saw people, or even signs of them, for weeks at a time. I remember how my heart would jump anytime we heard a plane in the distance. We would wade into the river just to wave hello. While it didn't strike me at the time, it is ironic that most of the planes that flew overhead bore oil company logos. One such fly-by is permanently etched in my memory. A single-engined craft buzzed us, tipping its wings hello. The bright red and yellow Shell Oil mark on its tail stood in stark contrast to the greens and browns and blues of the wilds. At the time it was a welcome sign, granting us a brief, high-altitude contact with other men. But in retrospect it was an omen, a bad omen, signaling the end of the wilderness as we were seeing it.

Over the next few years that same wilderness began to attract increasing numbers of visitors. Kayaking the Yukon became popular and the previously pristine woods were marred by the influx. The gold miners' cabins we had explored were destroyed. New camps sprang up along the Yukon—as well as the Mackenzie and Athabasca rivers—filled with new gold diggers: oil company men. Their growing presence shouldn't have surprised us, really. Government and private industry had been exploring these areas for oil since the 1920s. The seemingly overnight proliferation of so many oil men was due to the staggering rise in consumption in the Lower 48, which drove the search for domestic oil at an ever faster pace.

In 1969 Ole and I returned to the north and kayaked the Yukon once more. After an exhausting three months we reached the Arctic Ocean, exhilarated but penniless. We hired on with an Indian fire-fighting crew to earn money to fly home. By then the signs of exploitation that the oil explorations of the past few years had brought were everywhere. A refinery sat on the shore of Lake Athabasca. Many of the native trackers and hunters we'd met on previous trips were now employed dredging for oil. Branches of the rivers glimmered with a shiny new blue-black coat. The pipeline that would soon split the north in two was the talk of the region.

The pipeline would change Alaska forever. A steady migration of hopefuls—lured by promises of $90,000- and $100,000-a-year jobs—flocked north. The AlCan Highway was jammed with station wagons and pickup trucks loaded with people and their belongings, most from states with high unemployment. They'd come north with the understanding that the oil boom would last forever and that cheap land would go on sale soon. When state officials delayed the sale for months, many of the new immigrants lived out of their cars, in the woods and on the side of the road. It was like a scene from *The Grapes of Wrath*. The spirit of the place that I'd so admired was already waning. Competition, not cooperation, had become the predominant motive.

The next summer—between semesters of my secondary-school teaching job—I hitchhiked to Fairbanks, Alaska, from my home in Minnesota. I was stunned; the beautiful city that I had first seen in 1963 was now a nightmare. There was a bar on every corner, and the streets were a riot of cars bearing license plates from all over the United States and Canada. The sidewalks were filled with men, five and six abreast, waiting for their unemployment checks from back home. The spirit of Alaska that had so captured me was gone. I was forced to take my explorations deeper into the wilds.

But even as I forged further into the Arctic it became difficult to escape the signs of human intervention. In 1985 I dogsledded from my cabin near Ely, Minnesota, to Point Barrow, Alaska. For five months I sledded through incredible wilderness; little of it had ever been crossed by whites. But when I arrived at Point Barrow in May I was greeted by a brown haze. Smog, which plumed from smokestacks as far away as Siberia and floated across the ice-filled Arctic Ocean, hovered over the horizon.

I stood on the edge of the shore looking toward the North Pole, where, I imagined, was the clearest air in the world. In every direction my view was dulled by a scrim of manmade haze—a harsh signal that the twentieth century had finally caught up with the north. I was saddened by its arrival.

Over the past 25 years I've watched the north, and the people who live there, change inalterably. I've seen the wilderness shrink and become more polluted. I've seen the life-style of the natives change from a dependence on nature to a reliance on government. That's one of the reasons I went to Antarctica, to draw attention to one of the last remaining frontiers. My fervent hope is that the future does not hold the same end for the south, that humankind's role in Antarctica will be that of protector, not despoiler.

While preparing for spending seven months crossing Antarctica, I became convinced that many people don't fully understand just why the continent and its preservation are so important to the future of the planet. Most see it as a kind of cold hell anchoring the bottom of the globe. But Antarctica's links to global climatic and weather systems make it the best barometer of the globe's future that we have. The seas that surround the continent provide key nutrients to the rest of the world's oceans. Two thirds of the world's seals, a million whales, over 80 million penguins, and millions of other seabirds and fish call the deep seas that surround Antarctica home. Most importantly, Antarctica is a critical base for scientific study of the environmental problems that threaten the planet.

Despite such global importance, negotiations currently taking place behind closed doors could change—and severely damage—Antarctica's future. The international treaty that governs the continent is up for review in 1991. With that date in mind, the treaty's 39 signatory nations (and others that would like to have a say in the continent's destiny) are debating the future of Antarctica—and of the oil and minerals that are allegedly buried in abundance beneath the ice. An estimated 50 billion barrels of black gold permeate the rock and ice down under (as well as untold fields of coal, copper, iron, and a variety of precious metals), and representatives of nations from the United States to India are debating whether and how to apportion the rights to drill for those resources.

To date, Antarctica's guardian nations get high grades for their governance. But with Alaska as an example of exploration gone bad, we need to be increasingly cautious about Antarctica's future. Its ecosystem is fragile and should be maintained by a hands-off approach. The krill, a shrimplike animal that constitutes the world's largest marine food source, is already being heavily fished by the Japanese and Soviets. Blue and humpback whales are being harvested into potential extinction. There have been oil spills off the Antarctic coast, and the ice and surrounding seas are being polluted by garbage from research stations and passing ships. Tourists are flocking south in increased numbers; an Australian entrepreneur has proposed a hotel. Environmentalists have in turn suggested making the entire continent into a massive "world park," if only to protect it from humanity's greed.

Such unshackled greed has already caused a rash of environmental dilemmas. In recent years we have been exceedingly reckless in the way we treat the planet. For decades scientists have warned of the possible consequences of our environmental ex-

travagance. Few paid much attention, until now. Droughts, fires, garbage on beaches, earthquakes, ozone holes, the greenhouse effect, acid rain, and rain forests have become the subjects of news coverage and coffee shop conversation alike. The hundreds of millions worldwide who watch the evening news and read the news magazines are increasingly bombarded by stories about "our endangered planet." The commotion is good, because it's a daily reminder of the delicate balance that needs to be maintained in order to keep the planet on an even keel.

It seems wherever I go, whether to a big-city conference room or a backwoods stream, in my home state of Minnesota or an airport in Tokyo, I overhear conversations revolving around the accumulated horrors that face us. All of a sudden, it seems, the interrelatedness of these problems has captured the public's consciousness. The atmosphere that envelops the planet is being destroyed not just by car and industrial exhaust, but also by the destruction of the rain forests *and* the depletion of the ozone layer. Almost overnight, people have gotten the correct impression that the world's back is against the wall and that a multitude of environmental disasters is bearing down simultaneously. Everyone is searching for someone to blame. But headlines, magazine articles, and 60 seconds on the nightly news are often not satisfactory in detailing the causes and effects—not to mention the solutions—of the problems. The growing visibility of these problems has given birth to a corresponding need for straight talk—not scientific jargon—if people are to understand their roles in hurting the planet and in trying to save it.

Between now and the end of this century over a billion people will be added to the planet. As both populations and pollution continue to grow at alarming rates, as the systems from which we draw food and energy become more heavily burdened, we are reminded every day that we have only one Earth.

How long can that world endure as we know it? The answer is up to us.

Why am I so concerned about the world's environmental problems? Largely because I've been watching the environment change up-close since I was a boy. Nature has always been like a brother to me, something to wrestle with, enjoy, and love, not destroy. Witnessing the ruination of varying environments has given added incentive to my adventures; low-key protest against such destruction has long been one of my "jobs."

Born in 1944, I grew up into the economic boom that followed World War II and the urban sprawl that came close on its heels. That sprawl produced the community outside Minneapolis where I grew up, Richfield, which was the first suburb to sprout south of the Twin Cities. My childhood memories of the place are of cornfields and woods and a big swampy pond called Wood Lake. Muskrats, birds, and deer were everywhere, and there were plenty of open spaces to explore.

When I look back at my childhood I don't think I did any more exploring than the average boy. All kids have a natural fascination about the world, a natural need to investigate, to probe. Living in the "country" as I did and having access to a kind of "wilderness," I was fascinated by flowers, stars, and the skies. I think what's changed most in our world today is that kids—and many adults for that matter—lack such first-hand exposure to the outdoors. They live life vicariously (in climate-controlled confines) through television, computer games, and high-tech toys. They rarely see any kind of "wilderness" up close—whether they live in the suburbs or the cities—and rarely have a fingertip feeling and understanding of how the world around them works. I think that lack of instinctive understanding is one of the reasons we find ourselves facing so many environmental messes today. Technology has distanced people from the outdoors and the few fron-

tiers left. While my life has been shaped by my experiences outdoors, the lives of too many people today are formed by what they see on television. Computer games have replaced even such simple outdoor pastimes as "kick-the-can." I can't help but think that if people simply spent more time in nature they'd understand better how humankind pollutes it.

My parents still live in the house where I grew up, and I am amazed by how much the neighborhood has changed in my lifetime. I can remember watching the building of the freeway that now looms behind the house. In fact, its construction destroyed one of my favorite boyhood playgrounds. Wood Lake was a few blocks from home, and every day after school my friends and I would go down and raft there. We built our "crafts" out of logs or barrels and hid them in the weeds. We spent days exploring what to us seemed an unending body of water. Though it was a muddy, shallow, sometimes treacherous lake, it was our favorite playground, our home away from home.

But when I was 10 the state started construction on a six-lane freeway that would run directly over Wood Lake. They worked on it for five or six years. In place of after-school rafting our attentions were absorbed watching them excavate. They removed dumptruck after dumptruck of earth, then brought in tons of cement. At one point they accidentally scraped a hole in the side of our "home away from home." Overnight, Wood Lake was drained, our playground dried up.

My fascination with the wilderness wasn't thwarted by the cementing of my neighborhood, though. When I was 12, I worked as a volunteer during the International Geophysical Year (IGY). It was a monumental global scientific study that formally began on October 1, 1957; three days later the Soviet Union launched the first sputnik. The IGY's goal was to establish a community of scientists around the world who, working together, would study the planet's evolving air, land, and seas. They concentrated on the planet's changing environment and for the first time focused their eyes on the future of space exploration. The IGY also produced the treaty that still governs Antarctica. It was the first real global scientific project; none since has matched its spirit of cooperation.

One of my assignments was charting the northern lights. At that time no one really understood them. Some thought they were signals from another planet; my dad told me they were a reflection off the ice of the Arctic. It seems odd now that our scientific knowledge was then so archaic, but that was before satellites helped shrink the world to understandable size.

We lived in the southern suburbs and I gazed north over the city every night, watching from the back porch or out the back windows. The skies were clear, light pollution from the city minuscule. My job was to map the northern lights, write a report every third night, and send my reports to IGY headquarters in New York. If there was an unusually bright band of stars my parents were good about letting me stay up until 10 o'clock. If there was a lot of activity I would get up before the sun and continue my watch. I was fortunate during my monitoring to witness one of the biggest displays of northern lights of the century.

I also watched for—and mapped—shooting stars. During most of the sixth grade I would sleep next to the fireplace and set my alarm for one o'clock. My tools were a flashlight with a red cellophane cover and a map of the heavens. I'd stare at the skies, trying not to blink, and when I'd see a shooting star I'd write down the time, speed, and color and try to map its trail. I put in hundreds of hours, and once a month I'd make out a report. IGY headquarters would send me back a certificate, detailing how many hours I'd logged. The certificates were just little postcards with a special stamp, but they meant a lot to me and I kept those postcards for years afterward.

Watching the skies and stars was something I had always done. Throughout my childhood I kept meticulous weather logs; every day I would record the high and the low temperatures, note the cloud cover and any noteworthy weather events. I kept that up through high school, eventually collecting my own recording instruments. (I still use the barometer my dad bought me in high school.) Those hours spent monitoring the skies taught me a lot about the weather and have literally saved my life during my explorations, when I've been trapped in snowstorms thousands of miles from the nearest weatherman.

Shortly after the IGY, when I was 15, I began seeking adventures beyond the Twin Cities. Ever since, my life has been one adventure after another: I've kayaked more than 10,000 miles, dogsledded another 15,000, and hitchhiked over 100,000 miles. I've seen wilderness and horizons around the globe that will be seen by only a handful of men and women. Yet I remain just as curious and fascinated by flowers, stars, and skies today as I was when I was eight. But if my motives have not changed, the wilderness around me has. Many of the places I first explored are gone. The fields I roamed as a boy are under shopping malls. Kids no longer raft on Wood Lake. And because of the air and light pollution that hovers over the Twin Cities, I doubt you can see the northern lights from my parents' back porch.

In the 1970s I bought land north of Ely, Minnesota, and began living a self-sufficient life. I taught winter camping and outdoor skills to individuals and groups from all over Minnesota and the Midwest. I would give lectures for $25 in the city and recruit students from those who attended. I would meet them at the edge of my property, two miles from my cabin, and take them for three or four days deep into the woods.

I pared my needs down so that I was living on less than $2,000 a year. I used very little fuel and no canned goods, and I eliminated as many trips to town as possible. I grew a garden, repaired my own clothes, and did without a car. I'm sure some of the locals thought I was crazy. But it wasn't a faddish thing for me, as it was for some at the time. I truly wanted to live a simple life and learn to depend only on myself and nature.

In between classes I continued my explorations. By the end of the 1970s I had put together a team of top sled dogs, which gave me the means to explore the real wilderness, to travel to places I'd seen only in pictures, and to meet the native people who had lived there for generations. The kayak trips of my teens had introduced me to Canada, the Northwest Territories, and Alaska. The untouched, largely untraveled areas that now attracted me lay inside the Arctic Circle. While people had put their imprint on much of the rest of the globe, the north was one of those unmarked "white spots on the map" that have always drawn me. Now my adventures—by dogsled and ski, sometimes alone or with one other—introduced me to vast white wildernesses, thousands of miles from the nearest road.

I explored the upper reaches of Canada, the Northwest Territories, and the Arctic in a series of trips that eventually took me to the North Pole, in 1986. But I have always seen the north as a teacher, never as a personal challenge. I have never been motivated simply by getting from point A to point B. I crisscrossed the Arctic to see what I could learn, about the place and about myself. Each time that I returned from one of my trips I was a little bit wiser, a bit more experienced, and always revitalized, anxious to begin again. I saw some of the most beautiful hidden places on the planet and survived more close calls than I care to remember, but I also learned much from the people I met along the way. And I learned I could depend on myself, in virtually any situation.

While my curiosity has not been dampened over the years, the wild places that motivate me con-

tinue to disappear. Just as my boyhood haunts no longer exist, the first places I explored have changed forever. I can watch the results of mankind's overkill in my own backyard. Over the years I've continued to build north of Ely, on the fringes of Minnesota's Boundary Waters. But even that most wild of places has changed since I first guided canoe trips there in 1965. These days it is so crowded in the summer that people have to book their outdoor experience a year in advance. Today you have to make reservations to go to the wilderness.

One of my key motivations in going to Antarctica was to draw attention to its importance, both as an example of international cooperation and as an important place for the study of environmental problems.

My fascination with the continent goes back to the International Geophysical Year. One of the IGY's primary goals was to study Antarctica, which had been essentially devoid of human beings since the 1920s. During the IGY 12 nations agreed to set up 55 scientific observation stations on and around Antarctica, some of them deep in the interior. International staffs manned several of the posts; scientists from Argentina, Australia, France, New Zealand, the United States, South Africa, the Soviet Union, and other nations worked as a team.

As part of the celebration of the IGY, *National Geographic* ran spread after spread of pictures from Antarctica and documented the first crossing of the continent. In 1957 and 1958 British explorer Sir Vivian Fuchs led a team (which included the already-noted adventurer Sir Edmund Hillary) 2,158 miles by snowcat across Antarctica. Their story, and that of the IGY scientists who went to this barren place, inspired me. I wanted to know how they got there and what they found when they arrived. It was then that I knew that someday I would go to Antarctica.

The continent remains one of the planet's last great frontiers. Bigger than China and India combined, it is actually a desert covered by thick layers of ice. Temperatures can drop as low as 120° Fahrenheit below zero, and winds race up to 150 miles per hour. Most of the scientific bases are gathered in clumps along the rocky shores. Only a handful of trips have been made on foot to the South Pole, and only one expedition besides Fuchs's has traversed the continent. (Like Fuchs's team, a team led by British explorer Sir Ranulf Fiennes also chose a north-south route; they snowmobiled 2,254 miles across the continent in 1981.) Most of the route my expedition traveled—4,000 miles by dogsled and ski—had never been attempted during the seasons we were on the ice. It is a route I chose purposely not only to test men and dogs, but for the discoveries, scientific and psychological, that we would make.

Despite its isolated place at the bottom of the planet, Antarctica is one of the best scientific laboratories on Earth. Populated year-round by fewer than 2,000 scientists and support staff, it is also one of the best places on earth to study the effects of pollution. Adverse effects on global climate are likely to appear in Antarctica first, because of the central role the continent plays in the Earth's weather and because of the pristine nature of its physical environment. And its vast frozen crust, which accounts for more than 90 percent of the world's ice, contains an invaluable record of the Earth's climatic history. Ice cores drilled by scientists provide accurate information on increases in atmospheric carbon dioxide and other global pollutants going back 160,000 years.

But the environmental profligacies of the civilized world are beginning to take a toll even on Antarctica. The continent is shaped like the cross-section of a bottle cap; when it warms, ice flows to the sides and falls into the ocean. Today, with the global temperature rising and the ozone layer depleting, the ice shelves that surround Antarctica are breaking off more rapidly than in the past. This not only changes the saltiness and temperature of the teeming, fertile waters, but also causes the levels of the seas to rise, which leads to bigger ice shelves breaking off and drifting away. The increase in fresh water being added to the ocean ultimately leads to a raising of the water's temperatures, which may affect all sea life, from phytoplankton to krill to blue whales, and spark permanent changes in weather patterns around the world.

In the three years of preparation that led up to our arrival in Antarctica I talked with people from Minneapolis to Moscow who wanted to know more about Antarctica and were curious about its role in the planet's environmental future. That is reassuring. At times during those years I felt like a drowning man, as I tried to keep up with all the logistical planning, diplomatic and sponsorship negotiations, and team meetings involved in mounting the expedition. But whenever people asked me about the ozone hole, the greenhouse effect, or the future of the krill, I was reminded that my initial goal of educating people about the continent was still a priority, a necessity. People must realize that Antarctica is part of the world and one of the best teachers of how the Earth's mechanisms work. In many ways the ice of Antarctica holds the key to humanity's environmental future.

I first saw a need for this book—one that focuses on solutions to our environmental problems—in the early winter of 1988, when those three California gray whales were stuck beneath the ice outside Barrow, Alaska.

The whole world watched as millions of dollars were spent trying to "rescue" the surviving pair. (The third, a calf, disappeared after a few days.) Air Force planes and helicopters were commandeered, a Soviet icebreaker arrived, a bubbling machine was airlifted in to keep the hole in the ice from freezing over, and the world press camped out nearby. I've organized expeditions in the Arctic and I know how much it costs to get planes, ships, and the press into that region—millions of tax dollars and millions more from private pockets were spent, all for two lost whales. Here were people impeding again, attempting to "straighten out" a perfectly natural struggle—one that has been going on for centuries—between animals and the environment.

The story of the whales was inescapable, thanks to the representatives of 26 broadcasting companies and another hundred print reporters who made their way to Barrow. But that their plight became such big news caused me mixed emotions. I listened closely to how those around me reacted to the story. Some shed tears for "the poor whales"; others were outraged by the monies being spent. I couldn't help but wonder if the media—which seem to have become increasingly sensationalized in recent years—would have even made the trip north if the incident had happened just five years before. If they hadn't gone to Barrow, especially in such numbers, the matter would have gotten scant attention beyond the borders of that tiny Eskimo village.

Ironically, the event gave me hope. People rallied around those two whales as if they were the last on Earth. It led me to believe that if we could somehow whip up similar global concern about the harms caused by ozone depletion, acid rain, and toxic waste dumping, maybe we could retard their destructive effects. Perhaps, if we could show people that there are solutions to the myriad environmental problems that haunt the globe, they would exhibit compassion for their own communities, the way they did for those two whales.

During those two weeks in Barrow, people around the world were audience to a rare exercise in collective action and international cooperation. Americans worked with Soviets, soldiers with Eskimos, bureaucrats with the man on the street. We are just now attempting to harness those same energies with the goal of stopping the environmental degradation of the planet. International forums are beginning to churn out guidelines; government leaders are increasingly realizing that one nation's environ-

mental carelessness results in another's woes. Yet we are still a few years away from addressing most environmental problems from a truly global perspective. That perspective requires that our level of understanding be raised so that we truly understand the link between our everyday habits and our well-publicized environmental problems.

One of the problems in trying to educate ourselves about the environment is the sensationalist mentality that dominates today's media. One week the whales trapped in Alaska are on the tip of everybody's tongue, the next week they're forgotten. Our attention span is pulled and tugged, from oil spills to serial murders to political high jinks, day after day, week after week, each event invested with identical import. We concentrate on the spectacular and ignore the everyday. One night we see pictures of hundreds of acres of felled rain forest; the next it's a pristine lake destroyed by acid rain; the next, hundreds of starving villagers in Bangladesh. Such scenes are sandwiched between celebrity profiles and presidential photo opportunities; environmental stories often carry no more weight than the following 15-second commercial. With equal news value placed on issues of such varied importance society is numbed into complacency, convinced that there are no solutions, just ever more problems. People are overwhelmed by the sweep and enormity of the world's environmental problems, and they figure that there's little they can do to help.

I'm an explorer and an environmentalist, not a preacher. But it should be obvious to everyone that these problems won't reverse themselves on their own. Government, industry, and individuals must step in and take responsibility. In modern society, it is difficult to lead an environmentally "benign" life. (Tough questions come up every day. Do you make a scene and tell the fast-food helper to take his polystyrene box and shove it? Do you run the driver in front of you off the road for tossing soda cans out the window?) It is a full-time task to consider the environmental implications of every purchase you make. It is difficult to comprehend that when you do a simple chore like changing the Freon in your car's air conditioner, you are helping to destroy the ozone layer that shields the planet. But it is essential to remind yourself every day that people—you and I—are causing all this destruction; there is no one else to blame.

I moved to the wilderness in 1969, in part to gain a better understanding of the world around me. I had always had an interest in the atmosphere, the land and the water, and wildlife. Prior to that I taught science in secondary school, and had been teaching about ecology for some time. The first Earth Day took place during my last month of classroom teaching.

Many of my generation moved "back to the earth," and most claimed they were concerned about the environment. But we are as guilty as preceding generations for harming the world's ecosystems. In fact we may be more responsible because of the enormous consumption rate we have helped fuel. Today the United States uses 25 percent of the world's natural resources. The average American consumes 90 times the energy of a typical Kenyan; 45 times that of the average Indian, and 15 times that of the typical Chinese. We produce more garbage than any country in the world, and use more energy. It is our insatiable—and still growing—demand that is straining the world's ecosystems.

Slowing this demand, taking individual responsibility, is a key to stemming the world's environmental ills. The ultimate solution to every environmental problem from deforestation to ocean dumping is for each of us to take responsibility for our own acts and not to give up hope, despite the negativism that accompanies accounts of destruction from around the globe. It is easy to be a fatalist today, believing that polluted air, contaminated water, industrial wastes, and despoiled land are here to stay. My hope is that this book will convince people that by sacrificing just a little we can make an enormous difference. The goal for the upcoming decade should be to eliminate environmental ignorance.

For example, individuals who read this book can learn about things *they* can do. Maybe they'll decide to focus on a specific problem, something in their own backyard, like neighborhood recycling or planting trees or organizing car pools. Whatever action you take has to be done within the confines of your life. We can't expect the stockbroker living on the upper east side of Manhattan to chuck it all and go to forestry school. But maybe there are job-related things he can do—like promoting environmentally aware companies, doing pro bono work to help raise funds for a recycling facility, or most important, making sure his children understand the relationship between people and the environment.

Cleaning up the world's environmental messes and preventing future ones is going to require massive amounts of hope. If you convince yourself there is none, it's too late. What we have set out to do in this book is provide glimpses of hope, by examples from the United States, China, Brazil, and elsewhere. If those glimpses motivate enough people to care about the environment's future—just as so many around the world cared about those whales trapped under the ice—that may be enough to help focus the world's collective energies on slowing the destruction.

I have spent a lot of time in the past few years talking to groups interested in my experiences as an adventurer, and recently I've focused many of those speeches on my concerns around the environment. But while researching the problems of ozone depletion and the warming of our climate, I discovered a lack of sources that focus on the solution of our environmental problems. While there is an abundance of worthy material out there if you want to educate yourself on specific problems—from rain forests to toxic waste dumping to recycling—there exists no one book that explains in laymen's terms the problems that bombard us. I saw a need for such a source book, one that would explain the systems of the world—the interrelations of the oceans, the atmosphere, and the land, and how they are being sundered. This book explains the causes and effects of the problems, but its focus is on solutions. What can *you* do to stop the ozone hole from growing? What can be done to help *your* town reduce its garbage heap? What can nations do *together* to limit or halt environmental destruction?

The time is right for environmental action. A recent Gallup poll asked citizens what they would do if they had to choose between economic growth and environmental protection; two-to-one, citizens favored protecting the environment. Membership in conservation groups around the world has swelled in the past year. Governments appear ready to work together. The private sector is realizing finally that continued ignorance of existing laws will continue to heap eco-disaster upon eco-disaster.

Ultimately it is not technology that needs to be brought up to speed. In fact, the technology already exists to clean up oil spills and close the ozone hole. We have the expertise and intelligence to stop or slow most of the world's environmental problems. It is our *will* that must be encouraged. Unfortunately it may take more disasters to loosen the purse strings enough to focus those technologies, motivate those experts, and strengthen that will—disasters such as back-to-back droughts, oil spills, nuclear reactor leaks, billion-dollar cleanups, and even deaths.

Most importantly we need to combine the resources and energies available on a global level. The world's environmental problems will not be solved without international action. Any one country's efforts to change will be overwhelmed without global cooperation. If the seventies were marked by a series of innovative *national* laws aimed at addressing environmental problems, the nineties must be noted for comparable initiatives at the *international* level.

In a sense, such a move is already under way. An international accord aimed at stopping the depletion of the ozone layer has been adopted by more than 80 nations; meetings on what to do about global warming take place somewhere in the world every week. While international protocols and the burgeoning memberships of environmental groups around the world are encouraging, the motivation for cleaning up the world must still begin with the individual. Otherwise all those global protocols will go unheeded and those fine organizations will spin their wheels. Technologies will be untested and monies misspent. Until we commit to cleaning up our personal act, all the high-tech fixes and international forums won't make a difference.

One of my biggest concerns is that we are producing a generation that is out of touch with the world and its surroundings. I'm not suggesting that everyone needs to kayak the rivers of the Yukon or cross Antarctica to comprehend the problems we face. I admit it's tough to get to know nature if you live in a 30-story apartment building in the heart of a sprawling city. But we can't blindly continue to allow technology to race past us. We have to come to recognize its successes, but also come to grips with its dangers, so it doesn't race ahead so far that it destroys the Earth.

I'm concerned that while our generation thinks it is one of the most educated and informed, it doesn't understand the concept of saving the Earth, doesn't understand that nuclear waste generated in Great Britain may end up in Italy, that belching smokestacks in Buffalo may ruin lakes outside Montreal, that ocean dumping by Japan may lead to less food for Chile. You can be brilliant in mathematics or with computers, with great prospects on Wall Street or in Silicon Valley, but unless you understand the interdependency of the environment we live in, the planet is doomed. We can decide our fate in regard to the environment, but only if we fully understand the consequences of our actions.

The solution is education, although I know that is an abused word these days. I certainly don't think it's too late for adults to change their ways—they can. But soon it will be up to the children we're educating today to put the brakes on shortsighted environmental destruction. I already see changes in attitudes at schools where I talk and in conversations with young people who worked on the preparations for our Antarctic expedition. They say they want to do *something* about the environment, they want to do *something* with their lives, they want to do *something* for humanity, for the world. Some mention careers in forestry; others say they want to join the Peace Corps. Perhaps, in the next decades, earning six figures a year will start taking a backseat for our youth—out of necessity.

The key is for people to understand the connection between their daily lives and the environmental tragedies they read about in the papers. The Exxon oil spill in Valdez, Alaska, in May 1989 is a prime example. For months following the accident people were strident in their outrage. There were boycotts of Exxon and tens of thousands of people cut up their credit cards and mailed them back to the company. While those reactions were understandable, many of the protests missed the big picture.

While Exxon is an easy mark—and should be held responsible for cleaning up every inch of despoiled coast—the oil company is just a facilitator of our demands. The problem is much bigger than one tanker run aground. For example, look in your wastebasket right now. Do you see anything made of plastic? How about your driveway, any cars that use oil or gas? If you answered yes to one or both, you are oil dependent. Too often we forget just how intertwined our lives have become with the major forms of pollution in the world. We forget that our daily dependence on such simple things as cars and

plastic, fuels the industry we are so quick to blame. It is our out-of-control demand that allows tankers to travel through once-pristine Alaskan harbors to begin with. So before casting blame on Exxon, first look at your own life. Shoulder some responsibility. The only way changes are going to be made is when people understand that if they want those harbors to remain pristine, if they want cleaner air or less garbage on their beaches, they are going to have to make alterations at home, and in their mind.

While I remain hopeful about our environmental future, I believe we're facing the equivalent of World War III. It's ironic, since we always assumed the next war would be a nuclear battle or a space race turned ugly. Instead, we find ourselves locked in a battle between humankind and nature. And nature is losing ground fast.

What we need in this war are "armies" of people motivated by the goal of stopping the destruction, pushing to end the senseless "battle." Granted, ending the war is too big a job for individuals alone. Any such movement needs the weight of government behind it. I can't help but think back to the International Geophysical Year and the good it did, not just scientifically but morally. That kind of global effort is required for the environmental battles ahead. There are some recent shining examples—like the twentieth anniversary of Earth Day. The timing couldn't be better. Our energies—not to mention our monies—are no longer absorbed trying to match arms with the Soviets or race for the moon. Cooperation, not competition, must be the watchword of the nineties.

The next decade promises to be the most decisive 10 years in the history of this planet. How we proceed will dictate the world's environmental fate. It is a difficult challenge; our focus for the decade must be on solutions, with a constant eye on saving the only world we know. If I had to pass along a call to arms for the upcoming decade, I would borrow one from that respected environmentalist and futurist Buckminster Fuller: "Think globally, act locally."

ANTARCTICA AND THE EARTH

Since colder water contains more oxygen, the ocean that surrounds Antarctica is four times as productive as any other. Hundreds of species of fish, penguins, seals, and whales, and the largest gathering of seabirds in the world thrive there.

At the base of the Antarctic food chain are phytoplankton—microscopic plant life—that grow on the underside of sea ice. Each summer when that ice melts, hundreds of millions of phytoplankton are released into the water.

The floating phytoplankton are a rich bounty of food for the tiny crustaceans called krill, which swarm to eat them. In early summer the waters off Antarctica teem with ten million tons of krill.

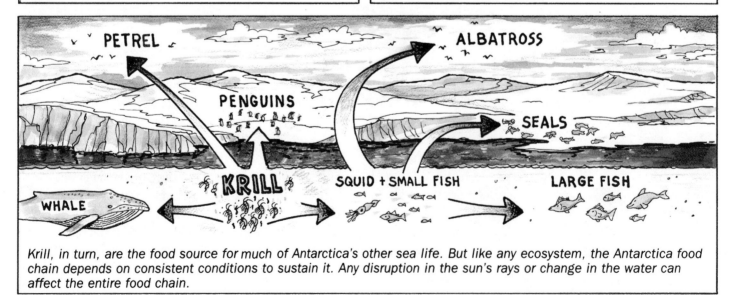

Krill, in turn, are the food source for much of Antarctica's other sea life. But like any ecosystem, the Antarctica food chain depends on consistent conditions to sustain it. Any disruption in the sun's rays or change in the water can affect the entire food chain.

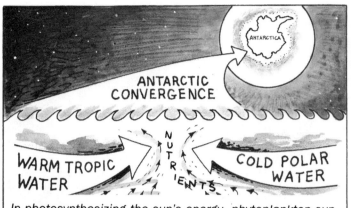

In photosynthesizing the sun's energy, phytoplankton supply much of the world's oxygen. At the Antarctica Convergence, tides churn up the nutrients formed by their decomposition, carrying them to other seas to feed marine and plant life.

Antarctica is also an integral part of the world's weather system. The cold polar stretches of Antarctica and the Arctic are the "engine" of global wind systems. Their white surfaces reflect the sun's energy, helping to cool the Earth.

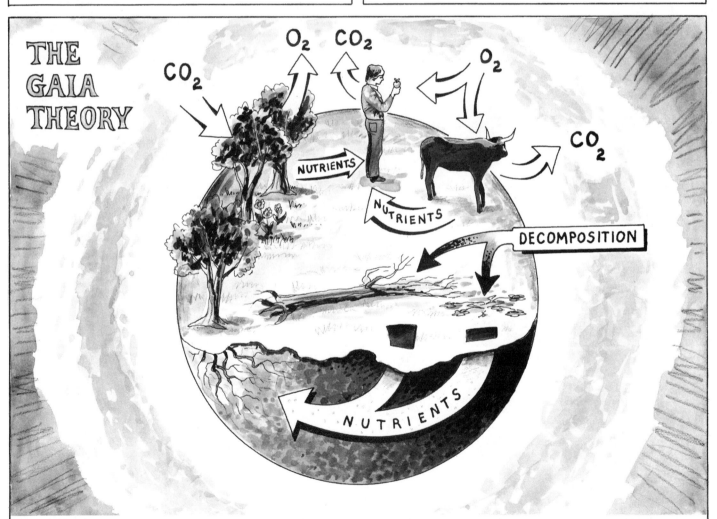

The world's ecosystems are constantly exchanging gases, heat, and nutrients. The Gaia Theory, originated by James Lovelock and supported by scientists and environmentalists worldwide, suggests that the Earth is itself a giant living organism, and that it is the various life forms themselves that regulate and maintain conditions necessary to sustain life as we know it.

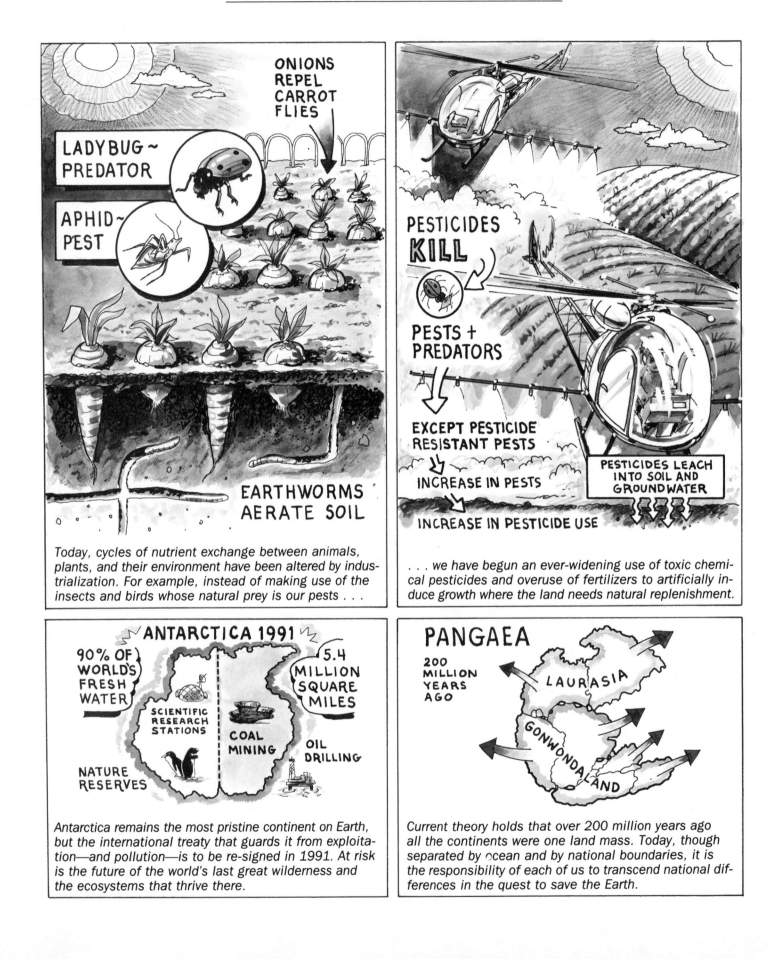

ONIONS REPEL CARROT FLIES

LADYBUG ~ PREDATOR

APHID ~ PEST

EARTHWORMS AERATE SOIL

Today, cycles of nutrient exchange between animals, plants, and their environment have been altered by industrialization. For example, instead of making use of the insects and birds whose natural prey is our pests . . .

PESTICIDES KILL PESTS + PREDATORS

EXCEPT PESTICIDE RESISTANT PESTS

INCREASE IN PESTS

INCREASE IN PESTICIDE USE

PESTICIDES LEACH INTO SOIL AND GROUNDWATER

. . . we have begun an ever-widening use of toxic chemical pesticides and overuse of fertilizers to artificially induce growth where the land needs natural replenishment.

ANTARCTICA 1991

90% OF WORLD'S FRESH WATER

5.4 MILLION SQUARE MILES

SCIENTIFIC RESEARCH STATIONS

COAL MINING

OIL DRILLING

NATURE RESERVES

Antarctica remains the most pristine continent on Earth, but the international treaty that guards it from exploitation—and pollution—is to be re-signed in 1991. At risk is the future of the world's last great wilderness and the ecosystems that thrive there.

PANGAEA

200 MILLION YEARS AGO

LAURASIA

GONWONDALAND

Current theory holds that over 200 million years ago all the continents were one land mass. Today, though separated by ocean and by national boundaries, it is the responsibility of each of us to transcend national differences in the quest to save the Earth.

SAVING THE EARTH

THE ATMOSPHERE

1
Global Warming

When James Hansen, director of NASA's Goddard Institute, appeared before the Senate Committee on Energy and Natural Resources, on June 23, 1988, he told the gathered crowd that, yes, it was fact, the Earth is getting hotter. That day he went further than any scientist of his stature had before by telling the committee that he was 99 percent sure that global warming was a real and present danger. His testimony confirmed what many suspected: that the so-called greenhouse effect—caused by an increase in atmospheric carbon dioxide and other gases—was threatening the future of the world's climate. For a world suffering through a summer of drought, fires, and searing heat, his words were all that people needed to hear. Media from around the globe leaped on Hansen's message. There it was, wrapped up in one neat phrase, a simple cause to explain the environmental problems that seemed to have cropped up overnight: the greenhouse effect.

Hansen's dramatic warning spawned immediate debate among meteorologists and prompted criticism from his peers. He was taken to task by skeptics, primarily for his attachment of percentages to science. Today the question still lingers: Is the world *really* getting hotter? As the twentieth century winds down, global warming—and the greenhouse effect's role in it—promises to be one of the most controversial, and potentially most disastrous, environmental problems the world faces in the century to come.

The theory is actually pretty simple. It suggests that a buildup in the atmosphere of carbon dioxide— and a grocery list of other gases, including meth-

ane, chlorofluorocarbons, nitrous oxide, ozone, and others—is causing it to warm. Why "greenhouse"? Because this growing accumulation of gases acts like a glass roof and traps heat, much as a garden greenhouse does. But instead of nurturing roses, as this atmospheric greenhouse grows hotter it could disrupt virtually every natural ecosystem humankind has grown to depend on. If its effects are as wide-ranging as predicted it would alter crop yields and water supplies, seas would rise, floods would swamp cities and wetlands, plant and wildlife habitats would shift, pests would proliferate, diseases would spread. The most sensational predictions have compared its potential disruptiveness to the aftermath of nuclear war.

Most of the greenhouse predictions have emerged from complex computer models that forecast the global climate. Current models predict that the average global temperatures will rise by several degrees Fahrenheit within the next century. By comparison, world temperatures rose just 1 degree in the past 100 years.

But these predictions are not unanimously accepted by the scientific community. They understand the public's need for a scapegoat for the unpredicted ills that have crisscrossed the weather map in recent years—including severe droughts, hurricanes, and floods—but most are hesitant to put all the blame on the "greenhousing" of the atmosphere. While they think they understand what's causing the Earth to warm, they are uncertain if it portends enormous disaster or if mother nature might step in and compensate for man's abuse. One of the major uncertainties arises from the fact that only 150 years of accurate weather information exist on which to base predictions. When that weather information is fed into supercomputers programmed to use it to "re-create" the past, the results rarely come out the same twice in a row. The simple truth is that climate change is very difficult to predict.

Part of the difficulty involves the complexity of the Earth's atmosphere. It is a constantly swirling sea of air currents whose flow, temperature, moisture, chemical composition, and intensity are governed by an equally complex interaction between the air, the sun, biomass (plant material and animal waste), and the oceans. There are some in the scientific community who argue that it is this complexity that makes predictions about the magnitude and timing of global warming nothing more than highly sophisticated guesswork.

Global warming is hardly a new phenomenon, though. During the past billion years, less than a quarter of the Earth's age, there have been at least four periods when ice covered most of the globe. At least nine times in the past million years alone, massive sheets of ice have blanketed North America and Europe. Each buildup of ice and each meltdown took thousands to tens of thousands of years. But the climatic shifts that set off those ponderous changes may have occurred quite rapidly—in as little as a few centuries.

For example, 95,000 years ago, in less than a century, sea levels abruptly rose 49 to 65 feet, probably because a large portion of the eastern Antarctic ice sheet suddenly slid into the ocean. Scientists know this because they have found marine plants and fossilized wood at high altitudes in the Transantarctic mountains, which suggests that the Antarctic ice sheet may have melted and reformed many times. If a similar event were to happen today the world's sea levels would rise over 200 feet. But no one is sure precisely how, or why, that would happen. "We are gazing into a very murky crystal ball," admits Stephen Schneider, director of the National Center for Atmospheric Research in Boulder, Colorado, and author of a major text on global warming.

So back to the question—is the world getting hotter? The question was first broached in the 1890s by Nobel Prize–winning Swedish scientist Svante Arrhenius, who tried to bring what he then termed the greenhouse effect to the public's attention. His concerns were prompted by the simple premise that the world was then burning a lot of coal and oil. He was apparently the first to publicly wonder what would be the lasting effect of all that carbon dioxide billowing into the skies.

His studies lay dormant until the late 1930s, when a British meteorologist cautioned that a warming induced by carbon dioxide was in fact already taking place. But his opinions were pooh-poohed by scientists who were convinced that there was plenty of room in the ocean to absorb any increase in the amount of atmospheric gases.

That ocean-as-bottomless-sink theory held firm for 20 years, until a pair of oceanographers from the Scripps Institute in California showed that the upper layers of the ocean were *not* absorbing carbon dioxide as fast as it was being produced. Their claim was bolstered in 1958, during the International Geophysical Year, by another Scripps scientist, whose monitoring device set high in the mountains of Hawaii showed that the amount of carbon dioxide in the atmosphere was climbing one part per million each year. (Since then it's gone up to 1.5 parts per million per year.)

Slowly the dire forecast began to gain the support of scientists from around the globe and predictions of impending natural disasters spread faster than Hollywood gossip. The consensus was that average temperatures would increase by *at least* 5 degrees. Heat would increase most at the poles, perhaps by 15 degrees Fahrenheit, said some studies. Sea levels might rise by 3 feet or more as a result of glacial and polar melting, predicted others. The resulting climatic shifts would be widespread. Droughts would become common across the grain belt. Forest and brush fires would spread. Coastal wetlands would be swamped. Wheat might grow in Siberia; Florida would become a desert. Bangladesh's floodplains—home to millions—would be underwater. Disease would spread; shipping would become impossible because harbors would flood; streets would buckle.

While concerns soared in the scientific community, it took NASA's Hansen to officially emblazon "greenhouse effect" on the world's vocabulary. Two months after his congressional pronouncement, Schneider, a one-time colleague and a supporter of Hansen's predictions, appeared before the same Senate committee. He attempted to explain the difficulty in precisely predicting the effects of any global warming, which everyone present was now convinced was just around the corner. Schneider asked committee members to imagine a pair of dice with 12,000 sides. Each roll of the dice, he proposed, determines the weather. "Most climatologists agree that the current evidence is strong that human activities are loading the dice with many more warm faces," he said. "And perhaps a few dry ones, too." But his point was clear: no matter how many supercomputers and how many climate models a meteorologist may have at his fingertips, predicting the future of the world's climate is still a gamble.

CAUSES

As we will see in the upcoming chapters, the causes of global warming are widespread. If one cause had to be singled out as the leader, though, it would be simply the number of people now crowding the planet. This growing mass of human beings—now just over 5 billion, and expected to double in the next 60 years—spews increasingly more greenhouse gases into the air every year. We do it by using

more energy, driving more miles, producing more garbage. While we struggle to improve our energy efficiency to slow the production of greenhouse gases, it must be kept in the forefront of both policymaking and action that controlling population is the ultimate environmental challenge.

Because global warming is fueled by so many different gases it may turn out to be the most difficult to cure of all the world's environmental ills. Ridding the globe of the multitude of activities that fuel the greenhouse buildup is impossible. Just getting up in the morning starts the cycle: When you turn on the bathroom light it probably uses electricity generated by the burning of fossil fuels, which pumps carbon dioxide into the air. The refrigerator that keeps your orange juice cold is lined with another contributor to the greenhouse shield—chlorofluorocarbons. Driving to work burns gasoline, which sends millions of particles of carbon dioxide into the atmosphere. The mahogany desk that you work at may have come from a tree in the rain forests, and that tree once helped absorb carbon dioxide from the atmosphere. Even the rice on your plate at lunchtime contributed, by giving off methane gas when it was grown.

These gases are not the result of some lab experiment gone awry. But as the world's population explodes, we pump more and more of them into the skies each day. (An easy way to think of the greenhouse is to compare it to a thick blanket. A blanket helps retain our body heat; in similar fashion, the gases that create the greenhouse "blanket" help retain the Earth's heat. The problem today is that the blanket of gases is too thick, and getting thicker.)

A common misunderstanding is that the greenhouse effect is all bad. In truth, it is one of the reasons life is comfortable in the first place. Without it the earth would be plunged into subzero temperatures. For at least the last 100,000 years, atmospheric carbon dioxide, naturally generated by animals and plants, accounted for a minute component of

Overpopulation is the primary cause of global warming. Increasing demand for food and transportation has led to spiraling numbers of livestock, acres of rice paddies, and automobiles, all of which emit greenhouse gases.

the Earth's atmosphere. Over the centuries the amount of carbon dioxide has risen and fallen, primarily coinciding with the spread and retreat of glaciers as ice ages have come and gone. Without this small but critical trace of gas to hold in heat, the globe's average temperature would be 0 degrees, instead of a pleasant 59 degrees. By comparison, the temperatures on Venus are very hot because its thick atmosphere is mostly carbon dioxide, and those on Mars are frigid because its atmosphere is very thin.

But even though this greenhouse effect is vital, the concern today is that the greenhouse shield is growing too thick, as a result of human activity. While the Earth has proven its resilience—as people have burnt it, bombed it, polluted it, and over-run it—this time we may be stretching its capacity to provide a comfortable home.

The thickening has not occurred overnight; it has been going on since the beginning of the industrial revolution of the late 1700s, which was marked by the introduction of power-driven machinery. Before that time the level of carbon dioxide in the atmosphere never rose above 280 parts per million. By the early 1900s, with business booming in the industrialized countries, those levels began a steady climb. At the end of 1989 they were at 345 parts per million, and by 2070 they are predicted to climb to more than 560 parts per million.

Carbon dioxide is the biggest contributor (50 percent) to the greenhouse shield; normally just .03 percent of the atmosphere, it has increased by 25 percent in the last century (to about .0375 percent). But it is not the sole contributor: methane, from such activities as growing rice and leaking from natural gas wells, accounts for 20 percent, while chlorofluorocarbons (15 percent), nitrogen oxides (10 percent), and ground-level ozone (5 percent) make up the rest of the greenhouse shield.

Carbon dioxide is released in large quantities when fossil fuels like coal, oil, and natural gas are burned.

Emissions from incinerators, waste treatment plants, electric power plants, factories, household furnaces, cars, and buses all contribute. The average North American is responsible for producing five tons of carbon dioxide a year; the worldwide average per person is under one ton. While the United States is the largest contributor, it may soon be passed by the Soviet Union and then China.

It's estimated that current worldwide carbon dioxide release from burning fossil fuels alone is 22 billion tons per year. Stabilizing the climate will require cutting that figure in half. But with the population soaring, that will not be an easy reduction to make without individual sacrifice. Here's why: Burning a gallon of gasoline produces around two pounds of carbon dioxide; using one kilowatt-hour of electricity from a coal-powered plant produces two pounds; flying one mile in an airplane generates a half pound of carbon dioxide per passenger. That doesn't begin to include the carbon dioxide that is produced by the energy used for the manufacturing of the odds and ends that sustain us through a day, from food packaging to facial tissues.

Carbon dioxide emissions have increased hand in hand with the industrialization and modernization of the world's economies. Today the developed nations contribute about 75 percent of the greenhouse gases. A study by the World Resources Institute (WRI), a Washington-based research group, suggests that consumption could be halved by a combination of conservation, improved efficiency, and worldwide belt tightening. So far that's not happening. Simultaneously, emissions in developing countries continue to grow, and fast, along with their expanding populations. Predictions are that the growth of both energy use and population means that the Third World will account for 50 percent of the global increase in energy consumption in the next few decades. As their economic development continues, so do their pollutions. (The WRI report argues that the two do not necessarily have to climb

Natural gas vapors, leaked directly into the atmosphere during their production and transport (above), and methane, produced in part, by the world's exploding population of termites, which feed on the remnants of deforestation (below), both retain solar radiation at 20 times the rate of CO_2.

together; promoting both sustainable development and energy efficiency is the key to slowing emissions.)

Methane is a big, and growing, contributor to the greenhouse shield. More than 425 million tons a year are generated by bacterial decomposition of organic matter—especially in landfills, flooded rice paddies, and the guts of cattle and termites—and by the burning of wood and fossil fuels. (New Zealand's 70 million flatulent sheep alone produce 2.5 million gallons of methane per week.) Despite methane's seemingly harmless origins, its abundance is no laughing matter—its concentration in the atmosphere has grown steadily as the Earth's population has grown, rising 1 percent a year over the past decade. According to figures compiled by NASA, methane in the atmosphere is increasing three times faster than carbon dioxide.

Chlorofluorocarbons (CFCs)—used in refrigerators, car air conditioners, home insulation, and a multitude of other everyday products—also contribute to the greenhouse shield (as well as the depletion of the ozone layer). They are completely manmade gases, solely a result of modern technology. While their production has climbed 5 percent annually in the past decade, it is hoped that a 1987 international mandate against their continued manufacture will slow their deleterious effects. Unfortunately they have a lifespan of up to 100 years and are estimated to be part of $135 billion worth of equipment (see Chapter Two).

Nitrous oxide emissions are burgeoning, too, with about a third of the total due to human activity. It is released when coal and other fossil fuels are burned and is a product of gasoline use and nitrogen-based fertilizer emissions. Its worst attribute is that it stays in the atmosphere in a stable condition for a long time—its full effects may not be felt for 200 years. Half of the world's nitrous oxide emissions come from just three countries—China, the Soviet Union, and the United States.

Ozone, a gas-powered engine emission, is a greenhouse shield contributor in the lower reaches of the atmosphere. Ironically, high in the sky it shields the Earth from the sun's most intense infrared rays.

(The indiscriminate cutting of rain forests contributes to global warming, too [see Chapter Five]. In the process of photosynthesis plants remove about 100 billion tons of carbon dioxide from the atmosphere every year, or about 14 percent of the total. As the rain forests are cut down, more and more carbon dioxide is left in the air. If adequate plans aren't made to reforest—before the rain forests are cut down—the result will be an ever greater buildup of atmospheric carbon dioxide.)

The scientific community continues to debate just how many of the world's environmental ills should be blamed on this thickening atmospheric shield. There are some who do not believe that the greenhouse effect is responsible for environmental problems at all. They cite temperature data gathered over the past century to bolster their arguments. *Their* figures show that despite strong industrial growth from 1940 to the late 1970s, temperatures decreased on average, or stayed the same. Fifty years prior to that, from 1890 to 1940—a period of significantly less fossil-fuel use—the Earth warmed by more than one degree.

Other climatologists believe the Earth is actually cooling, not warming. Still others contend that "feedbacks"—natural trade-offs that counter humanity's abuse—render the effects of the greenhouse nil. For example, they argue, the more the Earth heats up, the more clouds might form, and all that white cover will deflect the sun's rays before they ever have a chance to reach the Earth's surface.

But those that support the theory that the greenhouse effect is hastening global warming counter such arguments with a still-smoking gun. British scientists, using century-old records, claim that 1988 was the hottest year ever recorded. (In fact, the six warmest years ever recorded were all in the 1980s.) They, and many of their colleagues around the world, are convinced this warming will continue, and worsen, into the 1990s and beyond. They predict that by the middle of the twenty-first century, when the concentration of carbon dioxide in the atmosphere is likely to be 60 percent greater than today and double the level that prevailed before the industrial revolution, temperatures will average three to eight degrees warmer than today. That increase is equal to the entire rise in global temperatures since the glaciers last began their retreat more than 18,000 years ago. So far, their arguments—and predictions—are the most compelling.

EFFECTS

Everyone agrees that predicting the future of global warming is difficult, if not impossible. Thus predicting its effects is largely speculative. While more than a dozen major computer models in use around the world generally agree on its broad effects, they differ wildly when it comes to specifics like when, where, and how. Some scientists argue that we are already deep into a warming period, citing the hot 1980s as evidence. Others caution that it's too early to tell, that nature may yet be able to override many of the abuses we have heaped on the atmosphere. These differences of opinion have made it hard to focus international, national, or even local attention on what action should be taken to slow the warming.

No matter where they stand on the effects of global warming, the majority of scientists believe that greenhouse gases will certainly raise the planet's average temperature by the middle of the next century. (Just a five-degree rise would make the Earth warmer than at any time in the past 100,000 years.) What continues to befuddle those who study global warming is just how fast the warming will occur and which regions of the globe will be most affected.

Despite the use of sophisticated computer models, definitive answers to these questions have so far proved elusive. Scientific certainties are a long time in the making. While the causes and effects of global warming have been discussed and studied for almost a century now, that is a short time compared to the Earth's billion-year lifespan. Climatic shifts might simply prove unpredictable. But because of today's increased focus on global environmental problems—and a longing for easy solutions—this apparent unpredictability frustrates scientists, policymakers, and consumers alike. (An oft-used analogy, cited by scientists to illustrate just how iffy climate forecasting can be, is known as "the butterfly effect." Its nickname derives from the theory that a butterfly flapping its wings today in Nagasaki could conceivably influence storms next month in New York.)

Yet another problem in trying to predict the climate's future, suggests Stephen Schneider, is that we are altering the environment faster than we can predict the consequences. "This is bound to lead to some surprises," he says. Perhaps the biggest concern is that instead of a gradual warming—say, a degree or two per century—changes could come rapidly, within a decade or two.

For the sake of argument, let's say that Hansen, Schneider, and the other supporters of global warming are correct and that the world's average temperature climbs by five degrees in the next half century. If that happens, these are the kinds of changes we can expect:

The resulting doubling of the atmosphere's carbon dioxide content would raise temperatures enough to melt the edges of the Arctic and Antarctic ice sheets, raising sea levels around the globe. Coastal areas and islands would be inundated if that happened. Agriculture, water resources, fisheries, shipping, and energy use would all be disrupted. An area greater than the United States or China would be submerged worldwide (70 percent of that area in the Northern Hemisphere). Much of the Eastern Seaboard of the United States would be flooded.

Changes in Average Global Temperature

The graph shows how actual global temperatures have fluctuated from the expected temperatures over the last century. The increase in the "greenhouse gases," trace gases that absorb heat, seems to have influenced a trend in rising global temperatures. If these trace gases continue to increase in their concentration at today's rates, the world could face an average temperature rise of nearly 3 degrees Fahrenheit (or 2 degrees centigrade) by the year 2020.

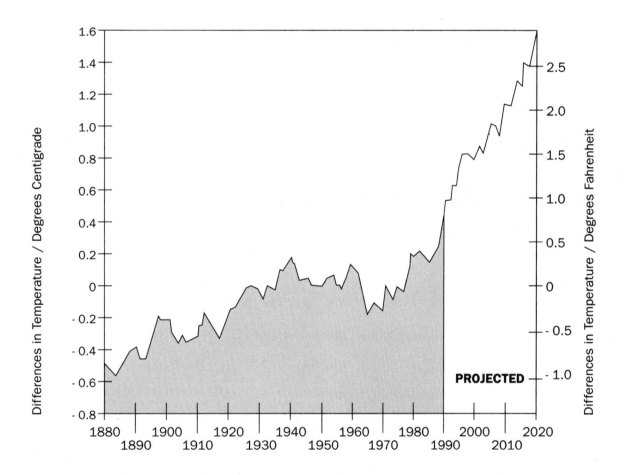

Gas	Contribution to Global Warming by the Trace Gases	Annual Rates of Increase in Concentration
Carbon Dioxide	50%	0.4%
Methane	20%	1.0%
CFCs	15%	4.0%
Nitrogen Oxides	10%	0.25%
Low-level Ozone	5%	N/A

Sources: Natural Resources Defense Council; Inform, Inc.; *The Challenge of Global Warming*, ed. Dean Edwin Abrahamson. Washington: Island Press, 1989.

Parts of the Soviet Union, Denmark, and the Ganges, Amazon, and Mekong deltas would be underwater. Much of Africa and New Zealand would be submerged. Beijing, Seoul, New York, and London would be flooded. Virtually all of the planet's islands would be uninhabitable. Egypt could lose 15 percent of its arable land. Cities surrounded by water—like Miami and Galveston—would be swamped. So would Atlantic City, Ocean City, and Myrtle Beach. Salt water flowing into the Delaware and Hudson river basins would poison the drinking water of Philadelphia and New York.

Those parts of the globe not flooded would get drier. Rainfall patterns would shift; parts of North America and Europe would dry up. Increased evaporation would lead to drier soils over much of the still-exposed land. Cold seasons would shorten, warm seasons lengthen. Strong winds, hurricanes, and assorted other storms, caused by shifting ocean currents and a rising sea level, would devastate cities and populations.

Ripple effects would show up, in changed soil conditions, lower crop yields, and less river water for generating hydroelectric power. There would be more droughts, and many more days above 100 degrees in some regions. Irrigation and food production would be radically altered. Many kinds of trees would die, as would other species of plants and wildlife. The world's food supply would be dramatically affected.

Many forests would turn to grasslands, water supplies would be tainted, recreational lakes would dry up, wetlands would flood. Higher water temperatures and rising sea levels would reduce fish and shellfish populations, and higher air temperatures would cause an increased demand for electricity. Fifty to 90 percent of America's salt marshes, swamps, and bayous—some of the world's most diverse natural habitats—would be destroyed. Devastating changes might occur in the oceans, which would be affected in ways no one can reasonably predict.

The social and political consequences of such warming-related environmental alterations are equally hard to predict. A change in climate would make certain geographical locations more conducive to living than others (it's unlikely people will continue to migrate to America's southwest if places like Phoenix are registering temperatures in the 130s and 140s). Fights over water would ensue. Political skirmishes would grow as shifts in resources—like food supplies—burgeoned.

Already, international corporate giants are starting to assess the potential effects to their businesses if such climate changes occur. According to *Fortune*, Weyerhaeuser, the giant forest-products company based in Tacoma, Washington is worried about their 2 million acres in Oklahoma and Arkansas, where some scientists are predicting a warm, dry trend that would kill off their investment. British Petroleum, which has spent $11 billion on oil and gas operations in Alaska, is also concerned because their drilling rigs, housing, and roads, and even the trans-Alaska pipeline, are all built on permafrost, which would most likely thaw in a warming trend.

Some states and nations are already making plans based on predictions of global warming. North Carolina has established a no-construction shoreline buffer zone. In 1988 Maine approved regulations allowing coastal development with the understanding that if sea levels rise enough to inundate a property, that property will revert to nature, with the owner footing the bill for dismantling or moving structures. But such legislation won't help every coastal area. Boston and New York would be safe only if surrounded by 10-foot walls.

The dikes that wind through the Netherlands illustrate what might happen if the seas rise dramatically. Nearly 60 percent of that country lies below sea level and each year the Dutch spend a larger proportion of their GNP—roughly 6 percent—than the United States spends on military defense, just to maintain the complex system of dikes, seawalls, and other structures that protect them from the sea. Seawall construction—to save airports, bridges, and wells—may become a booming global industry in the next century. But in a place like Bangladesh, where sandbagging and ditch digging and dike building would be impractical, not to mention unaffordable, the only solution may be picking up and moving. But only if there is enough warning . . .

Remember, all of these predictions are just that, predictions. There's no need to build your house on stilts, yet. Remember too that computer models, despite their sophistication, are still imperfect. No one knows for certain what the effects will be of global warming. So even though such predictions suggest a bleak environmental future, many scientists warn that such forecasts are alarmist. They point out that the drought of 1988, which originally sparked much of the public's awareness of the greenhouse effect, was later explained as largely the result of other natural forces.

There is also some evidence to support the theory that carbon dioxide and the other gases may not be the cause of the Earth's warming after all; rather, natural cycles might be causing the atmosphere to heat up. Scientists who subscribe to this school of thought cite the fact that 6,000 and 1,000 years ago average temperatures were apparently 1 to 3.5 degrees warmer than they are today. Since carbon dioxide levels were at a preindustrial level during those periods, it would be hard to blame that warming on a buildup of carbon dioxide or the other gases.

There are also those who think that nature can and will remedy even the most horrific abuses people impose on the planet. They cite "feedbacks," in which increases in pollutants cause climatic changes that, in turn, influence the level of those pollutants or modify their effects on climate. For example, a higher level of carbon dioxide in the atmosphere will promote faster decay of vegetation, releasing carbon dioxide even more quickly. Yet the same in-crease in carbon dioxide will also hasten plant growth, which will speed the removal of carbon dioxide from the air. Still others worry that urbanization—not the greenhouse effect—may be the reason the globe is warming. Some believe that replacing heat-absorbing forests and pastures with heat-radiating asphalt streets and concrete buildings paves the way for climatic change, regardless of the thickness of the greenhouse blanket.

It is not, however, just the rise in average temperature that is cause for concern. If warming occurs quickly, it will take only a handful of extreme storms (which could leave thousands dead) or two or three worldwide drought years in a row to prove that global warming can bring drastic change.

Wallace S. Broecker, a professor of geochemistry at Columbia University and an expert on global warming, believes such changes are inevitable and unstoppable, and that people should be doing everything they can now to slow them down. "My feeling is we overestimate our ability to predict," he says. "Many of the things that are going to happen to the planet will be surprises, like the ozone hole over Antarctica. Therefore, we should be much more careful about what we are doing and much more observant of how the system works."

SOLUTIONS

The greenhouse effect may be the preeminent environmental problem facing the world today. A variety of factors contribute to it—overpopulation, deforestation, ozone depletion, garbage dumping, and more—which we'll go into in detail in the chapters to come. But even though most experts believe that global warming is a certainty, there are many ways in which individuals can help slow its arrival. Consider:

• In Thailand, social worker Mechai Viravaidya promotes family planning—to help slow the country's population growth—by renting water buffaloes more cheaply to those who use contraception.

• Thomas Lovejoy arranges for congressmen (and anyone else) to accompany him to the rain forests of the Amazon, to educate them first-hand about the many problems caused by deforestation. Governments from Costa Rica to Peru have initiated "ecotourist" trips, aimed at enticing travelers to their country. Their intent is both to help explain the problems facing their nations and to beef up their economies with ecotourist dollars.

• In Canada, hundreds of car owners have switched to natural gas, to help cut down on nitrous oxide emissions. Cooperating service stations and fuel distributors are helping by setting up new pumps and new deliveries.

• Auto owners in the United States are being encouraged to seek out service stations equipped with recycling equipment that cleanses and reuses the car air conditioner's Freon, which is 100 percent CFCs. In West Germany, monthly rounds are made by city trucks to collect refrigerators, which harbor greenhouse-building and ozone-depleting CFCs.

• Luz International now operates seven solar electric-generating systems, which provide cheap energy to southern Californians on the hottest days of summer. The company's success has encouraged both smaller electric power facilities and individuals to rethink solar energy.

• The Highland (New York) Middle and High School Tree Committee has given away 5,000 evergreen seedlings and planted hundreds of large trees in its community. Similar programs are being duplicated around the world. Their goal is to help absorb excess carbon dioxide in the atmosphere and to provide shade, which cuts down on the demand for electricity for air conditioners.

It may prove helpful in the long run that global warming has so quickly become part of the world's vocabulary and encouraged so many individuals to try to help. This increased visibility should encourage the appearance of international laws and recommendations. International global warming forums are held weekly, it seems. Participants—whether scientists or policymakers—wrestle with the formulation of protocols and controls that should help governments reduce their nation's contributions to the greenhouse shield. The International Conference on the Changing Atmosphere, held in Toronto in the summer of 1988, for example, drew 300 delegates from 48 countries. It was the first large-scale attempt to meld the contributions of scientists and policymakers on a wide range of atmospheric problems.

The conference resulted in a call for both specific alterations and general preparation for the future. Regardless of their practicality, at least the recommendations started the ball rolling toward a united approach. The conference called for a 20 percent reduction of carbon dioxide emissions by industrialized nations by 2005, using a combination of conservation and reduced consumption of fossil fuels; a switch from coal or oil to other fuels; more funding for solar, wind, and geothermal energy; drastic reductions in deforestation and encouragement of local replanting; labeling of products whose manufacturer does not harm the environment; and elimination of CFCs.

There are certain policies that should be adopted across the board in all nations. Costs of fossil fuels should be raised, because current prices fail to reflect the environmental costs of pumping carbon dioxide into the air. Taxes on carbon dioxide emissions—a kind of user's fee—to be paid by anyone who buys gasoline, coal, or natural gas should be mandated. At the same time credit could be given companies—or individuals—if they plant trees. Incentives should be created to encourage switching from coal and oil to natural gas. Even methane has a potentially positive use. At the world's largest landfill, Fresh Kills on Staten Island, methane is being collected by a gas company and used to heat a few test homes. The technique essentially involves driving a pipe into the depths of the garbage and trapping the gas that rushes out. This technique could potentially be used at landfills around the globe.

For its part the U.S. Environmental Protection Agency has proposed a list of suggested reductions—only time will tell how many of them will become law. The agency's recommendations include doubling fuel efficiency standards; reducing the amount of fuel it takes to heat single-family homes to half the amount used in 1980; stopping deforestation; imposing fees on coal, oil, and natural gas to provide economic incentives to shift away from use of fossil fuels; accelerating research into solar power; increasing the use of sustainable wood and other vegetation, as a replacement for fossil fuels in the production of energy; and ending production of CFCs.

By now efficiency and conservation may sound like tired advice. It seems we've been instructed to do more of both nonstop since the energy crisis of the early 1970s. But they remain the only salvation if the planet is to maintain itself as we have become accustomed to it. Global warming is primarily a result of people using too much fossil fuel. Reducing our consumption is the only solution. That means using less electricity, driving fewer miles, making fewer babies. The Worldwatch Institute, a respected Washington-based environmental think-tank that annually publishes a report on the state of the world's environment, estimates that even a 1 percent annual increase in the rate of energy efficiency would still nearly double carbon dioxide levels by 2075, while a 2 percent annual increase in efficiency would keep levels stable, probably resulting in a much less catastrophic rise in temperatures. Solar, wind, geothermal, and hydropower—all of which have suffered from the continued availability of cheap oil—must

again be considered. Examples of successful solar and wind use abound. India—using systems developed in California—plans to develop 5,000 megawatts of wind power by the end of the century, providing energy for the needs of half a million homes. Solar water heaters are used in 65 percent of Israeli homes. Japan has about 4 million solar water heaters in use. More than 60 percent of Brazil's national energy use comes from renewable sources.

Reckless deforestation must be halted and the millions of rain forest acres already stripped to stumps and decay must be replanted. Roger Sant, chief executive officer of Applied Energy Services of Arlington, Virginia, is leading the way by example. His small utility company is helping to finance the planting of 50 million trees in Guatemala's rain forest. Sant became the first energy executive to take personal responsibility for his industry's pollution, and to step in with a cure. He contacted the World Resources Institute and was put in touch with CARE, Inc., an international relief agency. Over the next 10 years CARE plans to plant enough trees to remove 15 million metric tons of carbon dioxide from the atmosphere—roughly equal to the amount of carbon dioxide that Applied Energy's coal-fired plant in Uncasville, Connecticut, will have emitted during its 40-year lifetime. Similar tree-planting programs are already under way on city streets across the United States and in deforested regions of Indonesia, South Korea, and China. India has a goal of planting more than 12 million acres of trees per year. (Unfortunately, tree-planting alone is not a cure-all. A forestry expert with Resources for the Future, an independent research group, has calculated that it would take $186 billion to $372 billion to establish enough new forests to absorb the billions of tons of carbon dioxide poured into the world's atmosphere each year.)

Changing the balance of fossil fuels will help, too. Any shift to natural gas will lessen carbon dioxide

The carbon absorbed from the atmosphere by trees is released as carbon dioxide when trees are burned. The destruction of the Earth's tropical rain forests adds up to 2.5 billion tons of carbon to the atmosphere annually.

pollution because natural gas produces half the carbon dioxide of coal and about two thirds that of oil for the same amount of energy (though it will never completely replace coal or petroleum, simply because they are so abundant). Reducing the manufacture of greenhouse-contributing chlorofluorocarbons is already underway, thanks to an international agreement signed by more than 80 nations.

Toughening the fuel efficiency requirements of cars around the globe is a must. Between 1974 and 1987 the fuel efficiency of new cars in the United States nearly doubled, increasing from 14 to just over 26 miles per gallon, largely because of 1976 energy legislation spurred by oil shortages. If the United States were to double fuel-efficiency standards for vehicles again by the end of the century—a level that can be achieved with cars now on the market—global carbon dioxide emissions would drop significantly. A current EPA proposal calls for an international effort to require all new autos produced around the world to achieve an average of at least 40 miles per gallon. It also calls for automobiles in all industrial countries to have catalytic converters—mandated in the United States—to reduce tailpipe emissions, which produce both nitrogen oxide and ozone. If such measures are to accomplish any real good though, they must be international.

Governments around the globe are studying how they can help encourage reductions in greenhouse contributors. In Great Britain, Prime Minister Margaret Thatcher made her cabinet sit through a day of lectures from scientists about the coming heat wave. Prime ministers Brian Mulroney of Canada and Gro Harlem Brundtland of Norway have pledged that their countries will slow fossil fuel use and forgive some Third World debt, allowing developing countries to concentrate on cleaning up their environment, not paying off loans. West Germany's environmentalist Green Party recently obtained a governing role in West Berlin and may hold the balance of power in the next national election. Reducing the emission of greenhouse gases is one of their top priorities. The Greens' electoral power is growing in Italy and France, too, and making inroads in Budapest and Moscow, which gives hope to environmentalists around the world.

In the United States, the Bush Administration has given off mixed signals regarding global warming (mixed to the degree that they toned down the language of NASA's Hansen about the severity of global warming in testimony to the Office of Management and Budget). The Administration claims to be taking a wait-and-see approach, arguing that until the scientific community is certain of the effects of global warming, it's too early to rush solutions into law. The Administration's mid-1989 proposed amendment to the Clean Air Act does call for increased research on use of alternative fuels and for stricter fuel efficiency. But until more "proof" is in hand, Bush and EPA chief William Reilly remain hesitant to become party to any international treaty aimed specifically at slowing global warming.

The challenge of convincing developing nations to include conservation and efficiency in their growth plans still looms large. According to the Worldwatch Institute, some newly industrialized countries, such as Taiwan, South Korea, and Brazil, have begun to use state-of-the-art industrial machines and processes, accompanied by a broad array of energy efficiency standards and financial incentives. But most of the Third World lags far behind in terms of applying energy efficiency standards or encouraging reductions. Many countries are still going through the early, energy-intensive phases of industrialization, so their energy use is rising rather than falling. Few are ready to even consider policies to restrain consumption. Thus the challenge for any international forum is to explain fully why *all* nations must cooperate in seeking solutions if the global warming trend is to be slowed.

Arriving at restrictions fair to all countries is even harder than usual when it comes to greenhouse gases, though. How, for example, can developed nations expect that China, which has plans to double its coal production in the next 15 years in order to spur development, will be willing or even able to change course? Yes, the modernization of aging power plants around the globe would help—upgrading India's electric power distribution system, for example, could double the effective energy output—but who is going to pay for such change?

While Japan has its share of environmental flaws—they are the world's largest importer of rain forest wood—the country's energy efficiency stands as an example to all nations. The world's third-largest economy, it is one of the most efficient, despite or perhaps because of the fact that it has few natural resources. Both government and industry have long promoted energy efficiency. As a result, in 1986 Japan spent only 4 percent of its GNP to pay its fuel bill; the United States used 10 percent. The United States currently uses twice as much energy to produce a dollar's worth of goods and services as Japan does. The Soviet Union, with one of the world's least efficient economies, uses three times as much.

If Japan's example is to be duplicated in other countries, similar nationwide energy efficiency standards must be put in place immediately. Slowing the effects of global warming is a long, difficult process. It involves great will, both technically and politically. But we can't simply stand by as the world heats up; if we do, the greenhouse effect may prove the ultimate environmental catastrophe, rendering all others mere annoyances.

Neither can we wait while scientists argue over their forecasting abilities. There is enough evidence of a warming trend to show that action must be taken today—internationally, nationally, and individually. Unfortunately, as humanity has progressed the atmosphere has become something we take for granted. Global warming proves that nothing—particularly tomorrow's weather—can be taken for granted.

GLOBAL WARMING

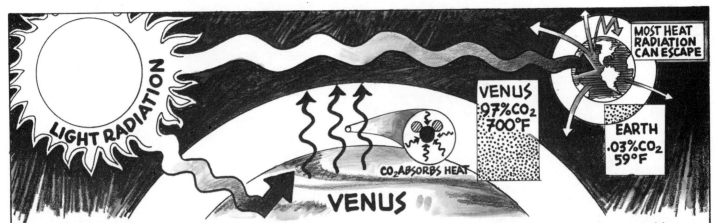

Venus receives roughly the same amount of the sun's energy as Earth, but its surface temperature is a scorching 700° F. The difference is due to the level of carbon dioxide in each planet's atmosphere. Carbon dioxide—which absorbs heat—makes up 97 percent of Venus's atmosphere. By comparison, only .03 percent of the Earth's atmosphere is carbon dioxide.

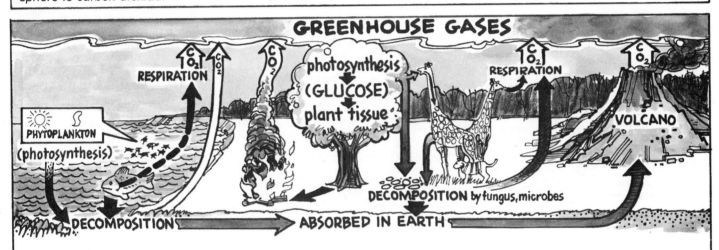

Carbon dioxide is continually recycled through the Earth's water and air, and animal and plant life. It contributes to the greenhouse effect along with other gases that absorb heat and influence the Earth's temperature.

But man's industrialization has upset the delicate balance of the atmosphere by spewing ever more greenhouse gases into it. The amount of carbon dioxide in the atmosphere (primarily a result of man's increased use of fossil fuels—coal, oil, wood—for energy) has grown by 25 percent since 1860.

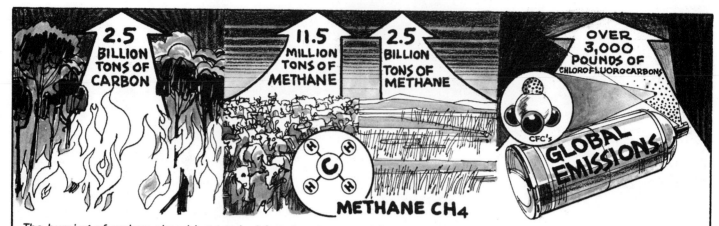

The burning of carbon-absorbing tropical forests releases additional carbon dioxide into the atmosphere. And there are other greenhouse gases besides carbon dioxide: Methane, excreted in enormous amounts by our herds of livestock and by bacteria in rice paddies; and chlorofluorocarbons, man-made chemicals used as refrigerants are both greenhouse gases.

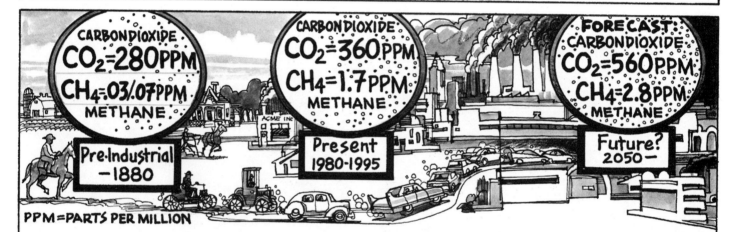

The result of these extra gaseous emissions is that the composition of our air has changed, and is changing. We add over 22 billion tons of carbon dioxide per year to the atmosphere, and it is predicted that the concentration of carbon in the atmosphere will have doubled by the middle of the next century.

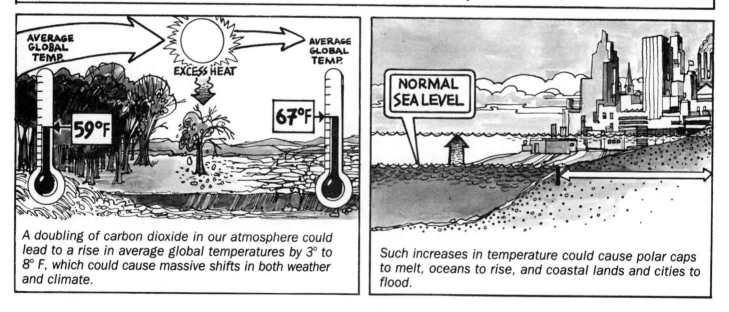

A doubling of carbon dioxide in our atmosphere could lead to a rise in average global temperatures by 3° to 8° F, which could cause massive shifts in both weather and climate.

Such increases in temperature could cause polar caps to melt, oceans to rise, and coastal lands and cities to flood.

Some scientists contend that nature will take care of itself, and eventually slow any global warming encouraged by man. An increase in clouds, they suggest, could help cool temperatures. But if the trillion tons of ice contained in the polar tundra and continental shelves were to melt, global warming could happen too quickly for nature to counter-balance.

The primary cause of global warming remains the burning of fossil fuel for energy. Thus each person can help slow global warming by reducing the amount of energy he or she uses—whether it comes from electricity, wood, or oil.

Planting trees—on the roofs of city buildings, along streets, or even within existing forests—is a simple way to help, because trees absorb carbon dioxide.

Switching to alternative sources of fuel for transportation will help, too. Methanol, natural gas, and even hydrogen produce fewer greenhouse gases. Riding bicycles, using mass transportation, and walking will help reduce the amount of pollution in the atmosphere.

Individual Action

1. Conserving energy in your daily activities is the most fundamental way to slow the production of gases that create the greenhouse blanket. From the simple (turning off lights not in use, even buying more efficient light bulbs) to the slightly more involved (like paying attention to the efficiency ratings of new appliances and insulating your home better), there are things everyone can do. If all Americans were to own the fuel-efficient refrigerators now on the market, for example, the resulting savings in electricity would be equivalent to the output of 18 large coal-powered generating plants. ("Energy efficiency," says the Worldwatch Institute, "will buy the greatest degree of climate insurance for the dollar.")

2. Proposals to require Detroit and other car makers to double the fuel efficiency of new cars are on the boards. Individuals can help by making fuel-efficient cars a priority. In the past few years, as oil prices have dropped, Americans especially have gone back to buying "gas guzzlers" and "muscle cars." It is that kind of behavior that is at the root of so many of the world's environmental problems. If there were no demand for such cars, automakers wouldn't produce them.

3. If you own a car, it is essential to keep it tuned up. Fuel-efficient cars produce less nitrogen oxide and ozone; those properly tuned create even less pollution.

4. Consider natural gas or a methane-blend fuel. (Natural gas sells for half the cost of unleaded gas.) Experiments with both are ongoing, from Canada to Sweden; U.S. automakers all have natural-gas powered prototypes. Special pumps are required, and so is conversion of your car's fuel tank. But with tax incentives for conversion, natural gas could easily become the fuel of choice, especially for fleets of both private and public taxis, trucks, and delivery vans.

5. To encourage continued experimentation with alternative fuels, higher taxes on carbon-dioxide-producing fuels should be encouraged. Individuals should lobby their local and national legislators to promote such legislation.

6. Smokeless forms of energy generation— like solar and wind power—should be encouraged, in part by an increase in federal funding for alternative sources. While putting a solar collector on your roof may sound like a sixties fad, it is actually more practical—and affordable—than ever. Write your legislator to suggest a recommitment to federal tax incentives for alternative energy sources instead of increased subsidies for the oil industry.

7. Landfills around the world are growing higher, and they may hold a unique form of energy. Siphoning methane gas from the interiors of landfills—and feedlots—has already proved a viable home-heating alternative. The process serves a dual role—eliminating the greenhouse-contributing methane gas and offering an alternative to fossil-fuel-generated power. Agencies in charge of local landfills should be encouraged to investigate.

8. Planting 400 million trees in urban areas of the United States is a goal of the American Forestry Association and others, and should be encouraged. A fast-growing tree can recycle 48 pounds of carbon dioxide each year, so tree planting is one of the most cost-effective, immediate and gratifying steps you can take to fight global warming. This applies to both country and city residents. If only 100 million trees were planted in urban areas of the United States to help shade residences it would result in a savings in air conditioning costs alone of $4 billion a year. That doesn't include the role of trees as "lungs," sucking carbon dioxide out of the atmosphere.

9. **Future production of chlorofluorocarbons** (CFCs) has already been drastically limited by international agreement. That agreement should serve as a model of international cooperation as international forums try to resolve environmental problems in coming years. But that agreement to phase out production of CFCs does not eliminate the problem—there are still billions of dollars' worth of CFC-related products in homes and offices. Caution must be taken when getting rid of a variety of goods, from automobiles to refrigerators, in order to prevent the CFCs they contain from leaking into the atmosphere. Recycling such goods is a growing business.

10. **Eat low on the food chain (i.e., less meat).** Cattle produce methane through anaerobic bacteria in their digestive tracts. The more fruits and

vegetables you eat, the fewer cows will be needed, resulting in less methane production. Also, try and buy locally grown produce. Buying and consuming local food supports regional agriculture, as well as requiring less transportation and the accompanying carbon dioxide emissions.

11. **Write state and national legislators to** encourage them to support bills aimed at curbing global warming. In the U.S. Congress two bills are pending: the Global Warming Prevention Act and the National Energy Policy Act. Both call for a 20 percent reduction in the nation's carbon dioxide emissions by the year 2000, placing heavy emphasis on increasing energy efficiency and accelerating the development of renewable energy sources. The Prevention Act also calls for tougher fuel consumption standards—45 miles per gallon for cars and 35 miles per gallon for light trucks—and an office of recycling in the Department of Commerce.

Government Action

1. **All nations should support the adoption of** an international treaty to limit greenhouse gas production. Such an accord is currently being negotiated under the auspices of the Intergovernmental Panel on Climate Change.

2. **New businesses should be required to reg**ulate their emissions so that there is no net increase in greenhouse gases. This can be done by energy conservation, by retiring older facilities that produce more carbon dioxide, or by investing in mass transit and tree planting projects.

3. **A national timetable for the phasing out of** fossil fuels and the implementation of alternative energy sources should be planned and adhered to.

4. **Environmental costs should be figured into** the cost of doing business. Currently, coal, oil, and natural gas prices are set without any reference to the environmental damage they may sow. Higher taxes on all three—matched to their role as pollutants—should be mandated.

5. **National and local governments should do** everything they can to promote energy efficiency and the use of non–fossil fuel alternatives. Budgets should include money for renewable energy sources, like solar, wind, and geothermal power.

6. **Higher standards of building insulation and** mandatory use of R4 insulating windows in new buildings should be legislated, and consumer purchases of minifluorescent light bulbs should be subsidized, as part of national goals towards energy efficiency.

7. Incentives should be legislated that en-courage moderate population growth.

8. Help—in money, technology, or manpower—should be offered to developing nations seeking alternatives to burning fossil fuels for energy.

9. The international treaty banning CFC pro-duction by the year 2000—signed by 81 nations—must be enforced, and its policies adopted by more nations.

10. Tree planting, in both urban and ruralareas, should be supported and funded.

Reading

Global Warming: Are We Entering the Greenhouse Century?, by Stephen Schneider. San Francisco: Sierra Club Books, 1989.

The Challenge of Global Warming, edited by Dean Abrahamson. New York: Island Press (with the Natural Resources Defense Council), 1989. (Call 1-800-628-2828, ext. 416, to order.)

The End of Nature, by Bill McKibben. New York: Random House, 1989.

A Matter of Degrees: The Potential for Controlling the Greenhouse Effect, by Irving M. Mintzer. Washington, DC: World Resources Institute, 1987.

The Potential Effects of Global Climate Change on the United States: Draft Report to Congress, edited by Joel B. Smith and Dennis A. Tirpak. Two volumes. Washington, DC: Environmental Protection Agency, 1988. Telephone 202-382-2090.

Global Climate Change Digest (newsletter). Elsevier Science Publishing, 655 Avenue of the Americas, New York, NY 10010. Telephone 212-370-5520.

The Greenhouse Gases, by Robin Clark. New York: United Nations Environment Programme, 1987. North American Office, Room DC2-0803, United Nations, New York, NY 10017. Telephone 212-963-8093.

"What's Happening to Our Climate?" by Samuel W. Matthews. *National Geographic,* November 1976.

Cooling the Greenhouse: Vital First Steps to Combat Global Warming. New York: Natural Resources Defense Council, 1989. 40 West 20th Street, New York, NY 10011.

Breathing Easier: Taking Action on Climate Change, Air Pollution, and Energy Insecurity, by J. J. MacKenzie. Washington, DC: World Resources Institute, 1989.

Organizations to Contact

Environmental Defense Fund, 257 Park Avenue South, New York, NY 10010, 212-505-2100.

Environmental Law Institute, Suite 200, 1616 P Street NW, Washington, DC 20036, 202-328-5150.

Global Greenhouse Network (c/o Foundation on Economic Trends), 1130 17th St. NW, Washington, DC 20036, 202-466-2823.

NRDC's Atmosphere Protection Initiative, Suite 300, 1350 New York Ave. NW, Washington, DC 20005, 202-783-7800.

Renew America, Suite 710, 1400 16th St. NW, Washington, DC 20036, 202-232-2252. (State-by-state breakdowns of carbon dioxide emissions from use of coal, oil, natural gas, and motor vehicles; carbon emissions from residential, industrial and commercial sources; forest cover; and the availability of programs to encourage energy efficiency, discourage acid rain emissions, and restrict emissions of chlorofluorocarbons and methane.)

Sierra Club, 730 Polk St., San Francisco, CA 94109, 415-776-2211. (Global warming poster—$5 for non-members; $4.50 for members, plus $1 shipping charge.)

United Nations Environment Programme, North American Office, Room DC2-0803, United Nations, New York, NY 10017, 212-963-8093.

2

Ozone Depletion

When was the last time you looked at the sky—really studied it, watched the clouds float by, followed a flock of geese, gazed at the stars? Too often in this fast-paced world we only look up when warned of a smog alert or if the afternoon skies are disrupted by thunderstorms. Day in and day out, nose to the grindstone, eyes locked on the path straight ahead, we rarely pause to consider the air we breathe—and pollute.

As complicated as the atmosphere truly is, there is a simple way to "visualize" its components, by dividing it into three fairly distinct layers, which differ chiefly by temperature. The lowest layer—the *troposphere*—extends from the land-water surface up to an elevation of about five miles in polar regions and 10 miles in the tropics. The higher you go in the troposphere the colder it gets. This layer contains about 75 percent of the atmosphere's total mass and virtually all of the water vapor and clouds. It is the layer where storms are produced and airplanes fly.

Above the troposphere is the *stratosphere*. Its ceiling is as high as 30 miles above Earth, and the higher you go, the hotter it gets. At the very top of the stratosphere—where it's at its hottest—is where ozone is created and the sun's ultraviolet rays are absorbed. Above the stratosphere is the *mesosphere*, which extends another 20 miles and is characterized by cooler temperatures.

It is the layer of ozone, hovering at the top of the stratosphere, that has gotten so much attention in the past few years. A man-made pollutant at ground level, ozone is a naturally produced, life-protecting shield 15 miles above the Earth's surface. A strong-smelling, slightly bluish gas, it is composed of three oxygen atoms (versus the two-atom variety we breathe) and is regarded as "the Jekyll and Hyde of the atmosphere."

About 90 percent of all ozone is located in the upper regions of the stratosphere; the rest is formed when emissions from automobiles and industries mix with the oxygen we breathe. Formed at ground level, ozone is one of the greenhouse gases responsible for warming the globe. But in the stratosphere, it acts as an umbrella, filtering the sun's most dangerous ultraviolet rays from the Earth, protecting humanity and nature from a handful of potentially disastrous environmental ills.

The reason this ozone layer has recently received so much attention is due to a kind of chemical experiment in the sky. In the mid-1980s it was confirmed—after years of suspicion—that the Earth's ozone shield is dissipating. The cause is laid primarily to man-made chemicals—chlorofluorocarbons (CFCs)—which are part and parcel of a variety of daily goods: from refrigerators to air-conditioners, aerosols to foam cushions. (Halons, carbon tetrachloride, and methyl chloroform also contribute to the depletion.) Originally regarded as "wonder chemicals," CFCs have in fact been proven "killers." Their first victim is the ozone layer over Antarctica, in which they have "torn" a 1.2-million-square-mile hole.

Patching this hole won't be easy. Worldwide, industry sells $2.2 billion worth of CFCs each year. Even if CFCs were banned today, it would take more than 100 years to rid the atmosphere of those already in existence. The danger is that as the ozone shield thins, the well-being of every person on Earth is threatened. This depletion serves as an example—both good and bad—of people's ability to deal with the unanticipated effects of a runaway pollutant. International negotiations to weigh the future of CFCs and other ozone-destroying compounds have produced some positive results. And the public appears ready to help. A 1989 study conducted by the Roosevelt Center for American Policy Studies in Washington, D.C., reported that four times as many Americans were worried about ozone depletion as they were about Communism's spread or the threat of a U.S.–Soviet nuclear war.

CAUSES

A combination of factors has made ozone depletion easier to isolate and address than other environmental problems. Unlike the variety of gases that contribute to global warming, ozone depletion is primarily the responsibility of one, comparatively simple chemical compound. The number of countries that produce the chemical is relatively small. Already, 81 nations have called for the discontinuation of CFC manufacturing by the year 2000. But despite the apparent ease and quickness of those efforts, the challenge of finding an adequate substitute for this valuable chemical is great. And the impossibility of ridding the ecosystem of those that have already been produced, means the potential for disaster lingers.

When CFCs were first developed in the 1930s, they seemed like a chemist's dream: odorless, non-flammable, noncorrosive, nontoxic. They cooled refrigerators and air conditioners and cleaned delicate electronics. They are used in manufacturing plastic foam, in home insulation, and throwaway food containers. In the United States, they also propelled aerosols in everything from deodorants to whipped cream, until they were banned in 1978. They were literally dubbed a "wonder chemical."

Their environmental hazard was not foreseen by their inventor, Thomas Midgley, an American chemist whose dubious legacy also includes the idea of adding lead to gasoline. In 1930, working for the Frigidaire division of General Motors, Midgley hit upon CFCs as nontoxic coolants to replace poisonous ammonia in refrigerators. (His first compound was actually Freon, the Du Pont brand name for CFCs.) People quickly found hundreds of uses for the chemicals and Midgley scoffed at any suggestion that they were hazardous. In fact, before an audience he once inhaled a mouthful of them and blew out a candle to prove that they were indeed nontoxic and noncombustible. CFCs were considered completely safe: they didn't react with other substances or break down easily, and would remain stable for up to 150 years.

But if CFCs were the "perfect" chemical on the ground, they pulled a Mr. Hyde–like transformation in the stratosphere. After drifting high in the sky, the compound acted like a high-altitude Pac-Man, devouring all the ozone it could, destroying it. The reaction is simple: Once split apart in the stratosphere by solar UV radiation, a chlorine atom in a CFC molecule plucks off one of the three oxygen atoms in ozone. A single chlorine atom can, over time, destroy more than 100,000 ozone molecules.

For years the concern that CFCs were "eating away" the ozone layer was one held by just a smattering of atmospheric scientists. The inconclusiveness of stratospheric studies provided a ready excuse not to act against CFCs, even though by the early 1970s a handful of scientists around the world were beginning to question what would happen if CFCs destroyed more and more of the ozone layer. The companies that manufactured the chemicals balked at slowing production, insisting no solid evidence pointed to a serious environmental problem.

It wasn't until 1974, when two scientists at the University of California at Irvine—Sherwood Rowland and his assistant Mario Molina—studiously traced the path of CFCs after they were released into the atmosphere, that their devastating potential was unveiled. (By then millions of tons of the chemical compound had spiraled into the atmosphere.) Rowland and Molina claimed that 99 percent of all CFCs released would end up in the stratosphere, where they would survive for many decades. Once at that elevation, CFCs would be broken down by ultraviolet radiation and release chlorine atoms, which would then trigger the chain reaction leading to the destruction of ozone. This trail of events troubled the scientists and they sounded the alarm: if CFC emissions were not stemmed, they warned, the stratospheric ozone shield would be drastically depleted by the middle of the twenty-first century. The result would be exposing the Earth to untold levels of dangerous ultraviolet radiation.

Rowland and Molina called for an immediate ban on CFC aerosol propellants, but their theory was disputed vigorously both by colleagues and the chemical industry. Opponents demanded proof, insisting the Californians' theory was just that. Du Pont—the world's largest manufacturer of CFCs—asked Congress to delay any action until further studies were conducted. The Governing Council of the United Nations Environment Programme believed Rowland and Molina enough to convene a panel of experts to examine the problem in 1977. The next year Canada, Sweden, and the United States banned the use of CFCs in aerosol sprays.

The smoking gun, providing absolute proof that CFCs were responsible for destroying sizable amounts of ozone, was not found until almost a decade later. The ultimate clue was a large hole in the ozone layer, discovered over Antarctica by a British survey team in 1984. This was no pinprick; according to their studies, a hole the size of the United States was opening every summer over the seventh continent.

Ironically, the chief of the British Antarctica Survey, Joseph Farman, had first noticed a thinning of the ozone shield as far back as 1977. His studies showed that beginning in September, the atmosphere over Antarctica would lose more and more ozone, until November, when the stratospheric winds would change and the hole would disappear. But Farman was convinced his studies were an aberration, since none of the sophisticated satellite monitors or computer models employed by NASA and other global scientists were transmitting the information that he was seeing. Finally, convinced that he was correct and frustrated by his lone stand, Farman went public with his findings in 1985, writing about them for a British science magazine. While his colleagues were initially skeptical of the report they nevertheless rushed south to confirm whether or not he might be right.

His discovery was soon verified, even by NASA scientists who claimed that their satellites had, in fact, spotted the depletion in 1984, but that they had dismissed it as a computer malfunction because of the drastic nature of the decrease in ozone levels. While it was clear that Farman's finding was, as one report dubbed it, "the monitoring scoop of the century," and that the ozone shield was thinning, no one was sure what was to blame. CFCs were immediately suspected, but not everyone was immediately convinced they could cause such severe damage. Other theories emerged, but all were found to have holes of their own. While scientists searched for a rationale, the ozone depletion over Antarctica worsened: Farman's 1985 study showed it dissipating by 50 percent. In 1987, the dissipation rate jumped to 60 percent, and the hole remained open longer than ever before, spreading toward South America, New Zealand, and Australia.

Eventually, there were two potential leading culprits: CFCs or the extreme cold and wind characteristic of the skies over Antarctica. In May 1988, 200 researchers from nine countries who were meet-

CFC Emissions Around the Globe

CFCs, or chlorofluorocarbons, broken up into ozone-destroying compounds by UV radiation from the sun, are carried to the poles on global winds created by the movement of the Earth. Western Europe and the United States contribute most of the world's CFCs.

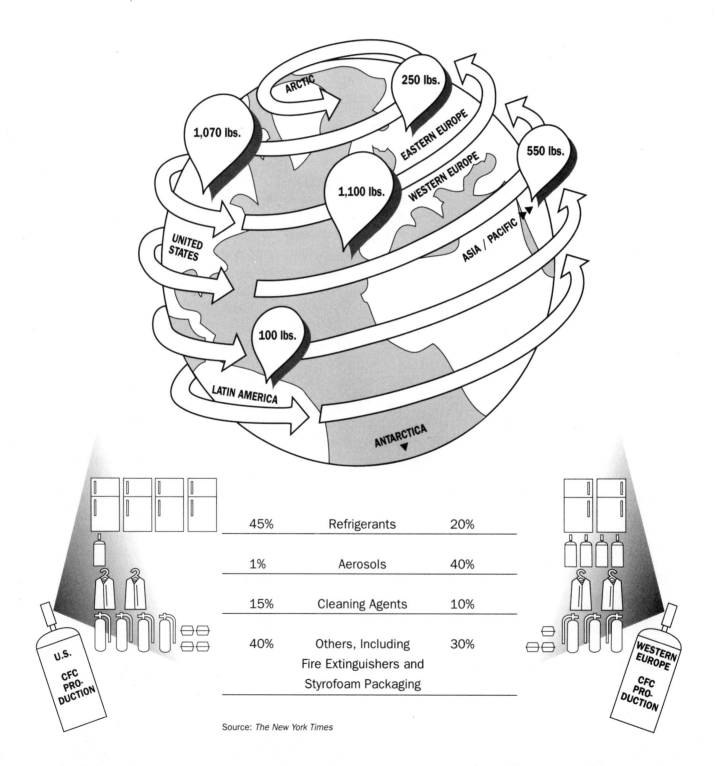

45%	Refrigerants	20%
1%	Aerosols	40%
15%	Cleaning Agents	10%
40%	Others, Including Fire Extinguishers and Styrofoam Packaging	30%

Source: *The New York Times*

ing in Colorado reached a consensus, based on several years of newly gathered data from probes carried aloft by balloons, instruments aboard NASA satellites, and even from a supersonic jet flying directly into the heart of the open hole. The ozone layer over Antarctica was thinning, they agreed, and CFCs were responsible.

It turned out that the compound's very stability—one of its early selling points—had turned it into a man-made nightmare. Aerosols were not the only culprit, however. Air conditioners, refrigerators, foam insulation, fast-food containers, and hundreds of solvents all leaked CFCs into the atmosphere. (One common misunderstanding is why all the "bad" ozone produced by automobile exhaust doesn't rise through the atmosphere and replace the ozone being destroyed in the stratosphere. That would be nice, but impossible. The ozone produced by car emissions simply doesn't drift that high, and after a few days, actually reverts back into oxygen.)

While scientists and industry became similarly convinced that CFCs were thinning the ozone layer, their hope was that the problem would be confined to the cold, thin air over Antarctica. Their optimism was dashed by a second report, this time by NASA in 1988, which showed that an ozone hole roughly the size of Greenland was opening annually in the Arctic. Worldwide, said this report, the Earth's ozone shield was estimated to have thinned by between 1.7 to 3 percent since 1970, affecting Europe, North America, and the Soviet Union. All of a sudden, this thinning was no longer an isolated problem over Antarctica, but a global one.

EFFECTS

The loss of just a percent or two of the ozone layer may seem paltry, but it could have unhealthy repercussions for people and nature. The problem with ozone loss is that it increases the amount of one form of ultraviolet light—UV-B—that reaches the Earth. Each 1 percent drop of ozone allows 2 percent more UV-B to reach the ground. This, in turn, increases the potential for skin cancer by 3 to 6 percent. If ozone depletion continues at the current rate, and if CFC usage continues unabated, the EPA predicts more than 60 million additional cases of skin cancer and about one million additional deaths among Americans born by the year 2075. Currently, populations most at risk are those who live closest to the giant hole that opens over Antarctica every September through November: in Argentina, Australia, Chile, and New Zealand.

A diminished ozone layer may also make people more vulnerable to a variety of infectious diseases—including, perhaps, malaria, according to researchers at the World Resources Institute. The EPA also predicts an additional 17 million cases of cataracts if the ozone layer is allowed to deplete at its current rate.

But increased UV-B radiation doesn't only harm humans, it will disrupt the food chain as well. As UV-B levels increase, the life cycle of plants will be altered and billions of dollars' worth of crops destroyed. (Indicative of the Reagan-era EPA, when the CFC destruction was confirmed, then–Interior Secretary Donald Hodel proposed coping with the dangers of ozone depletion by wearing sunglasses and hats. David Doniger of the NRDC chided that it was hard to put sombreros on crop plants—which may be the hardest-hit victims.)

The impact on the ocean may be even worse. In jeopardy are microscopic organisms necessary to maintain all marine life. In the waters surrounding Antarctica, scientists have already found that increased UV-B has hurt the photosynthesis and metabolism of the plankton at the base of the marine food chain, caused mutations in some marine organisms, and harmed the eggs of others.

Ozone depletion may also disrupt the Earth's climate. Some climatologists fear that a loss of ozone in the stratosphere will cool that layer, perhaps

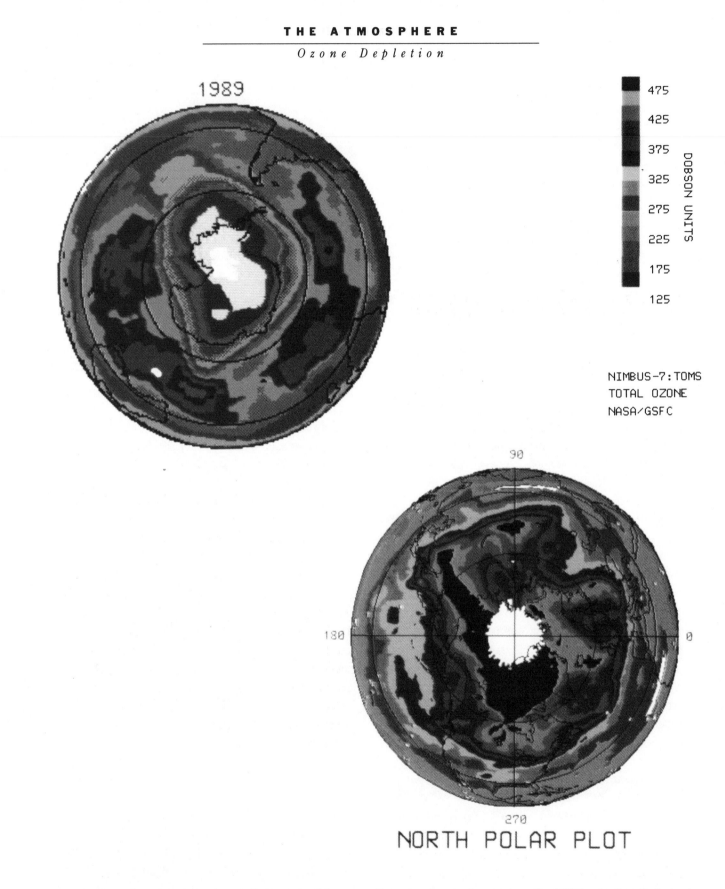

In 1984, a huge hole in the atmosphere's ozone layer was discovered over Antarctica. By 1989, another hole had opened up over the North Pole. The large white areas in recent photographs taken by the Total Ozone Mapping Spectrometer show the sizes of the holes in 1989. (South Pole above, North Pole below)

altering global wind patterns. Shifting winds will change the weather in ways that not even the most advanced computers can project. Not only will the oceans be affected, but the deserts and forests will suffer too. And ultimately, a diminished ozone layer will help heat up the atmosphere, adding to the threat of global warming.

SOLUTIONS

The ozone hole above Antarctica is nature's way of giving us a warning. It is one of a string of environmental "surprises"— not dissimilar to the accumulations of DDT that killed off bird populations in the 1960s, or the fire on the Cuyahoga River in Ohio, a result of its being filled with toxic waste—that have unexpectedly, and potentially irreversibly, shocked one of Earth's life-support systems. Michael Oppenheimer of the Environmental Defense Fund suggests that the ozone hole may stand for decades "as a red light flashing a warning every spring against irreversible tampering with the atmosphere."

Given what we now know about the destructive potential of CFCs, it would appear that getting rid of them would be simple. Unfortunately, they are scattered everywhere around industrialized societies. If you live in a modern home or apartment, or work in a modern building or large manufacturing plant, they are in the insulation. They are used in air quality control systems, air conditioning, and refrigeration. When you eat perishable foods that were transported in refrigerated trucks, or shop at supermarkets with refrigerated storage containers, or if you have a refrigerator, freezer, or air conditioner at home, you are a CFC user.

CFCs are used to help regulate climates in zoos, hockey rinks, art galleries, museums, homes, and offices. If you've been hospitalized, CFCs have probably been used to help sterilize surgical instruments and cool X-ray equipment. They are found in cleansers used in airplanes, communications systems, and electronic components. In many countries of the world they are still used to propel aerosols. While the United States, Canada, and several Scandinavian countries banned aerosol sprays in 1978, other nations, including France, Japan, and many in Eastern Europe continue to propel products with the chemicals. As a result, aerosol cans are still the largest source of CFC emissions worldwide, contributing as much as one third of the ozone-eating compound.

Recent international response to the discovery that CFCs were responsible for creating the hole in the ozone has been remarkable. Soon after the theory was confirmed, 30 nations signed a treaty known as the Montreal Protocol, which called for the reduction of CFCs manufactured around the world.

Almost immediately, politicians, scientists, and environmentalists argued that the treaty wasn't sufficiently strict. It called for only a 50 percent cut in CFC production by the year 2000—"too little, too late," said the Natural Resources Defense Council and other environmental groups. Simply to stabilize CFCs at their current atmospheric levels would require annual emissions cuts of 85 percent, estimated the EPA. And because the two most widely used forms of CFCs stay in the atmosphere for 75 to 100 years, even if the chemicals were banned tomorrow it would take the planet 100 years to cleanse the ozone destroyer from the stratosphere.

In January 1989, twelve European nations announced they would ban production and use of all CFCs by the year 2000; the next day, the United States said it would enact the same deadline. (Between the 13 countries, they produce 75 percent of the world's CFCs.) Two months after the London meeting, 81 nations gathered for four days in Helsinki and agreed on a complete ban of all CFC production by 2000. (The declaration also calls for provisions to assist developing countries to develop CFC replacements through the funding and transfer of technology.) Such agreements are an indication that the world's leaders recognize the problem of ozone depletion. But working with industry to meet the proposed deadline will be a monumental task.

Both the Montreal Protocol and its revisions serve as exemplary models of how international environmental agreements can be forged (though admittedly it is much easier to deal with an environmental problem that is the result of essentially one industry, as opposed to something like global warming, which entails hundreds of major industries and dozens of chemicals). Discussions about what to do about ozone depletion have fostered a variety of national and international cooperative efforts. The United States and Soviet Union have agreed, for example, to collaborate on further scientific investigations of the atmosphere over Antarctica. The agreement calls for the United States to provide 50 packages of ozone-monitoring equipment and balloons, which the Soviet Union will fly over their Molodezhnaya station. Currently, two British bases and one American base in Antarctica are conducting similar tests.

In the United States more than two dozen ozone protection bills have been passed. Los Angeles requires all service stations and auto repair shops to recycle CFCs. Connecticut's legislation prohibits the sale of new CFC-laden products—from refrigerators to dry cleaning solvents—after July 1, 1992. Vermont's law bans all cars equipped with CFC-using air conditioners by 1993.

Perhaps the most comprehensive law was passed by the city council of Irvine, California—a suburb of Los Angeles. The law prohibits the use of nearly all CFCs in most industrial processes, except in the manufacturing of drugs and medical devices, and when military specifications require them. It bans the sale and use of plastic foam food-packaging and prohibits the use of building insulation containing the compounds. It also requires service stations and auto repair shops to capture and recycle Freon.

The Irvine bill was passed at the behest of the town's mayor, Larry Agran, who estimated before its passage that about 500 of the town's 5,000 businesses would be affected by the law. But he felt it was a "moral obligation" to eliminate the approximately half-million pounds of ozone-depleting chemicals that were being sent into the skies over his community every year. While other communities have banned CFC-made packaging—including Tempe (Ariz.), Portland (Ore.), Berkeley, Newark, and San Francisco—Irvine's law is the most explicit. It covers CFC-related compounds, including halons (used in fire extinguishers), carbon tetrachloride, and methyl chloroform, all potential ozone depleters. Locals were not surprised by Irvine's tough stance—the city has long had curbside recycling programs and strong ordinances regarding the disposal of hazardous waste.

Irvine's action met with disgruntlement from the businesses that will be affected by the ban. Most argue that until replacements are developed for CFCs, they are essentially handcuffed, and must continue using them. Parker-Bertea Aerospace, which employs 3,500 in Irvine, uses Freon and other CFC compounds for cleaning precision components. The company's manager, Kevin Clark, argued that the one year given companies to find replacements was too short. "Down the road there will be replacements," said Clark, "but they aren't ready yet."

In 1988 Du Pont—which produces 25 percent of the world's CFCs and 75 percent of the CFCs in the United States—spent $30 million on process development, market research, testing, and production of CFC alternatives. The company has promised to phase out production of the CFCs by the year 2000, and is planning seven plants solely to produce CFC alternatives. They have also patented a Freon substitute that could replace CFCs in existing car air-conditioners by 1993, at a cost currently seven times that of Freon.

The solvents used for cleaning computer chips and other electronics equipment are made with chlorofluorocarbons (CFCs), which are soon to be phased out by international agreement. Here, an engineer at a Du Pont lab tests potential alternatives.

Those who produce the chemicals are being joined by the world's biggest consumers of CFCs in their efforts at reducing demand. AT&T, one of the world's biggest users of CFCs, says that it will quit using them entirely by 1994. The company will replace the 3 million pounds of CFCs it uses each year in the manufacturing of computer chips and circuit boards, with alternatives yet unknown. This announcement was preceded by similar plans by Northern Telecom of Canada and Seiko Epson of Japan. Dow Chemical is discontinuing its use of CFCs in foam-insulation manufacturing; American electronics firms are experimenting with exotic alternatives to CFCs, including compounds derived from petroleum distillates and crushed orange peels.

But the obstacle to CFC substitutes is cost, not chemistry. Du Pont estimates that there is now more than $135-billion worth of installed equipment dependent on the current CFC products. Virtually all of this equipment, some of it with a remaining useful lifetime of 20 to 40 years, could require replacement or modification.

Until replacements are available, prices for CFCs are expected to double over the next decade as their supply shrinks. Some auto mechanics and hospital administrators are already hoarding CFC products while they are still available—and affordable. Though some manufacturers may absorb these increased costs, until satisfactory alternatives are on the market consumers will inevitably bear the price of continued research. The price of cars with air conditioners will rise, and so will that of refrigerators. Companies that require large amounts of CFCs in their products, such as manufacturers of foam insulation for buildings, will be stunted if they don't find replacements.

In nearly every case to date, the few substitute products on the market are inferior, more expensive, or more dangerous than CFCs. Propane, for example, can be used as a refrigerant. But it is combustible and requires heavy tanks, which makes it impractical for most buildings and all cars. Alternatives to CFC-filled blown-foam have been found to include cancer-causing ingredients. Fiberglass and cellulose insulation are less efficient than CFC-containing polyurethane. Alternatives to CFC-containing plastic materials are more flammable.

Needless to say, experiments continue. But whether or not Du Pont, or any other chemical maker, can find and produce CFC substitutes fast enough to bridge the gap created by the new legislation, is still an open question. The only certainty in the race to save the Earth's ozone is that the costs will be borne by everyone.

While industry struggles with substitutes for CFCs, recycling them appears to be the wave of the near-future. By the turn of the twenty-first century, the big chemical companies will most likely have developed substitutes. Those that remain in use—in refrigerators, automobile air conditioners, and elsewhere—will hopefully be recycled and reused, indefinitely.

The first recycling effort that will be available to the average consumer may be for the CFCs in automobile air conditioners. David Gillis, who works for Draf Industries in Bedford, New York, has built one of the leading prototypes of such recyclers, or "vampires," as they're known. His work is hardly secret—engineers at a half-dozen companies around the country have built similar machines. Their shared dream is that by the early 1990s, car owners around the world will be on a first-name basis with their inventions.

Gillis's invention, dubbed simply the "Draf 1400," is a squat, metal box-on-wheels. Three on/off buttons, two pressure gauges, and two cylindrical glass tubes are the only disruptions on the machine's flat surface. Drooped from the front are two 3-foot-long hoses, one marked "Inlet," the other "Outlet." Viewed with its rear door swung open, the inside of the contraption is similarly noncomplex: the hoses lead into two metal cylinders. At first glance, the machine looks most like an industrial rug cleaner, or, more precisely, something you'd find at the corner service station.

The vampire's job is simple. Hooked up to a car's air conditioner, it sucks out Freon, purifies it, and renders it reusable, either in the car it's connected to, or another. Previously, car air conditioners were emptied by the simple twist of a valve. A mechanic or do-it-yourselfer turned that valve under the hood, and three pounds of clean, odorless Freon escaped into the air. Gillis and his competitors hope that letting that gas just hiss into the air will soon be illegal. His machine—which will sell for $2,995—has recently gotten the approval of the Underwriters Laboratories, a consumer products testing company, and production is gearing up. White Industries of Indianapolis markets a similar machine for $2,900 under the brand name K-Whit Tools. The company's vice president, John P. Hancock, tells potential customers it will pay for itself after just 300 cars. John Tyson's company in Muskegon, Michigan, recently signed a deal with General Motors that would make his "vamps" available to all of its 10,000 dealers by the 1991 season. (The EPA has told the auto industry that if it is not encouraging recycling satisfactorily by 1992, the agency will mandate it.) The acceptance of these recyclers—after some push and tug with both industry and Congress—gives encouragement to environmental entrepreneurs around the globe.

So far, the service station operators who will soon be required by many states to buy the machines are optimistic about their payback ability. Richard De Silva, who owns an 11-bay auto air-conditioning service in Detroit, began using recyclers in early 1989. He estimates that the machines paid for themselves within eight months. Industry watchers guess that operations like De Silva's are the wave of the

future. It's not yet known how customers—who will most likely have to pay $5 to $10 to have their Freon recycled—will respond.

Car air conditioners are not the only products that are being retrofitted to adapt to a CFC-less world. Experiments with helium (long used for space and military refrigerators), rigid foam, and vacuum insulation (like that used in Thermos bottles) continue, Petroferm, a small California biotech company, has developed a solvent to replace CFCs used to clean delicate electronics. Most manufacturers of plastic-foam food containers have switched to non-CFC compounds.

Companies that make fire extinguishers are also scrambling to find substitute chemicals. Most extinguishers today are filled with a compound called halon, which is three to ten times as destructive to high-altitude ozone as CFCs. Though produced in much smaller quantities, halons could account for up to one sixth of the eventual ozone depletion. Recycling of halons is already under way, and Du Pont—the biggest halon manufacturer in the world—says its sales of the compound are dropping and they are searching for alternatives. Meanwhile, sales of automatic sprinklers and dry, non-ozone-depleting chemicals are picking up.

Car designers from Detroit to Tokyo are scratching out new concepts, based on the potential changes in auto air conditioners. Side vents and tinted windows are being considered, as are a variety of solar-powered ventilation systems. But as a sure sign that environmental issues have invaded all corners of life, even the sports world is responding to the concern over ozone depletion. FIFA, the world soccer governing body, has urged its teams to keep the use of painkilling sprays to a minimum, since the aerosols are propelled by CFCs.

OZONE DEPLETION

The chain of events that leads to the destruction of the Earth's ozone layer may begin with something as simple as a refrigerator.

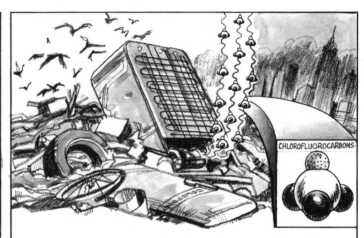

Discarded at the local dump, punctured and disintegrating, the refrigerator leaks a gas composed of chlorofluorocarbons, or CFCs.

Once emitted into the air, CFCs make their way up through the layers of the Earth's atmosphere, a process which can take several years.

In the upper reaches of the atmosphere, the CFC molecules bump up against the layer of ozone molecules, which form a protective blanket around the Earth and shield it from the harmful ultraviolet rays of the sun.

The ultraviolet rays splinter the CFC molecule, splitting one chlorine atom off. It is that chlorine atom that combines with the ozone molecules to "destroy" the ozone layer.

One tiny chlorine atom can destroy thousands of ozone molecules. This chemical reaction results in the thinning of the protective layer of ozone, creating the "holes" that allow ultraviolet rays to reach the Earth.

The problem on Earth if this loss of ozone continues is that as more ultraviolet (UV) rays pass uninhibited to Earth, they can harm animals, plants, and humans.

One result of increased levels of UV rays is the killing off of the delicate species of plankton on which the oceanic food chain is based, thus altering the feeding system of all ocean life.

Excessive UV rays may also increase the risk of skin cancer and weaken man's immune systems.

Scientists are just beginning to understand the effects of ozone loss on the world's weather systems.

UV radiation can also mutate the genes of plants, potentially destroying billions of dollars' worth of crops—fruits, vegetables and other produce—affecting our food supply.

But the refrigerator is hardly the only culprit. Harmful CFCs are found in thousands of products—many that we use daily around the house, from packaging to solvents and foam cushioning.

Individual Action

1. If you drive a car with an air conditioner, keep the cooling system leak free. More ozone-harming CFCs escape into the air from leaking systems than they do from systems being recharged.

2. Encourage the discontinuation of the one-pound cans of Freon sold at department stores and service stations by not buying them. Though still relatively inexpensive, they encourage drivers to simply add a one-pound charge when a system is low, rather than having it properly serviced, its leaks repaired, and Freon recycled.

3. If your local service station doesn't have, or know about, Freon reclamation units, suggest them. Or take your car elsewhere. Stations that offer such recycling will soon display signs advertising the service.

4. If or when your car ends up headed for a junkyard, be sure its Freon is emptied prior to junking. The same goes for refrigerators—several towns in West Germany are already operating collection services for used refrigerators. Encourage your local recycling center to investigate these services.

5. Refrigerators made without CFC coolants and insulation aren't on the market yet. Until they are, the best advice is to keep your current model running properly until recycling programs are set up. Cleaning the coils regularly and checking door seals for damage will help.

6. When building a new home or an exten-sion find out about different insulation options. Rigid foam insulation is full of CFCs, which will someday escape into the atmosphere. Alternatives include fiberglass, fiberboard, cellulose, gypsum, and foil-laminated board. If you use cellulose-fiber insulation, look for a label indicating that the material meets the standards of the Cellulose Industry Standards Enforcement Program.

7. Try and get used to sitting on slightly harder car seats and couch cushions until an alternative is found for the flexible foams that fill them. CFCs are emitted from these foams almost immediately upon manufacturing, because of their open-cell construction.

8. Refuse to buy products that come in poly-styrene containers, such as eggs, fast foods, and meat from grocery freezers. Look for "Non-CFC" markings on similar-looking packaging. Plenty of alternatives are available to do the same job, including molded pulp and paperboard. Many foam plastics are now being made from a CFC-alternative called HCFC-22. This material contains only five percent as much ozone-depletion potential as the original compound. But it's still a good idea to eliminate foam cups, plates, and other such products from your purchases. Also, stay away from packing chips and ice chests made from polystyrene: the CFCs are secure in the plastic foam until it is broken and discarded, and they are then released into the atmosphere.

9. Encourage the use of non-CFC disinfec-tants in hospitals, offices, and computer cleaning. Check the labels of those you use to see if they contain chlorofluorocarbons. In most cases, water- or alcohol-based solvents will do the same job.

10. If you have a home fire-extinguisher, make sure it does not use a chemical called Halon 1211, a CFC product. Most use dry chemicals, which do not include halons, but it's worth a check. If you have halon fire extinguishers, the best recommendation is to keep them until somebody comes up with a way to recycle them.

11. Though most aerosol spray cans have been banned in the United States, Canada, Norway, and Sweden for over a decade, worldwide, aerosol cans are still the largest source of CFC emissions, contributing 224,000 tons annually to the skies. Most countries have either reduced the use of aerosol sprays or are planning bans, but technicalities in the law have enabled some aerosols to stay on the market—notably for spray confetti, VCR-head cleaners, film-negative cleaners, and boat horns. Other aerosols have been reformulated so that they don't include CFCs. It's best to check labels, or not buy these products at all.

Government Action

1. Either the use of CFCs in packaging and ozone-depleting chemicals in solvents used for electronics applications should be banned immediately, *or* labels on product packaging should be required to inform consumers whether the product they are buying contains or was made with any ozone-depleting substance.

2. Grants should be issued to corporations and businesses that are developing recovery and recycling methods for ozone-depleting substances.

3. A national permit system for businesses using, producing, or importing CFCs could be established, and the permits gradually limited. Such a system would raise prices of CFCs, encourage the development of alternatives, and induce industry to recycle ozone-depleting substances from production processes.

4. Governments should support, in developing countries, the researching and marketing of technologies that are not reliant on ozone-depleting substances, so as to dissuade them from beginning the heavy use of CFCs.

5. The scientific study of ozone depletion over the Antarctic and Arctic circles should be continued and funded.

6. The Montreal Protocol, the 1987 agree- ment to limit production of CFCs and related chemicals, should be strengthened.

7. The import of products made with CFCs and halons from countries that refuse to adopt equivalent phase-out rules should be banned.

8. Service stations should be required to re- cycle Freon.

9. Businesses should be prohibited from using foam packaging.

10. Building codes should be established that prevent the use of building insulation containing CFCs.

Reading

Protecting the Ozone Layer: What You Can Do: A Citizen's Guide to Reducing the Use of Ozone Depleting Chemicals, by Sarah Clark. New York: Environmental Defense Fund, 1988, 257 Park Avenue South, New York, NY 10010.

Global Lessons from the Ozone Hole, by Michael Oppenheimer. Environmental Defense Fund, ibid.

Protecting Life on Earth: Steps to Save the Ozone Layer, by Cynthia Pollock Shea. Worldwatch Paper 87, Worldwatch Institute.

"Solo flights into the ozone hole reveal its causes," by Ellen Ruppel Shell. *Smithsonian,* March 1988.

"Company policy in the face of global concerns: The ozone issue as a model," by Joseph P. Glas. Du Pont Company, B-13225, Wilmington, DE 19898.

How Industry Is Reducing Dependency on Ozone-Depleting Chemicals. U.S. Environmental Protection Agency, Stratospheric Ozone Protection Program, 1988.

The Ozone Layer and *The Changing Atmosphere,* by Robin Clarke. New York: United Nations Environment Programme, 1987. North American Office, Room DC2-0803, United Nations, New York, NY 10017.

Saving the Ozone Layer: A Citizen's Action Guide, New York: Natural Resources Defense Council, 1989.

"Politics of the Ozone Layer," by David Doniger. *Issues of Science and Technology,* Volume IV, No. 3, 1988.

Organizations to Contact

Air Conditioning and Refrigeration Institute, Suite 600, 1501 Wilson Blvd., Arlington, VA 22209, 703-524-8800.

Association of Home Appliance Manufacturers, 20 North Wacker Dr., Chicago, IL 60606, 312-984-5800.

Environmental Defense Fund, 257 Park Avenue South, New York, NY 10010, 212-505-2100.

International Mobile Air Conditioner Association, Suite 1300, 2100 North Highway 360, Grand Prairie, TX 75050, 214-988-6081. (For information on recyclers in your area.)

Natural Resources Defense Council, 40 W. 20th St., New York, NY 10011, 212-727-2700.

3

Smog

Dirty air is everywhere. In São Paulo (Brazil), Athens, Rome, and Budapest, the air is so polluted that cars have been banned from their city centers. Kraków is enveloped in a stationary cloud of smog 135 days a year; the facades of its buildings are crumbling as a result. In West Germany, where many stores are ordered to close at 6:30 P.M. and lawn mowing is banned on Sunday, there are no auto-emission controls. As a result Hamburg, Berlin, and other urban areas are mired in smog. In a recent study the Global Environmental Monitoring System (GEMS, a long-term project of the World Health Organization and the United Nations Environment Programme) ranked Milan as the city with the world's highest air levels of sulfur dioxide, just ahead of Shenyang (China), Teheran, and Seoul. The same study proclaimed that New Delhi's air had the most overall "particulate matter"; Paris had the most carbon monoxide (Los Angeles was fourth, New York sixth); and Tel Aviv the most nitrous oxide. Sydney, Santiago, and Hamilton (Ontario) followed closely. While thorough, the GEMS report was hardly complete: Vast areas of Africa, Asia, and South America were not monitored. Mexico, home of the dirtiest air in the world, refused to cooperate. And the report did not even track ground-level ozone, perhaps the worst urban air pollutant.

In the United States the list of cities darkened by smog has grown each year since 1970. In 1989, the biggest offenders—Los Angeles, New York, and Houston—were once again ordered by the federal government to meet new standards of cleanliness. They have until sometime next century to meet the deadlines. The summer of 1988—when James Hansen propelled the greenhouse effect into a global concern—was the dirtiest ever, according to the EPA. Safe ozone levels were exceeded in 96 cities, including 28 that had never before made the list (including Kennebec County, Maine, home of George Bush's summer White House). In Los Angeles, almost half the days on the calendar exceeded safe ozone levels; New York City's air exceeded some federal standard one out of every two days; and Washington's air was bad on one out of three. More than 150 million Americans now live in areas that exceed EPA standards. In big cities—and increasingly, smaller ones too—smog has become as accepted as the sun rising in the east.

Slowly, governments around the globe are putting into place laws and regulations they hope will cut through the smog. In the United States, the Clean Air Act of 1970 is being tinkered with and retooled for the 1990s. While the original legislation is credited with doing some good during the past two decades, it hasn't been enough.

It is either a great irony or a coincidence that the then-monumental legislation was passed during a 14-day Washington, D.C. smog alert. It was an incredibly popular law—the Senate passed the law unanimously and there was but one "nay" vote tallied in the House. Its goal was to attack the mounting problem of air pollution, specifically smog, which was then beginning to muddy the skies over urban areas across the country.

The law's history has been marked by success, as well as missteps and miscalculations. Since its adoption, airborne lead has been reduced by 90 percent, primarily due to the reduced sale of leaded gasoline. It is generally conceded that if the bill had never been passed, skies across the country would today be even more shrouded by a thick blanket of man-produced smog.

Still, many big cities in the United States have never met even the law's initial air quality standards. Today, dirty air plagues big cities and rural counties around the globe; like most pollutants, smog knows no boundaries. It usually originates over big, sunny, gridlocked cities. But increasingly, it drifts downwind: Thus, northern New England is often treated to pollution that originates as far away as Baltimore. Italians breathe smog-filled air, compliments of industries and automobiles in West Germany. Rangers in Maine's Acadia National Park recently recorded ozone levels so high that they would have triggered a smog alert in Los Angeles. Perhaps the best illustration of the problem is photographs from Arizona where from sources as far away as Los Angeles, a daily white haze of smog gathers over the Grand Canyon.

On the optimistic side, the technology exists to clean up the air. Theoretically, if every car in the world used available pollution-reducing technology and was in good repair, smog would decrease. The 150,000 new cars that roll off America's assembly lines each day produce on average just 4 percent as much pollution as 1970 models. (The auto industry, of course, argues that smog would go away if everyone just bought a new car. . . .) Scientists, engineers, and designers tinker with new technologies constantly, with a goal of improving fuel efficiency and controlling emissions even more.

Still the air is dirtier. Why? Because there are many more cars on the road, being driven many more miles. According to the National Highway Traffic Safety Administration, the number of motor vehicles in the United States rose to 183 million in 1988 from 147 million in 1977, an increase of about 25 percent. The number of trucks increased 40 percent in the same period, to a total of 41 million, many of them with soot-belching diesel engines. The accompanying increased amount of engine exhaust—though cleaner than in 1970—accounts for 66 percent of the nitrous oxide and one third of the hydrocarbons that produce smog. While fuel-efficiency rates climb, cheap oil prices have driven up consumption. (In the United States, cars burn one out of every six barrels of oil consumed.)

(While cars are the chief culprits behind our dirty air, they aren't the lone contributors. Aerosol sprays, barbecue lighter fluid, dry cleaning solvents, and oil-based paints all emit the chemicals that combine to create smog. Rules and regulations controlling the use of such compounds are already on the books in many communities and their number is growing. It may be that efforts to clean up our air in the next decade may affect what's under your sink more than what's in your driveway.)

Automobiles remain a particularly American obsession. There are an estimated 387 million cars scattered around the world—83 million of them in the United States. By comparison, Brazil has around 11 million cars, China less than one million, and Kenya fewer than 150,000. But their growing popularity, and hence, pollution, is a global nightmare.

Until the late seventies, for example, trains, trucks, and buses dominated the transportation network of the Soviet Union and Eastern Europe. Today, *perestroika* may lead to an increased emphasis on consumer goods, with the automobile near the top of the list. In fact, the Soviet Union plans to double its present annual production of 1.4 million vehicles by the year 2000. Car ownership in the Third World has also risen sharply in the past decade, especially in Latin America and Southern Asia. (Argentina, Brazil, and Mexico account for almost half the cars in the developing world.) According to the Worldwatch Institute, the only places where automobile emissions are not yet a problem are

Air pollution is a growing concern everywhere, not only in the car-choked cities of western industrialized nations (above). Despite the smaller number of cars in China, the city of Beijing (below) suffers from smog caused by growing industry.

China and India. Although 38 percent of the world's population lives in the two countries, they own scarcely half of one percent of the world's cars. (In China there are 540 bicycles for every car, one bicycle for every 4 people.) It's not a lack of desire, but poverty, that keeps cars out of many people's reach.

The growth in global automobile sales is particularly ominous because virtually all countries lag far behind in auto-emission standards. In Western Europe, there are no mandated standards for the emissions for small- and medium-size cars, 10 million of which are sold each year. Attitudes about emissions controls vary from nation to nation: Britain, France, Italy, and Portugal discourage any anti-pollution laws; West Germany, Scandinivian countries, Austria, Switzerland, and the Netherlands have at least encouraged unleaded gas, though it remains nearly impossible to find off the main roads of Europe.

One of the biggest stumbling blocks in cutting down auto-produced smog is that so far most efforts have focused on the control of tailpipe emissions instead of the development of solutions to prevent their formation in the first place. Over the past decade, legislative bodies and oil and auto industries have haggled over mile-per-gallon increases in fuel efficiency and the raising of speed limits. Much of that effort would have been better spent trying to figure out ways to eliminate dirty emissions altogether, and promoting alternative transportations, from buses and trains to bikes and skateboards.

Although government and industry have controlling roles in the problem, the general public must shoulder much of the responsibility for all this dirty air. Lawmakers have not acted more boldly because although voters say they want clean air, they don't want to pay for it through restrictions on driving and tougher, costlier auto-emission standards. The oil and auto industries have, in turn, spent millions fighting each proposed change. Lack of convenient and affordable mass transit for commuters exacerbates the problem. The result is that places like Los Angeles, Milan, and Rio de Janeiro—with levels of smog that threaten to permanently blot out the sun—may soon adopt stringent laws of their own, banning cars and trucks from downtown streets, and limiting the kind of paints, lighter fluids, and chemical solvents that can be sold.

Still, there are some who virulently oppose greater spending on clean air measures. Those who oppose increased spending suggest that higher costs will be absorbed by the poor through higher food, electricity, and transportation bills. Objections not withstanding, more spending to control air pollution is indeed on the horizon. The Bush Administration wants a $30-billion-a-year increase—$2 to $8 billion to clean up acid rain; $1 to $6 billion to clean up toxic air pollution, and $8 to $20 billion to clean up smog.

The Administration's proposed amendment to the Clean Air Act sent automakers and oil producers scurrying, experimenting in a way not seen since the early 1970s with alternative ways of doing business. "The party's over," admitted Robert Lutz, president of Chrysler Motors Corporation. "We are making a mess out of our environment, and the sooner we clean it up, the better."

Carmakers have already proven they can adapt to tighter emission controls—*when they have to*. In the mid-1970s they developed catalytic converters and other means of limiting exhaust pollution because Congress told them they *had* to. They also experimented with lighter engines, controlling fuel and air ratios, and perfecting spark timing—all of which have helped. Advances have continued almost as fast as car sales. Today the most advanced engines—turned out in Detroit, Japan, Sweden, and West Germany—are fuel-injected, their combustion processes controlled by electronic ignitions and computer modules. Engine exhaust flows through new and improved catalytic converters. Some cars even contain sensors that tell the engine how well it is burning gasoline and are capable of adjusting the combustion process for greater efficiency. But until car *buyers* concentrate on the smog their cars create and reevaluate their habits, all the technology in the world won't slow the polluting. Industry won't budge until it feels a push from consumers.

CAUSES

The yellowish-brown smog that drapes most urban areas of the world is a hazy mixture of microscopic droplets, solid particles, and gases. It contains more than 100 different chemical compounds, many of them irritant, toxic, or carcinogenic. Cars and trucks emit more than half of the smog-producing chemicals from tailpipes and fuel intake. Most of the rest are produced by fires (including wood-burning stoves), waste treatment, oil and gas production, industrial solvents, paints, and coatings.

The dozens of ingredients that contribute to smog include carbon monoxide, particulates such as dirt, soot and dust, and ozone. But the basic recipe calls for three elements—hydrocarbons, nitrogen oxides, and sunlight—to be mixed together in the lower atmosphere.

• Hydrocarbons result from chains of carbon atoms linked with each other and with hydrogen atoms. They are present in engine exhaust and are created by the incomplete burning of the fuels. Gasoline consists of mixtures of hydrocarbons, so vapors escaping when it is spilled or leaked also contribute to the smog buildup.

• Nitrogen oxides are created with any high-temperature combustion involving air. The two main components of air—nitrogen and oxygen—combine at high temperatures to form nitrogen oxides, which are pollutants.

• Sunlight serves as the oven for this concoction, "baking" all these atmospheric pollutants into ozone. (Ozone is comprised of three oxygen atoms and is the same compound that, high in the stratosphere, protects the Earth from ultraviolet rays.) Close to the ground, ozone combines with hydrocarbons to form the family of compounds that make up smog. As long as sunlight pumps energy into the mixture of hydrocarbons and nitrogen oxides, smog continues to form. There is no way to scrub it out of the sky. Although the process stops at sunset, the ingredients remain in the atmosphere, and the "baking" process resumes the following morning. The greater the number of cars and miles driven, the greater the ozone pollution. The problem is expected to worsen as the greenhouse effect warms the atmosphere.

Diesel engines and leaky gas station pumps are big smog contributors. Diesel engines produce carbon-based soot particles, each of which can attract upwards of 10,000 chemicals, including toxic substances such as lead, cadmium, and benzene. A major contributor to the number of hydrocarbons in the atmosphere is gasoline vapor that escapes during refueling and while vehicles are in operation. To deal with escaping vapors, an increasing number of gas pumps are being equipped with recovery hoses.

Every year humans pump more than 450,000 tons of lead into the air (nature adds just 3,500 tons). More than half of that human contribution is from lead in gas—added to improve its combustion—which is released in fine particles. While the United States has virtually eliminated leaded gas, in the Third World unleaded gas is unheard of.

Some headway has been made in the past two decades toward reducing causes of smog. Since the passage of the Clean Air Act, for example, there has been a 90 percent reduction in emissions of hydrocarbons and carbon monoxide from the average car in the United States and a 75 percent reduction of nitrogen oxides. This has been made possible through the development of the catalytic converter (which transforms dangerous gases into

Power plants fueled by coal or oil emit small carbon particles that can "absorb" other pollutants in the air and carry them for long distances. Here, a Navajo, Arizona power plant spews "innocent" wisps of smoke into the air.

less harmful ones), improved engine designs, reduction of the lead content in gasoline, and improved fuel-efficiency standards.

Still the smog thickens. The campaign to control it is losing ground because of the enormous increase in the number of cars and trucks on the road. Henry Ford II's boast in 1971 that "mini-cars mean mini-profits" appears to be a sentiment shared by many in the automobile capitals of the world today. Big cars are back in vogue and setting sales records. Too often the auto industry concentrates its efforts on pollution tradeoffs instead of on improved technologies. (One recent example in the United States involved carmakers attempting to "trade" air conditioners that did not contain ozone-depleting CFCs for lower fuel-efficiency ratings.) Powerful industry lobbyists prowl the halls of Congress, pushing for higher speed limits and lower fuel-efficiency standards.

While automobile emissions get most of the attention when the pollution in question is smog, increasingly, legislation is surfacing that will limit other smog contributors. These include cleaning solvents, gasoline-powered lawn mowers, starter fluids for backyard barbecues, hair sprays, windshield cleaners, and even bakeries, where yeast growing in bread dough emits alcohol vapors. If alternatives are not found to replace them, many household items may be banned, and soon. (See Chapter Seven.)

EFFECTS

The real tragedy of smog pollution is that it is one of the most immediately felt environmental problems. The greenhouse effect and acid rain take their initial toll on nature. Smog makes people sick. Not in some far-off decade, but right now. It takes direct aim at human health and is the cause of a variety of aches and pains, from the bothersome (eye irritation) to the deadly (lead poisoning and lung cancer).

These unhealthy effects may be best exemplified by Mexico City, where smog pollution is the worst in the world. According to the United Nations Environment Programme, ozone levels there tripled between 1986 and 1988, to 60 percent above World Health Organization standards. The reasons are easy to see—the crowded city has 2.8 million vehicles and 36,000 factories. And the problem worsens every year. The nation's heavy foreign-debt burden— some $100 billion plus—makes it prohibitive to retool the state-owned oil industry to produce gas with less pollutants, to replace fleets of smoke-belching buses, expand subway systems, or enforce existing pollution controls.

The result of all this bad air has been disastrous for the 18 million residents of Mexico City. The continued sooty burning of nearby rain forests adds to the city's pollution and noxious air, as does open sewage dumping. (Thirty percent of the residents do not have sewage service and dispose of their waste wherever they can. The U.N. estimates that 600 tons of solid human waste are dumped into the streets daily.)

The city's futile attempts to cope with the pollution can be observed everywhere. Newspapers are filled with ads for home and office air purifiers, and hotels a few hours away promote "clean air" weekend escapes. Some people on the street wear protective masks. The main victims of the smog, however, are the elderly and children. Many foreign embassies and businesses consider it a dangerous place to live, and employees who relocate there receive "hazard" pay and are discouraged from bringing children.

Health problems result from the fact that the body has limited defenses against smog, which irritates and inflames delicate pulmonary membranes, producing a host of symptoms, including chest pains, coughing, and throat irritations. Smog also lowers the lungs' resistance to infection, colds, and pneumonia, and can trigger asthma attacks and aggra-

Fine particles of flyash oil (inset) and flyash coal are emitted by power plants and the incomplete burning of fossil fuels. Suspended in the air, they can absorb toxic metals. Many of the chemical reactions that form photo-chemical smog take place on the surface of these tiny particles.

vate chronic heart disease. The worst effect, though, is that ground-level ozone whittles away at an individual's lung capacity. Once in your system it may remain there for a week and can permantly scar lung tissue as badly as cigarette smoke.

One of the most harmful atmospheric pollutants to human health is carbon monoxide, which emanates mostly from car exhaust. A colorless, odorless gas, it robs the body's tissues and organs of life-sustaining oxygen. It interferes with blood's ability to absorb oxygen, thus impairing perception and thinking, slowing reflexes and causing drowsiness, unconsciousness, and even death. Inhaled by pregnant women, carbon monoxide may threaten the growth and mental development of the fetus. Long-term exposure is suspected of aggravating arteriosclerosis and vascular disease.

For many years smog was thought to be chiefly a problem for people suffering from asthma, emphysema, and other respiratory diseases. But in 1988, Dr. Thomas Godar, president of the American Lung Association, told Congress that a growing body of research showed that "ozone can cause immediate short-term changes in lung function." Simultaneously, federal environmental officials reported that smog pollution was a "serious health threat," particularly to children. Today, asthma sufferers are cautioned to stay away from Milan, Teheran, Seoul, and other urban areas blighted by smog.

The lead in gas is also a debilitating compound when it's released into the atmosphere. Between 75 and 95 percent of that lead is inhaled or ingested and accumulates in bones and other tissues, potentially causing irreversible brain, nerve, and kidney damage and high blood pressure. Young children are most vulnerable because their nervous systems are still developing.

It should be obvious that smog-related health problems are not just a public nuisance but constitute a true health crisis. But some worry that illnesses resulting from pollution are neglected because they are primarily an inner-city, or poverty-related problem. Moreover, the symptoms are difficult to assign specifically to the air we breathe—people often blame stress, late nights, or fast-food diets when they feel run down. In fact, their ills may be a result of too much dirty air.

Increasingly, smog is extending beyond urban borders. Carried away from city skies by big, slow-moving, low altitude weather systems, it can kill trees and crops, as well as inflict harm on people and buildings. One recent EPA study concluded that ozone pollution was reducing crop yields by $2.5 to $3 billion a year in the United States, and it is estimated that farmers can lose as much as 30 percent of a potential crop from ozone pollution, even when that pollution is at federally permitted levels.

Smog infects soybeans, wheat, tomatoes, peanuts, lettuce, and cotton. It enters plant leaves through their gas exchange pores and, once inside, the powerful chemical combination virtually burns cell membranes and the membranes of interior cell structures. Crop yields drop as a result, because plants expend most of their energy, energy needed for growth, repairing the damage. In a suggestion straight from the pages of science fiction, it is predicted that weather forecasters may someday give farmers a couple of days' warning before plant-choking ozone conditions arrive. Farmers could then apply chemical protectants now being developed to save especially vulnerable plants from killer smog.

SOLUTIONS

Since the United States is the biggest manufacturer of cars—thus the biggest polluter by exhaust—it is up to federal and state governments, industry and individuals, to lead the way in limiting smog creation. In the past year, a variety of innovative community actions have been developed which promise to be the wave of the future for air pollution control.

☼

The European community and others are watching closely as the new decade begins.

At the same time that laws discouraging auto exhaust pollution are being drafted, a growing number of other smog-contributing chemicals are soon to be regulated. Most are produced from stationary sources such as backyard barbecues, dry cleaners, and giant petrochemical plants. As a result, local governments—city councils, town boards, boards of supervisors—are mandating changes in the chemicals used to make everything from house paint to kitchen cleaners. Less embattled by high-priced lobbyists, such legislators may provide the incentive to start cleansing the air at a local level.

Prime examples of such moves toward clean skies have surfaced in Los Angeles and Denver (ranked 1, 2 in America's "dirtiest skies" competition). L.A. sits in a basin, Denver in a valley, and the horizons of both are blocked by a dirty brown haze every other day.

In Denver, the inversion of cold air traps warm, smoggy air below, and during late-afternoon rush hours in winter months the city is bathed in a toxic haze. Carbon monoxide levels are twice what is deemed safe by the EPA. In recent years, city and state governments have tried a variety of measures, with only marginal success. They've experimented with mandatory use of oxygenated fuels in the wintertime, and year-round Daylight Savings Time (which in winter helps get people home before air cools and traps bad air). Drivers have even been asked to leave their cars at home one working day a week.

Finally, in the winter of 1988, they tested a program which mandated cleaner-burning fuels. Vehicles were the target, because they produce 75 percent of the area's carbon monoxide (most of the rest comes from wood-burning stoves). In effect from January 1 until February 28, along the 125-mile corridor from Colorado Springs to Fort Collins, the program required that stations sell gasoline containing one of two additives: ethanol (made from corn), or the slightly less efficient MTBE, a petroleum product.

It was not the first time mandatory controls had been used in the United States. Similar programs have been tested in Phoenix, Salt Lake City, Albuquerque, and other hazy urban areas. And it seems to have had an effect. After the initial season's testing, carbon monoxide levels over Denver fell by 12 percent, and plans were made to broaden the test to include power plants and wood-burning stoves.

But the most sweeping clean air initiative, more inclusive than any federal law since the original Clean Air Act, was proposed in Los Angeles in mid-1989. That shouldn't be surprising, since California is credited with spurring many clean air initiatives (as well as leading the way in smog pollution). It is the only state with its own vehicle emissions standards, and has been the leader in introducing most of the major technological advances in automobile pollution control, such as catalytic converters. Today, new cars in California run eight to ten times cleaner than cars sold 20 years ago. But on a rare smogless day in March 1989, L.A.'s city council went further than any city in the world, and launched an effort to clean up the skies over Southern California. They proposed stringent new laws to reduce the brown haze that has become as much a symbol of the city as surfing and Hollywood. Their three-tiered plan attacked every source of air pollution, big and small, and proposed more than 160 specific bans, regulations, and mandates.

The plan's immediate changes—to be implemented within the first five years—would affect everyone in the 6,600-square-mile Los Angeles basin. Parking fees would be raised. Buses would run free in the summertime. Van pooling would be required for companies with more than 100 employees. Single-occupant vehicles would be banned from the freeway system. New swimming pools would have to be equipped with solar heating panels. Barbecue fuels would be banned. The number of cars a family could own would be limited. The cost of registering cars would be raised. Gas-powered lawn mowers would be banned. Control equipment for dry cleaners and bakeries would be required. Bias ply tires, which introduce more rubber particles into the atmosphere than radials, would be banned.

The second tier of the plan would convert 40 percent of passenger vehicles, 70 percent of freight trucks, and all buses to clean fuels—methanol, natural gas, ethanol, electricity—by 1998 and reduce by half the hydrocarbon emissions from consumer products, locomotives and construction equipment.

The last phase would virtually eliminate combustion from vehicles and ban almost all ozone-forming compounds in solvents, paints, and coatings by 2007. The plan is expected to cost the city a total of $2.8 billion a year for the first five years—at an average expense to residents of $220 a year—and another $20 billion-plus to implement the second and third phases.

L.A.'s legislation is acknowledged to be a model for municipalities—and nations—around the globe. Yet, after its proposal, few expect the law to be adopted without lengthy and expensive battles. Many of the proposals are simply impracticable, according to critics. Others say the expectations are based on highly speculative projections of emission reductions and technological advances. Backers of the plan fear that economic and political realities may water down the proposal. Corporations, individuals, and special interest groups of every stripe have fought each of the 160-plus changes.

Though the substance of L.A.'s law may change before adoption, its example quickly spawned imitators. By year's end a coalition of eight northern states—New Jersey, New York and six New England states—proposed clean air rules of their own. (It makes sense that those would be the first areas of the country to react; they have the dirtiest skies and the most cars. Of the 10.5 million new cars registered in the United States in 1988, 1.9 million—18.5 percent—were in the eight northeastern states; 1.2 million—11.5 percent—were in California.) The northeastern states' first goal was to tighten automobile pollution standards. Currently, the national emissions standards apply only to cars with 50,000 miles, or less, on their meters. Some 60 percent of the cars on the road, however, have more miles than that. And while older cars with more miles account for a small fraction of the miles driven each day, they produce 70 percent of the pollution. The states' proposal called for applying standards to cars with 100,000 miles or less, lowering the emissions-per-mile standard for several pollutants, including nitrogen oxides, hydrocarbons, and carbon monoxide, and recommended fines for factories not meeting new emission standards (up to $5,000 per ton).

While such recommendations on the local level may be an indication of future reforms, it is still up to national governments to wrestle with the heavyweights—the auto and oil industries. The Bush Administration, led by a self-proclaimed environmentalist, soon after inaugural day proposed the biggest amendments to the Clean Air Act since its adoption. The smog-control bill was two-staged: It required auto manufacturers to comply with emissions standards by 1993 using existing technology, and strongly encouraged oil and auto companies to use alternative fuels, such as methanol, ethanol, or natural gas. Industries' first response was a loud moan—but that is the same reaction both industries have voiced to every presidential air quality suggestion since the 1960s.

Specifically, the amendment required the gradual introduction of cars powered by "clean fuels," like methanol or natural gas. It asked that 500,000 of these prototypes be sold by 1995, and that a million a year be sold after 1997—about 10 percent of all new cars sold. (Those sales would be concentrated in the dirtiest areas: Los Angeles, Houston, New

Major Contributors to Smog

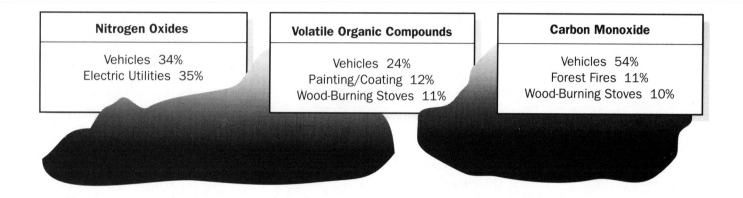

Nitrogen Oxides	Volatile Organic Compounds	Carbon Monoxide
Vehicles 34% Electric Utilities 35%	Vehicles 24% Painting/Coating 12% Wood-Burning Stoves 11%	Vehicles 54% Forest Fires 11% Wood-Burning Stoves 10%

U.S. Urban Areas with More Than 20 Days in 1988 above Smog Safety Levels*

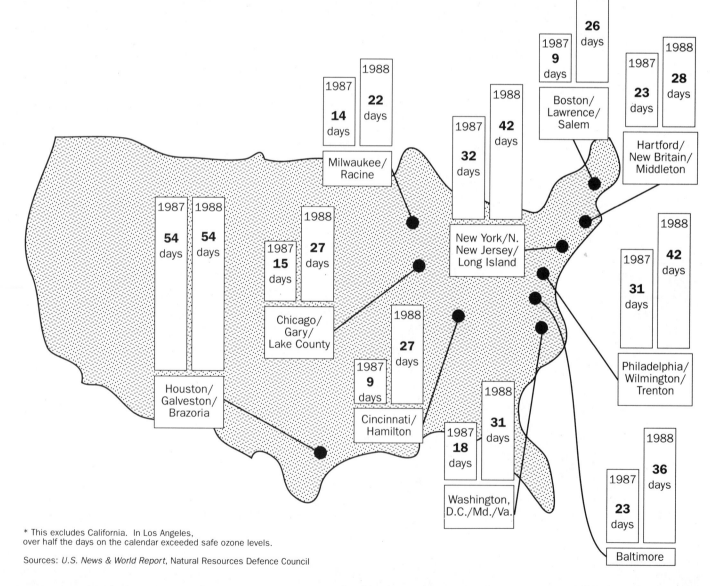

Milwaukee/Racine — 1987 **14** days, 1988 **22** days

Boston/Lawrence/Salem — 1987 **9** days, 1988 **26** days

Hartford/New Britain/Middleton — 1987 **23** days, 1988 **28** days

New York/N. New Jersey/Long Island — 1987 **32** days, 1988 **42** days

Houston/Galveston/Brazoria — 1987 **54** days, 1988 **54** days

Chicago/Gary/Lake County — 1987 **15** days, 1988 **27** days

Cincinnati/Hamilton — 1987 **9** days, 1988 **27** days

Philadelphia/Wilmington/Trenton — 1987 **31** days, 1988 **42** days

Washington, D.C./Md./Va. — 1987 **18** days, 1988 **31** days

Baltimore — 1987 **23** days, 1988 **36** days

* This excludes California. In Los Angeles,
over half the days on the calendar exceeded safe ozone levels.

Sources: *U.S. News & World Report*, Natural Resources Defence Council

York, Milwaukee, Baltimore, Philadelphia, the Connecticut suburbs, San Diego, and Chicago.) While some of the clean fuels proposed may pose new environmental hazards, and none are economically competitive with gasoline, the amendment suggested that now is the time to start refining new technologies.

The Bush plan also asked automakers to lower tailpipe emissions (although environmentalists complained not by enough!), called for stricter inspection programs, mandated vapor-recovery nozzles on gas pumps, and required the regulation of such consumer products as paint thinner. In a separate proposal, the administration also called for improving fuel-efficiency rates from 26.5 to 27.5 miles per gallon—but allowed companies to average the rate of all cars they sell, not require that efficiency for each of them.

The carmakers' immediate reaction was "no-can-do," since any such changes would require substantial investment in the redesign of both cars and engines. The oil companies also protested, because new fuels mean potentially less demand for oil and gas. Independent service station owners also cried foul because new fuels could mean substantial and costly investments in new equipment.

The plan drew criticism from the environmental community as well. In part, critics were concerned that switching from gasoline to fuels like methanol, which are made from coal or natural gas, would not be an optimal trade-off, since these sources too are non-renewable fossil fuels. They also worried about pollutants emitted by alternative fuels, like formaldehyde from methanol. For their part, officials in city and state governments were concerned that if the Bush plan wasn't sufficiently strict they would soon have to adopt their own legislations, such as banning cars from certain areas, prohibiting older vehicles without pollution controls, restricting the number of cars within city or freeway systems, and imposing higher tolls.

Despite criticisms of the plan, environmentalists were encouraged by the administration's effort. En-

vironmental regulations were so lax during the Reagan Administration that by 1987 the three leading American carmakers—General Motors, Ford, and Chrysler—had dismantled many of their programs researching smaller, more fuel-efficient cars. According to a lengthy assessment of Reagan's disregard for the environment (*A Season of Spoils*, Pantheon, 1984), in August of 1981, then–Vice President Bush led the administration's drive to abolish regulations against leaded gas by 1982. This drive was undertaken despite evidence that lead levels in blood had dropped 37 percent from 1976 to 1980, concomitant with a reduction in gasoline lead levels from 190,000 tons per year to 90,000. Lobbied by small refineries and lead-blending companies, Reagan, Bush, and then–EPA chief Anne Gorsuch tried to revoke the ban. Better heads at the EPA eventually won out over the White House team, but the struggle was indicative of the administration's contempt for environmental protection programs.

Later, the Reagan Administration proposed repealing fuel-efficiency requirements altogether. The effort was mildly successful, and beginning in 1986 industry requests to lower standards were granted each year. Although by 1985 the mandatory fuel-efficiency standards of 27.5 miles per gallon had been achieved, the EPA allowed them to revert to 26 miles per gallon between 1986 and 1988. As a result, some carmakers have been able to meet and even exceed the standards, and earn credits with which to offset lapses in future years.

The priority of the Bush plan, and the suggestion that provoked the most controversy, was for an immediate improvement of "clean fuel" technology. These are the options:

• *Methanol*—three parts hydrogen, one part oxygen, one part carbon—may be the most likely substitute for gasoline, simply because it's made from coal or natural gas, both of which are abundant in

North America. It burns more cleanly than gasoline and produces only 20 to 33 percent of the ozone-creating gases.

Methanol has flaws, however. It is more expensive than gasoline or natural gas; when spilled, it forms pools, creating a safety hazard; its production results in carbon dioxide formation, which contributes to the greenhouse effect. When the gas burns it produces formaldehyde, a carcinogen that must be removed by a catalytic converter, and is 25 percent more dangerous than gasoline. (As with many pollutants, alternative fuels have to be evaluated in terms of risks and benefits—e.g., is the carbon dioxide emitted by methanol production less or more harmful than the nitrogen oxides emitted by gas-powered engines?) A California state agency is currently conducting large-scale testing of methanol engines and there are already a scattering of methanol pumps at stations across the country.

• *Ethanol*—made from corn—is also more expensive than gasoline, but experiments are underway to generate it from other plants and even garbage. Carmakers are now refining experimental engines that can run on a variety of fuels, which the driver would select by simply flicking a switch on the dash. According to the *Wall Street Journal,* Ford has designed a Taurus that can run on ethanol, methanol, or gas; General Motors has converted its mid-sized Lumina to operate on any of the three; and Chrysler is experimenting with a methanol/gasoline LeBaron.

Ethanol is being tested publicly by a handful of bus companies across the United States. In Des Moines, the first ethanol-powered buses have been on the streets since mid-1989. They were developed by Midwest Power Concepts, in nearby Radcliffe, Iowa. The company first designed the technology for farmers to use in diesel tractors and combines, using alcohol squeezed from an abundant supply of corn. "Our findings could revolutionize the way mass transit systems are fueled in the future," said K. Stephen Spade, general manager of the Des Moines Metropolitan Transportation Authority. He claimed that ethanol would reduce hazardous emissions by 50 percent while getting diesel-equivalent fuel mileage.

Perhaps the most successful ethanol experiment so far is underway in Brazil, where ethanol made from sugarcane has provided half of the country's automotive fuel since 1986. Despite the program's initial success, it is uncertain whether or not ethanol use will increase. The program was heavily supported by state funds and fueled by the country's massive amounts of sugar beets and sugarcane. It is estimated that for the United States market to switch to ethanol, 40 percent of the country's annual corn harvest would have to be earmarked for fuel.

• *Natural gas* is viewed by many to be the fuel of the future. In some places, it is already widely used—more than 500,000 natural gas vehicles are already on the road worldwide, with a similar number expected in the next 10 to 15 years. In British Columbia, more than 5,000 drivers of Fords and Chevys that have been converted for natural gas (a simple procedure) pull into service stations and, instead of pumping gasoline, open their car hoods and attach what looks like an air hose. More than 200 of the Brooklyn Union Gas Company's fleet of corporate sedans, vans, and trucks are currently equipped to run on two fuels—just flick a switch on the dash and they'll run on either unleaded gasoline or natural gas.

The potential future use of natural gas is great, because it produces no soot (the bane of diesel fuel) and less carbon monoxide, nitrogen oxide, and hydrocarbons than gasoline. Its supply far exceeds demand, and unlike oil it can be readily produced in the United States and Canada. Natural-gas-powered vehicles already meet emission standards without the catalytic converters needed on gasoline-powered vehicles. The cost of converting a car to natural gas today is still prohibitive, though—roughly $1,500 to $2,000. Recently, one manufacturer, Cummins Engine Company, built the first natural-gas-only bus engines, which are being tested by Columbia Natural Gas Company in Columbia, Ohio.

Although they are few, natural gas does have flaws. Natural-gas-powered vehicles would have a relatively short range (they'd have to be filled about twice as often as gas-burning vehicles), and special fueling stations would have to be built. Like electric cars, they generally don't accelerate as fast as gas-powered cars. Though tens of thousands of utility vehicles are currently powered by natural gas, and buses around the world are testing it, regulations restrict its use in tunnels and on bridges because of its explosive potential. And, for now, it's expensive.

Its immediate future use may be best left with taxis, delivery vehicles, and older cars. As increasing numbers of vehicles experiment with it, more gas stations will make it available. Home refueling tanks are also on the horizon. Tapped into the line feeding a home's heating unit and cooking appliances, and powered by a $2,000 compressor, cars can be filled overnight.

(One unexpected result of the push for alternative fuels is that at least two oil companies—with the backing of Detroit—have proposed "reformulated" gasoline as an option. But even though such gases are aimed at older, more polluting cars and they are cleaner burning than leaded gas, they still can't match methanol or natural gas for cleanliness. The oil companies are pushing the reformulated gas—which they insist is 20 percent cleaner—because they can produce it at existing refineries. Atlantic Richfield and Sun Oil lead the way, with the support of General Motors, Ford and Chrysler.)

Other options, which hold less potential, include:

• *Hydrogen* ultimately promises to be a great source of power for cars and trucks. Canada, Japan, and West Germany are already experimenting with it. Its beauty is that it could be used as either liquid or compressed gas, and can be made from water. It's easy to generate by using electricity to break up water molecules. But so far, the amount of energy needed to produce hydrogen fuel exceeds the amount created when it is burned. Recent advances in the efficiency of solar cells, which convert solar energy into electricity, are increasing hydrogen's potential.

• *Electric* cars have been experimented with for decades. They produce near-zero pollution, can be driven up to 70 miles on a single charge and are ideal for stop-and-go traffic because they use no energy when "idling." They are quiet and efficient, but the currently available batteries take many hours to charge, do not carry enough power for extended operation, and have a limited lifetime. Stronger batteries are on their way, but for now they are expensive. Today, electric cars are used mostly by electric utilities and the postal service. Their major flaw is that they depend on yet another fossil-fuel-driven energy source—electricity—which creates pollution problems of its own.

• *Diesel* is one fuel that should be phased out rather than encouraged. Currently, no diesel engine can meet emissions standards and manufacturers are not sure they can ever modify engines completely. Unfiltered, diesel engines emit roughly 30 to 100 times more particulates than existing gas-powered engines. (Yet, new diesel truck purchases have increased 10 to 15 percent annually over gas-powered trucks, largely because diesel is a less expensive fuel and gets 20 to 40 percent better gas mileage.) There is a good chance that diesel engines will not become obsolete, however. Experiments to convert them to methanol-burning engines are underway, and a process capable of eliminating nitrogen oxides from diesel exhaust has been reported.

Ironically, it was the encouragement of diesel-powered cars by Detroit that proved one of the car

Although automobile tailpipe emissions have been vastly improved in the United States in the past 10 years, the proliferation of cars on the road over the last decade has led to a worsening of urban air pollution. For nearly half the days in 1988, the air over Los Angeles (below) exceeded safe smog levels.

and oil industries' major miscalculations. In the early 1980s, Detroit began to roll diesel cars off the assembly lines, encouraged by consumers who liked diesel fuel's lower price. At the behest of Detroit automakers, oil companies spent bundles installing diesel pumps at gas stations across the United States. The automakers dropped the ball technology-wise—the cars they churned out sold well enough, but gave their buyers constant trouble. Diesel cars' sales plummeted as quickly as they had soared, angering the oil companies who had gambled on their potential. (Despite the misstep, not all oil companies oppose experimentation with alternate fuels. Exxon, for one, has vast coal and natural gas holdings.)

Despite the progress in developing alternative fuels, there are major roadblocks both to their development and use. A "chicken-and-egg" argument is promoted by both oil and auto industries when debating the future: Without a plentiful supply of alternative fuels, they argue, motorists are reluctant to convert. But without vehicles bought and paid for, fuel suppliers hesitate to make the investment in distribution operations.

Carmakers could produce enough alternative-fuel-powered cars by 1995 to meet the Bush Administration's goals, but they remain skeptical about consumers' willingness to buy them. Cost—to the consumers—is a concern, too, and carmakers argue that if alternative-fueled cars are much more expensive than gas-powered cars, they will be a very tough sell, no matter how environmentally sound.

There may also be a problem at the pump with any switch to alternative fuels. If, indeed, there are soon to be several million methanol or natural-gas-powered cars on the road, the nation's 93,000 service stations will have to install new pumps, tanks, and other equipment, at an estimated cost of $5 billion. For their part, automakers have a preference for which "clean fuels" they'd like to see, if any. They prefer alcohol-based fuels over natural

gas or propane, since gases have to be stored in thick-walled tanks under enormous pressure. They also offer substantially less driving distance than alcohol.

Gas stations, both the "mom-and-pop" variety and the big chains, are also playing a role in smog control. In fact, pollution controls have already been legislated at the pump in California and Washington, D.C. Called "vapor-recovery nozzles" (they resemble big black accordion hoses), these gas pumps capture and recycle polluting gas vapors. Conversion to the pumps costs stations $12,000 to $20,000 for 9 to 12 nozzles and requires digging up the station's driveway to install pipes that return vapors to storage tanks. But they have proven so effective that New York, New Jersey, Connecticut, and Massachusetts have recently adopted laws requiring them.

No matter which way the public—or Congress—leads the auto and oil industries, companies are gearing up for change. In the waning days of the Reagan Administration, General Motors had just 15 staff engineers working on alternative fuels; now it has an entire manufacturing division and three parts units concentrating on their development. Ford already makes ethanol-powered cars in Brazil and propane-powered trucks used in Louisville, Kentucky. Despite all their lobbying against alternatives, American automakers know that if the use of such fuels become mandated, or strikes the public's fancy, they will have to be ready, otherwise foreign competitors will take *all* the business.

Automakers are already focusing on ways both to reduce emissions and improve efficiency, by experimenting with lighter cars and using more plastic. Cadillac's new V-8 engine is 100 pounds lighter than the cast-iron version. GM's minivans use plastic body panels that are glued to lightweight metal frames. The companies are also experimenting with four-valve engines, already standard on Japanese cars, and electronic automatic four-speed transmissions that can be programmed to shift at the optimum engine speed to save miles per gallon. And they are working on improved catalytic converters—the original of which may be the auto industry's best environmental solution ever.

Foreign governments and carmakers are wrestling with the same set of problems as smog levels rise worldwide. Speed limits, improved mass transit, increased restrictions on car use are all being considered across the European community. In Denmark, all new cars sold after October 1, 1990 will have American-style emissions standards. Those have already been adopted in Austria, Sweden, Switzerland, and Norway. Oslo plans to build toll gates at approaches to the city to discourage driving. Long delays—while buses whiz by—may help. Some French-built cars, notorious polluters, are being considered for banning by some neighboring countries. Britain's labor party is lobbying for higher taxes for vehicle use, restrictions on car use in central cities at peak hours, and improved mass transit. Some British companies are adding catalytic converters to cars—which are not mandated in any country but the United States—at no charge to the purchaser. Even the royal family has jumped on the bandwagon, retrofitting all of its vehicles to use unleaded gasoline. Some Western European countries have added a dollar-a-gallon gasoline surcharge to discourage gas-guzzlers. (Comparatively, U.S. gasoline prices are cheap. U.S. tax per gallon is just 29 cents. In Japan it's $1.61, in France $2.44, and in Italy, $3.31.)

Japan's standards—implemented between 1975 and 1978—are similar to those in the United States, as are those in Australia, Canada, and South Korea. Japanese carmakers responded first to meet the efficiency demands of clean air laws at home: Honda's CRX gets over 50 miles per gallon, as does Suzuki's Sprint, Mitsubishi's Mirage, and Subaru's Justy. The most efficient car sold in the United States is the Geo—marketed by GM, and produced by Toyota. Volvo is experimenting with increasingly lighter materials, like magnesium, to reduce the weight of its cars. German manufacturers are fiddling with improved aerodynamics, weight reduction, and new engines that burn cleaner, and considering the introduction of engine blocks made of lightweight ceramics.

Ultimately, all such experimentation—with alternative fuels, lighter engine blocks, sleeker aerodynamics—are merely stopgaps until we become less dependent on fuel-powered cars. The simple fact that cars today are traveling more miles per year and idling in traffic for many more hours than their predecessors, should be a clear sign that the goal is to reduce driving as well as emissions. Mass transportation is the most obvious remedy to both.

A promising sign may be the success of a group called Transportation Alternatives, a New York City bicycle club. Representing the more than 70,000 New Yorkers who use bicycles for transportation, the group has been lobbying for more parking space, bike lanes, and other initiatives for several years. In a recent mayoral election, the group sent surveys to each of four Democratic candidates, attempting to gauge their attitudes towards bicycles, and all four responded. "The bicycle is the only vehicle that can address all the problems we've inflicted on ourselves," says the Worldwatch Institute's Marcia Lowe, who recently authored a paper on the subject, "such as air pollution, congestion in our cities, and still give us an individualized way of getting around."

As with so many of the environmental messes in which we find ourselves, we have let smog back us into a corner. National governments are having a difficult time regulating the problem, so states and big municipalities have no option but to legislate change. Other last-resort options that should be encouraged include limiting the number of cars that families can own, forcing manufacturers to reformulate cosmetics and paints, and outlawing gas-powered lawn mowers, charcoal lighter fluids, and a host of everyday products. (In New York, paint makers have been told to cut down on the volatile, oil-based chemicals that help paint and varnishes dry quickly, but pollute the air. Manufacturers are seeking national standards for paints, varnishes, stains, shellacs, and rust- and fire-inhibitors. "In the trade-off between the environment and whether the bathroom ceiling remains pristine, it might be that we can put up with a little discoloration," said Donald Smith, vice-president of Pratt & Lambert, a national paint company.) Long-debated plans to restrict or bar private automobiles from crowded, dirty places, such as Manhattan and the Los Angeles freeways, may be a necessity before the turn of the century.

Perhaps the true wave of the future is in the head of planners like 40-year-old Peter Calthorpe. In an effort to battle both suburban sprawl and urban pollution, he has designed what he calls the Pedestrian Pocket. It is actually a well-conceived urban/suburban strategy for a series of high-density small towns linked by light rail, which encourages leaving the car at home, and walking or taking the train to shop, work, or play.

No matter what the solutions are, they must be adopted globally, and soon. Because even if the skies over Los Angeles or Denver, London or Oslo were to miraculously clear, those above Melbourne, Ankara, Mexico City, and many others would still be hazy.

SMOG

Bakeries, dry cleaners, and cars have one thing in common: they produce hydrocarbons, one of the key components of smog.

Released into the air by fermenting yeast, evaporating dry cleaning fluid, or car exhaust (and dozens of other sources) hydrocarbons combine with other noxious emissions—including carbon monoxide and nitrogen oxides—in the atmosphere close to the Earth.

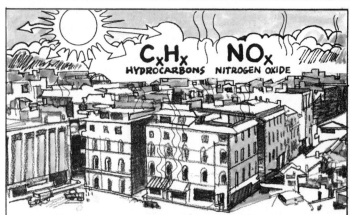

Airborne, these gases mingle and are "baked" by the sun's heat to create photochemical smog, the brownish haze that hovers over many of the world's cities—and increasingly the countryside.

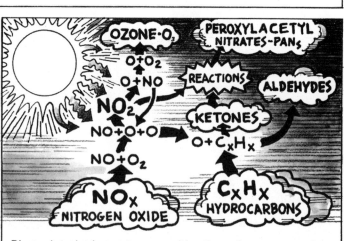

Photochemical smog—a combination of peroxyacetyl-nitrate, ozone, and other toxic gases and particles—is created by a complex series of reactions.

In addition to hazardous fumes, smog is made up of tiny particles of toxic metals and particles emitted by industry, building construction, even oil-based paints, which make it an even more dangerous health hazard.

Smog inflames the lungs, causing chest pain, making breathing difficult, triggering asthma attacks, and can be as damaging to lungs as cigarette smoke, permanently scarring lung tissue.

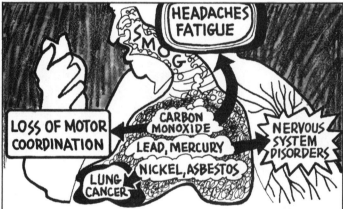

Absorbed through the lungs into the bloodstream, smog (especially carbon monoxide) decreases the blood's ability to absorb oxygen. Other toxic metals and pollution particles can cause a variety of health problems.

In a process known as "temperature inversion," smog accumulating in valley areas like Los Angeles and Denver can be trapped close to the ground whenever a cold front pushes a layer of insulating warm air above the smog.

Borne by prevailing winds to suburbs and farmlands, smog can enter the pores of plants and "burn" their cell membranes, severely stunting growth. The result is billions of dollars of crop damage every year due to smog.

Although tailpipe emissions have been improved in recent years, the growing number of cars on the road, and their nitrogen oxide and hydrocarbon emissions, continues to raise smog levels to new highs.

Los Angeles, known for its smog, is trying to implement strict new laws to curtail air pollution. The laws—including bans on many household items and mandating alternative fuels—may establish precedents for the world to follow.

Some cities, including São Paulo, Athens, Rome, and Budapest—have banned cars from their inner cities in order to cut down on smog. Using mass transportation, riding your bike, or burning cleaner fuels will help reduce the necessity of such bans in other cities.

An emphasis on car-pooling and mass transportation is chief among Los Angeles's encouragements, both for their fuel and pollution savings.

There are a variety of things you can do around the house to help cut down air pollution: using vinegar and baking soda instead of most commercial cleaners can help cut down on pollutants in the air.

Individual Action

1. If you drive a new car, be sure it is in tune and that the spark plugs and oil are clean.

2. Use mass transit if it's available. If not, try walking, biking, or skateboarding.

3. Car pools may be mandated in the future, so it's not too early to start one today.

4. Do not leave your car idling when you run into the 7-Eleven or post office—12 percent of smog contribution comes from idling.

5. Once, taking a leisurely Sunday afternoon drive seemed the "All-American" activity. Today, such "entertainment" spins just add to pollution.

6. After your pollution-controlled car is inspected and cleaned, put it in the garage. Take the bus or ride with a friend. Only 20 percent of the driving done in the United States is pleasure- or vacation-related. The rest is spent driving to work or running errands. If we don't reduce both driving and consumption, it won't matter how "clean" we make our cars or their fuel.

7. The EPA is considering taxing some of the thousands of contributors to ozone pollution, such as solvents used by auto body shops. If you use solvents or paints in your business, investigate whether there are less environmentally-harmful alternatives—or be prepared to pay more for the tools of your trade.

8. Speaking of taxes, don't be surprised if someday soon there is a sticker tax on new cars that don't meet fuel efficiency standards. If you're considering getting a new car—or used car, for that matter—buy one that gets *at least* the average fuel economy.

9. There is a possibility that if the proposals in Los Angeles are successful, such niceties as barbecue lighter fluids and gas-powered lawn mowers will be banned. There are already alternatives to both: electric charcoal lighters, paraffinated briquets, and electric mowers. It would be helpful if those kinds of switches were now made voluntarily.

10. There are also a variety of air-polluting chemicals in household cleaners beneath your sink. Everything from glass cleaners to aerosol anti-perspirants contains dangerous, air-polluting chemicals—and the options to them are cheap and simple. Baking powder and vinegar are great cleaners and there's nothing wrong with roll-on deodorants.

11. When you buy a can of house paint, buy a water-based one, not oil-based. The oil paint contains a rash of pollutants and requires air-dirtying solvents to clean brushes afterwards.

12. When considering where to live, take into account the pollution caused by driving to work, shopping, and school. Communities planned around easy access to all three—and more—are environmentally sound and represent the lifestyle of the twenty-first century.

Government Action

1. Stricter emissions standards for all vehicles should be imposed.

2. Governments should allocate increased funding for the research of alternative auto fuels—including methanol, ethanol, natural gas, and electric-powered vehicles.

3. The conversion of fleets to cleaner-burning fuels, like ethanol or natural gas, should be encouraged by legislation.

4. Increased public transportation should be encouraged by providing tax incentives to operators and imposing higher registration costs on private vehicles. Sales taxes on bicycles should be removed in order to encourage their use.

5. Inspections of private vehicles should include emissions testing.

6. Tighter standards for diesel engine emissions, in both cars and trucks, should be imposed, and the replacement of diesel buses with those that burn alternative fuels should be encouraged.

7. Governments should require the installation of controls on gas pumps to capture and recycle vapors which escape during refueling.

8. National emissions standards for a number of the hydrocarbon solvents (including paints, household cleansers, pesticides and other chemical compounds) formulated and manufactured for nationwide sales should be adopted.

9. Similar national emissions standards need to be applied to dry cleaners, furniture makers, paint shops, and bakeries, all of whose businesses produce smog-contributing chemicals.

10. The clean air laws already on the books should be enforced. Where such proposals are not law, they should be encouraged and legislated.

Reading

"Air: An Atmosphere of Uncertainty," by Noel Grove. *National Geographic,* April 1987.

"Rethinking Transportation," by Michael Renner. *State of the World 1989: A Worldwatch Institute Report on Progress Toward a Sustainable Society.* New York: W. W. Norton & Co., 1989.

"L.A. Fights for Breath," by Alan Weisman. *The New York Times Magazine,* July 30, 1989.

"New Tactics Emerge in Struggle Against Smog," by Malcolm W. Browne. *The New York Times,* February 21, 1989.

The World Resources Report, compiled by the World Resources Institute. 1709 New York Ave. NW, 7th Floor, Washington, DC 20006. (Available at most libraries.)

A Who's Who of American Toxic Air Polluters: A Guide to More Than 1500 Factories in 46 States Emitting Cancer-Causing Chemicals. NRDC, 1989.

The Bicycle: Vehicle for a Small Planet, by Marcia D. Lowe. Washington, DC.: Worldwatch Institute, 1989.

Organizations to Contact

Air and Waste Management Association, Box 2861, Pittsburgh, PA 15230, 412-232-3444.

Air Pollution Control, Bureau of National Affairs, Inc., 1231 25th St. NW, Washington, DC 20037, 202-452-4200.

INFORM, 381 Park Ave. South, New York, NY 10016, 212-689-4040.

National Audubon Society, 950 Third Ave., New York, NY 10022, 212-832-3200.

Sierra Club, 730 Polk St., San Francisco, CA 94109, 415-776-2211.

State and Territorial Air Pollution Program Administration/Air Pollution Control Officials, Suite 306, 444 N. Capitol St. NW, Washington, DC, 20003, 202-624-7864.

U.S. Public Interest Research Group, 215 Pennsylvania Ave. SE, Washington, DC 20003, 202-546-9707.

4

Acid Rain

Acid rain may be the most insidious of all airborne pollutions. Unlike smog, it is invisible; unlike chlorofluorocarbons (CFCs), it does its damage not in the upper reaches of the atmosphere, but right here on Earth. Acid rain also serves as perhaps the best example of how a form of pollution can cause global environmental damage, as well as transboundary political strife. The product of invisible gases—sulfur dioxide and nitrogen oxide, produced primarily by coal-burning plants and automobile exhaust—acid rain is carried by winds of the upper atmosphere from state to state, nation to nation, without regard for boundaries. It may originate in Ohio or Great Britain, but it carries its destruction to lakes and forests as far away as Ontario and Norway. The resulting devastation has caused lakes to die, forests to shrivel, and spurred rifts between governments that may take decades to repair.

Though acid rain was first detected more than 150 years ago, its cause remains an issue of contention between scientists, policymakers and environmentalists. Although man-made emissions were a recognized contributor, some experts claimed that decaying vegetation, forest fires, bacterial decomposition, volcanoes, and even lightning, were equal parties to the acid-heavy rains. In the past two decades, however, after years of intensive research and international study, sophisticated tracking of polluted air masses has proven that man-made emissions are in fact the worst offenders. Since that scientific verification, some of the dirtiest emissions have been slowed in North America and parts of Europe. Coal-burning—which produces the highly acidic sulfur

dioxide—is leveling off in a handful of industrial countries as a result of utility companies switching to low-sulfur coal, installing scrubbers on smokestacks, and using coal "washed" clean of its worst pollutants. Measures adopted by the auto industry have also helped to lessen acid rain, including the production of a growing number of fuel efficient cars, the use of unleaded gasoline and, in the United States, catalytic converters.

Despite such technological improvements, acid rain pollution in Eastern Europe, China, the Soviet Union, India, and Third World countries is worsening. By the year 2000, sulfur dioxide emissions in Eastern Europe (two thirds contributed by coal-burning electrical power plants) are expected to be twice as high as those in the United States, although it's one seventh the size. China's plans for per-capita energy-consumption suggest that it will soon be burning a third more coal annually than the U.S.'s current annual consumption of 900 million tons. Coal consumption in Brazil and India has almost tripled in the past decade. Sales of nitrogen-oxide-laden leaded gasoline continue to soar across South America. And the deleterious effects of acid rain have even been felt in such non-urban settings as the jungles of western Africa and Southeast Asia.

Acid rain captured the attention of lawmakers, the media, and the public in the past decade, as conclusive reports from scientists proved that rains and snows were poisoning streams and lakes. Studies showed how, once captured in huge weather systems, the acid-forming pollutants could travel 500 to 1,000 miles from their point of origin. Today, concerns about acid rain have broadened to include threats to fresh water, forests, and public health. And while there is still some skepticism about acid rain's effects—some scientists suggest that air pollution is so insidious that it is difficult to separate the effects of any one chemical reaction—there is clear consensus that acid rain is no overnight sensation, but a long-term threat to the world's ecosystems.

The history of "acid precipitation" dates back well over a century. The term "acid rain" was first used in 1852 by an English chemist, Robert Angus Smith, to describe the sooty skies of industrial Manchester and the acidity found in local precipitation. Yet 125 years later, when America's Clean Air Act was first amended, acid rain was not addressed. Its causes and effects were still not well understood.

Smith's studies were neglected until the 1950s, when a Canadian ecologist tried to generate interest in what he perceived as a worsening problem. But the first detailed scientific reports of the acid rain problem to gain wide acceptance did not emerge until 1967 from Sweden. Over the next few years, lakes and streams in North America and Europe (their beds low in acid-absorbing limestone) began to wither. Although fish and vegetation were dying, scientists could only guess at the reasons. Then, in the early 1970s, mountaintop trees in the Black Forest of West Germany exhibited signs of inexplicable abuse: needles and leaves became discolored and fell, growth slowed, roots shriveled, insects and disease were rampant. In the early 1980s, similar signs of unnatural decay surfaced in forests in the Appalachians and Vermont's Green Mountains. By 1982, almost 40 percent of the trees on Mount Mitchell in North Carolina were defoliated and 7 percent died. Scientists around the world became convinced that the devastation they were seeing in lakes and streams—and the inexplicable dying of forests—was yet another outcome of man-made chemicals in the atmosphere.

By the mid-1980s, debate over acid rain had touched off international furies, pitting state against state, nation against nation. Canada's prime minister, Brian Mulroney, called the acid rain mess a "rapidly escalating ecological tragedy" and blamed much of the destruction in his country on coal-burning power plants in the American heartland. In Sweden, acid rain pollution was called "an undeclared act of war" —since most of the acidifying chemicals damaging Swedish lakes and forests originated in the sulfur dioxide emissions of West Germany and other European nations. The estimated worldwide cost of dealing with just half of the causes of acid rain ranges from \$16 to \$33 billion.

Even while data are being collected to prove (or disprove) exactly how *much* of the blame can be attributed to acid rains, it is apparent that ignoring the problem is one of the most short-sighted global environmental blunders of all. We've been watching it worsen in North America for more than a decade, and in Europe for almost 20 years. Ultimately, acid rain threatens both plant and animal life in tens of thousands of lakes and streams. Around the globe, millions of acres of forests that have thrived for over 300 million years are slowly being decimated by the nitric and sulfuric acids that rain on them.

Cost is the primary rationale cited by industry and politicians for failing to tackle acid rain. Powerful lobbies have fought proposals that would mandate adding high-tech cleaners to power plants and cars. Lawmakers from coal-mining regions argue that the potential loss of tens of thousands of mining jobs is sufficient reason for being cautious. Everyone agrees that increased cleanup costs will eventually be borne by consumers. Yet environmentalists and lawmakers around the world are slowly prodding industry to change. A large section of the Bush Administration's proposed amendments to the Clean Air Act was aimed at reducing the main contributors to acid rain. Predictably, coal, car, and utility industry representatives denounced the Bush proposal as "harmful to business"; environmentalists, on the other hand, claimed that the plan "did not do enough."

The specific recommendations of the amendment's plan to reduce acid rain pollution include halving sulfur dioxide emissions by the year 2000. Nitrous oxide emissions—mostly from cars' tailpipes—would be reduced by 2 million tons, or about 10 percent. Implementation of new technologies is encouraged, including "cleaning" the pollutants from coal before it is burned. The bill's most innovative proposition would permit the buying and selling of "pollution rights," in order to allow companies to reduce pollution in the most cost-efficient manner. After receiving considerable input from industry and environmentalists, Congress began drafting the legislation. Regardless of the law's final provisions, its initial impact won't be felt until 1995.

CAUSES

While there is residual debate over the effects of acid rain, its origins are now certain. Sulfur dioxide and nitrogen oxides are the chief contaminants, and so far acid rain has been primarily a problem of the heavily industrialized eastern half of North America and western Europe.

Seventy percent of the sulfur dioxide in the air is emitted by coal-fired power plants, which annually pump 100 million tons of the gas out of their tall stacks into the atmosphere. (The worst offenders in North America are in Ohio, Michigan, Pennsylvania, central Ontario, and Quebec.) Ironically, the pervasiveness of acid rain is partially a result of past pollution legislation in the United States. The taller stacks required for power plants by the Clean Air Act of 1970 just send the chemicals higher into the sky, where stronger winds can carry them further, to distant lakes and forests. Smelters, especially in southern Canada, are big contributors, as are garbage incinerators.

Nearly half of the nitrogen oxide pollution comes from the growing fleet of automobiles worldwide. (It is also a residue of the emissions of coal and other fossil-fuel-burning power plants.) Despite efforts to clean up car exhaust, nitrogen oxide emissions have tripled in North America since the 1950s, and doubled across Europe. The brown haze of smog is the chief result. The increased focus on alternative fuels—like methanol and natural gas—is aimed at reducing nitrogen oxide's role in both smog and acid rain. But nitrogen oxides do not pollute just the air. According to an Environmental Defense Fund study (the New York–based group that helped the Bush administration write their clean air proposal), deposits of nitrogen oxides—25 percent of them rained down from the skies—are one of the key pollutants stimulating algae growth in the waters of the Chesapeake Bay. The proliferation of algae there has become so extensive in recent years that it is killing fish and shellfish, and rapidly accelerating the aging of the bay.

Natural causes, such as forest fires, volcanic eruptions, bacterial decomposition, even lightning, pump an additional 75 to 100 million tons of nitrogen oxides into the air each year. But acid rain's major contributors are still man-made: a large coal-fired plant can emit in a single year as much sulfur dioxide as was blown out by the 1980 eruption of Mt. Saint Helens—some 400,000 tons.

Part of the problem in studying air pollutants is that they are difficult to visualize. If you were to stare at the stacks of your local electric company power plant all day, or watch your car's tailpipe for several hours, you wouldn't see a single sulfur dioxide or nitrogen oxide particle emerge (though the average electric plant emits over 8,000 tons of them a month). Although they are invisible, these particles hover above the city or industrial plant that spawned them, and create clouds that occasionally settle locally. Most, however, are sent spiraling high into the atmosphere; their flight may last days

☼

and take them thousands of miles away. En route, the pollutant molecules interact with sunlight, moisture, oxidants, and catalysts, to change into new, acid-laden compounds of sulfur and nitrogen.

After traveling considerable distances, the now highly acidic chemicals return to earth in the form of rain, snow, fog, frost, or dew. A drop of rain—or snow, fog, frost or dew—so altered can contain 30 times more acid than normal. It can damage vegetation and wildlife, ruin painted finishes on cars and homes, and tarnish shiny new skyscrapers and centuries-old buildings.

Tracing acid rain back to its source is difficult, which is one reason for governments' reluctance to respond to the problem. (The Reagan Administration refused to recognize acid rain as a problem because there was no "conclusive" proof of its source.) No doubt *all* air pollutants have a negative impact on wildlife; it has been proven that ozone created by car exhaust is more damaging to forests and trees than acid rain. Skeptics (especially industries not eager to make large financial investments in cleaner technologies) prefer to blame drought, disease, and insects for the recent devastation of lakes and forests. Unfortunately, the destruction is often evident only after the damage is extensive and before a specific chemical can be indicted. But after decades of study scientists are convinced that acid rain is high on the list of man-made chemical combinations devastating the world's ecosystem.

EFFECTS

The question of whether or not acid rain is killing the world's lakes and forests is complicated by the biological complexity of both systems. Differences in topography and winds can alter the effects on forests and streams within miles of each other. Since scientists have measured cloud water as acidic as battery acid, however, and found heavy trails of acidity in soil and water, especially in northeastern

North America and across Europe, they are convinced of acid rain's damaging potential.

It is now projected that the problem could increase tenfold by the end of the century. (That's partly because it's estimated the world has an abundance of relatively inexpensive coal waiting to be mined. And the relatively high price of oil insures we will use it.) The concentration of sulfur and nitrogen in rain and snow in the eastern United States, for example, is currently 10 to 15 times greater than in remote areas of the Southern Hemisphere. But as China and other developing countries become increasingly industrialized, the effects of acid rain will spread. Soon, acid rain will become an even more unmanageable global pollution problem than it is today. Thus, the emphasis should be on finding workable ways to reduce the pollutants that build it—in effect, laying the groundwork for nations still unharmed by acid rain.

The effects of acid rain are diverse. Affected lakes and streams are no longer able to sustain many kinds of fishlife. Spawning waters are threatened. Acid-heavy water leaches important plant nutrients out of the ground and activates heavy metals such as cadmium and mercury, which contaminate water supplies. Man-made monuments—from the Statue of Liberty to the Acropolis—are etched and worn. Statues and tablets made of bronze, limestone, marble, and sandstone are slowly wearing away. Mayan ruins in the Yucatan of Mexico have turned black from acidic rains. The multi-billion-dollar global timber industry has been hurt by weakened forests and both commercial and recreational fishing businesses have been affected.

"Potential of hydrogen"—or pH—is the measure used to determine a substance's acidity. The scale runs from 1 to 14 (and can be estimated by anyone, using litmus paper and a measuring scale bought at your local drugstore—see "Individual Action"). The more acid in a substance, the lower the number: natural rainfall averages between pH 5.0 and 5.6;

The corrosive effects of acid rain can be seen here in the rapid deterioration, between 1982 and 1985 (inset), of the Mayan monument The Queen of Palenque in Mexico.

Coca-Cola has a pH value of 4; vinegar, 2.2; and battery acid has a pH of 1. A pH reading of 4 is *10 times* more acidic than 5. Acid rain has a pH of less than 5.

The first signs of acid rain's long-range ecological damage appeared in Scandinavian lakes during the 1960s. Fish populations were dwindling, and in some lakes disappearing entirely. Similar evidence of devastation grows annually. In the 1970s, New York's Department of Environmental Conservation (DEC) reported that more than 200 lakes in the western Adirondacks had already become too acidic for fish to survive, and that many more appeared threatened. In a recent study, the DEC reported that fully 25 percent of the lakes and ponds in the Adirondack Mountains are now so acidic that they cannot support fish and another 20 percent have lost most of their acid-buffering capacity and appear doomed.

Across the border in Massachusetts, almost 20 percent—over 800—of the state's ponds, lakes and rivers are vulnerable to acid deposition, including drinking-water reservoirs near Boston. Data show that more than half of the state's 34 reservoirs have lost much of their acid-buffering capacity since 1940. The largest, Quabbin Reservoir, has lost almost three quarters of its buffering capacity; the state estimates that in 20 years it will not be able to neutralize any acids and will be unusable for humans.

The Pennsylvania Fish Commission estimated in 1987 that half of the state's streams will not be able to support fish life by the year 2000 unless acid depositions decline. Ironically, Pennsylvania's emissions of sulfur dioxide are the second worst in the country, and its powerful coal industry and other industrial emitters have opposed most cleanup regulation. Environmental Protection Agency studies also show increases of acidity in rainwater in Virginia, Delaware, Maryland, West Virginia, the Great Smoky Mountains, and in lakes in Wisconsin and Minnesota, the Pacific Northwest, Colorado's Rockies, and the Pine Barrens of New Jersey.

It wasn't until the early 1980s that scientists suggested that the same acid rains—as well as ozone and other man-made pollutants—were beginning to kill off the upper reaches of forests. By 1984, West Germany reported that more than half of its forests were damaged. Today, the Black Forest of Bavaria has lost one third of its trees, and damage to the country's timber industry is estimated at $800 million per year, plus $600 million in agricultural losses due to diminished soil fertility. West Germans believe that half of the acid rain that falls on their forest comes from outside their borders. A word has been created to describe the devastation: *Waldsterben,* or forest death.

Mountain forests—those closest to the acidic clouds—best illustrate the long-term effects of acid rain: growth is stunted, leaves and needles drop inexplicably, frailer species die. The effect of pollution on trees has been compared to human physical exhaustion—they are weakened, and more susceptible to disease. Many scientists studying the problem feel that air pollution does not kill trees directly, but rather weakens them to the point where they are no longer able to withstand normal periods of moderate drought, insect infestation or disease.

Extensive forest destruction was first documented on European mountaintops in the 1970s, but has since been seen in lower altitudes as well. Although conifers seem especially vulnerable to acid rain, hardwoods also suffer. The far-reaching effect is that the soil is weakened to a point where it cannot sustain any new growth. While more clearly evident in the tighter confines of the Eastern European countryside, the effects of acid rain have taken a toll on U.S. mountain ranges, from the Appalachians to the Sierra Nevadas.

In the past few years, fingerpointing between states and nations over responsibility for acid rain has increased. The United Kingdom, heavily dependent on coal power (and destined to remain so into the foreseeable future because of its large coal re-

Acid Rain and the pH Scale

The pH scale measures how many hydrogen ions are in a substance. The more hydrogen ions, the lower the pH value, and the more acidic a substance is. Each unit decrease in pH value corresponds to a *tenfold* increase in acidity. Under continual acid precipitation, a lake gradually loses its "buffering capacity" against acidity, the pH value of its waters begins to drop, and its ecosystems are threatened.

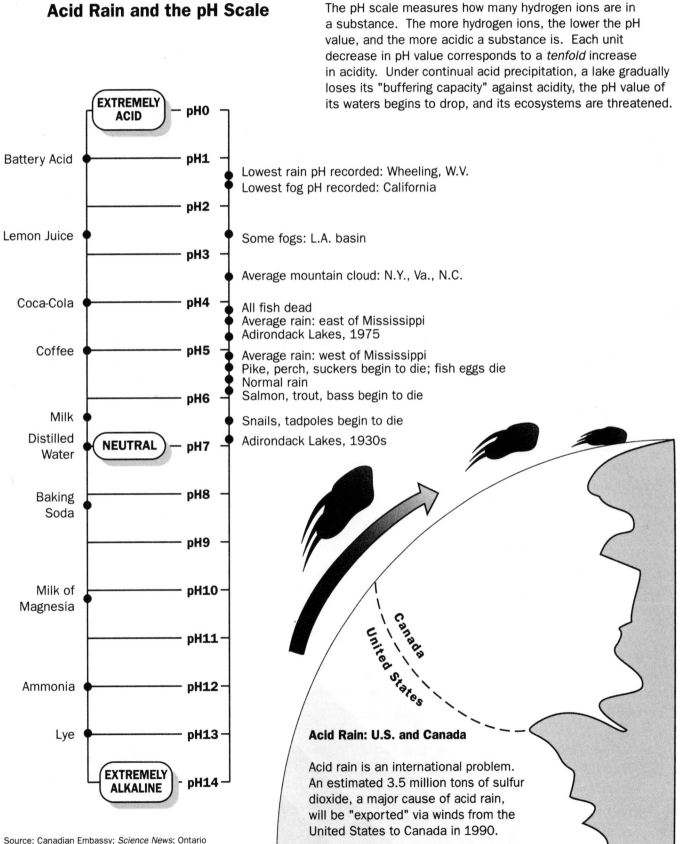

EXTREMELY ACID — pH0

Battery Acid — pH1

Lowest rain pH recorded: Wheeling, W.V.
Lowest fog pH recorded: California

pH2

Lemon Juice — pH3

Some fogs: L.A. basin

Average mountain cloud: N.Y., Va., N.C.

Coca-Cola — pH4

All fish dead
Average rain: east of Mississippi
Adirondack Lakes, 1975

Coffee — pH5

Average rain: west of Mississippi
Pike, perch, suckers begin to die; fish eggs die
Normal rain
Salmon, trout, bass begin to die

pH6

Milk

Snails, tadpoles begin to die

Distilled Water — **NEUTRAL** — pH7

Adirondack Lakes, 1930s

Baking Soda — pH8

pH9

Milk of Magnesia — pH10

pH11

Ammonia — pH12

Lye — pH13

EXTREMELY ALKALINE — pH14

Acid Rain: U.S. and Canada

Canada
United States

Acid rain is an international problem. An estimated 3.5 million tons of sulfur dioxide, a major cause of acid rain, will be "exported" via winds from the United States to Canada in 1990.

Source: Canadian Embassy; *Science News*; Ontario Ministry of the Environment; Pacific Northwest Laboratory.

serves), contributes more acid rain to Norway than Norway itself, and is the largest external source of Swedish air pollution. It is estimated that over half of Canada's acid deposition arrives from the United States. Documented forest damage in Czechoslovakia, the Netherlands, Switzerland, Romania, France, and Italy all has its origins across national borders. Hundreds of acres of forest in Finland have been damaged by the annual discharge of several hundred thousand tons of air pollution from smelters in the Soviet towns of Monchegorsk and Zapolyarny. Soviet authorities, admitting their responsibility, say they will try and reduce by half the annual pollution by 1993.

The effects of acid rain are not confined to industrial nations. As Third World economies boom, fuel consumption rates and associated pollution increase as well. Far from the industrial belt, in Australia and Brazil thousands of lakes are already lifeless, their deaths blamed on acid rain. But the cause and effect of high acidity rates varies from country to country. Recent measurements in China, for example, show that precipitation there tends to have high concentrations of sulfates and calcium, but relatively low acidity. That's because most of China's acid rain pollution comes from home heating and cooking; the chemicals are not sent high into the sky by tall stacks but instead remain closer to the ground. Also, many of the country's homes and buildings are constructed with limestone, which absorbs much of China's acid rain.

Perhaps the greatest problem of acid rain falling on lakes and streams is that acid lakes don't really die; instead, their ecosystems are irrevocably changed. If acid deposits continue unabated, plant and animal life eventually shrivels. An overload of nitrogen feeds marine algae, which bloom into vast blankets that can block sunlight and deplete the oxygen supply, smothering fish, crustaceans, and plantlife.

The early days of spring are often the days of highest acidity in the world's waterways. The bulk of fallen acids reside in the top layers of snow, hence, the greatest infusion of acid a stream will receive during the entire year comes from melting snow, when great rushes of acid water flow from streams into rivers and lakes. The result is a brief but dangerous springtime acid surge that coincides with the point at which many aquatic species are beginning to reproduce.

As researchers' knowledge of the consequences of acid rain has improved, they have also begun to identify its effects on animals. Scientists in New York report that frog and salamander populations completely disappear from some acid lakes and streams. In an extreme test, Canadian scientists sacrificed an entire lake in a remote sector of western Ontario by purposely metering in acid, to learn more about acid rain's effects on wildlife. Freshwater shrimp died first, followed by crayfish; as acidity increased, everything from snails to insect larvae disappeared. Other reports indicate that acid deposition may be playing a role in declines in waterfowl and other bird populations that feed in now-acidic lakes. Acid rain's most foreboding effect, however, is not the loss of one species or the killing of one variety of plant, it is the shakeup of the food chain that may never be completely reordered.

The effects are not limited to nature either. According to Dr. Phillip Landgrigin, Director of Environmental and Occupational Medicine at Mount Sinai School of Medicine in New York City, "the pollutants in acid rain are probably third after active smoking and passive smoking as a cause of lung disease." Both sulfur dioxide and nitrogen oxide emissions from cars and industry have been linked to increases in occurrence of asthma, heart disease, and lung disease, primarily among children and the elderly. The American Lung Association estimates between $16 and $40 billion is spent annually on illnesses directly related to air pollution.

While most efforts to stem the problems of acid rain have been aimed at industry, recent reports have identified another man-made source far from smokestacks and freeways. Scientists working in western Africa have discovered alarmingly high rates of acidity in rains over the lush jungles, caused by man-made fires that rage for months across thousands of miles of savannas. For centuries, farmers and herdsmen have set fires to clear shrubs and stimulate the growth of crops and grass. Now, added to already slightly polluted skies, smoke from those fires has raised the level of acidity in soil and rainwater to 10 times the norm. While scientists and governments ponder this new source of pollution—and ways of dealing with it—the fires burn on.

SOLUTIONS

Everyone agrees that acid rain is a problem. Academy of Science reports, EPA studies, international panels, United Nations data, and more, insist that sulfur and nitrogen oxide emissions must be slowed. Yet just how is still hotly debated.

Acid rain is one pollution problem over which individuals have little direct control, other than the common-sense daily habit of saving energy at every turn. (The less electricity used, the less sulfur dioxide spewed from power plants; the fewer miles driven, the fewer nitrogen oxide particles emitted from tailpipes.) The burden of solving the problem of acid rain must be shouldered primarily by industry and government, albeit under the watchful eye of scientists and citizens alike, whose monitoring and lobbying efforts have been the motivating factors behind many of the changes to date.

There are some shining examples of industry taking the initiative for stemming dirty emissions before they are commanded to by law. Perhaps the leader in the United States is the Minneapolis-based Northern States Power Company. The utility produces electricity for over a million customers, and

since the early 1980s has spent more than a billion dollars on pollution controls. At the same time, the company's profits have more than doubled. Northern's success has come at the encouragement of the company's president and chief executive officer, James Howard, who rationalizes their emphasis on sound environmental planning very simply: "You have to be environmentally responsible to have hope for success or longevity."

Northern States installed scrubbers, to clean sulfur from smoke and gas, on two of their plants before they were federally mandated to do so. They began buying low-sulfur coal—which emits less pollutants—back in 1972, years before it was recommended by the president or Congress. Recently they have begun experimenting with high-tech combustion systems, which burn a mixture of coal and limestone, as a way of reducing sulfur content and its acidity before it goes up the smokestack. The company is also looking into ways of generating fuel from garbage, and a furnace that creates energy from whole trees. Their success, in efficiency and especially profitability, pokes holes in arguments that pollution controls cost utilities and their stockholders potential earnings. Northern States' example should encourage others to jump before they are pushed. As Joseph Wall, the company's environmental sciences manager, says, "You have to start to take steps a little bit at a time. You don't want to wait to act until you fall off the cliff."

Northern States' example has hardly swept the acid-rain-producing industry by storm. For years, opponents of tighter controls—primarily electric power plant operators, coal manufacturers and automobile makers—have debated the conclusiveness of environmentalists' and scientists' claims about acid rain. They have argued that agriculture-related runoff is as responsible for the pollution of lakes as acid rain, and that ozone's impact on forests is far worse than the acid precipitation. They were able to hold their ground for years, largely because acidi-

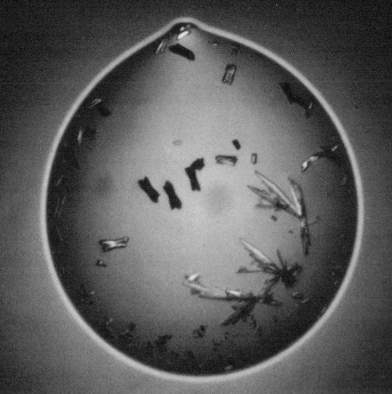

Flyash trapped in cloud droplets may enhance acid rain production. In a laboratory experiment, a water droplet is injected with flyash from an electric power plant (above), and the sulfurous particles react with the water to create needlelike sulfate crystals (bottom). A similar reaction probably occurs in acid-affected marble deterioration and leaf damage.

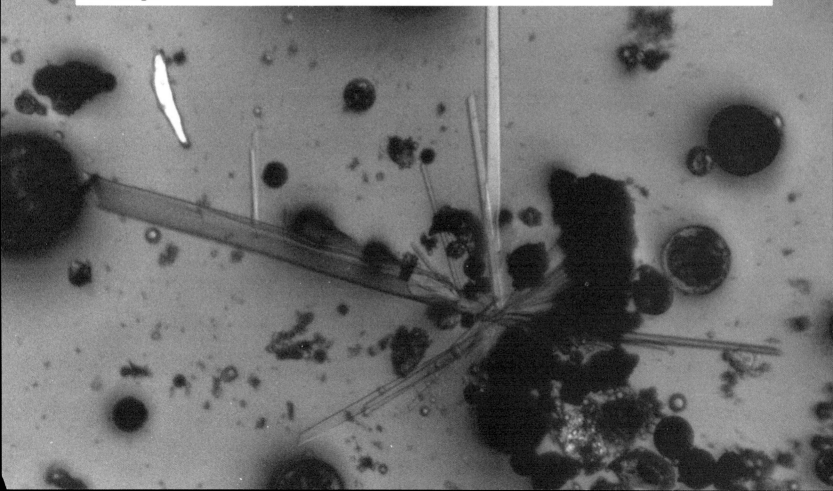

fication is so subtle that widespread damage is not immediately evident. Moreover, chemical compounds naturally present in lakes, streams, and watersheds can neutralize acids, often for many years. Only when those neutralizers are depleted will a lake begin to acidify.

Forest destruction can also take years to surface. Scientists have learned that visible symptoms of forest destruction become obvious only after damage is well underway. And in some cases—as acid rain legislation opponents are quick to point out—if acid damage is not too severe, lakes can rebuild themselves once acid input drops. But the recovery of a lake depends on the extent of damage. If sufficiently weakened, the lake's natural recovery mechanism is overwhelmed by increasing amounts of acid and other pollutants.

The latency period between acid rain pollution and the manifestation of its consequences has provided a fascinating case study of the relationship between environmental science and environmental policy. Encouraged to outlaw the pollutant, politicians have been waiting for science to deliver a clear indictment. Although eager to comply, scientists have had an extremely difficult time providing definitive proof.

As evidence mounts against acid rain pollution, the debate rages over the *best* ways to remove it from the skies: Environmentalists are convinced washing can remove satisfactory levels of sulfur from coal before it is burned, that stack scrubbers can eliminate sulfur from power-plant emissions, and that new ways of burning can reduce both sulfur and nitrogen oxide emissions. Coal and power plant lobbies continue to fight such legislation, arguing that it could cost in excess of $100 million for each poorly controlled fossil-fuel-burning power plant. They are promoting instead "clean coal technologies"—still in the research and testing stages—that could control pollution in the combustion process at much lower costs. Ultimately, the burden of paying for

any such changes falls to utilities and their rate payers, carmakers and their buyers. Higher taxes on electricity rates and gasoline are most likely one result of any acid rain legislation.

Environmental groups in the United States and Canada pushed hard for the Bush-proposed amendments to the Clean Air Act, and were generally satisfied when they were announced. They were happier, however, with the proposed reductions in sulfur dioxide than with nitrogen oxide reductions. The proposal calls for a 50 percent reduction in sulfur dioxide than with nitrogen oxide reductions. utilities have until 1995 to choose between scrubbers or clean coal technologies. Conversely, the law calls for only a 10 percent reduction in nitrogen oxide emissions during the same period.

The proposal's most innovative approach to pollution control, though, is the so-called "trading" of pollution rights. As the Bush administration proposed the law, emission limits would be set and then utilities would be allowed to decide how to meet them. They could choose to invest in scrubbers, switch to low-sulfur coal, "clean" high sulfur coal, or use various market-driven incentives, including permits that would allow the "selling" or "trading" of pollution limits.

Here's how that "trading" would work: Utilities would be issued permits to pollute, with emission levels based on past rates of discharge. (Plant A, for example, would be allowed to spew 100 units of sulfur dioxide into the air each year.) They would be allowed to buy or sell those rights in order to bring plants in certain communities within mandated limits. (If Plant A only used 90 units, it could sell its remaining 10 units to Plant B, which polluted "over" its limit.) This is the kind of proposal that sounds good on paper, certainly innovative, but could result in more paperwork than pollution control. There is speculation that outsiders—even environmental groups—would buy those "rights," with a goal of retiring them and eliminating air pollution in that area altogether. That's fine. The biggest flaw in such a proposal, however, is that if plants concentrate on buying and selling rights, they are likely to spend less time and energy developing new technologies and conservation efforts. The plan also does not have provisions for cleanup of already dirty lakes, streams or forests.

The most obvious way to lessen the components of acid rain is conserving energy. Recycling helps by reducing electricity demands at the power plants. Wind, solar, and renewable power sources should continue to be explored as alternatives to sulfur-dioxide-producing coal burning. Efficiency standards for household appliances—adopted in the United States in 1988 for fluorescent lights and household appliances—should be mandated worldwide. (As should similar ratings for plumbing, showerheads and standard lighting. It's estimated that the energy produced by 40 to 100 large power plants can be saved simply by the strict efficiency standards now mandated of new water heaters, refrigerators, room and central air conditioners.)

In the United States, the Department of Commerce Bureau of Economic Analysis estimates the overall cost for air pollution control exceeds $32 billion a year. Cleanup efforts already proposed around the world would require an investment of billions of dollars more, and even then, emissions might be reduced by only a third. So the goal is to develop *economical* as well as efficient methods to reduce acid rain pollutants. While industry and science continue to fiddle with solutions to the big picture, a variety of stopgap measures are already helping.

In Sweden, the government spends more than $50 million a year trying to stabilize the effects of acid rain by adding prodigious amounts of acid-neutralizing lime to their lakes. "Liming," currently being tested in the United States in an estimated 100 projects from the Adirondacks to the Great Lakes, offers a way to stave off permanent harm until there is a solution. It can also restore the health of lakes and streams where life has already been destroyed by acidification, though it works best and is least costly in small water systems. In Sweden, about 500 lakes are limed each year, and the results have been dramatic. Waters are miraculously returned to near neutral state. Unfortunately, liming's success has been championed by some power-plant representatives, which can be read only as foot-dragging. While inexpensive—roughly $10 to $15 an acre-foot per year—liming remains a stopgap effort, not a solution.

The most promising technology, one which coal and utility industry representatives are watching anxiously, is the "washing" of sulfur from high-sulfur coal. If it works as well as experiments suggest, it could allow coal-burning electric utilities to cut air pollution linked to acid rain without installing costly scrubbers. Instead of filtering sulfur dioxide from smokestacks, the process removes the potential for pollution before the coal is burned. Tests, currently being conducted under a Department of Energy grant by TRW, Inc., in California, suggest that 90 percent or more of all sulfur could be removed by such washings. While hardly a new process—it has been done in limited form for more than 100 years—it is expected to be successful, especially for older, expensive-to-retrofit power plants.

(In a backwards approach to pollution control, scientists in several countries are experimenting with what they call "curative" approaches. They are breeding acid-tolerant fish and crops, and coating valuable structures and artwork against corrosion. This is hardly a solution, just a novel experiment.)

A handful of government initiatives around the globe are also pointing in new directions, especially important as U.S. lawmakers wrestle with new laws. For example, in 1968 the Japanese government issued stringent sulfur dioxide controls and mandated the use of low-sulfur fuels and desulfurization; by 1975, sulfur dioxide emissions had plunged by 50

Although excess acidity in a pond, lake, or stream can kill any fish (top), the acidity can be countered by spraying lime into the water (bottom), which neutralizes the acid gradually and eventually renders the water habitable again. However, liming acid lakes will not necessarily bring back the full complexity of their ecosystems.

percent even as energy consumption doubled. Since then, even stricter limits have been set, and nearly 1,200 scrubbers installed. While U.S. industries have complained that higher energy rates brought on by scrubbers and washing would diminish their competitive edge on the world market, similar restrictions in Japan haven't resulted in a competitive disadvantage. In West Germany and the Netherlands, new power plants are required to have scrubbers; in 1985, Canada passed legislation calling for a 50 percent reduction of sulfur dioxide emissions by 1994. In the United States several states, including Minnesota, Massachusetts, New Hampshire, New York, Vermont, and Wisconsin, have passed tough emission laws.

But the fact that acid rain recognizes no boundaries remains a stumbling block to solutions. For every acid raindrop saved in Japan through tough government laws, two more are created in China, where laws are lax. Solutions must be hammered out simultaneously in every nation if the problem is to be resolved. Another nagging world dilemma is that only Canada and the United States require catalytic converters on cars, which have demonstrated the ability to drastically reduce acid-rain-contributing nitrogen oxide emissions.

The larger lesson to be learned from acid rain

pollution is that energy efficiency can save more than merely fossil fuels. Irreplaceable natural resources such as forests and lakes can also be targets of conservation efforts. Worldwide, man-made emissions of sulfur dioxide have soared past the 100-million-ton mark per year. Cutting the United States' portion of that waste by 10 million over the next decade will help, but that will happen only if consumption also drops and new laws are enforced.

Unfortunately, international protocols like the one adopted to help slow ozone depletion will not work for the acid rain problem, since each nation produces, or receives, acid rain in varying levels. Several international agreements on sulfur dioxide emissions have been attempted between the United States and Canada, and the European countries, but they have proven more successful as research initiatives than laws. International guidelines for nitrogen oxide emissions—recommending they be kept at 1987 levels—exist, but have not been uniformly met. But even if a single global mandate is not the solution, nations must continue to exchange successful technologies and laws in an effort to control their emissions. Acid rain does not carry a passport—its ignorance of borderlines has made it our most international of pollutants.

ACID RAIN

The world's 400 million cars are the main culprits contributing to the growing problem of acid rain.

Each year, automobiles and the thousands of electricity-producing utilities around the globe pump over a hundred million tons of acidic particles into the atmosphere.

Nearly invisible, the dustlike particles of sulfur dioxide (SO_2) from power plants and nitrogen oxides (NO_x) from car exhaust combine with the water vapor in the sky to form acid-laden clouds.

These new compounds can travel hundreds of miles through the air—across national boundaries—before returning to Earth in the form of dangerously acidic fog, dew, snow, and rain.

While acid rain may look harmless, it is not. It can destroy lakes and forests, ruin buildings and affect man's health.

Absorbed by the soil, acid rain dissolves nutrients necessary for plants and trees to grow.

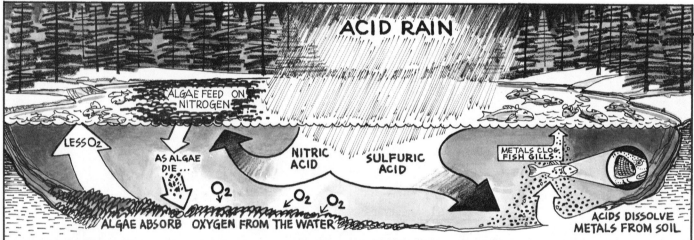

Acid rain will dissolve harmful metals from the soil at lake and river bottoms and excess acidity will encourage algae growth, both of which will harm aquatic life and their ecosystems.

Acid rain can also affect our drinking water. Falling into reservoirs or seeping into groundwater, it can eventually pollute the water that comes from your kitchen tap.

On its way to the kitchen the acid can also corrode plumbing. Toxic metals are then dissolved into the water we drink and bathe in.

Acid rain has already caused billions of dollars of damage by corroding buildings, highways, bridges, and priceless works of public art.

It can take a human toll, too. The pollutants in acid rain contribute to lung cancer and there is mounting evidence of links to respiratory illnesses such as asthma, especially in children.

So far, acid rain's toll on nature has been the worst. In Sweden a third of the lakes are acidic, and half of West Germany's forests have been damaged.

The only real solution is reducing our reliance on the sources of acid rain. Non-polluting, alternative forms of energy may be the best hope.

Individual Action

Many of the remedies for reducing acid rain emissions are similar to those of other atmospheric pollutions. We can all help by using fossil fuels more wisely. Car pools and mass transit help; so do fuel-efficient cars and trucks. Using smart, efficient appliances at home and work helps, as well as turning off lights and appliances when not in use.

Acid rain is a pollution that *industry* needs to address, but that *individuals* need to help keep in the public eye. One simple way to draw attention to the problem is by monitoring the acid levels in the rainfall (or snowfall) in your own backyard. The tools required for at-home testing are simple, and though the results may not stand up in a scientific lab they should give an indication of whether or not there are high levels of acid in your community's rainfall.

A simple pH test on pond or stream water can be conducted by using pH (litmus) paper, which is available at most drugstores. Use a clean glass jar or container to collect the water sample; collect the water from the middle of the pond or mid-depth in a stream to get a representative sample; dip a piece of pH paper into the sample; immediately compare the color of the wet pH paper to the color chart that is provided with the pH paper to determine the approximate pH value.

For a more accurate test, here's a step-by-step guide similar to that used by the National Audubon Society's Citizens' Acid Rain Monitoring Network. (The key to the accuracy of this test is to avoid contaminating the sample, so approach any effort cautiously.)

1. When selecting a site, it is extremely important that there be no obstructions directly above the mouth of the collection pail, such as tree branches, powerlines, building walls, or eaves. Clean off and place a roughly *four-foot-by-four-foot plastic sheet* on the ground. Weight the corners with bricks or stones, in case of high winds.

2. Put a collection pail in the center of the plastic sheet and put a tightly sealed plastic sandwich bag filled with rocks, gravel, sand, or dirt in the pail to keep it from tipping over.

3. In order to insert a collection bag inside the pail without contaminating the inner surface, wear a new *sandwich bag* inside out, as a glove.

To avoid contaminating the inner surface of the sandwich bag "glove" as you put it on, grab it on the bottom with the hand that will wear it, and begin pushing the bottom through the mouth of the bag. You may use your other hand to help pull the bag over as long as it doesn't touch the newly exposed surface.

Using the gloved hand, insert and spread open the collection bag inside the pail. Your other hand may be used to steady the pail as long as it does not touch the inner surface of the bag.

Secure the bag over the mouth of the pail using a *rubber band*.

4. Record the date and time of day when you put out the rain collector. If possible, the collection pail should be set out just as the storm is beginning. If it is set out too long before the rain begins, it may increase the potential for contamination of the rain sample. You may begin testing the rainwater as soon as the rain stops, but no longer than 24 hours from the time the bucket was placed outdoors.

5. Bring the collector indoors.

6. Remove the rubber band and use a twist tie to close the bag. In doing so, do not touch the rainwater or the inner surface of the bag (any such contamination will ruin the test). Allow the sample to come to room temperature. Leave the bag in the collector during this step.

7. "Re-baggie" your hand, and lift the rain sample out of the collection pail. Remove the twist tie and place the bag on the table, and carefully roll down the sides of the bag, folding them under. Continue to roll the sides down until the bag is as flat as it can be without allowing the rainwater to spill out.

8. Using your gloved hand, place a strip of *pH paper* in the rainwater in the plastic bag, being careful not to touch the color patches. Lean the strip against the edge of the bag, and leave it there for 15 minutes.

The three colored paper patches should be completely immersed in the water during this time. If the entire strip submerges, you can either "glove" your hand to remove it or leave the strip there and use a new one for the test.

Do not wait any longer than 15 minutes to take your reading, or you may get a false, low reading. If the strip has been immersed longer than 15 minutes, simply discard it and try another strip.

9. After 15 minutes, carefully remove the strip of pH paper and compare it with the color chart on the pH strip container. Be careful not to touch the colored patches on the pH paper. If the color patches seem to be between the divisions on the color chart (for example, between 5.0 and 5.5) use your best estimate.

(A similar test can be done with carefully collected snow.)

If you are interested in more complete monitoring of acidity levels in lakes or rain in your area, you can join the Citizens' Acid Rain Monitoring Network mailing list and receive monthly data to compare to your own. (Write: CARMN, c/o National Audubon Society, 950 Third Ave., New York, NY 10022)

Government Actions

1. Companies that reduce the amount of emissions contributing to acid rain should be given credits, which can then be bought and sold.

2. The costs of any reduction in sulfur diox-ide emissions—current efforts are attempting to cut them in half—should be apportioned fairly among the worst polluters, not paid for in across-the-board assessments.

3. Laws to reduce nitrogen oxide emissions from car tailpipes should be toughened.

4. Sulfur dioxide emissions in the U.S. should be maintained at a level 12 million tons per year less than 1980s standards.

5. The EPA should adopt a National Ambient Air Quality Standard for acid rain to fairly assess acid deposition and try and trace its source.

6. Scrubbers should be mandatory on all coal- and oil-burning power plants and ore smelters.

☼

Reading

Worldwatch Paper 58: "Air Pollution, Acid Rain, and the Future of Forests," by Sandra Postel. Worldwatch Institute, 1776 Massachusetts Avenue NW, Washington, DC 20036.

"Air: An Atmosphere of Uncertainty," by Noel Grove. *National Geographic,* April 1987.

"Forests Are Dying, But Is Acid Rain Really to Blame?" by Jon R. Luoma. *Audubon,* March 1987.

"Acid Murder No Longer a Mystery," by Jon R. Luoma. *Audubon,* November 1988.

Fact Sheet on Acid Rain. Canadian Embassy Public Affairs Division, 1771 N Street NW, Washington, DC 20036-2879.

Environmental Education Report and Newsletter, April 1987, Volume 15, Number 4. American Society for Environmental Education, PO Box 800, Hanover, NH 03755-0800. (Detailed reading list of more than 80 books and pamphlets, valuable for teachers, students, or the curious.)

"Effects of Acid Rain on Freshwater Ecosystems," by D. W. Schindler. *Science,* Vol. 239, January 8, 1988.

Acid Precipitation Digest (newsletter), Elsevier Science Publishing, 655 Avenue of the Americas, New York, NY 10010.

Organizations to Contact

The Acid Rain Foundation, 1630 Blackhawk Hills, St. Paul, MN 55122.

Acid Rain Information Clearinghouse Library, Center for Environmental Information, Inc., 33 S. Washington St., Rochester NY 14608.

American Bass Association, Inc., 886 Trotters Trail, Wetumpka, AL 36092, 205-567-6035.

Department of the Interior, U.S. Fish and Wildlife Service, National Ecology Center, Leetown, Box 705, Kearneysville, WV 25430.

Edison Electric Institute, 1111 19th St. NW, Washington, DC 20036.

Electric Power Research Institute, 3412 Hillview Ave., Box 10412, Palo Alto, CA 94303.

Izaak Walton League of America, Level B, 1401 Wilson Blvd., Arlington, VA 22209, 703-528-1818.

National Academy of Sciences/National Research Council, Attn: Environmental Studies Board, 2010 Constitution Ave. NW, Washington, DC 20418.

National Acid Precipitation Assessment Program, Program Coordination Office, 722 Jackson Place NW, Washington, DC 20506.

National Clean Air Coalition, 530 7th St. SE, Washington, DC 20003.

National Coal Association, 1130 17th St. NW, Washington, DC 20036.

National Wildlife Federation, 1412 16th St. NW, Washington, DC 20036.

US Environmental Protection Agency, 401 M St. SW, Washington, DC 20460.

U.S. Geological Survey, 419 National Center, Reston, VA 22092.

THE LAND

5

Rain Forests

Just as we are wantonly destroying the Earth's atmosphere, people are wreaking similar havoc on the land. The best example of this may be the destruction of the world's rain forests. In just the last 30 years, more than 40 percent of the tropical forests that belt the equator have been felled or burned. Dubbed the "Earth's deposit box" for the millions of plants and animals they spawn and protect, rain forests are disappearing at such a rapid rate that scientists predict all may be razed by the end of the twenty-first century. Harvard biologist E. O. Wilson calls this "the greatest extinction since the end of the age of dinosaurs."

If acid rain is the most clandestine of pollutants, the destruction of rain forests may be the most public of environmental debacles. Their preservation has become the *cause célèbre* of the hip and famous the world around. Celebrities by the dozens have lent their names and images to the cause. Sting showed up in face paint and posed with South American natives deep in the forest. Pop artist Keith Haring bought land in Brazil to help preserve a piece of the forest and encouraged others to do the same. Virgin Records released an album called "Spirit of the Forest," featuring a battery of international pop stars. Several of the songs were actually recorded in a Brazilian jungle. Ben and Jerry's introduced "Rain Forest Crunch" ice cream. American composer Philip Glass teamed up with avant-garde theater director Gerald Thomas to create a rain forest–inspired opera, which premiered in Rio de Janeiro. Polish-born sculptor Frans Krajcberg devoted an entire exhibition to 24 burned and broken

wood sculptures and panels inspired by the destruction. A gaggle of celebs, led by Madonna and members of the Grateful Dead, hosted a fund-raising evening of song and dance at the Brooklyn Academy of Music, dubbed "Don't Bungle the Jungle." Even Kermit the Frog got in on the action, starring in a film called "Save the Rain Forests." The list of similar celebrity-for-the-rain-forest actions goes on and on.

Yet, despite all the glamorous publicity, the rain forests continue to burn. In Brazil alone, an area the size of Nebraska—76,000 square miles—is decimated each year. Whether the attention excited by $500-per-head benefits or well-intended testimonials makes a difference is hard to assess. But while the rain forests continue to be destroyed by a combination of misdirected government policy, greed, heart-rending poverty, and ignorance of the most basic environmental concerns, any hint of public awareness should be welcomed.

At first glance, rain forests can be off-putting. The jungles are soggy, humid places crawling with bugs and reptiles. A dense canopy 200 feet overhead screens out most sunlight, and is so thick a heavy rain takes 10 minutes to trickle down to the ground. The "rain" in the forest's name is well-deserved. The green band of tropical woodlands that encircles the earth 10 degrees north and south of the equator receives more than 80 inches of precipitation each year. If the appeal of the rain forests to the celebrity set remains something of a mystery, their necessity is not; though they account for just seven percent of the Earth's land surface, they contain almost half of all its trees and more than 10 million species of plants and animals.

The forests' role on the planet is simple: for hundreds of millions of years they have nurtured and protected a multitude of life forms. Because green plants convert carbon dioxide to oxygen, they serve as a kind of sponge, helping to soak up the excess man is pumping into the atmosphere. But today, thanks to humankind's insatiable greed for land and profit, and the planet's rapidly proliferating population, the rain forests' days are numbered.

Rain forests once dominated Indonesia, Zaire, Papua–New Guinea, Burma, Malaysia, the Philippines, Peru, Colombia, Bolivia, and Venezuela. These nations share not just tropical forests, but overwhelming national debt, high unemployment, and a large percentage of foreign investment in their arable lands.

But it is the forests through which the Amazon River flows in Brazil that have captured so much of the public's attention, in part because the region (two thirds the size of the continental U.S.) is the most biologically diverse wilderness on the globe—and because its management has proven to be an ecological nightmare.

A tenth of the world's species, most of them still unidentified, live in the jungles of Brazil. An Amazon pond the size of a tennis court may contain more species of fish than all the rivers in Europe combined. New trees and insects are discovered there daily. More than 50,000 plant species and 3,000 types of fish are part of the Amazon ecosystem. (By comparison, North America has about 17,000 plants, and Europe only 150 types of freshwater fish.) During burn season, August through October, more than 5,000 fires rage across the region each day, reducing once-lush forests to little more than charred deserts. Farming, ranching, logging, mining, and road-building are rapidly taking their toll. In 1975, just 0.6 percent of the Amazon was deforested. Today more than 12 percent has been cut. Since every acre is different, the destruction of even a small area can result in the extinction of uncounted, and some as yet unnamed species.

Estimates of worldwide losses vary widely. Some say 50 million acres are lost each year, the United Nations says *only* 17 million. The World Wildlife Fund says 25 to 50 acres a minute are cut or burned. But concrete numbers are not necessary to affirm the destruction of the rain forests—or to predict a future without them.

The decimation of forests is hardly new. Before people learned to grow their own food roughly 10,000 years ago, the Earth boasted 15.5 billion acres of forest and woodland. As civilization expanded, that acreage has shrunk by a third. When newly shorn lands are mismanaged, the result has inevitably been the same worldwide, whether in the tropics or on snow-covered mountains: soil loss, droughts, floods, disrupted water supplies, and a legacy of unproductive land.

Because of the wildlife they nurture and the carbon dioxide they absorb, the destruction of the tropical woodlands may be the most dangerous deforestation we have yet witnessed. British environmentalist Norman Myers insists, "If patterns persist, it may be the worst biological debacle since life's first emergence on the planet 3.6 billion years ago."

The contemporary plunderers of the Amazon jungle are following a tradition that began when rubber was discovered in the river basin in the early part of this century. The potential for profit attracted thousands of "investors," including Henry Ford, who bought up millions of acres of rain forest and named it Fordlandia. But the spread of disease among the Indian workers and abuse of the forests quickly killed off the rubber business in South America. Malaysia then became the primary source, and 90 percent of the rain forests there have since been cut.

The effect of rain forest loss is simple yet wide-ranging. When the trees are cut down, sunlight and dry, hot winds pour in. Tropical soil is poor—most

The Costa Rican rain forests (above), home to vast numbers of wildlife including 103 species of bats, are being destroyed at rates up to 175,000 acres per year (below) mostly to provide grazing pasture for cattle, some of which are used for fast-food hamburgers. Although inexpensive, the land is unsuitable for long-term grazing, and much of the cleared land turns to scrub after just a few years.

of the nutrients in the rain forest are stored not in soil, as happens in temperate forests, but in the trees themselves. So a slight change in moisture or temperature can hold drastic results for the shallow-rooted trees. Once the trees are gone, so is shelter for plants and animals. Since few saplings are re-planted, devastated rain forests resemble deserts, littered with the charred debris of burned and rotting timber.

Next to birth control, few biological activities are as important to the future of the planet's environment as thriving rain forests. Each year the Earth's population—all users of wood products in one form or another—grows by 85 million people. Every year, 5 million acres of tropical woodland are cut for firewood. Ninety-five percent of the next 5 billion people will be born in developing countries, population watchers estimate. That growth implies continued devastation of the rain forests, as 40 percent of the world still uses wood as a primary source of heat.

Preservation of the planet's fragile ecosystems depends on long-term sustainable development. But "sustainable development" and "ecosystems" mean little to governments of poverty-riddled countries, desperate for cash to pay huge foreign debts. Developing nations have accumulated debts totaling $1.3 trillion; Brazil's is the largest at more than $124 billion. In countries where forests are ravaged by peasants seeking food, preserving ecosystems has not been a priority.

Overpopulation is a big problem—and an environmental problem—in most developing nations, and contributes to their perilous economic situations. More than half of the globe's population now lives in countries that are in part tropical, and where the standard of living is declining. According to UNICEF estimates, more than 14 million children under the age of four starve to death each year in tropical and subtropical countries. Every day more than 40,000 young children die from starvation and associated diseases—and very few of them or their family members understand the concept of sustainable development.

Protecting rain forests—like many conservation efforts—is a monumentally complex task. It is important for celebrities to rally around tropical forests, and may be essential to sensitize others to their destruction. But it is equally important to understand the squalor that encourages debt-ridden governments to condone the destruction and allow it to continue. Sustainable *economic* growth must become the priority in these tropical regions—but at the same time, we must all help lay the groundwork for their protection.

CAUSES

The cycle of rain forest destruction is driven by myriad pistons: bad governmental policies, poverty, growing worldwide demand for timber, and greed. Many leaders of developing nations view their woodlands as a kind of "instant cash" machine. Far too often, environmental issues enter into their policy-making as an afterthought.

The push to settle and industrialize rain forests around the world, and to reap the benefits of their abundant gold and minerals, oil and gas, hardwoods, and products from nuts to oils, began in earnest in the mid-1960s. Slash-and-burn agriculture, logging, mining, hydroelectric projects, clearing for plantations, and cattle ranching have decimated the perimeters and eaten ever deeper into the woods since. An explosive wave of people has marched in and pillaged the rain forests, usually with government encouragement. (In Brazil it is joked that anybody with a chain saw and a match can become a farmer.) An underlying goal of the local governments in the forested regions is to sweep the jungles of their riches before other nations or multinational companies can beat them to it.

For all their diversity, rain forests are incredibly fragile. Farmers who move in and chop them down typically clear-cut the jungle, harvest a few seasons' crops, and turn the fields over to cattle ranchers. Herds graze for just a few more years, and when the land is exhausted and barren it is abandoned. The once-lush forests rarely grow back, and when they do, it's with only a percentage of their original diversity.

For regions beyond the tropics, woodland destruction also poses a loss. Rain forests function like giant utilities. They serve as both filter and cleanser by extracting carbon dioxide from the atmosphere, separating and recycling oxygen, and storing the excess carbon in their wood, leaves, roots, and surrounding soil. The decline of these "utilities," plus the billions of tons more carbon dioxide pumped into the atmosphere as the forests are burned, is credited with hastening the warming of the Earth's atmosphere. Fires in the Amazon contribute approximately 10 percent of all global carbon dioxide emissions.

Poverty, which drives people into the woods for fuel, food, and work, and the world's growing demand for wood and wood products, encourage the continued rape of the rain forests. Consumption of tropical hardwoods is 15 times greater than in 1950, and Japan accounts for about 60 percent of the new demand. (Japan imports more wood—especially wood chips used in making boxes for stereos, televisions, and VCRs—than any other commodity but oil.) Logging accounts for almost a quarter of the destruction in Brazil's rain forests, and as supplies of wood dwindle in Southeast Asia, Japan is looking closely at Brazil's remaining acres. (The Far East is far from alone in its appetite for foreign hardwood. The United States imports $2.2 billion worth every year.)

Global demand for other forest products is also growing. Much of the wood used in building construction, furniture manufacturing, the making of plywood and fiberboard, weaving materials, gums, resins, oils, charcoal, even chop sticks—45 million a month are shipped to fast-food restaurants in Japan—originates in the rain forests. The raw materials for latex, Brazil nuts (the United States buys $16 million worth of them a year), oils, spices, houseplants, edibles from avocados to vanilla, 25 percent of prescription pharmaceuticals, and 70 percent of anti-cancer drugs also come from tropical woodlands. Much of what Americans eat, including corn, wheat, rice, sugar, coffee, and tea, originates in tropical regions. The rain forest's most abundant product though, is tin.

The insatiable demand for timber can be explained in part by the almost half of the world that still depends on wood as a source of energy. More than two thirds of Third World countries use wood for cooking and heating, and in Nigeria and many African nations it's used almost exclusively. According to the Worldwatch Institute, in rural parts of the Himalayas and Africa, women and children spend between 100 and 300 days a year gathering firewood. In Tanzania and Thailand people burn between one and two tons of firewood a year. The growing popularity of wood stoves in industrialized countries has only increased the demand.

Recognition that this demand is costing the loss of a valuable natural resource has yet to stop the uncontrolled harvesting. Japan continues to support plans to build more roads across western Brazil, largely to obtain logs quicker and cheaper. Environmentalists warn that new roads will open up the western Amazon to the same kind of commercial exploitation that has already destroyed regions to the east. The International Tropical Timber Association, headquartered in Japan, insists that greater demand for Amazon's timber is unstoppable. "Even if world consumption remains stable, Indonesia and Malaysia should run out of commercial species in the next 20 years," the association claims. Japan's unabashed push into the Amazon—smoothed by loans of "undesignated" money to Brazil to be used "however the country sees fit"—has prompted the U.S. State Department and international environmental groups to appeal to the government in Tokyo to slow its demand for trees.

In its role as rain forest protector, the United States faces a charge of hypocrisy, though. The only American tropical rain forest still standing is facing extinction also. The jungle covering the mountainside of Mauna Loa on the island of Hawaii is being cut down to make room for a geothermal power plant. Its destruction has allowed developing nations to question how the United States can preach the importance of protecting tropical rain forests if it can't even save its very last.

The best-publicized example of rain forest destruction remains the Amazon of Brazil. As big as five Texases, Brazil's Amazon River valley encompasses half of all the world's tropical forest. Since 1964, when the military government first commanded 15,000 miles of highway be cut through the forests for the sake of "national integration," the jungle's management has been controversial. The government's goal was to prod some of the country's 30 million dirt-poor natives away from the coastline, and to persuade large investors to clear the forest and produce beef. According to Alex Shoumatoff, author of many books and articles about the Amazon, some Brazilian leaders suggested at the time that *all* forests be cut down, because they stood in the way of development.

The government saw the opening of the forest frontier as a way to bolster the economy through agriculture—with a heavy emphasis on cash crops. The nation's "bravest, brightest and best" were encouraged to relocate in the western half of the country in the mid-1970s. "Colonization" moved slowly until the World Bank paid for the paving of a massive highway through the state of Rondonia to its capital, Porta Velho. Tin miners, speculators, and prospectors looking for gold quickly headed into the malaria-ridden river valley. So did homesteaders given 250-acre parcels each to clear and farm. Cattle ranchers were lured to the region by a variety of incentives: interest rates below inflation, tax bene-

fits, and other concessions. Ranchers from the south and multinational companies were enticed by promises of big, cheap profits.

From the beginning of the settlement programs, neither the government nor the new farmers and ranchers gave much thought to the destruction of the environment. Gangs armed with chain saws and bulldozers leveled forests, carving roads and clearing land, and started the biggest fires in history. Environmental problems surfaced quickly. As early as 1972, at a United Nations conference on the environment in Stockholm, Brazil was cautioned about its environmental profligacy. Representatives from Brasília stood firm, informing the gathering that if Brazil wished to abuse its land and pollute its waters, the nation had every right to do so.

While some loggers, miners, and cattle ranchers have prospered, the march into the jungles has been disastrous for the environment. When forests are clear-cut for farming, only a few years of successful rice or corn crops can be cultivated. Once the trees are felled, the surrounding ecosystem collapses. Because of the low quality of the soil, there can be no such thing as "permanent" farming in the rain forests. Soil shrivels under the sun and is blown or washed away by the pounding rains. Most of the farmers who took advantage of the resettlement found that after one good year, crops failed, and they abandoned the land and moved back east, or plunged deeper into the forest, repeating their disastrous mistakes.

Once the peasants moved off the land, much of it was turned over to big cattle operations, which profited more from tax breaks and land speculation than from selling beef. (In fact Brazil imports more beef than it exports.) About five years later, after the tax incentives are depleted, the ranchers also abandon the land, leaving it a wasteland.

A variety of other ills simultaneously tax the beleaguered rain forests. When the government showed there was an abundance of mineral wealth

The carbon and ash resulting from the slash-and-burning of rain forest land gives the soil a temporary boost in nutrients. After a few years of farming, however, the nutrients in rain forest soil are used up and the land is usually abandoned.

under the topsoil, the land boom cranked up another notch. Hopeful prospectors bulldozed their way to the sites. Gold, tin, and oil prospecting proliferated, triggering both environmental destruction and violence between rival miners and natives. Rain forests continue to be flooded for hydroelectric-dam reservoirs, providing inexpensive power but threatening hundreds of thousands of acres of woodland across South America. More construction, new industry, and people attracted by cheap power only promise more damage for the fragile forests.

Most of the people who live in and continue to migrate to the rain forests are desperately poor, and their numbers are growing. (Political refugees from neighboring Central American countries have fled to Costa Rica, for example, exacerbating the problems in its already crowded jungles.) By clearing the land, the settlers can grow food crops, if only for a couple of years, and selling hardwood provides another source of income for the poor. When the world's policymakers and environmental leaders sit down to plot the rain forests' future, they must keep in mind that many of the people destroying the forests have a simple goal: survival.

EFFECTS

The forests' future does not look bright. Those that are still standing in 2001, except for some expanses in Brazil and Africa, are likely to disappear or be severely damaged within the following 25 years. If nothing is done to check world population growth and control tropical deforestation, there may be only 20,000 square miles of rain forest left on the globe by 2050, nothing by 2100.

The destruction of forests in the Amazon basin has been replicated around the world. Land is cleared, farmed, and then abandoned. What's left is now blanketed by clay and covered with a scrubby layer of vines, weeds, and stumps. Wildlife is gone; the

very conditions that nurtured life in the first place have vanished.

In their natural state, rain forests are an infinitely renewable resource. High, consistent levels of heat and moisture foster the enormous variety of organisms that prosper in them. But slash-and-burn agriculture makes renewal nearly impossible. After fires torch the trees, only a very thin layer of ash is left for crops to grow in. The sparse nutrients in the ash and topsoil are soon taken up by the crops, or washed away by the warm rains, and the land becomes virtually worthless. Rain forests can regenerate after 50 to 120 years, but most of the obliterated species will never come back.

Slash-and-burning affects the uncut areas, too. Typically, forests hold rainwater, and allow it to soak in and recharge underground aquifers. But when forests are leveled, rains run off too quickly and water is unavailable to the thirsty trees that remain. Water tables fall, streams flow unpredictably, erosion and sedimentation fill reservoirs with silt, and the remaining trees suffer.

Technological advances and encroachments other than slash-and-burning are also hurting the forests and their inhabitants.

• In Brazil half a million prospectors have joined the gold rush into the jungles, and are exhuming more than 70 tons of the metal each year. Their machinery spews filthy exhaust into the air; mercury used to extract gold from the sand poisons rivers and fish.

• In steep areas, logging not only destroys the forests, but rapidly erodes bare ground. During rainfall, soil is washed into the sea, leaving forest inhabitants with no trees to sell, no soil to till, and life on the river inexorably changed. Heavy siltation has clogged hydroelectric reservoirs, irrigation canals, and coastal harbors. (The reservoir that provides water to fill the Panama Canal's 50-mile

After forests are razed, much of the rain in tropical areas that was once absorbed and recycled by rain forest trees instead runs off the land, carrying soil and nutrients with it into nearby waterways. Madagascar's Central Plateau suffers massive erosion of topsoil due to deforestation.

waterway, for example, is slowly filling with topsoil. There is concern that someday there may not be enough water to float tankers through the locks.)

• Many valuable chemical compounds are created in the jungles. Alkaloids from the rosy periwinkle, a small plant that originated in Madagascar, have proven very effective in treating Hodgkin's disease and childhood leukemia. Curare, made from a plant that grows only in the Amazon, is used in heart operations as a muscle relaxant. More than 225 rain forest plants from Costa Rica alone are thought to be potential anti-cancer agents. Many scientists believe that solutions to AIDS may very well lie somewhere in the rain forests. Unfortunately, as the forests are cut, many of these potentially life-saving tropical plants disappear forever.

• Hardly the least of concerns is that these intrusions deep into the rain forests have scattered or decimated the native Indians. More than 1,000 tribes of indigenous peoples are thought to be close to extinction. Colonists have brought in alien diseases including malaria, and homelands are being destroyed. The encroachment has led to repeated violence and lives lost, most notably among the native rubber tappers who have fought the roads and settlers since they first appeared, and who have been driven deeper into the jungle. Leaders of the tappers and workers alike have been threatened—and some murdered— by landowners, cattlemen, and hired guns.

• Perhaps the most destructive legacy of the burning forests is their contribution to the greenhouse effect. Deforestation releases more than a billion tons of carbon into the air annually. When trees are cleared, the carbon they contain, as well as some of the carbon in the underlying soil, is oxidized and released into the air. This release occurs rapidly if the trees are burned, but slowly if they decay naturally.

• Not surprisingly, given what we know about the magnitude of illegal drugs emanating from South America, coca-growing also contributes to the devastation of many forested acres. In Peru, coca growers are credited with destroying more than half a million acres of tropical forests, much of this publicly owned. Unfortunately, few details about such destruction exist because organized gangs and native rebels guard the coca-growing regions.

The importance of rain forests to the global environment is immeasurable. They are linked to weather and climate patterns we still don't fully understand. Yet, nearly every second another acre is lost to logging or farming. Perhaps the greatest irony in their destruction is that since 1900, the average rainfall in the forests has decreased by as much as 10 percent. Deforestation is the cause; fewer trees mean less water rising into the air in vapor form, and so less returns to the trees as rain. Someday soon, like the buffalo of the American West, rain forests may live only in legends and Tarzan movies.

SOLUTIONS

So much of the global rain forest has already been destroyed that some ecologists believe no amount of conservation can impede disaster—that by the middle of next century, small parks and preserves may be all that is left of the forests. Restoration projects are underway in Costa Rica and elsewhere, but restoring entire ecosystems is impossible. Many species are gone forever. Fortunately—in part because of the high level of publicity their plight has received—a variety of people and groups are working successfully to save patches of rain forests.

• Dozens of scientists and ecologists have made the rain forests their homes in recent years, studying the tops of the canopies and the soil of the Earth for clues as to how to save them. Amos Bien is an American ecologist who moved to Costa Rica in 1979, to gather data for his master's thesis. Six years later he bought 1,500 acres of forest land, intent on creating the first "economic model of rain forest conservation for profit." At the site, Rara Avis, he has built a tramway along the top of the foliage, and attracts "ecotourists" who are coming more frequently to see the rain forests for themselves, in case they disappear for good. Bien's goal is to turn his acreage into a hot spot for the harvesting of wicker, tree ferns, flowers, and even pacas, large rodents that make for delicious soup.

• A variety of government efforts are helping to slow destruction in some tropical countries. In Indonesia, fines have been imposed and forestry concessions revoked if companies are found cutting trees smaller than law dictates, or taking more than they are licensed to. So far, the country's minister of population and the environment says that 121 million acres have been protected as primary forest and national park land, and another 158 million set aside for regulated use by the timber industry. Indonesia has also set out on a 50-million-acre reforestation project.

Over the past 15 years, similarly "protected" rain forest acres have more than tripled. Today, Brazil and Indonesia actually protect as much as countries all over the globe did collectively in 1972.

• In Korea, a government-enforced fuelwood ban has reduced consumption of wood for energy from 55 percent of the nation's total energy demand in 1966 to 19 percent in 1979, primarily through introducing more efficient heating techniques.

• In the past two decades in Zambia, almost 100,000 acres of tree plantations have been planted, equal to the country's industrial timber needs until the end of the century.

• In Australia, where rain forests have been felled by extensive logging and land clearing for over a century, novel appeals are being made to UNESCO's World Heritage Convention for help. Claiming its rain forests are of "outstanding ecological value," Australia wants to gain inclusion on the World Heritage List, which would obligate the country to "protect, conserve, and rehabilitate" forests and make them off-limits to development. The list already includes 288 natural treasures, including Mt. Everest and the Great Barrier Reef. If Australia is successful in winning this "protection," it may set a precedent for other nations.

• In San Francisco, the plight of the rain forests has led public officials into direct, if distant, action. The Department of Public Works there is donating parking meters to all Bay Area zoos. Refitted with pictures of anteaters or jaguars, the meters are used in the zoo parking lots. Meter returns go to a save–the–rain forest fund. The zoos' goal is to buy land in Costa Rican national parks to help preserve it from devastation. They calculate that $300 will buy 2.5 acres—and the 200 orchids, 10,000 mushrooms, 200 frogs, 1 million ants, and 4.7 billion raindrops that come with the land, as well as assorted anteaters, tapirs, and jaguars. Given the 114 million zoo visitors in the United States each year, "If every visitor put 50 cents in the meter instead of buying a bag of peanuts," says San Francisco zookeeper Norm Gershens, "we could purchase and protect 4.8 million acres each year."

• Tourism—"ecotourism" to be exact—is credited with helping some nations save their rain forests. Costa Rica, under the banner of "Costa Rica, It's Only Natural," claims tourism as their number three source of income, and government and private industry are taking steps to maintain what's left of its pristine jungle to keep those tourist dollars coming. In Belize, aquatic and forest parks and new hotels are luring tourists. In Manaus, Brazil, the president of the state tourism agency predicts that visitors will be the largest single source of income in the Amazons in the 1990s. They come to the forests to birdwatch, hike, sightsee, and visit cultural sights, and give conservationists a growing army to protest continued devastation.

Tropical nations contend that the industrialized countries developed by exploiting Third World minerals and forests, and blame many of the planet's environmental problems on the First World. If the forests are to be saved, those same developed nations must provide massive support and research.

Our primary goal must be to reduce the use of fossil fuels, including firewood. Slowing population growth is almost a must. But those efforts won't be enough. A global effort must be made to reforest *and* to raise the quality of life in countries which are rapidly destroying their forests.

Most equatorial nations argue that they face more immediate demands than environmental problems, like getting a handle on massive debts. Ultimately, no amount of external coercion will relieve the poverty that is the major cause of tropical rain forest loss. Among the pressing needs many of these countries face is satisfying increasing fuelwood demands and stabilizing soil and water resources. Planting trees for these purposes would meet the combined need of reforestation and help to extract more carbon from the atmosphere. Such tree-planting programs are most effective, though, when local people are involved in the planning and implementation and perceive their own interest in doing so. Rain forests must be saved or replanted with *local* commitments, even if they are *internationally* encouraged. As Brazil's leaders have said so succinctly in the past, "You can *recommend*, but you cannot *tell* us what to do."

Environmentally conscious government rule and increased public awareness are a big part of the solution. (This is where Sting and Madonna play an important role.) We must greatly increase the interest in tropical forests and make their preservation the global issue it deserves to be.

As is typical when it comes to global environ-mental issues, however, it isn't easy to gain consensus on how best to provide for the future of the rain forests. At a recent meeting convened by the United Nations Environmental Programme to discuss "the conservation and wise utilization of tropical forests," international opinion was divided. African governments, backed by France and Japan, encouraged continued exploitation, in order to get the most production out of the forests and promote foreign exchange and jobs. Norway, Sweden, and the Netherlands deplored the continuing destruction. The United States urged definitive (if broad) goals: By 1992, a significant reduction of forest loss, accompanied by strong laws for sound management; for 2000 and beyond, a stable situation with select forests providing all wood products, and others left completely untouched.

Several specific mandates have been launched since then in the United States. Secretary of State James Baker's first public statement called for international efforts to promote reforestation as a way of combating the global warming trend. The United States Congress has passed legislation requiring federal agencies to protect tropical forest and species diversity by regulating financial dealings with other countries. Colorado senator Tim Wirth is exploring ways to create a 25-million-acre forest preserve—the size of Ohio—under Brazilian sponsorship.

That much of the rain forest destruction was funded and encouraged by industrial nations cannot be ignored simply because new "policy" statements are being distributed. Much of the money to finance dams, roads, logging, and mass resettlement projects has come from temperate-zone countries in the form of loans from the World Bank and others. In the past, banks made such loans with little or no consideration for environmental consequences, and without regard for the displacement of thousands of native people. Despite criticism from governments and environmental groups alike, the Inter-American Development Bank (IDB) recently funded the paving of a road as far as Rio Branca, deep into the Amazon, while its position papers claim the bank was "looking at ways to promote more reserves and form cooperatives to commercialize forest products." The international banking community must be persuaded not to invest in projects in the tropics without strict conservation guarantees attached.

But the worst enemy of nature is not banks, it's poverty. In order to restructure the management of rain forests, there must first be a shift in the kind of aid given to tropical nations. The focus must be on how to improve the income and quality of life of the 200 million small farmers living in the forests. Setting up preserves and parks may be a start, but hardly the end. Economic growth must go hand in hand with environmental protection.

Forgiveness of much of the Third World's $1.3 trillion hard-currency debt through officially sponsored settlements is viewed as inevitable. The Bush Administration forged a path by forgiving over $4 billion owed by African nations in mid-1989. The international banking community followed suit by writing off several billion owed by Mexico. If such settlements are linked to enforceable preservation commitments, the forests may yet be granted a reprieve.

One of the more experimental approaches to preserving rain forests is debt-for-nature proposals in which debts are written off in return for specific promises to spare rain forests. The first such deal was struck by Conservation International, a Washington-based environmental organization. Its terms were simple: they bought $650,000 of Bolivia's $4 billion debt at a discounted price of $100,000 from banks anxious to be rid of loans they never expected to collect. In exchange, Bolivia set aside 3.7 million acres of river country, home to a variety of endangered species.

In Costa Rica the American Express Bank sold $5.6 million in Costa Rican IOUs to the Nature Conservancy for $784,000. The Washington-based environmental group then traded the paper back to the Costa Rican Central Bank for $1.7 million in local currency bonds. A similar deal was struck to help finance Costa Rica's Guanacaste National Park. Because of those successes, Ecuador announced it was seeking foreign benefactors. The success of these swaps is still uncertain; no one knows for sure whether they can effectively halt, or even slow, development.

In Brazil, which holds world records for both debt and deforestation, the country's leaders stubbornly continue to plan new highways, farms, and mines in hopes that someday profits will overtake its foreign debt. President José Sarney adamantly maintains that the destruction of his country's rain forests is not so extensive as environmentalists claim. He places the blame for most pollution—industrial waste, acid rain, carbon dioxide—on developed nations and has rejected any debt-for-nature swaps to buy down the country's $124 billion foreign debt. To combat international opinion running against his government, in 1989 Sarney proposed 35 laws and decrees aimed at protecting the forests, including set-aside programs, temporary suspension of raw-timber exports, regulation of toxic chemicals used in mining and agriculture, and the creation of seven million acres of park land. He estimated the cost of his program at $350 million in the first two years. While the program was greeted skeptically by environmentalists, Sarney bought time for public opinion to change the minds of either international leaders, or his countrymen.

Solutions other than throwing money at the problems vary. One simple goal is for consumers to use restraint when buying products that are known to contribute to continued destruction, from mahogany to hamburgers. The Rainforest Action Network is mounting a boycott of tropical timber imports and a campaign to ban such imports into the United States. Other proposals encourage more ecotourism, which replaces income from hardwoods with tourist dollars. Several Central American countries have designated forests as national parks and encourage tourists to come to see their hundreds of species of birds, butterflies, reptiles, and amphibians. Sustainable cultivation must be encouraged so that the products like spices, tea, coffee, chocolate, vanilla, and sugar can still be produced and marketed.

The best example of the use and preservation of rain forests may be that carried out daily by the 300,000 people who still live by collecting rubber, nuts, resin, and other forest products in Brazil. They have proven over the decades that using and preserving rain forests can go hand in hand—and may even be profitable. Sadly, many of the rubber tappers have been driven from their homes by encroaching development and greedy landowners.

There are many preservation lessons to be learned from the native cultures still living in the rain forests. The Kayapo Indians of Brazil practice an amazingly sophisticated form of sustainable agriculture; they clear small plots, plant them with a range of species in careful patterns, and for a month or two each year they move about the Amazon planting food along the trails. Their "plot" may cover an area the size of France and delivers renewable produce year after year.

The last peoples carrying on Mayan culture also still plow the rain forests of Central America. They work small two- and three-acre plots in 20- to 30-year rotation. Annual burnings control pests. A wide variety of species is planted and productivity is comparable to North American corn operations.

The Kuna Indians, who live along the west coast of Panama, maintain successful plots alongside the rain forest and receive assistance from Aid to International Development to protect their farmlands from destruction.

Techniques for growing hardwood forests that allow for easier reforesting and less erosion should also be encouraged, because reforesting *is* possible, if slow. One of the best examples, in fact, sits just beyond the edge of the forest on the Atlantic coast of Brazil. The rain forests surrounding Rio de Janeiro were completely cut in the 19th century and today they are back, in all their damp, lush glory.

In an effort to better understand exactly how rain forests work, international scientists are experimenting with small, isolated plots to determine just how much rain forest is necessary to keep various species of plants and animals alive.

Perhaps the most compelling argument for saving the rain forests emerged from a just-completed three-year study by a team of scientists in Brazil that found that woodlands are worth more if left standing, than if cut for timber or cattle grazing. The study's conclusion, reported first in *Nature* magazine, claimed that revenues generated by harvesting edible fruits, rubber, oils, and cocoa from 2.5 acres returned nearly twice the value of either timber or cattle. "People who wanted to save the forest using environmental arguments have not been very persuasive because many of these nations have a large debt," the team's leader, Charles Peters, head of the Institute of Economic Botany, told the *New York Times*. "But our findings offer a very powerful argument for forest conservation."

Their study showed that 12 products, including fruits and latex, were worth $6,330 if sold in local markets over 50 years. The same land would produce just $3,184 if cut for timber, or just $2,960 if converted to cattle pastures.

Along with fines and more strict government control, nature itself may in the end prove to be its own best protector. In 1989, forest burning slowed dramatically in Brazil, largely due to the heaviest rains of the past decade. According to pictures taken by a National Oceanic and Atmospheric Administration satellite, fires destroyed 37 percent fewer acres than in the previous year, down from 80,000 to 50,000 square miles. Government officials take some credit, citing increased fines given landowners who allowed burning without permits, suspension of tax

The Rain Forest, in Dollars and Cents

A scientific team from the New York Botanical Garden assessed, in U.S. dollars, the profits that could be made over a 50-year period from harvesting and selling the natural products of trees and plants found in an untouched hectare (2.471 acres) in the Amazonian rain forest in Mishana, Peru. Compared to the potential profits from using an equivalent area for cattle ranching or for timber production, the rain forest is twice as valuable if left standing.

One Hectare of Rain Forest Can Be Used for

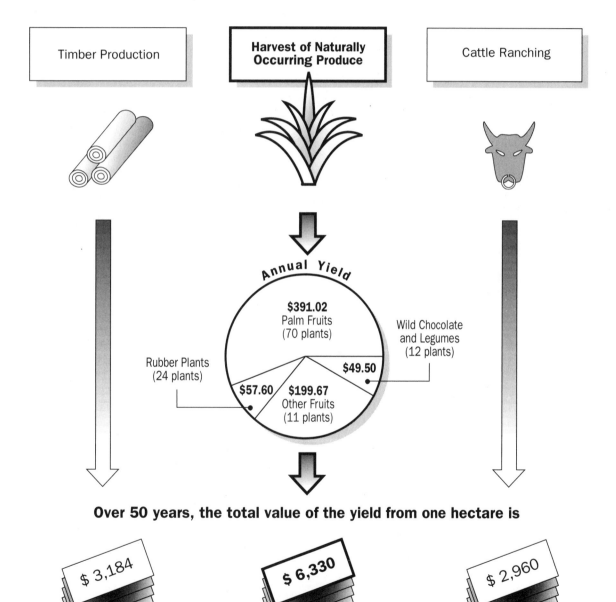

Timber Production

Harvest of Naturally Occurring Produce

Cattle Ranching

Annual Yield

$391.02
Palm Fruits
(70 plants)

Wild Chocolate
and Legumes
(12 plants)

Rubber Plants
(24 plants)

$49.50

$57.60 **$199.67**
Other Fruits
(11 plants)

Over 50 years, the total value of the yield from one hectare is

$ 3,184

$ 6,330

$ 2,960

Source: *Earthwatch*, December 1989.

incentives for cattle ranching, and changes to the country's constitution, which allowed landowners to go unpenalized for unproductive land. But ultimately, the savings must in part be credited to an act of God.

As for the celebrities and superstars who have lent their names to saving the rain forests, though few will ever stoop and replant a tree in the Amazon, their efforts should not be discouraged. Public opinion *can* alter the chain of events and encourage changing standards for groups as diverse as multinational corporations, lending institutions, and legislatures. So more power to the Dead and Madonna, Sting, and the rest. If we are lucky they will lend their names to other, less romantic pollutions, like smog and garbage. Because without public agitation it will take a political revolution to reverse the destruction of the rain forests, and war, like poverty, is hardly conducive to environmental protection.

RAIN FORESTS

The Earth's vast stretches of tropical rain forest—which wrap around the equator in a humid band—are home to over half of the world's species of life.

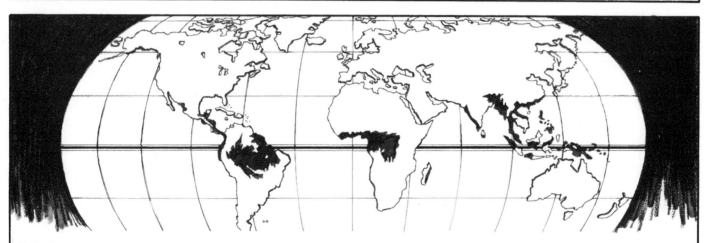

Rain forests dominate Central America and the Amazon regions of South America, as well as Indonesia, Zaire, Papua—New Guinea, and Burma. Although they cover only 6 percent of the Earth's surface, their role in the world's weather and ecosystems is immense.

Man and other animals absorb oxygen (O_2), exhaling carbon dioxide (CO_2). Green plants absorb this CO_2, producing more life-sustaining O_2. Tropical rain forests play a vital role in this global cycle, absorbing a large percentage of the world's carbon emissions.

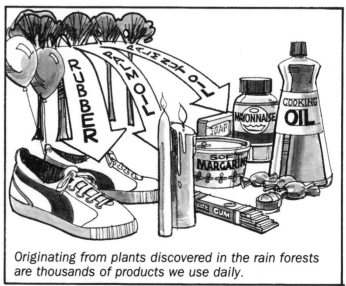

Originating from plants discovered in the rain forests are thousands of products we use daily.

More than a quarter of all prescription drugs are made from substances that originate in rain forests. The pareira plant found in South American rain forests is the source of tubocurarine, a muscle relaxant.

The rain forests are home to over ten million species; many have not yet been identified or named. Cures for some of the world's most baffling diseases—from cancer to AIDS—may lie deep in the equatorial jungles.

But this refuge for plants and animals is being destroyed; cut down and burned at the rate of a football field per second, largely to provide living space and food for an expanding population.

Once cleared of trees, rain forest land has few nutrients left, and is not adequate for long-term farming.

As the destruction drives deeper into the forests, the land that has been cut and farmed for just a few years is abandoned. Much of it is converted to low-yield ranching operations.

Wood from the rain forests is used worldwide, much of it by industrialized nations with huge appetites for paper and hardwood, to make everything from furniture to disposable chopsticks. Much of the beef raised on the barren ground is used for fast-food hamburgers.

As forests are cut and burned at increasing rates the vast stockholds of carbon contained by the trees are released into the atmosphere, adding to the problem of global warming.

At the current rate of destruction the Central American rain forest will be gone by the year 2000. Yet recent studies show that if the forests were harvested naturally, profits would be bigger than if they were cut down and sold.

One of the simplest methods of counteracting the loss of our carbon-absorbing trees is replanting. But the thousands of plant and animal species that are lost forever when an acre of rain forest is cut can never be replaced.

Individual Action

1. Citizen diplomacy plays an increasingly important role in pushing governments to stem environmental degradation. Environmental groups around the world have joined hands to influence global policies, and several well-organized groups represent the concerns of rain forest devastation. The Rainforest Action Network is pressuring development banks not to fund projects that destroy the remaining rain forests. The Environmental Project on Central America is organizing American support for Central American "Peace Parks." The Rainforest Alliance organizes letter-writing campaigns and monitors government actions worldwide. Support them by joining and telling a friend.

2. We all play a part in the decline of tropi-cal forests. We demand special hardwoods like meranti, teak, and ebony at unrealistically low prices. Don't buy rosewood or mahogany furniture. Skip wooden toilet seats made from tropical hardwoods, too. If you're a carpenter or contractor, don't buy plywood made from timber clear-cut from rain forests. Refuse to use disposable chopsticks (bring your own). Great Britain's branch of Friends of the Earth has put together a tropical hardwood products list and a guide to other rain forest products that can be avoided called the "Good Wood Guide." The Rainforest Action Network is encouraging a boycott of all tropical hardwoods and has published "Tropical Hardwoods Handbook" to explain the issue.

3. Don't eat fast-food hamburgers or processed beef products, *if they came from rain forests of Central or South America.* Each year the United States imports over 120 million pounds of fresh and frozen beef from Central American countries. Two thirds of these countries' rain forests have been cleared to raise cattle, whose stringy, inexpensive meat is exported to profit the U.S. food industry. Deciphering where the beef you buy comes from is complicated, because most is not labeled with its country of origin upon entering the United States. Write to the Secretary of Agriculture (14th St. and Independence Ave. SW, Washington, DC 20250), and let him know you want a beef labeling law to specify the country of origin.

4. International lenders are helping rain for-est destruction to continue by funding costly dams and roads and saddling poor nations with mountains of debt. Write the World Bank, one of the prime lenders, in protest and encourage them to include environmental concerns in the planning of each and every project they initiate (Barber J. Conable, Jr., President, World Bank, 1818 H St. NW, Washington, DC 20433.)

Lobby legislators to restrain government agencies and lending institutions that invest in the tropics from encouraging environmentally harmful development. For example, bills are pending in Congress to set aside Agency for International Development funds to foster sound environmental practices, hire consultants, and spend at least $2.5 million annually on new biological diversity projects overseas. Congress has also proposed legislation encouraging the World Bank to promote preservation of tropical forests. The protection of U.S. tropical forests, on the other hand, has not received similar congressional attention. It should. A campaign is underway to help protect America's last tropical rain forest in Hawaii. Information about that action is available through the Rainforest Action Network.

5. Plant trees. A single forest tree absorbs 26 pounds of carbon dioxide, and an acre can convert 2.4 to 5 tons a year. Tropical forests lose 500,000 trees every hour of every day, so it will take a lot of planting to match their loss—but every seedling helps.

6. The key to saving the rain forests rests in helping Third World nations achieve sustainable development, Those areas that have already been cleared should be addressed first, but global cooperation is required to illustrate to the native peoples of the rain forests just how important their lands are. Forgiveness of national debt is a significant indication of how seriously the developed nations take the rain forests' plight. Lobby your congressmen to promote such debt reductions.

7. Educational programs are important tools to inducing local peoples to save their own forests. An international environmental version of the Peace Corps has been suggested, which could spread conservation expertise throughout the Third World. "Rainforests Resources Pack" is a comprehensive teaching package for primary and secondary school children (Living Earth, 37 Bedford Square, London, WC1B 3EG England, $75). "Trouble in the Tropics" enables students to design their own solutions to rain forest problems using Kipling's *Jungle Book* characters. For grades K-12. (Cognetics, EIRC, 700 Hollydell Ct., Sewell, NJ 08080, $5.)

8. The World Resources Institute has a color brochure, "Keep Tropical Forests Alive," which details the value of tropical forests, the severity of their destruction, and what you can do to help. For a single free copy write to: Tropical Forest Project, World Resources Institute, 1735 New York Ave. NW, Washington, DC 20006.

9. Help organize and attend rain forest bene-fits in your community, school, or workplace.

10. Because of the medicinal values and bo-tanical secrets locked in the rain forests, doctors have proven effective lobbyists for forest protection. Encourage your doctor and local hospital to get involved. The Rainforest Alliance has details about some of these efforts.

11. Consider visiting a rain forest yourself. The knowledge will help you, and your tourist dollars will help the developing countries you visit.

12. If you have any contacts in your local media, pass along information about the rain forests and encourage stories from a local angle (maybe carpenters who refuse to use tropical hardwoods, neighbors who have visited rain forests, etc.).

Government Action

1. Developing nations should be encouraged to change economic and other policies that stimulate deforestation and land misuse, such as tax incentives and subsidies which encourage development in forested areas.

2. Policies advocating sustainable forest land and resource use, such as land tenure reform and

incentives for proper forestry management and reforestation, should be promoted.

3. The development of energy policies in de-veloping countries which do not rely on the destruction of rain forests for immediate sources should be encouraged. Four-lane highways provide easy access to the jungle and massive dams generate needed power, but both threaten the future of rain forests and should be built with great caution. The U.S. is the primary financial contributor to many of the banks and lending agencies that support these projects; any money headed for the rain forests should come attached with proper warnings that discourage deforestation.

4. The importation of tropical hardwoods should be banned, unless the wood comes from properly managed reserves. The import of rain forest beef should also be immediately banned.

5. Reforesting must be encouraged by loans, grants and technical assistance.

6. Local environmental groups in rain forest areas must be strengthened so they can play a larger role in shaping local policymaking.

Reading

"Deforesting the Earth," by Sandra Postel and Lori Heise. *State of the World 1988,* The Worldwatch Institute.

In the Rainforest, by Catherine Caufield. New York: Knopf, 1984.

Lessons from the Rainforest, edited by Suzanne Head. San Francisco: Sierra Club Books, 1990.

Amazonia, edited by Betty Meggers. Chicago: Aldine, 1971.

In Southern Light, Trekking Through Zaire and the Amazon, by Alex Shoumatoff. New York: Simon and Schuster, 1986.

The Rivers Amazon, by Alex Shoumatoff. San Francisco: Sierra Club Books, 1978.

Running the Amazon, by Joe Kane. New York: Knopf, 1989.

Biodiversity, edited by E. O. Wilson. Washington, DC: National Academy Press, 1988.

Before the Bulldozer: The Nambiquara Indians and the World Bank, by David Price. Seven Locks Press, 1989.

The Good Wood Guide, Friends of the Earth, London, 1988.

The Primary Source, by Norman Meyers. New York: W. W. Norton, 1984.

"Clear-cutting the tropical rain forest in a bold attempt to salvage it," by Jake Page. *Smithsonian,* April 1988.

"Crisis in the Rain Forests," Mother Earth News, July/August 1987.

"Brazil's Imperiled Rain Forest," by William S. Ellis. *National Geographic,* December 1988.

"Cause and Impact of Deforestation," by Peter H. Raven, in *Earth '88: Changing Geographic Perspectives,* National Geographic Society, 1988.

"Murder in the Rain Forest," by Alex Shoumatoff. *Vanity Fair,* April 1989.

Environment Bulletin, Environment Department, World Bank, Room 2-5029, 1818 H St. NW, Washington, DC 20433.

Organizations to Contact

Conservation International, 1015 18th St. NW, Suite 1000, Washington, DC 20036, 202-429-5660.

Earth Island Institute, Suite 28, 300 Broadway, San Francisco, CA 94133, 415-788-3666.

Environmental Project on Central America, 349 Church, San Francisco, CA 94114, 415-552-1619.

Friends of the Earth, 530 Seventh St. SE, Washington, DC 20003, 202-543-4312.

Global Releaf, c/o the American Forestry Association, PO Box 2000, Washington, DC 20013, 202-667-3300.

International Society of Tropical Foresters, 5400 Grosvenor Lane, Bethesda, MD 20814, 301-897-8720.

The Nature Conservancy, 1815 N. Lynn St., Arlington, VA 22209, 703-841-5300.

Rainforest Action Network, 301 Broadway, San Francisco, CA 94133, 415-398-4404.

Rainforest Alliance, Suite 1804, 295 Madison Ave., New York, NY 10017, 212-599-5060.

The World Bank, 1818 H St. NW, Washington, DC 20433.

World Wildlife Fund, 1250 24th St. NW, Washington, DC 20037, 202-293-4800.

THE LAND

6

Garbage

Perhaps no pollutant is argued about more vociferously among environmentalists, politicians, and the man on the street than garbage—not the simple litter that lies in gutters and gathers along roadsides, but bulky, plastic-bagged and dumpster variety trash that accumulates on the edges of town, in piles bigger than most city halls. What we throw away may be the closest we come to our pollution of Earth. We never really touch the acid in acid rain, or spot those dangerous CFCs. Garbage, on the other hand, you can easily touch, see, and smell. This growing accumulation of rubbish depresses land values, increases truck traffic, and ruins health, aesthetics and the necessities of life—the air we breathe and water we drink.

Debate about trash, especially what to do with it, fills small-town newspapers and provokes long-running arguments in coffee houses and meeting rooms around the world. The talk focuses on the fact that we're running out of room. Every day, the people of the United States churn out more than 432,000 tons of garbage. Over 80 percent of it is carted to landfills and covered with a patina of clay. It is bad enough that we so casually send dead refrigerators, old tires, plastic bottles, commercial junk, mounds of food scraps, and household trash to the local dump; what's worse is that this burgeoning mass is accompanied by an increasing load of hazardous chemical waste.

Around the globe this torrent of waste—toxic and non-toxic—has run smack up against the NIMBY mindset. "Not In My Back Yard" is a shout heard around the world. Proposals for new landfills arouse stiff local opposition and fights drag on for years. Shipping trash across state lines and international boundaries has become a lucrative business for some, but the mood in communities at the receiving end is increasingly inhospitable.

Our garbage problem worsens because most consumer goods are designed, in the words of the Worldwatch Institute's Cynthia Pollock, "for a one-night stand." They are bought, used, and tossed with little regard for their lasting potential. America's biggest misconception was that the limits on dumping were endless—a naivete that encouraged history's biggest throwaway society.

We should have known that the immense and growing bulk of refuse would spell trouble sooner or later. But as with so many of our environmental problems, we chose an "out of sight, out of mind" attitude toward garbage. Now that the crisis is here and starkly evident, states and localities, rightfully concerned about water and air contamination, methane gas leaks, and sheer ugliness, have begun to close up the dumps.

Now, more than half of the landfills in the United States boast "Closed" signs. In West Germany, 35,000 to 50,000 landfill sites have been declared potentially dangerous because they threaten groundwater supplies. Few developing nations have the instinct, motivation, or expertise to make solid waste disposal a priority, as a result, trash heaps are developing faster than industries in some nations.

The symbolic turning point in our changing attitudes toward the world's dumps is the garbage barge *Mobro 4000*—and its 3,186 tons of garbage—

which became an international joke, then dilemma, in 1987. Its cargo, initially rejected by an overflowing landfill in Islip, New York, floated up and down the Atlantic for nearly six months, seeking a home. It was systematically rejected by North Carolina, Florida, Alabama, Mississippi, Louisiana, Mexico, the Bahamas, and Belize. Finally, after a 6,000-mile voyage, the *Mobro*'s garbage found a resting spot—after being reduced to 400 tons of ash in a New York City incinerator—in the same landfill that first rejected it. The plight of the *Mobro* snapped the world to attention. Its message was clear: We are running out of places to put our garbage.

That message is now being sounded emphatically around the globe, from the wealthiest nations to the poorest. In California the problem is nearly epidemic. The state produces roughly 8.5 pounds of waste per person every day. State Assemblywoman Delaine Eastin describes her fellow Californians as possessed of a "TWABAL" mentality. "There Will Always Be a Landfill" is their idée fixe, she claims. As the state's population continues to grow by 600,000 people a year, California is running out of room, for people and garbage. All of Los Angeles' landfills are expected to close by the mid-1990s. Chief executive of the state's Waste Management Board, George T. Eowan, voices the concerns of many when he warns that Californians can't pick and choose among alternative solutions. "We've got to do everything," he says.

In equally populous if less prosperous locales the problem is the same. In Beijing, Shanghai, Tianjin, and other large Chinese cities, garbage piles grow by 10 percent a year. Great Britain landfills close to 90 percent of its consumer waste and is running out of dump sites. In Mexico City, most of the 20,000 tons of trash collected daily is thrown into open dumps where it nourishes huge populations of flies and rats. In the United States, Chicago's 33 dumps will be closed by 1991. Many New England towns already truck refuse 24 hours a day to Pennsylvania

and Ohio. States and nations have resorted to shipping their garbage across international borders, playing the zero-sum game of trash-swapping.

Thankfully, as a result of journeys like the *Mobro*'s and growing local protest, more and more people around the globe are ripping the wax paper out of cereal boxes, rinsing bottles and cans, and bundling newspapers and cardboard into neat piles for recycling. Ten states in the United States already have mandatory recycling, and more than 1,000 communities have instituted curbside pickup programs. In Woodbury, New Jersey, non-compliance results in fines of up to $500. In Austin, Texas, peer pressure and pride have resulted in 85 percent compliance. Oregon requires cities of more than 4,000 to pick up recyclables at curbside and offers tax incentives of up to 50 percent on equipment that processes or uses secondhand materials. Rhode Island has given home owners bins to store bottles, metal, and glass. If the trash isn't sorted, it doesn't get collected. Bright blue recycling cans line some streets of brownstones in Brooklyn and Queens, and fancy new collection trucks, paid for by the city's sanitation department, roam the streets. And in Islip, Long Island, home of the *Mobro*, mandatory "garbage coupons" are now sold. It costs 50 cents for each bag dropped at the dump. It is fitting that garbage is becoming a municipal priority since the average city of 100,000 pays as much for waste disposal as for its police department.

Seattle stands out as a shining example of what the future portends. More than 60 percent of households participate in the city's five-year-old recycling program. More than 30 percent of all household garbage is recycled. Those who recycle receive lower monthly trash bills—and those who don't pay twice as much. Most residents can simply dump newspapers, cans, and bottles into one container, and private collectors pick it up once a month. Sorting is done at processing centers. The city's goal is to recycle 50 percent of all household garbage.

But even 50 percent is nothing to the residents of Wilton, New Hampshire. Their landfill was a long-accepted institution. Housed in an old stone quarry, its controlled fires kept the growing piles of garbage at reasonable levels. But in the mid-1970s the state began pressuring the town to close the dump. It sat on the edge of the river and was oozing dangerous chemicals and garbage into surface and groundwater, the state said. Dump fires were clouding the otherwise pristine skies. The town fathers were encouraged to open a "proper" landfill, export the waste, incinerate it, or recycle it.

Town counselor Greg Bohosiewicz, an economist by trade, decided Wilton's decision should be based primarily on keeping taxes low. After studying the options he quickly hit on recycling as the path of least resistance and highest savings. "The only thing I knew about trash at the time was that it magically disappeared some place," he told an interviewer.

He encouraged, cajoled, lobbied, and convinced a half-dozen surrounding towns to open a joint recycling center. That was in 1979. Today, about 65 percent of the area's population recycles, an especially high participation rate for a program based around a drop-off center. Wilton now spends about $36 per ton to dispose of its waste, compared with $120 per ton in a neighboring town that does not recycle.

Globally, the transition from user state to conserver society is slowly getting underway. The European steel industry reuses scrap metal, copper, and aluminum, resulting in energy savings up to 95 percent. In Norway the price of a new car now includes a disposal cost of about $100, redeemable when the junked car is turned in at an approved receiving center. The Netherlands runs the world's largest composting operation, producing 125,000 tons of compost annually. In France more than 100 composting facilities generate in excess of 800,000 tons of compost annually. The Chinese reuse 2.5 million tons of scrap iron each year, and recycle another million tons of waste paper. And in West Germany, public recycling programs in which citizens can either drop off recyclables at corner depots or have them picked up in front of their homes have been in place for many years, in part because the country is strapped for both raw materials and space.

In Japan, a country the size of Montana and home to 121 million people, recycling is a must. Oil shortages in the mid-1970s spurred recycling of raw materials from 16 percent to 48 percent in just five years. Over 100,000 tons of garbage are converted back into valuable material annually. "This year's Toyota is last year's Ford," goes the local recycling fable. As an indication of just how well the Japanese recycle, suffice it to say that when two noted U.S. "garbologists" studied the country's system, the resulting book was titled *Garbage Management in Japan: Leading the Way.* Today, Japan recycles 95 percent of its newspapers, 55 percent of its steel, 66 percent of its bottles, and 40 percent of its aluminum. In fact, recyclables there are not perceived as garbage. In much the way that Americans often sell or give away old cars, clothes, and books, Japanese citizens set aside materials such as glass, paper, metals, and household hazardous waste for processing and reuse.

Citizens divide their discards into four categories: combustibles, noncombustibles, recyclables, and hazardous waste. Each of the different categories of refuse is collected by private contractors on different days. In some towns, garbage trucks weave through the streets playing classical music and children's songs. In others, the arrival of the garbage truck is announced by loudspeakers, a signal for citizens to swap bundled newspapers for free rolls of toilet paper. Cans, bottles, and newspapers are collected by volunteer or private industry groups. Some bulk items, like broken furniture, appliances, bicycles, and toys, are taken to centers where they are repaired and sold. People who want to get rid of a refrigerator or television set make one phone call to the sanitation department. In general, only non-recyclable wastes are picked up by municipalities and taken to incinerators or landfills.

Allen Hershkowitz and Eugene Salerni, authors of *Garbage Management in Japan,* cite the example of Mari Hatano, who lives near the city of Kyoto. She separates her waste into six categories: paper and kitchen waste, plastics and incombustibles, glass and cans. They are collected on different days of the week. Pickup is not at her home but at a centralized collection point a block away. Newspapers and magazines are collected door-to-door by a citizens' group, and bulky waste is picked up at her home once each month. While she admits that separating waste requires extra effort, and that she doesn't particularly enjoy it, especially after working all day and coming home late, she wouldn't think of not recycling, though there are no fines or penalties.

Once the garbage to be landfilled arrives at the dump, the Japanese treat it differently than most other nations, report Hershkowitz and Salerni. Unlike most American dump sites, Japanese dumps are constructed with sturdy plastic liners and use high-tech collectors to prevent toxic pollutants balled up in the garbage from leaking into groundwater. What isn't recycled or landfilled is burned for energy. Potentially toxic ash that remains after garbage is burned is insulated from groundwater by burying it in leak-proof dump sites. And if Kyoto residents are interested, they can check a 24-hour, digital scoreboard in the middle of town, which registers the level of emissions from local incinerators.

Hershkowitz and Salerni conclude that Japan's success is due to extraordinarily close coordination among national, regional, and local governments. Yet even in Japan, problems in garbage management are beginning to crop up. Room for landfills is growing tighter, and is expected to run out completely by 1995. The recycling efforts of individuals (especially the young) and corporations (especially in bigger cities) are slacking off. Apparently, as the East

adopts more and more Western traditions, attitudes toward garbage are changing there, too. Perhaps the most telling symbol of even Japan's struggle with garbage is that as the value of recycled magazines and newspapers has dropped, their local governments are now considering doing away with their toilet paper for trash incentives.

CAUSES

The collection and disposal of garbage has a long history. The first organized dump is reported to have been set up outside Athens in 500 B.C. Citizens were asked to dump no closer than a mile from the city's walls—a much more sophisticated approach than that of the Parisians, who well into the fourteenth century were still tossing their trash out the window. As far as can be discerned, the first systematic incineration of municipal refuse was tested in Nottingham, England, in 1874. By the late 1800s New York City scavengers were paid to "trim" the garbage of materials they could sell off and in the mid-1890s the city's street cleaning commissioner, George A. Waring, tried to recapture some of these resources for the city to help defray the cost of waste disposal.

By the turn of the century garbage was already threatening human health worldwide. Giant refuse incinerators were built and modern recycling was born. In 1903, workers picked useful items from New York's garbage as it passed by on conveyor belts. In Milwaukee a trash-burning plant began producing electricity in 1913.

During World War II, the scarcity of raw materials gave recycling a big boost. Households routinely saved tin cans, glass, and other products. At least one third of all paper was recycled, along with copper, aluminum, and other "strategic" materials. Glass bottles and jars were refilled as many as 40 times.

But when international trade resumed after the war, recycling efforts fell off. In the 1950s and

1960s urban "source-separation" programs were cut back, and by the mid-1960s most cities were collecting mixed garbage. Separation of materials was considered too expensive compared with the relatively low cost—and apparent abundance—of landfills. Recycling made forays into the public consciousness in the early 1970s when it first became apparent that natural resources and landfill space were diminishing. But such efforts were scattered, and confined mostly to "back-to-earthers" and "hippies."

In the past decade the world has fully realized the effects of the Disposable Society. "Throwaway" and "disposable" have become sales incentives. Radios break and we throw them away. Flashlights come with irreplaceable batteries. Watches cost more to fix than to replace. The same goes for toasters, irons, and VCRs. More than 7.6 million television sets are thrown out every year in the United States alone, each loaded with parts made of rubber, metal, wood, plastic, glass, and synthetic chemicals.

Altogether the United States produces 160 million tons of garbage a year. That's a crude figure and doesn't include millions more dumped illegally. Of this waste stream, 34 percent is made up of containers and packaging, 26 percent is items *designed* to be thrown out, 18 percent is mown grass and raked leaves, and up to 13 percent is food. In just one year America buries enough metals to build two million automobiles, enough wood to construct one million homes, enough paper to publish all the daily newspapers in the country, enough aluminum to manufacture 500,000 trailer homes or rebuild the entire American airfleet 71 times. The total pile fills 11 million garbage trucks each year. Babysitting all this trash costs $20 billion a year.

The dangers of our profligacy began to become obvious over a decade ago. Since 1978 an estimated 14,000 solid waste landfills have closed in the United States. Another 2,000 are expected to close in the next five years because they are leaking danger-

ously. In some cases, as landfills close, those that are still open have raised their "tipping" fees more than 200 percent.

While such wanton wastefulness is not solely an American dilemma, most other nations lag behind in terms of pure physical volume. Individuals in the United States create 3.5 pounds of waste each day; by comparison the typical West German throws out 2.5 pounds, the average Japanese 2.2 pounds. Despite those numbers, a recent Gallup poll reports that 42 percent of all Americans say they or other family members regularly recycle. (Only 15 percent said recycling was required in their community.) But they also did not consider waste disposal as serious an environmental problem as the contamination of drinking water or the pollution of marine life and beaches. Just 41 percent suggested that waste disposal was a source of "great concern."

EFFECTS

Perhaps the most ominous vision of the world's garbage future sits on New York's Staten Island. The 3,000-acre Fresh Kills landfill is without doubt the most significant monument to our seeming disregard for the trashing of the globe.

The 40-year-old dump is listed in the *Guinness Book of World Records* as the largest anywhere. Its height and volume challenge the pyramid of Khufu, the grandest of the great pyramids of Egypt, as well as most of the best-known urban landmarks of the world. When it closes sometime soon after the turn of next century, it will have risen to more than 500 feet tall, and will rival the Great Wall of China as the largest man-made structure in the world.

The landfill, built on a swampy lowland, became a dump in 1948. Three years later a report to the mayor concluded that "the Fresh Kills landfill project cannot fail to affect constructively a wide area around it. It is at once practical and idealistic." Today it contains an estimated 100 million tons of

Garbage dumped at landfills does not just rest benignly. Rain washes hazardous waste from paints, household cleaners, and batteries into the soil; decomposing garbage emits volatile methane; and plastics and other solid refuse are carried by winds to the waterways.

oozing, leaking garbage. (When 17 garbologists dug into it recently, they came up with everything from ham to newspapers that looked as fresh as on the day they were discarded.) Fresh Kills will soon be the tallest "mountain" on the Atlantic coast between Florida and northern Maine. When it closes, the city plans to turn it into a grass-covered park. Its peak will be reached by a curving two-lane paved road and will be served by power lines.

Perhaps the most dangerous factor in the growth of the world's landfills is their contamination of nearby drinking water. Toxic chemicals bound up in the garbage we throw away every day eventually leach from landfills into nearby aquifers, streams, and lakes. This deadly cocktail moves slowly through surface water or down through the soil into groundwater, which is the source of drinking water in most communities. Fresh Kills alone leaks more than one million gallons of such toxic "juice" directly into nearby waterways every day.

Examples of such contamination abound and some are horrific in scope. In a small Florida town near Miami, a 291-acre lake is flanked by a now-inactive landfill, which was open for less than 20 years and accepted mostly construction site waste. Today, if a healthy fish is thrown into the water, it dies in less than 30 seconds. Poisons clog the region's aquifers and foul its air. Cleanup is estimated to cost more than $100 million. In 1984, a landfill in Old Bridge, New Jersey, simply collapsed under the weight of its non-precious collection. Waves of mud rushed down a slope, knocking down supporting structures and allowing contaminated water to escape into nearby waterways. (See Chapter 9, Freshwater Pollution.)

One alternative to landfilling, incineration, has been argued about by communities around the world. For the good it promises—reducing the bulk weight of garbage by 75 percent—its potentially dangerous effects have prevented such plants from blossoming like dandelions. The process sounds good, but the air emissions of sulfur and nitrogen oxide, hydro-

chloric acid, heavy metals and dioxins from burn plants are as dangerous as the leaking landfills they replace. The toxic ash residue often requires a separate home (although in Los Angeles toxic ash is mixed with mainstream waste), and must be transported and dumped in hazardous-waste landfills, which are often in another county or state.

SOLUTIONS

The primary solution to the world's mounting garbage problem is "source reduction." Its definition is simple: The less we create, the less we have to throw away. Reducing the amount of waste generated by placing limits on packaging or restricting the use of disposable products should be at the top of every nation's, community's, and individual's list of environmentally wise "things to do." For example, a community might ban the use of polystyrene (as did Suffolk County, New York, and Berkeley, California), or taxes might be levied on excess packaging or frequently purchased disposable products, which has been proposed in a handful of state legislatures and city councils.

Next, we must begin to reuse as many products as possible, from bags to boxes, and anything else that may have a life other than in the dump. Third, recycling must be emphasized at home, work, and in every neighborhood. It is no longer a chore for hippies only. Instead, what is gradually emerging across the country is a broad recycling structure initiated by government, private enterprise, and new technology. Various urban governments are designing new systems for separating the variety of recyclables. States, localities, and private companies are building or contracting for such systems. Mandatory recycling laws are being passed in communities worldwide. Solid waste management is finally in a state of transition.

The success of recycling depends largely on the willingness of public officials to create new, long-term programs in the face of current pressures to build incinerators. Recycling is sometimes described as competing with incineration because it reduces the amount of waste incinerator operators receive and are paid for, and many communities guarantee incinerator operators a minimum volume of trash. Success also demands that markets be found or created for the materials once they have been separated.

Most people in the industrialized world are literally surrounded by recycled materials, whether we know it or not. In your house, the gypsum board for the inside walls, tar paper for the roof, and thick waxed paperboard under hardwood floors are probably made from recycled goods; ditto for the materials in the glove compartment and door panels, sun visors, and backs of the upholstered seats in your car. In West Germany, highways are lined with sound barriers made out of old tires, newspapers, and construction debris. The walls of a playground in Chicago are made of roughly 300,000 compacted milk jugs and soda bottles, shredded by a plastics recycling company in Iowa Falls, Iowa.

A new zeal for recycling has proven to be a boon for both entrepreneurs and foresighted businesses and corporations around the world. Some have jumped on board out of a sense of civic pride, others at the behest of consumers, still others are forced by law.

Several thousand waste-paper dealers and brokers and hundreds of thousands of individual "scavengers" have turned paper collecting into their main source of income. Eight paper mills in the United States depend solely on waste paper. But the real money-makers are those who collect cardboard boxes, which bring about $100 a ton, and high-quality paper like computer printouts, which can go for as much as $200 a ton. Corrugated cardboard boxes are currently the Port of New York's biggest volume export at 800,000 tons a year, much of it headed for South Korea and Japan, where it's recycled for new boxes for televisions, stereos and VCRs.

• In Atlanta, 28-year-old Jack Lupas empties trash for 150 Atlanta firms, collecting almost 200 tons a month. He pays three cents per pound for the high-grade paper and resells it for 12 cents a pound. He got his start in 1983, by drawing up a potential client list culled from the "help wanted" ads of the *Atlanta Constitution*. He made a blanket offer to buy from his clients what they obviously no longer wanted: the computer paper they were tossing in their wastebaskets.

• On a smaller scale, when 66-year-old Milly Zantow heard that space was running out at the town dump in North Freedom, Wisconsin, she cashed in an insurance policy and set up her own recycling center, staffed mainly with volunteer senior citizens. Zantow has just a few pieces of rudimentary equipment—a magnet for pulling out tin cans, a baler, and a glass crusher—but reprocessors who melt the stuff down take all the sorted and reprocessed materials she can supply.

• At the truly grass-roots level, "at-home" recycling systems promise to become a booming trade, and several entrepreneurs are leading the way. In Woodstock, New York, David Goldbeck and his wife Nikki spent a year designing an "environmentally aware" kitchen. The redesign cost $400. To catch vegetable scraps, for example, they cut a 6.5-inch-square hole in a little-used section of the kitchen countertop, and covered it with a swiveling plastic lid. Underneath, they installed a garbage can to catch the scraps. The insulated space, which is laminated to protect against moisture, is linked by a passageway to the outside of the house. To transfer the container's contents to the compost bin, one simply opens a door outside the kitchen. Similarly, to store recyclable bottles and cans, they concealed a 17-by-31-inch space behind bifold doors, hiding a garbage container and a freestanding rolling wire trolley. An outgrowth of their grand experiment is a book, which illustrates how everyone can ready their house for recycling.

If we are to halt the encroachment of, and leaching of toxic liquids from, landfills onto valuable lands such as these endangered wetlands (above), recycling is a necessity. Around the globe, the number of recycling stations (below) is growing.

• In response to increased recycling pressure on the real-estate industry and carting and waste disposal companies, Red Hook Recycling in Brooklyn, New York, processes demolition and construction waste for builders. Michael Cosola, the company's president, said it took five years to plan and build his plant to handle the debris. He expects to recover 80 percent of the waste brought in. The final, salable products will be mainly scrap metal, wood chips, and stone and concrete particles, which can be sold as landfill or road pavement base.

Most of the sorting is done by machines, not hand. The plant's main structure is a hangarlike building 200 feet long and 45 feet high. A series of machines, grates, and screens designed to break down and sort the material are connected by a system of conveyor belts. A huge shredder and sorting machine (which separates lighter materials, like cloth, sponges, and plastic) dominate the center of the space. A tower at the end of the room serves as command central, and is equipped with a bank of television monitors.

• On the corporate level, McDonald's has switched from prepackaged orange juice to frozen concentrate (reducing packaging by 75 percent) and has figured out a way to repackage their frozen french fries—instead of 36 pounds to a package, they now pack 39, saving two million pounds of packaging a year. The company is also experimenting with incinerators at some of its stores, and with in-store separation of recyclables. Canada's largest supermarket chain, Loblaw's, has sold more than $5 million worth of "environmentally friendly" products in the past year, from unbleached coffee filters made in Sweden to biodegradable cleaning products from Belgium. Based on studies the store has commissioned, Loblaw's president is convinced that some day, 50 percent of the goods sold in his stores will bear a "Green Line" stamp of approval.

Around the globe, people are taking different approaches, but are aiming for the same result. Conservation and the reuse of goods, while not quite epidemic, are finding growing numbers of converts. As the world's population continues to boom, the conservation experiments of today may have to become the necessities of tomorrow.

• In Shanghai, garbage from an apartment house is carried by miniature tractor to the outskirts of town and dumped into a commune's compost heap. From the pile run thin, clear plastic pipes, which are hooked up to individual kitchens. When a spigot is turned in the house, methane gas generated by the compost fills fuel tanks.

• Danish refuse is collected in moisture-resistant paper sacks, which allow moisture to evaporate. By the time the garbage collector comes, the bag already weighs less. He leaves an empty bag whenever he takes a full one. In Moscow, garbage is dropped through apartment house chutes into an underground vacuum pipeline and shuttled at 60 to 80 feet per second to a central collecting station. (A similar system operates in Disney World.) In Germany and France, firms have developed laser techniques that sort materials by color, texture, weight, toxicity, and other factors. The technology isolates plastics, which are in heavy demand by recyclers.

• In many developing nations, garbage is not only a recyclable good but a livelihood. Every morning in Colombia (and Sri Lanka, Manila, Jakarta, and other cities and countries across Asia and South America), hundreds of scavengers converge on new "mountains" of refuse. Paper, clothing, cans, and glass jars are picked out, cleaned, and sold. In Mexico City, thousands pay to belong to the scavengers union. Some then pay more to overseers at the dump to insure a good location.

• In Cairo, flattened and baled cans are sold to craftsmen who recycle them into shiny pots and pans. Squatters, called *wahis,* have controlled the garbage flow in the city for the last 100 years. Men and children collect, while women stay home sifting and sorting the trash into piles of paper, glass, textiles, bones, and metals. Food waste is reserved for feeding the families of pigs the *wahis* raise as their main cash crop. Most live in indescribable squalor, but without this system, much of the city's waste would not get collected.

Those who study landfills—and it is a growing preoccupation, as scientists, environmentalists, and governments ponder how to resolve the garbage dilemma—find that a handful of items dominate the world's trash. If we could just find a way to better recycle, reuse, or reduce our need for these things, the world's landfills would last longer.

• Paper is the biggest portion of the globe's garbage; newspaper makes up 10 percent of all solid waste. Figuring out ways to better recycle pulp products, and creating a bigger demand for the end-product is a major challenge. Today, paper is the most recycled waste, but markets for recycled newspaper are shriveling. Right now, prices are expected to drop, especially as urban recycling programs expand. The glut is understandable. Americans alone bought 13.2 million tons of newspapers in 1988, then put 4.7 million tons out on the curb to be recycled. Recycled newsprint is used to make more newsprint, cereal boxes, construction paper, egg cartons, insulation, paper board, animal bedding, and cat litter. But mills that recycle paper say they can't absorb it all—yet.

In Hurley, New York, a glutted newspaper recycling market has put Ernest Myer Elementary School's paper collection–recycling project "out of business." In 1989, principal Frederick Wadnola tried to make arrangements to have the school's stock-piled newspapers picked up. The firm that had bought their papers for the previous decade turned him down. Wadnola learned, like everyone else who has tried to recycle papers in the past couple of years, that newspaper just isn't in big demand anymore. Instead, the company told Wadnola they wanted to be paid to take the newspapers away.

A similar fate has befallen organizations from the Boy Scouts and Lions Clubs to municipalities. The push is on to figure out how to use recycled paper better, especially since 10 states have already approved laws for 1990 that will ban newsprint and other recyclable items from landfills and incinerators. (One suggestion is that newspapers themselves print more on recycled paper. *The New York Times,* for example, uses just 8 percent recycled paper.) In New York City, the Office Paper Recycling Service, run by the Council on the Environment, helps organizations develop cost-effective waste paper–recycling efforts (for bond, computer, newspaper, and corrugated paper) and is developing plastic-recycling programs. The program has been used successfully by companies including Merrill Lynch, *The New York Times,* and AT&T.

• Recycling of plastic is still in its infancy. The Society of the Plastics Industry estimates that 20 percent of all plastic products manufactured in the United States in 1984 were recycled, compared with 54 percent of all aluminum cans. The process is stymied because there are currently more than 50 different types of plastic in use, many made with a variety of toxic dyes and chemicals. As a result, not all plastic can be successfully melted down and recast. Polystyrene foam (better known by its trade name, Styrofoam) takes thousands of years to decompose, and is difficult to recycle. There are 25 billion such foam containers made each year in the United States alone. Though convenient, they are a major contributor to landfills. Plastic-recycling solutions are desperately needed: The EPA estimates that the amount of plastic trash will double by the end of the century.

Laws regarding the use of plastic are being met with mixed reviews and much contention. Early in 1989, the Minneapolis city council adopted an ordinance that would ban most throwaway plastic food packaging from grocery-store shelves and fast-food outlets. It permits retailers to sell milk in plastic jugs and soft drinks in plastic bottles only if the city can work out an acceptable recycling program. Prior to that proposal, the most ambitious plan for limiting plastics was adopted in Suffolk County, New York. The community wanted to ban polystyrene foam plastic—the kind used in fast-food containers and meat packaging—entirely. Both measures have been postponed indefinitely, due to hard-fought battles by manufacturers, grocers, and retailers.

A handful of companies are experimenting with bio- or photodegradable plastic bags, grocery bags, and plastic film. Sixteen states already require degradable yokes for beer and soda six-packs. But some environmentalists are concerned that if people think all plastic is biodegradable, they won't recycle. Scientists themselves are not certain what happens to the percentage of polystyrene and other chemicals that is left after biodegradable plastics degrade. Until the process is refined further, the residue is simply another toxic by-product mixed in with the waste stream. Plastic manufacturers and recyclers agree that degradable plastics and recycling technologies are not compatible, in part because even a small amount of degradable plastic may contaminate and make a whole batch of plastic unfit for recycling. So degradable plastics may be best reserved for high litter items that could never be made recyclable. (Even naturally biodegradable materials, like paper and food, don't break down in many landfills because of the lack of moisture, oxygen, or warmth. It is possible to find newspapers in readable condition after two decades in a landfill.)

Nonetheless, plastic waste is increasingly being reused to make durable products such as plastic lumber for low-maintenance fences and pier supports, and insulation for sleeping bags and jackets; even park benches are molded from recycled yogurt containers. National Waste Technologies of New York and Advanced Recycling Technology of Belgium have teamed up to produce a synthetic lumber dubbed "syntal," made from recycled plastics. They process an estimated 120,000 pounds of plastic a day, and turn out everything from boat docks and retaining walls to flower boxes and picnic tables.

Procter and Gamble is test-marketing a new cleanser container that can be reused 100 times. Refillable plastic milk bottles are being auditioned in upstate New York. Fast-food operators are looking for more degradable plastics and most have given up on polystyrene.

Dow Chemical and Domtar, Inc., of Montreal have formed a new company to reuse plastic bottles. Seven polystyrene makers, including Atlantic Richfield, Amoco, Mobil, and Dow, have put $14 million into the National Polystyrene Recycling Company. They contend the plastic is as recyclable as glass—it just needs to be separated from other waste more carefully because there are so many different types. Their first targets are schools, hospitals, and restaurants. Material collected will be ground into small pieces and washed with hot water. Once dried, it will be reduced to fluff and melted at high temperatures to a waxy consistency. After filtration to remove dirt and other contaminants, the plastic will be cooled and chopped into small pellets for reuse, in cafeteria trays, trash containers, and office products. In West Germany, a move is on to make all bottles—glass and plastic—interchangeable, thus easier to reuse.

At a demonstration plant in Brooklyn, bags of trash from 19 McDonald's restaurants and several nearby school cafeterias are loaded into hoppers, carried by conveyor belts that chop, sort, and separate the refuse. Flakes from former coffee cups and

Big Mac boxes will be recycled into construction materials and hard plastic products like office in-baskets and cafeteria trays. The project is funded by Amoco, Rubbermaid, and McDonald's.

• Lawn clippings make up about a fifth of all garbage in landfills. Wisconsin, Illinois, Florida, and Minnesota will soon enforce statewide bans prohibiting landfills from accepting leaves, brush, and grass clippings. Instead, this "refuse" should be used as compost or left on the lawn. Community compost heaps should be encouraged, like the one in Fairfield, Connecticut. The town hopes its new $3 million composting center will reduce its annual collection of 4,000 tons of sewer sludge to usable compost. The system occupies a two-acre building and is driven by computers. Six concrete troughs are loaded with sewage sludge mixed with chopped leaves, grass, and branches from thousands of lawns and parks. The town plans to use the compost to finish capping its landfill, and then turn it into a park laden with ball fields and meadows.

• Medical waste, especially infectious waste (or "red bags"), is a growing problem. The burgeoning flow of waste from walk-in clinics, doctors' and dentists' offices, nursing homes, dialysis centers, blood banks, and home care has doubled in the past decade, as the use of disposables grows. When added to the tons of waste generated, and mostly incinerated, by hospitals, it's yet another significant contributor to the garbage pile. "More people are exposed to emissions from substandard hospital incinerators than from wash-ups on the beach," says Jacqueline M. Warren, staff attorney for the National Resources Defense Council, a New York–based environmental advocacy group.

• Tires are designed to last, and their durability has become a big problem. Over 2 billion unretreadable scrap tires are stockpiled across the United States and another 200 million are discarded each year.

They stubbornly refuse to remain buried, continuously rising to the surface of those landfills that will still take them. Burning tires creates noxious fumes. Recovering oil from them—called pyrolysis—works in laboratories, but never outside of them. There are options, though. When shredded, they can be reused, on the bottom of thick-soled sandals for instance, and even in some asphalts.

In Babbitt, Minnesota, a state-financed company, Tirecycle, is beginning to reduce 3 million of the state's discarded tires into gaskets, storage bins, railroad crossing pads, even new tires, by converting tire waste into a raw material and then combining it with virgin rubber and plastics.

• More than 16 billion diapers containing an estimated 2.8 million tons of excrement and urine are dumped into landfills each year. The feces and urine may contain any of more than 100 viruses, including polio and hepatitis, and can spread through groundwater or may be carried by flies; plastic liners can take 500 years to decompose. Most diapers are buried in landfills, and they make up about three percent of the waste stream.

Diaper makers around the world are experimenting with better products. Procter and Gamble is working with a company in St. Cloud, Minnesota, to compost 2 to 3 tons of Pampers and Luvs diapers a day. Mixed with sewer sludge, the diapers move through 120-foot-long drums, 12 feet in diameter, which rotate 24 times an hour. Essentially, all this procedure does is hasten the biological process. The remnants are screened and cured for weeks before being sold as fertilizer. (Similar processes are used across Europe, for a variety of discards.) Other companies are experimenting with diapers that are 96 percent biodegradable, or are made completely from cotton, but the best bet from a disposal point of view is to use cloth diapers.

• To some people, incineration is the cure for the garbage problem. Certainly Rand Burgner thought

Even if rusted, much of the metal and other material stockpiled in U.S. car graveyards is recyclable. The 200 million tires discarded every year in the U.S., however, produce noxious fumes when burned and can't be melted down. Efforts to recycle them by shredding are gaining momentum; scraps are used for soling shoes and making storage bins and railroad crossing pads.

so. As deputy director of the Solid Waste Management Authority in North Hempstead, New York, he wanted to put the embarrassment the *Mobro* brought to his region behind him. He wanted North Hempstead to be recognized for garbage innovation, rather than garbage malaise. The solution, he thought, was to build a $135 million incinerator, which would convert garbage into energy. Citizens and environmentalists on Long Island have spent more than a half million dollars trying to thwart his dream.

The two groups, Burgner's followers and the environmentalists, represent the poles of a growing debate. To burn or not to burn? The environmentalists have commissioned studies that suggest the town could be recycling 71 percent of its waste within five years and argue that toxic air emissions and ash disposal problems would increase with incineration. The town fathers say, "Okay, but with our landfills closing fast we still have to burn some of our garbage." To date, the wrangle has cost the town $1 million in taxpayers' money. Similar fights are being waged in small towns and municipalities around the world.

Incineration is problematic, in part, because there's no such thing as a small or inexpensive mass-burn plant. Incinerator furnaces can reach up to six stories and emission stacks may climb 500 feet into the sky. Tall cranes transfer garbage from the trash pit to hoppers, where it is funneled down a moving grate. Such plants burn upwards of 3,000 tons of garbage a day—and can cost up to $500 million to construct.

Whenever a new incinerator is proposed, hackles are raised because of the additional environmental threats the plants pose. Garbage is difficult to burn because it's so moist and it generates potentially toxic ash and a range of pollutants, including contributors to acid rain such as sulfur dioxide, nitrogen oxide, as well as carbon monoxide and hydrocarbons. Incinerators may also emit dangerous levels of dioxins and furans, the most toxic man-made substances, which are more threatening than the emissions from coal-burning plants.

Studies show that every burn plant, whether in the United States, Japan, Switzerland, the Netherlands, Germany, or Canada, emits poisonous dioxin gases. And no one knows for sure what level of dioxin emissions is dangerous to life. Some argue that such emissions could result in just one case of cancer per 10 million; others insist it's somewhere between 17 to 270 per million. Currently, the United States has no dioxin exposure standard and the EPA is conducting studies to determine whether one is necessary. The only recent sign that dioxin emission levels may be too high came from Sweden in 1984. The Swedes stopped burning for six months when high levels of dioxin turned up in crabmeat and mother's milk. But in 1986, the moratorium was lifted, with the recommendation only that new emission controls be established and standards raised.

Community protest against incinerators is becoming more vocal, especially as the NIMBY mindset proliferates. Victorious community groups set precedents and encourage others to fight. Opponents argue that the plants are too expensive (especially compared to waste reduction or recycling), and that they discourage or preclude recycling, pollute the air, and create toxic ash. Incinerators are very difficult to site and hard to regulate. Like nuclear reactors, they are also difficult to build. It can take decades to obtain a permit and construction may then last another three to four years. Another major flaw is that incinerator operators can just as easily burn a drum of dangerous chemicals as they can grapefruit rinds. Most incinerators have no adequate screening process that will weed out hazardous waste before it goes up in flames. Instead of burn plants, opponents say, monies and energies should be spent encouraging garbage reduction.

Despite such concerns, incineration is viewed by many communities as a viable last resort. Landfills are closing and recycling isn't yet widespread enough to reduce our mass of refuse. Connecticut already burns 60 percent of its garbage. New scrubbers and "smokestack bags" have helped limit airborne pollutants. Local governments in 38 states have committed to building massive incinerators. More than 90 are already in operation, and another 100 are planned. They are in common use across Europe, where landfill space is even more scarce.

Garbage burning is studied most in Europe, because Europeans have incinerated for decades. In Sweden, where the average citizen produces a pound less of garbage a day than people in the United States, 27 mass-burn plants torch 50 percent of the nation's garbage. In West Germany, 34 percent of all garbage is burned; in Switzerland, about 75 percent. All three countries report they find landfills harder to control and that leaching is more difficult to monitor than emissions from the burn plants' tall stacks. Incinerators are used best in combination with a strong recycling program, a well-maintained landfill, and close monitoring. Used optimally, incinerators can reduce by as much as 70 to 95 percent the volume of garbage that would otherwise have to be landfilled and can supply small amounts of energy.

NRDC's Allen Hershkowitz is an incineration expert. His 1986 study of burn plants across Europe and in Japan concedes that such technology can be efficient—but only if the waste is properly prepared by an educated public and pollution-control devices are watched over by highly skilled workers. Unfortunately, he says, the U.S. government and individual states have yet to coordinate the full range of standards that a successful plant requires. Poorly operated incineration plants pose an expensive and continuing crisis in waste management. Despite any apparent "success stories," the most telling example of incineration's future may be in New York City. The proposed Brooklyn Navy Yard incinerator, which environmentalists and local activists have fought hard against, would burn 3,000 tons of garbage a day, and reduce it to 900 tons of ash containing concentrated toxics. The ash would have to be hauled to secure hazardous-waste landfills (costing up to $1 million an acre to construct), which are few and filling fast.

If the garbage problem is ever to subside, manufacturers of consumer products must cooperate. Reducing packaging and disposables should be an intrinsic part of every manufacturing and sales effort. Unfortunately, far too often, industry pays lip service to solid waste problems by offering things like biodegradable disposable diapers and plastic bags that may never decompose in tightly packed landfills.

Manufacturers and retailers understandably prefer plastic over glass because it is lightweight, cheaper, microwavable, durable, and more resilient. Consumers like it because it's secure, strong, and waterproof. Environmentalists hate it because it's hard to recycle. Less than two percent of all plastic is currently recycled. The packaging industry, the largest user of plastics in the world, produces 40 percent of all plastic waste.

Reducing packaging and encouraging recycling appears to be inching up on the agendas of most major corporations (in many instances, just a step ahead of legislation that would require them to be responsible for disposal of their products). A recent Gallup poll commissioned by the Glass Packaging Institute showed that more than 50 percent of Americans would change their purchasing habits to buy food and beverage containers that recycle. London's *Financial Times* reports similar trends in Britain. Some McDonald's franchises ask their customers to separate garbage before throwing it away. Procter and Gamble is using containers made of 20 to 100 percent recycled plastic for a number of its products. The Scotch Corporation, a chemical manufacturer in Dallas, has introduced plastic pouches of concentrated household cleaners that consumers can mix with water and use to refill empty spray bottles.

Ruffies and Good Sense are plastic bag brands that are photodegradable. Anheuser-Busch now uses only photodegradable plastic yokes to hold six-packs together. Varta, a West German manufacturer, makes batteries that contain no air-polluting cadmium or mercury.

Smart manufacturers are capitalizing on the nascent signs of a swing towards more recycling, by including "Recycled Goods" or "No CFCs" on product labels. The best labeling approach, and one already in use in Germany, Canada, and elsewhere, is a kind of universal code that guarantees a product is environmentally benign or recommended. Dorothy MacKenzie, director of product development at a New York and London–based consulting firm, has studied such movements in Europe and North America and is convinced they will proliferate. "Just as the 1980s saw a proliferation of 'lite' products designed to meet growing consumer health awareness, the 1990s will be the decade of 'green' products designed, packaged, and marketed with a strong environmental perspective," she told a reporter.

The symbol used in Canada boasts three intertwined doves. Surveys show that Canadians are prepared to pay more for environmentally friendly products that carry this symbol. Standards require that the products be nontoxic, derived from renewable resources, recyclable and/or biodegradable, and sold in packaging that meets criteria established by a 14-member products advisory board.

In Japan, environmentally approved products carry a logo called an Ecomark. The West German mark is called the Blue Angel, and has been awarded to 2,000 consumer products over the past 10 years. In Sweden, newspaper ads boast 100-percent recycled goods from paper to toothpaste containers, all without excessive packaging. In the United States, supermarket chains including A&P, Winn-Dixie, Kroger, and Safeway sell products with a "Recycled" label (three arrows following each other around a circle). A loose coalition of industry and environmental groups is pushing for one international logo, which would be recognized worldwide as the sign of an environmentally sound product.

Garbage has long been one of the world's greatest bargains—easy to accumulate, just as easy to get rid of. Now we're paying the price for past negligence. If we are to stem the sweeping tide of trash, we must adopt integrated, organized, solid-waste management. It doesn't sound very sexy, but it's a must.

Experts believe that we should ultimately be able to reduce at least 10 percent and recycle more than 50 percent of consumer waste, given proper technology, careful handling, and lots of cooperation. Recycling processes have their own flaws—glass making, paper pulping and bleaching, and steel, aluminum, and copper smelting all produce toxic emissions and residues that must be disposed of. Water pollution from these industries is also a concern, as are the currently limited markets for recycled goods. Still, reduction and recycling should be the goal, and both should be promoted over incineration.

"What we need to do is get rid of the garbage, not just move it through one more machine," says Thomas Webster, research associate at the Center for Biology of Natural Systems at Queens College in New York. "To get high levels of recycling you have to work hard. You need legislative strategies and you need political will. But once you have the systems in place, you've solved the problem."

The world's future economic stability depends on how we use three things: energy, raw materials, and money. Governments now spend far too much collecting and disposing of garbage. Billions more are spent on the environmental damage caused by out-of-control consumption. Making the transition to a sustainable, recycling society will result in both better economies and healthier environments.

People are not without power. By reducing the amount of waste they produce and recycling a large

A discarded tire on the beach in Santa Monica, California, is just a fraction of the one billion tons of waste discarded by humans each year.

share of their discards, individuals can have an effect. But consumers cannot effect change without the support of government and industry. The degree to which people and nations work together to conserve raw materials and resources will determine the rate at which the global environment is altered.

The challenge does not lie so much with more "technical fixes" but with our approach to the world around us. "There will always be another landfill" cannot be the words we live by, because we are simply running out of room. The time for the shift from throwaway society to conserving society has arrived.

GARBAGE

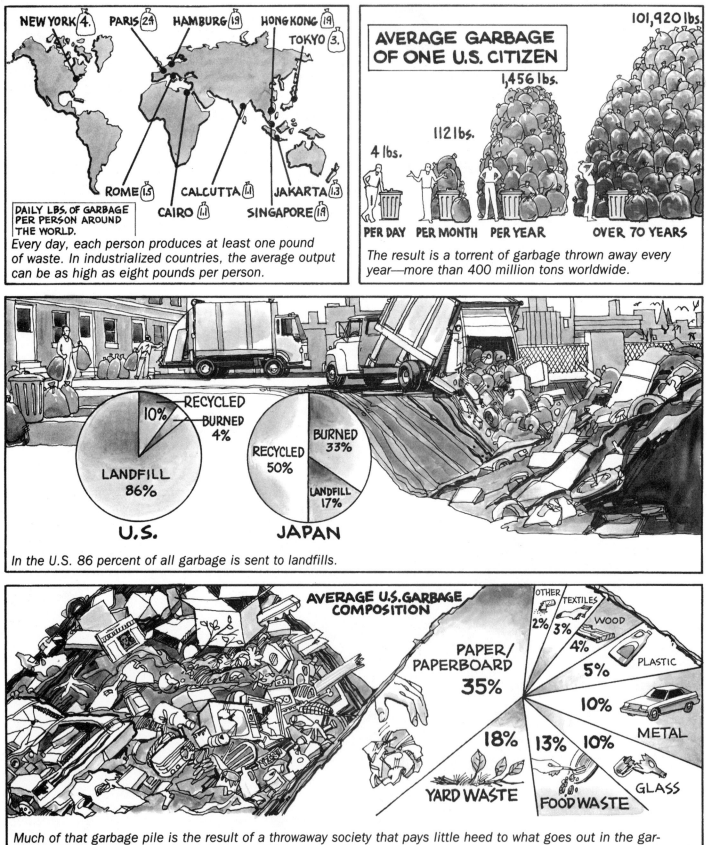

DAILY LBS. OF GARBAGE PER PERSON AROUND THE WORLD.

NEW YORK 4.   PARIS 2.4   HAMBURG 1.9   HONG KONG 1.9   TOKYO 3.   ROME 1.5   CALCUTTA 1.1   JAKARTA 1.3   CAIRO 1.1   SINGAPORE 1.9

Every day, each person produces at least one pound of waste. In industrialized countries, the average output can be as high as eight pounds per person.

AVERAGE GARBAGE OF ONE U.S. CITIZEN

4 lbs. PER DAY   112 lbs. PER MONTH   1,456 lbs. PER YEAR   101,920 lbs. OVER 70 YEARS

The result is a torrent of garbage thrown away every year—more than 400 million tons worldwide.

U.S.
RECYCLED 10%
BURNED 4%
LANDFILL 86%

JAPAN
RECYCLED 50%
BURNED 33%
LANDFILL 17%

In the U.S. 86 percent of all garbage is sent to landfills.

AVERAGE U.S. GARBAGE COMPOSITION

PAPER/PAPERBOARD 35%
OTHER 2%
TEXTILES 3%
WOOD 4%
PLASTIC 5%
METAL 10%
GLASS 10%
FOOD WASTE 13%
YARD WASTE 18%

Much of that garbage pile is the result of a throwaway society that pays little heed to what goes out in the garbage. Much of the world's waste heap could be prevented.

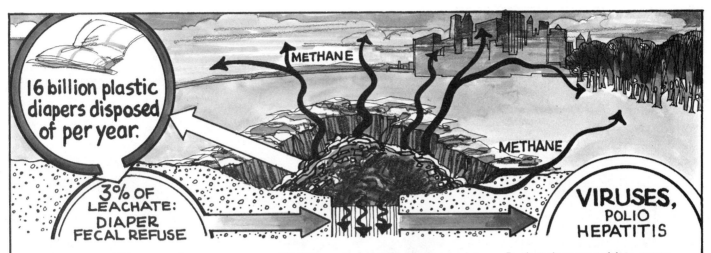

16 billion plastic diapers disposed of per year.

METHANE

METHANE

3% OF LEACHATE: DIAPER FECAL REFUSE

VIRUSES, POLIO HEPATITIS

Once in the landfill, waste decomposes, provided there is enough air and moisture. During decomposition, some waste produces methane, a volatile gas which can leak into the soil, killing vegetation, and seep into nearby buildings.

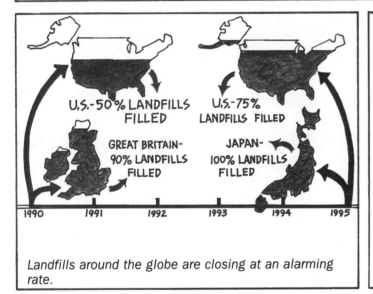

U.S.-50% LANDFILLS FILLED

U.S.-75% LANDFILLS FILLED

GREAT BRITAIN- 90% LANDFILLS FILLED

JAPAN- 100% LANDFILLS FILLED

1990 1991 1992 1993 1994 1995

Landfills around the globe are closing at an alarming rate.

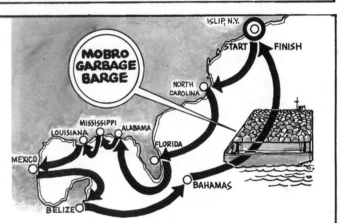

MOBRO GARBAGE BARGE

ISLIP, N.Y.

START FINISH

NORTH CAROLINA

MISSISSIPPI ALABAMA

LOUISIANA

FLORIDA

MEXICO

BAHAMAS

BELIZE

As a result, garbage is increasingly transported to dump-sites across state and national borders. In 1987, one garbage barge spent a six-month, 2,000-mile journey in search of a dumpsite.

ACID RAIN

ELECTRICITY & STEAM PRODUCED BY BURNING WASTE

SULFUR DIOXIDE AND NITROGEN OXIDES

CARBON MONOXIDE AND HYDROCARBONS

DIOXINS TOXIC ASH

SMOG

HAZARDOUS WASTE

WASTE BURNING PLANT

One highly debated alternative to landfills is incineration. Although such burn plants can produce electricity or steam for heat and power, they may produce more pollution, especially in the toxic ash left after burning.

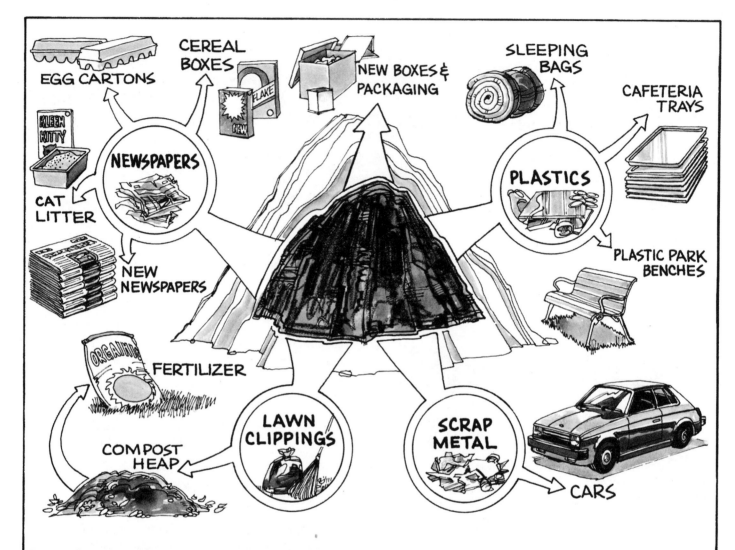

CEREAL BOXES

EGG CARTONS

NEW BOXES & PACKAGING

SLEEPING BAGS

CAFETERIA TRAYS

NEWSPAPERS

PLASTICS

CAT LITTER

NEW NEWSPAPERS

PLASTIC PARK BENCHES

FERTILIZER

LAWN CLIPPINGS

SCRAP METAL

COMPOST HEAP

CARS

Recycling is increasing around the world. Estimates are that we could recycle at least one third of the garbage we throw away, which would limit the growth of the world's garbage heap.

Excess packaging is one of the key waste products that needs to be reduced.

About one quarter of all waste is disposable goods. The only real solution to the garbage problem is to concentrate on making products reusable or recyclable.

Individual Action

1. Learn what is and is not recyclable, and what products recycled goods are used in. Remember, just because it's collected doesn't necessarily mean it's recycled. There are warehouses around the country filled with newspapers and plastic milk jugs waiting to be recycled. If your community doesn't have a recycling program, it should. Lobby whomever necessary, from state senators down to town clerks.

Glass: Clear, amber, and green glass is recyclable; milk-white glass, plate glass, light bulbs, fluorescent bulbs, and crystal are not. Before taking bottles or jars to the recycling center rinse them out; labels can stay on. Remove metal rings, separate by color and do not break. Roughly 90 percent of all old bottles can be made into new bottles, or used for glasphalt to pave streets and in bricks, tiles, and reflective paint for road signs.

Paper: Recycle all newsprint, corrugated boxes, egg cartons, junk mail, telephone books, computer cards, and print-out paper. Waxed or plastic-coated cellophane cannot be recycled. Stack and tie newspapers, break down cardboard. Recycled paper comes back as game boards, record jackets, grocery store food boxes, book covers, gift boxes, jigsaw puzzles, paper matches, game/show tickets, and more.

Aluminum: Recycle all cans, foil, TV trays, ice-cube trays, aluminum siding, storm doors, windows, gutters, and lawn furniture. One hundred percent of recycled cans can be made into new cans. Other aluminum items are made into similar products or castings for car parts.

Metals: Test all metals with a magnet. If the magnet *does* stick to them, they can be recycled. Most ferrous metals, like cast iron, steel sheet metal, tin-coated metals and bi-metal cans, can be recycled. For non-ferrous metals like nickel, bronze, copper, brass, and lead, first check with your recycler.

Plastics: Recycle all plastic containers. Rinse them, remove metal caps. The recycled product is used for fiber-filling for jackets, flowerpots, paintbrush bristles, and plastic strapping for shipping.

2. Reuse items whenever possible. Avoid bulky, disposable items. Buy products in reusable containers. Reuse wrapping paper, plastic bags, boxes, and lumber. Give clothes to friends or charity. Donate old appliances to Goodwill, or a local charity.

3. Encourage source reduction. In industrial countries, packaging contributes about 50 percent of the volume of household waste. Keep this in mind when shopping. When buying toothpaste, for example, consider if it is really necessary that it comes in a box and goes home in a paper or plastic bag, too.

4. Precycle. A new concept, it implies simply that you should consider the end result of everything you buy and where it will eventually rest. Choose products carefully, consider the environmental impact of each: Is it safe? Is it reusable? Is it recyclable?

5. Compost. Food and yard waste are second in the volume of landfill space they occupy after packaging materials. If you don't have room at home, encourage your community to establish neighborhood compost heaps.

6. Burning anything, from leaves to computer paper, creates toxic emissions. Incinerate only as a last resort.

7. **First Investors in New York encourages its** employees to pick up at least one piece of trash or litter on the way to and from work and toss it in the nearest trash can. If every company and school encouraged similar programs, streets would be cleaner.

8. **If your community doesn't recycle plastic,** urge them to.

9. **Refillable glass bottles only require a thorough** washing after each use, and are designed for 30 round trips from the store shelf to the consumer. Consider them when possible over plastics.

10. **Shop where you can get fruits and vegetables** without plastic wrapping.

11. **At cookouts, wash and reuse plastic silverware** and plates, or use paper plates instead of Styrofoam.

12. **Don't buy tampons with plastic applicators.**

13. **Save paper whenever possible. Make** double-sided copies when photocopying, reuse paper bags, reuse scrap paper for notes.

14. **Encourage your local grocery store to** carry both paper and plastic bags; better yet, carry your own string bag, which you can reuse many times, to the store.

15. **Encourage your elected officials to levy** a tax on packaging used for food prepared for immediate consumption (e.g., fast-food containers).

16. **Buy durable products, like cloth napkins,** silverware, cloth diapers, multiple-use razors, lighters, and pens, rather than disposables.

17. **When things break—from televisions to** tricycles—fix them rather than dump them.

18. **Share newspapers, magazines, and catalogs** with others. Don't subscribe to any you don't read.

19. **Have garage sales or charity pickups** rather than simply throwing away household goods you've tired of.

20. **Consider having your milk delivered by** a dairy, in refillable bottles. If you buy spring water, use a service that delivers large refillable bottles instead of buying individual bottles at the store.

21. **Buy nickel-cadmium batteries for your** Walkmans and cameras, and recharge them. Also, though alkaline batteries cost more, they last longer than carbon-zinc batteries and are a better value.

22. **Don't be afraid to speak out, whether in** your community or by letters to manufacturers, about the importance of source reduction and recycling.

23. **Find out what scrap processors in your** community will take, or buy. Investigate all the various recyclable markets—for cans, paper, household scraps, tires, etc.

24. **Consider designing or redesigning your** house/life style to accommodate recycling. Two books that will help are: *Redesigning the American Dream,* by Dolores Hayden (Norton, 1984) and *Smart Kitchen: How to Design a Comfortable, Safe, Energy-Efficient and Money-Saving Workspace,* by David Goldbeck (Ceres Press).

25. **Encourage recycled and recyclable goods** at work, including all stationery, brochures, and catalogs, as well as buying recycled packaging.

26. **Be a smart, determined shopper. If you're** not happy with your grocer because he/she refuses to stop using polystyrene to wrap meats and vegetables, organize a group to talk to the store manager. Also encourage him/her to put more "recycled" and "recyclable" products on the shelves.

27. **If you really want to watch what you buy,** write the U.S. Council on Economic Priorities, which distributes "Shopping for a Better World," a 128-page booklet that rates 138 U.S. companies and their products in 10 areas of social performance, one of which is the environment. (Send $5.95 to 30 Irving Place, New York, NY 10003, 212-420-1133 or 800-822-6435. In Great Britain, *The Green Consumer Guide* (London: Victor Gollancz, 1989) provides similar information. Seventh Generation's catalogue offers environmentally sound household cleaners, children's items, biodegradable diapers, energy efficient lightbulbs, and more. Send $2 to 10 Farrell Street, South Burlington, VT 05403, 802-862-2999.

28. **Anyone can buy recycled printing and** writing paper. The largest brokers in the United States are Conservatree Paper Company, 10 Lombard Street, Suite 250, San Francisco, CA 94111, 800-522-9200, or 415-433-1000 (in California), and Earthcare Paper Company, PO Box 3335, Madison, WI 53704, 608-256-5522. Both will send catalogs, and Earthcare specializes in small orders.

29. **Encourage reverse vending machines in** your neighborhood. They make recycling aluminum cans a breeze. Just put the cans in, and get a deposit back. They save retailers time and money. More than 12,000 are in use worldwide. Sweden has one third of the total, and most of the rest are in Norway, France, and the United States. Most read universal codes and come in indoor and outdoor models. Bottle bills should also be a priority of all state and national legislatures, requiring deposits on cans and bottles.

30. **Carry clean forks, knives, spoons, even** plastic straws in your purse, briefcase, or car so that when going to a fast-food restaurant, you won't have to use their plastic utensils.

31. **If your community burns or is considering** incinerating garbage, organize or join the opposition.

32. **Save margarine tubs, Styrofoam trays,** juice cans, toilet paper, and paper-towel rolls for children's arts and crafts. Encourage teachers to reuse household supplies in the classroom.

Government Action

1. **Recycling laws should be adopted in every** nation, state and community.

2. **Recycling operations should be provided** with guarantees of minimum supplies, similar to those already offered to incinerators and landfill operators.

3. **Deposit laws for bottles and cans should** be mandated in all states.

4. **Garbage collection should be paid for by** user fees—which more fairly distribute the costs—instead of through property taxes.

5. **Higher taxes should be imposed on non-**recyclable or disposable products.

6. **Non-degradable plastics should be banned.**

7. **Packaging standards for both retail and** wholesale merchandise should be required.

Reading

Worldwatch Paper #76: "Mining Urban Wastes: The Potential for Recycling," by Cynthia Pollock. Worldwatch Institute, April 1987. 1776 Massachusetts Ave. NW, Washington, DC 20036.

Garbage Management in Japan: Leading the Way, by Allen Hershkowitz and Eugene Salerni. INFORM, Inc., 1986. 381 Park Ave. South, New York, NY 10016, 212-689-4040.

"Solid Waste Management: The Garbage Challenge for New York City," INFORM (see above).

Garbage Burning: Lessons from Europe, by Allen Hershkowitz. INFORM (see above).

"No Time to Waste: Starting Waste Reduction, Recycling and Reuse Programs to Stop Incineration and Landfilling. A Citizen's Guide," by Walter L. T. Hang and Steven A. Romalewski. New York Public Interest Research Group, 9 Murray Street, New York, NY 10007, 212-349-6460.

"The Fascinating World of Trash," by Peter T. White. *National Geographic,* April 1983.

"Recycling: Coming of Age," by Barbara Goldoftas. *Technology Review,* November/December 1987.

"The Trashing of America," by Ellen Kunes. *Omni,* February 1988.

"Trash Clash," by Paul Frumkin. *Restaurant Business,* May 20, 1989.

To Burn or Not to Burn, by Dan Kirshner and Adam C. Stern. Environmental Defense Fund, 257 Park Ave. South, New York, NY 10010.

Coming Full Circle: Successful Recycling Today, Environmental Defense Fund (see above).

Garbage: Practices, Problems & Remedies, by Joanne D. Underwood, Allen Hershkowitz, and Maarten de Kadt. INFORM (see above), 1988.

Proven Profits from Pollution Prevention (316-page book of case studies). Institute for Local Self-Reliance, 2425 18th St. NW, Washington, DC 20009.

How to Recycle Waste Paper, American Paper Institute, 260 Madison Ave., New York, NY 10017.

Recycling: 101 Practical Tips for Home and Work, by Susan Hassol and Beth Richman. Snowmass, CO: The Windstar Foundation, 1989.

Blueprint for a Green Planet: Your Practical Guide to Restoring the World's Environment, by John Seymour and Herbert Girardet. New York: Prentice-Hall, 1987.

Organizations to Contact

Center for Plastics Recycling Research, Rutgers, The State University, Building 3529, Busch Campus, Piscataway, NJ 08855.

Environmental Defense Fund Recycling Hotline, 800-CALLEDF.

INFORM, Inc., 381 Park Ave. South, New York, NY 10016, 212-689-4040.

Institute for Local Self-Reliance, Publications, 2425 18th St. NW, Washington, DC 20009.

National Association of Recycling Industries, 330 Madison Ave., New York NY 10017.

National Center for Resource Recovery Inc., 1211 Connecticut Ave. NW, Washington DC 20036.

Polystyrene Packaging Council Inc., 1025 Connecticut Ave. NW, Suite 513, Washington, DC, 20036, 202-822-6424.

Resource Conservation and Recovery Hotline, 800-424-9346.

Society of the Plastics Industry, Literature Sales, 1275 K St. NW, Suite 400, Washington, DC 20005, 202-371-5200. (Request *Plastic Bottle Recycling Directory,* $5).

U.S. Environmental Protection Agency, Office of Solid Waste Management Programs, 401 M St. SW, Washington, DC 20460, 202-382-4627.

THE LAND

7

Hazardous Waste

All of the pollutions we've considered so far have involved "hazardous emissions" of some kind or another. The greenhouse effect is fueled by inordinate discharges of carbon dioxide, hydrocarbons, and other chemical compounds; the ozone hole widens as releases of chlorofluorocarbons increase; acid rain and smog are created by dangerous man-made chemical combinations; the forests and the oceans are threatened by poisons of man's creation. The hazardous emissions that are the subject of this chapter are not invisible chemical compounds. Instead they are bulky, toxic wastes that are too often dumped in ponds behind manufacturing plants, carted to landfills, or sitting beneath your kitchen sink.

While the volume of dangerous wastes is becoming a bigger percentage of the garbage heap, their disposal continues to be by and large an afterthought for both manufacturers and consumers. They drift up into the air and are poured (some legally) directly into rivers and streams. Manufacturers dump them in on-site landfills or pay big money to have them shipped across state lines or to another country. At home we nonchalantly toss half-full cans of paint thinner and pesticides into the garbage, their destination the local dump. Sooner or later all these "disposed of" chemicals seep into the groundwater and are headed for the kitchen tap. They do not discriminate in their injuries. Whether they leak from abandoned waste sites underground or industrial dumps or are washed down the kitchen drain, they pose a serious threat to the health of both the environment and people.

Recognizing the problem is simple; eliminating hazardous waste is not. Despite its tenacity (like a bad cold, hazardous wastes can be very difficult to shake) there are a variety of ways this pile of dangerous waste can be reduced. Solutions are even within easy grasp of the individual. First, one simple rule should apply when dealing with all chemicals, whether they come in 65-gallon drums or are packaged as bathroom air fresheners: the fewer we use, the fewer we have to throw away. As with the other effluvia we send to the landfill, *reduction* of hazardous waste should be the goal—and responsibility—of government, industry, and consumers.

CAUSES

Because of its mysterious effects and potential "explosiveness," hazardous waste seems a more frightening pollutant than acid rain, which works its harm relatively unobtrusively. Yet the attitude that has allowed the hazardous waste problem to grow over the years is an extension of the Disposable Society's "out of sight, out of mind" credo: Bury it, burn it, inject it deep into the ground, anything so that we don't have to face it. But facing it, reducing the piles, slowing its production, must now be done.

In the early 1970s, dirty skies and polluted streams made the headlines, not hazardous waste. Public protest helped encourage the passage of laws aimed at protecting the air and water. Some protests and laws indirectly addressed the problem of hazardous waste, but it got less attention—until the morning in 1978 when leaking barrels of toxic chemicals surfaced from their burial grounds at Love Canal, near Niagara Falls, New York. That day, hazardous waste became a front-page story.

Over the previous four decades Hooker Chemical and the Olin Corporation had disposed of 22,000 tons of toxic chemicals in an old canal at the edge of the U.S.-Canada border town. By the mid-1970s, barrels of dangerous poisons filled the 3,000-foot-long, 60-foot-wide ditch. The company's purposeful malfeasance surfaced in surrounding neighborhoods, in the alarming rates of miscarriages, birth defects, blood disease, epilepsy, hyperactivity, and cancer.

Today, there are thousands of "Love Canals" scattered around the world. Many cover much larger areas and involve more potent substances than were dumped near Niagara Falls. Unfortunately, many are discovered only after sickness and disease begin to fell dump-site neighbors.

Industrial chemicals are used everywhere, and their ubiquity is the basis of the problem. They are used to make steel, paper, wood products, plastics, pesticides, and much else. The list of *dangerous* chemicals we come in contact with every day is long and runs the gamut from "A" to "Z," from acetaldehyde, used in making plastic, drugs, and dyes, to zinc, used in car parts, electroplating, batteries, electrical products, and fungicides. More than 80,000 different industrial chemicals are used worldwide. These materials are costly to make and expensive to get rid of. And the costs, whether in terms of human health, damage to the environment, or the pocketbook, are borne by everyone. Taxpayers' money is spent to protect the environment, cover increased health costs, and in attempts to revise damage already done to water and air. In the United States, Congress has appropriated $4.5 billion since 1980 to clean up the 1,175 worst toxic-waste dumps under the banner of the much-publicized Superfund. Only half of that money has been spent, and only 34 of the waste sites have been cleaned up. According to a study by the Rand Corporation's Institute for Civil Justice, as many as 30,000 more dumps will eventually need to be cleaned up.

Hundreds of millions of pounds of hazardous waste are produced each year around the world. Hard figures are difficult to come by, because every nation defines hazardous waste differently. The debate on how best to dispose of it all has become a full-time occupation for thousands of government and industry employees and environmental watchdogs. In the United States, the Congressional Budget Office estimates that two thirds of our hazardous waste is disposed of in injection wells, pits, ponds, lagoons, or landfills. Another one fifth is discharged directly into rivers and streams. Only a small percentage is recycled or detoxified. (By comparison, West Germany detoxifies 35 percent of the hazardous waste it collects.) But even if treatment, recycling, or detoxification efforts were to increase 100-fold, the only way to stem the tide of poisons is to use fewer chemicals, and thus produce less hazardous waste. Rather than spend time and money figuring out how to get rid of their leftover phenol, manufacturers should simply come up with ways to use less phenol, perhaps by substituting a less toxic chemical. Consumers should buy recyclable batteries instead of throwing their Walkman retirees into the garbage. We should substitute baking soda or any of the half-dozen nontoxic alternatives for Drano.

The hazardous waste challenge is hardly peculiar to the United States. In Poland and the Soviet Union, towns have been declared "unfit for human habitation" due to dangerous toxic dumps. In Nepal, hardly a major industrial center, rivers and streams are polluted eyesores, thanks to the spread of battery manufacturers, chemical companies, paint and dye producers, and textile mills. England dumps much of its hazardous waste down old mines and directly into the North Sea. Italy, Sweden, and other nations pay to have their toxic waste burned on roaming, seaborne incinerator ships. East Germany sells the right to dump toxic waste to just about anyone in the international community, and buries it in crude pits. Such nonchalance can be life-threatening, as the Japanese town of Minamata illustrates. The effects of mercury dumping near the town's groundwater have been felt since the 1950s. A disfiguring paralysis has ruined the lives of 800 people so far, and is expected to affect thousands more in the coming years.

According to the Conservation Foundation in Washington, D.C., urban areas like Mexico City, São Paulo, Seoul, Jakarta, Lagos, Lima, and Calcutta are threatened by hazardous waste pollution because these cities are poor, densely populated, and boast fast-growing industrial sections. India now has an estimated 4,000 chemical factories and most of its toxic waste goes to landfills or directly into rivers or streams without treatment. China produces 400 million tons of industrial waste each year, much of it hazardous, which is dumped on the outskirts of cities or released into surface waters. Far too many people on the planet are surrounded, according to one environmental theory, by an inescapable "circle of poison."

Eventually, hundreds of billions of dollars will be spent on cleaning up the thousands of hazardous waste sites discovered since the disclosures at Love Canal. Fingers can be pointed in all directions. The Department of Defense is a major contributor; so are giant international companies like Westinghouse, Dow, General Electric, Monsanto, and Union Carbide.

To date, cleaning up hazardous waste has proven to be a difficult task, and banning the burial of wastes is rarely effective. If one state outlaws such burial (as California has), there's always another state (like Nevada), or a foreign nation that will gladly take it. Stiffer regulations help; so do fines. But according to one EPA official, "60 percent of major disposal facilities don't obey the laws and regulations anyway, nor pay the fines."

The increasingly common practice of shipping hazardous waste across state and international borders is perplexing. It is nothing more than a high-stakes game of "juggle the poison." It answers none of the problems, just creates new ones. Americans generate roughly 275 million tons of hazardous waste each year, more than a ton per citizen. The United States is one of the leading exporters of toxic waste. (That doesn't include the thousands of tons that are sent into the atmosphere from the exhaust pipes of cars, waft from toxic dump sites, or otherwise go undetected or unreported.) Most of the measurable mass is legally burned or buried. The rest, up to a third, is shipped and trucked to Canada, Mexico, India, South Korea, Nigeria, and Zimbabwe. "Out of site, out of mind."

Toxic waste exportation is practiced worldwide. According to the Organization for Economic Cooperation and Development, 100,000 to 120,000 international shipments of toxic waste, amounting to 2.5 million metric tons, originate each year in Western Europe alone. So far laws against these exports are thin and hard to enforce.

Another by-product of modern civilization that continues to haunt the environment is nuclear waste. It is dumped in the ocean, buried in land, and shipped from country to country. While generally more tightly controlled than chemical waste, leaks of radioactive materials have occurred in many countries. The most horrific example of such accidental release in the past decade occurred in the Soviet Union at Chernobyl in 1986. Contamination from the accidental reactor meltdown spread over much of Europe, contaminating the food chain for many years to come. The long-term health effects remain uncertain, but estimates suggest that 5,000 to 50,000 additional cancer deaths may result over the next 30 to 60 years.

Siting radioactive waste dumps has proven extremely difficult. The U.S. Department of Energy spent $7.8 billion on creating new nuclear weapons in 1988, yet the department estimates it will take between $4 and $17 billion to clean up the high-level radioactive waste at just one production site, its Hanford nuclear plant. The department faces monumental challenges as it attempts to come up with a safe and satisfactory way to get rid of all the dangerous waste that is piling up. The opening of the first underground repository for nuclear waste has been postponed, due to both public protest and infrastructure concerns. (Cracks in the underground facility are surfacing two to three times faster than expected.) While the delay has allowed more time to address safety concerns and to meet regulatory requirements, it has caused additional problems for the department, which is quickly running out of storage space. The $700 million repository, dug 2,000 feet below the desert surface near Carlsbad, New Mexico, may not be ready for some years, if ever. For the time being plutonium-contaminated waste generated at the nation's largest nuclear weapons plant at Rocky Flats, near Denver, is stored in Idaho. But Idaho shut its doors to shipments in 1989. Rocky Flats may be shut down if new storage space can't be found.

In the meantime, approximately 15,000 metric tons of spent uranium fuel, still highly radioactive but unusable, is sitting in huge pools of water at the 106 licensed nuclear power plants across the United States, waiting to be transported to a permanent—and safe—home. The Department of Energy estimates that by the turn of the century, wastes will have mounted to 50,000 tons. By then, current storage will be maximized, and the repositories will be dangerously radioactive for at least 10,000 years.

Finding a home for even low-level radioactive waste continues to frustrate officials. Generated by nuclear reactors, hospitals, research centers, and companies licensed to handle radioactive materials, such waste includes items like workers' clothes, tools, machine parts, and resins. Communities around the globe are fighting the location of such dump sites in their backyards, options are narrowing, and the problem mounts.

The results of the first National Inventory of Toxic Releases into the Environment—an effort to quantify the toxic waste that is dumped each year into the air, land, and sea—was distributed in April 1989, and showed that manufacturers required to report their activities released or disposed of at least 22.5 billion pounds of toxic substances in 1987. The report concluded, understatedly, that industry in the United States "is putting a startling and unacceptably high" volume of toxic substances into the land, air, and water. (Thirty companies said they each spewed at least a million pounds of hazardous waste. Eastman Kodak Company, of Rochester, New York, took the prize as top emitter of a single toxic air pollutant that year. The company sent more than 8.9 million pounds of methylene chloride into the atmosphere.)

The report admitted that its conclusions did not give a true indication of total emissions. Twenty-five percent of the companies required by law to fill out the report did not. Those that did reported on only 300 chemicals. The figures also did not take into account car and truck emissions or runoff from farms and city streets, and did not include what are known as "small quantity generators," those who produce under 100 pounds of hazardous waste a month and were not required to report.

Responses to the mind-boggling figures were hardly muted. "We are assaulting the environment with toxic emissions. . . . ," concluded one senator. An environmental toxicologist working for the National Wildlife Federation, the nation's largest conservation group, said the inventory proves that "[our] program for controlling toxic pollution has failed."

A major source of hazardous waste remains virtually unregulated, and uninformed—you, me, and the person next door. Four million tons of hazardous waste a year come from our careless disposal

Radioactive Waste in the United States

Radioactive wastes, which are generated at each stage of the processing of nuclear materials, are divided into five categories by the U.S. federal government. The total accumulations of radioactive waste in the United States, including wastes from defense uses, are shown below.

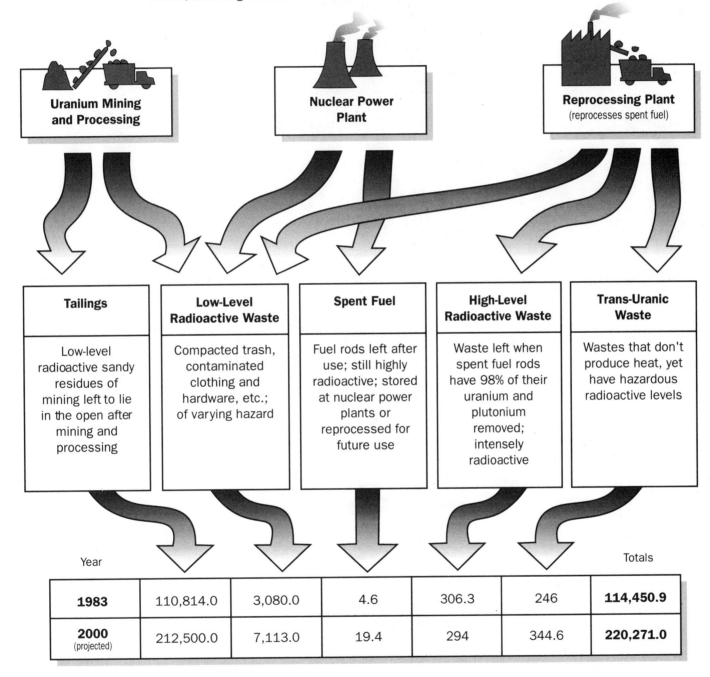

	Tailings	**Low-Level Radioactive Waste**	**Spent Fuel**	**High-Level Radioactive Waste**	**Trans-Uranic Waste**	
	Low-level radioactive sandy residues of mining left to lie in the open after mining and processing	Compacted trash, contaminated clothing and hardware, etc.; of varying hazard	Fuel rods left after use; still highly radioactive; stored at nuclear power plants or reprocessed for future use	Waste left when spent fuel rods have 98% of their uranium and plutonium removed; intensely radioactive	Wastes that don't produce heat, yet have hazardous radioactive levels	
Year						Totals
1983	110,814.0	3,080.0	4.6	306.3	246	**114,450.9**
2000 (projected)	212,500.0	7,113.0	19.4	294	344.6	**220,271.0**

Accumulated Radioactive Waste in the United States, from Commercial and Defense Use, in Thousands of Cubic Meters*

* Cubic Meter = 1.308 Cubic Yards
Sources: Natural Resources Defense Council; *Worldwatch Paper 75*: "Reassessing Nuclear Power : The Fallout From Chernobyl," by Christopher Flavin. Worldwatch Institute, March 1987.

Until we discovered that it caused lung cancer, asbestos was thought to be a perfect building material and was used widely. Workers today are especially trained and equipped to deal with its removal, transportation, and storage. But hundreds of chemical products are still introduced each year without adequate testing.

of insect sprays, antifreeze, chlorine bleach, nail polish, and dozens of other household effluents. Only a handful of the nation's 15,000 municipal landfills separate out these household hazardous wastes before they seep from landfills and into groundwater, or are incinerated.

It may help to visualize the problem this way: Hazardous household waste composes only half of 1 percent of the garbage thrown out in each house. That may not seem like much, but it adds up. Each person in the United States throws away one ton of garbage annually; the New York City metropolitan area, with a population of 18 million people, throws away about 90,000 tons of hazardous waste, from nail polish to battery acid, every year.

EFFECTS

The health costs of our reckless disposal of hazardous waste continue to grow. Of the 80,000 chemicals in existence, just a small percentage have been adequately tested as to their potential for harm to both the environment and human health. Little is known about the effects of chemicals when they are mixed, whether in groundwater or in an industrial pond. And each year, 1,500 new chemicals are introduced, their potential dangers unknown.

The long-term effects of hazardous and radioactive waste are felt every day, if subtly. While Chernobyl, Bhopal, and Love Canal may stand out, smaller leaks and dump sites are affecting people's health around the globe every minute. For example, a school in Jersey City, New Jersey, was closed in 1989 after more than a third of students tested showed high levels of dangerous chromium in their urine. Chromium dust blown from nearby vacant lots used for years as the dump sites of local refineries was found in air ducts, the library, the gym, cafeteria, and swimming pool. State health officials told the children and their families that so little research had been done on exposure to such dust that they couldn't even guess at its dangers.

It is this lack of knowledge that leaves policy-makers on shaky ground when it comes to regulating one chemical or another. The testing process is arduous. Even though up to 90 percent of industrial chemicals may be hazardous (according to the Natural Resources Defense Council), banning or outlawing them is difficult. Unfortunately, only accidents—and deaths—are taken seriously enough to encourage stricter laws.

SOLUTIONS

Despite the threat of impending toxic clouds and silent poisonings that discussions of hazardous waste inevitably invoke, there are many successful efforts being made to both clean up and reduce hazardous waste. Breaking poisonous compounds down into nontoxic waste is one approach. Better monitoring of waste disposal is another. Environmentalists who are encouraging industry to use fewer toxic chemicals in their manufacturing processes have made some headway. Ultimately, this is the key to eliminating the toxic waste threat. Individuals can make a difference, too, whether by reducing the amount of hazardous materials in their own home, making purchases based on whether or not dangerous chemicals or pesticides were used in a product's creation, or forcing industry's hand by protesting the spread of toxic waste dumps.

People who have studied hazardous waste disposal for years say the technologies and methods now exist to cut the generation of industrial waste by a third or more. Their optimism is fueled by growing public awareness, protests by communities and individuals, and increasing corporate and government recognition that simply dumping hazardous waste is no longer an option.

In 1985, homemaker Carol Boykin complained to the South Carolina highway department about an increase in heavy truck traffic along her rural road. When she learned that the trucks were feeding a hazardous waste dump, which was growing along with the traffic, she decided that filing a noise complaint was not nearly enough. She organized her neighbors, and launched a movement that may end up banning hazardous waste dumping statewide.

Boykin and two others founded "Citizens Asking for a Safe Environment " to protest the dump, which sat atop the Santee-Cooper lakes system and aquifers supplying most of southern South Carolina's drinking water. Initially, twelve people marched to protest the dump. Four years later, after pressuring local officials and resisting inertia, the group has more than 7,000 members. The dump closed for good in 1989, and the South Carolina legislature is considering a law which would ban all hazardous waste disposal in the state after 1991. "Unless we speak up," says Boykin, "we'll end up with something that is not only dangerous and harmful, but just plain wrong."

Similar actions are taking place in communities worldwide. Across Europe, Green Party politicians and activists have stopped the construction of several nuclear reactors and toxic dump sites and are trying to slow the export of hazardous wastes. In California, "Residents Against Pollution" successfully blocked a plan to use jet engines to burn hazardous waste in the center of Van Nuys. In Florida, "Concerned Citizens of Suwannee County for Safe and Progressive Community Development" shouted down a proposed hazardous waste incinerator in just six days. "Lincoln Park Area Concerned Citizens" in Colorado hired their own advisers with an EPA grant, to help coordinate a nearby Superfund cleanup.

Taking a different avenue toward the elimination of toxic wastes, scientists in industry and government are excited by recent successful experiments with so-called "plasma arc" torches, which can generate temperatures as hot as 10,000 degrees Fahr-

enheit. They can be used for torching otherwise hard-to-destroy compounds, like PCBs. The torch works like an arc welder, except that it reorders the dangerous waste into simple, nontoxic materials.

Such torching methods are being tested at the Love Canal site. The more than 22,000 tons of chemical wastes left behind, along with 17,000 gallons of toxic sludge in nearby holding tanks, are slowly being reduced to compounds that can safely be landfilled. Local officials regard the process as a dream come true. "Nobody in the world would accept that waste," said Norman Nosenchuck, New York State director of solid and hazardous waste.

Across the Hudson River in New Jersey, companies are being forced to clean up their own messes. Before corporations are allowed to sell property, they are required by the Environmental Cleanup Responsibility Act to cleanse any contaminated soil. The Burroughs Corporation, for example, had to spend nearly $1 million to remove tons of soil contaminated with diesel fuel. So far, $52 million has been spent by companies in the state on relatively simple cleanups at 600 sites. At 167 more sites, industries are spending another $73 million on cleanups. No state loans or grants are available, and while the effort has produced positive results, some companies have opted for bankruptcy over cleaning up.

Scientists are also experimenting with a process that separates organic chemicals from inorganic contaminants, using giant electrodes. When they are plugged into the ground or sludge, an electrical current is passed through the waste. What's left are piles of harmless solid waste, and a pile of radioactive atoms, which are easier to dispose of in this condensed form.

Still others are experimenting with a variety of biological processes. Tiny microbes dropped into contaminated water and soil neutralize the toxics as they eat the chemicals. Scientists at General Electric are confident they've developed a two-step bacterial process that can reduce PCBs in rivers and lakes by more than 70 percent in four to eight weeks.

But stumbling blocks remain on the road to slowing hazardous waste pollution. Waste continues to be burned around the globe, and, like garbage burning, is provoking loud and growing public protest. While a small percentage of hazardous waste is suitable for burning if properly policed by trained professionals, opponents are concerned that incineration just creates "landfills in the sky." Incineration simply creates more toxics, critics argue, and discourages waste reduction and recycling.

About 10 percent of all hazardous waste in the United States is legally disposed of in another questionable manner—it is pumped down injection wells thousands of feet deep. Under high pressure, treated waste is shot down steel pipes clad in concrete through layers of dense clay and into sand nearly a mile below the ground. A deep bed of hard shale lies below. This may sound like a satisfactory solution, but its main flaw is that the waste may hit cracks and crevices on its way down—and it almost assuredly does—and can then seep into the groundwater from which we drink.

As for the "export" of hazardous waste from state to state and country to country, many states and nations are clamping down on how much, if any, waste they will accept. The United Nations Environment Programme has proposed global standards for regulating such shipments. A treaty signed by Canada, France, Spain, Norway, Saudi Arabia, Mexico, Venezuela, the Philippines, and others will soon regulate hazardous waste shipped across national boundaries. In May 1988, the Organization of African Unity passed a resolution condemning the practice of accepting toxic chemicals from the industrial world, and various of its member nations are taking action to implement the declaration. That same month, the European Parliament urged its govern-

ments to adopt national legislation insuring that recipient countries can properly and safely handle the wastes. (So far only Belgium, Greece, and Denmark have adopted the directives as law.) In the United States, Congress is considering measures that would severely restrict such exports.

But some environmentalists oppose such restrictions. They feel that setting any standards or limits is a step backward, because it would still allow dangerous toxics to be shipped across national borders rather than eliminating them. Greenpeace and other environmental groups are calling for the industrialized countries to agree to a total ban on the export of both hazardous wastes and some pesticides. Until such a ban is accepted, they are calling for the international acceptance of the principle of "prior informed consent." This requires that wastes or restricted products not be exported unless importing countries fully understand the history—and potential dangers—of the chemicals.

Several European countries use innovative, if not quite perfected, systems to treat, detoxify, or incinerate much of their hazardous waste. In Denmark, toxic waste from 21 transfer stations is trucked to one giant treatment facility near the country's geographic center. An additional 300 smaller collection units gather paints, solvents, and other household hazardous wastes. Only a fourth of what is collected is landfilled. The rest is sent to the central system where it is turned into steam to heat the town's heating system, detoxified and released into the sewer system, or burned and sent into the atmosphere.

A similar system is employed in the West German state of Bavaria. Companies are charged anywhere from $38 to $368 per ton (the more toxic, the higher the fee) for accepting hazardous wastes. Industries are *required* to send their wastes to the treatment facilities, and the systems in both countries are financed by state and municipal governments. Critics of this approach say that energy is

In Western countries, landfill regulations for hazardous waste are being tightened and improved. For example, using this three-layered-plastic-lined pit prevents leakage (above) and specially trained toxic waste handlers wear protective garments (below). However, much of our hazardous waste is still disposed of irresponsibly.

still focused on waste "management" instead of waste "reduction."

In some respects, corporations are leading the way in waste reduction. Companies around the world are experimenting with changes in their manufacturing processes, operational reductions, new equipment, new formulas, or different chemicals to reduce the amount of compounds they use. (Admittedly, many are doing so before laws mandating such reductions sneak up on them.) Current efforts still affect just a small percentage of the dangerous waste industries churn out, but they are steps in the right direction:

• By changing production processes, 3M has reduced wastes by 50 percent over the past decade, saving more than $350 million in the process. The company reduced the amount of chemical solvents used in the coating phase of its tape-making operation, and now uses safer solid coatings instead. 3M also sells its ammonium sulfate to fertilizer makers, who convert the corrosive by-product of videotape manufacture into plant food.

• Cleo Wrap in Memphis, Tennessee, the world's largest producer of holiday wrapping paper, completed a six-year waste-reduction conversion project in 1986. Rather than relying on organic, solvent-based printing inks, all its operations now use water-based inks. The firm has virtually eliminated its generation of hazardous waste and saves $35,000 a year in waste disposal costs.

• A Borden Chemical plant in Fremont, California, has reduced the organics in its wastewater by 93 percent since 1981 through four changes in its handling of phenol and urea resins. The manufacturer took action after being told by the local sewage treatment operators that they could no longer handle the plant's highly toxic waste. Borden investigated other methods of treatment, including setting up their own sewage treatment facility, but

finally opted for eliminating as much phenol from its manufacturing processes as possible, and it worked.

• General Motors has begun storing auto-making supplies in reusable bulk containers, and now has fewer 55-gallon drums to dispose of.

• Dow Chemical has instituted a company-wide program called "Waste Reduction Always Pays," which emphasizes source reduction and recycling. Plants boast full-time WRAP coordinators and steering teams.

• In Sweden, pharmaceutical-maker Astra substitutes water for some solvents and has cut toxic wastes by half.

• At a pesticide plant in Colombia, Du Pont has introduced new equipment which recovers chemicals used in making fungicides, and as a result estimates that waste discharges have been cut by 95 percent.

While no company has solved all of its hazardous waste disposal problems, and while no country has figured out how to reduce its output to zero, research continues. The French government provides matching funds for companies researching waste-minimizing technologies. The Netherlands spends about $8 million annually on waste reduction research. Denmark recently spent $7.1 million on a three-year plan aimed at clean manufacturing technology. And in West Germany, a 1986 law tightening treatment and disposal requirements is expected to at least double, and perhaps triple, waste management costs, encouraging reduction.

In the United States, not enough energy is spent by government on waste reduction. Some states administer their own programs, but a coordinated national effort—and money—are needed. The EPA's 1988 budget request for waste "minimization" activities (rather than waste "reduction") totaled just $398,000. This kind of inadequate allocation was a

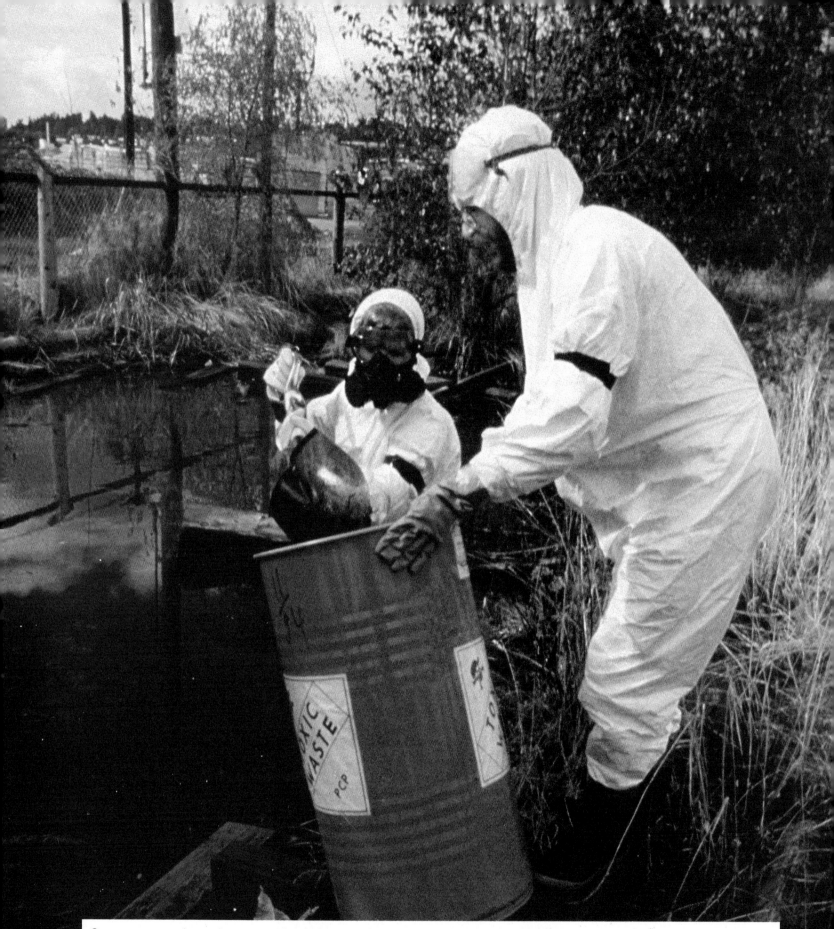

Greenpeace workers clean up toxic sludge at a paper mill. Paper mills and other industries use chlorine to bleach paper, thus producing a hazardous byproduct—dioxins, which have been linked to serious skin disorders, cancer, and immune system problems in humans.

holdover from the Reagan Administration. Its rationale was that a nation that had voted for less government would tolerate less protection of the environment. As a result of such policy-making, a growing accumulation of hazardous waste must now be disposed of. Hopefully new agendas—initiated by governments, corporations, and private citizens—will help slow the accumulation.

HAZARDOUS WASTE

Modern homes are warehouses for dangerous chemicals: they come in paints, cleansers, and dozens of other products. Asbestos has been found in baby powder and pesticides in shampoos. This abundance of poisons is harmful to the health of both the environment and man.

More than half the world's hazardous waste—produced by industry, thrown away in household garbage, or a by-product of nuclear energy—is dumped irresponsibly. At landfills, toxic liquids can seep into the groundwater; industry pumps hazardous chemicals into the sky; and some toxic wastes are stored in corrodible containers or poured directly onto the land or surface water.

Man-made chemicals permeate our environment. Studies indicate that small amounts of PCBs and dioxins (widely used industrial chemicals) are in the tissues of humans and animals worldwide.

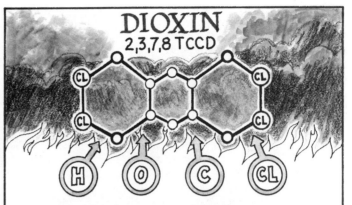

Dioxins may be industry's most hazardous chemical by-product, produced by a wide range of processes, including garbage incineration. Some dioxins have been found to be 30,000 times more carcinogenic than certain laboratory drugs used to give mice tumors.

Whether spewed from incinerators, floating in the water or buried in a landfill, dioxins affect the land, water, animals, and man. A dioxin leak from a chemical plant in the town of Seveso, Italy, forced the town's evacuation and, in the years following, was blamed for crop failures, birth defects, and an increased cancer rate.

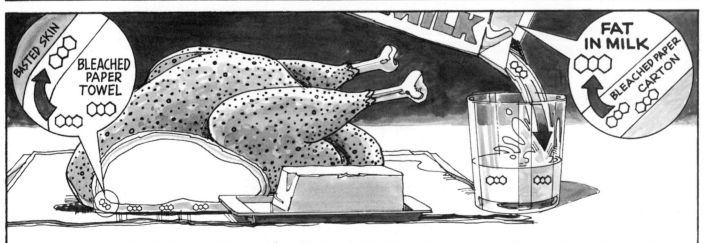

Dioxins are not confined to industrial emissions. Created during bleaching processes, they are found in paper towels, milk cartons, and writing paper. Dioxins are easily absorbed by fats, such as milk fat or the butter used to baste a turkey.

Of the 80,000 chemicals on the market, only a small percentage have been tested for their effects on man and nature. A good many have not even been named. Worldwide, 1,500 new chemicals are invented each year. Monitoring them all is necessary in order to predict their potential harms.

Incineration is one way to dispose of hazardous waste, but this produces more dioxins, pollutants, and toxic residue. Alternatives are being explored—some microbes (microscopic organisms) have been found that can eat toxics and convert them into harmless compounds.

These new methods are costly and experimental. The most efficient way to cut down on hazardous waste is by substituting benign for toxic chemicals. Simply using nontoxic cleaning agents at home is one way each individual can help.

Individual Action

Unlike acid rain or the greenhouse gases, the disposal of hazardous waste has a hands-on solution. Granted, you can't shovel the toxic waste created by chemical companies into a pit in the empty lot next door and be done with it. But the individual can help by being responsible for his/her own backyard. The first step toward lessening the amount of hazardous waste around us is to rid our households of dangerous wastes and to be careful not to accumulate more.

Throwing out toxic materials with the rest of the trash is a recipe for contaminated soil and groundwater. But each home continues to discard about 10 pounds of hazardous material each year, so the problem is growing. The only long-term solution is to reduce use.

Following the example of the Department of Defense or 3M, the goal at home should be waste reduction. If, like most, you know there are dangerous chemicals in your house, garage, or workshop that you don't know how to get rid of safely, find out about "amnesty days" and hazardous waste collection services. In many West German cities, brightly colored trucks loaded with barrels for solvents, acids, and chemicals make monthly rounds. In Japan, collection days are posted at recycling centers and people drop off everything from car batteries to mothballs. In Sweden and Switzerland, consumers may now return their used car batteries to retailers or to designated drop-off sites.

Collection days for toxics have been established in the United States since the early 1980s, though they are not yet widespread. (Roughly 2,000 have been held across the country since 1981; 600 were held in 1989.) Collection days have gained a higher priority in some states than in others. In Florida, for example, the state's environmental regulation department offers $500,000 in grants to help coun-

ties set up year-round collection sites for household hazardous waste. Florida's concern is great because of the region's vulnerable groundwater supply, which provides 90 percent of the state's drinking water, and which is susceptible to dangerous leakages from landfills and manufacturers. In California, San Bernadino County runs the nation's first permanent household hazardous waste collection center, and more than 25 other states now have programs aimed at developing collection programs.

Single collection days can be expensive. Sponsoring groups may spend from $5,000 to $100,000 to dispose of the items they collect at the appropriate toxic landfills, or to have it burned. More and more such groups are investigating detoxification of their collections, or recycling.

But even collection days or centers are not the ultimate solution. As worthy as these seem, the toxic chemicals gathered are still dumped or burned, and the cycle of pollution continues. With that warning in mind, we've laid out some simple suggestions on how best to reduce your dependence on hazardous chemicals and how to get rid of those that are lying around the dark corners of your garage or hidden in musty basements.

The first thing you should do is check with your local landfill (if it is still open), because some will take items like car batteries and hold them for recycling. Remember too, that an alternative to collection, dumping, or recycling is to give that half can of paint to a neighbor who might use it, rather than tossing it into the trash.

Keep chemicals (paints, solvents, acids) in their original containers and don't mix chemical products before disposing, recycling, or turning them in for collection. If you insist on throwing these things in the garbage, wrap waste in newspaper and two layers of plastic bags. Be particularly careful about dumping any chemical down a toilet or sink, especially if you're on a septic tank system rather than a sewer, because it could wreak untold damage to the entire system.

HOUSEHOLD HAZARDOUS WASTE

In the Kitchen

1. Instead of loading up on every imaginable sink cleaner, window washer, and toilet bowl scrubber that the grocery store stocks, consider that most household cleaning needs can be met with six simple ingredients: vinegar, soap, baking soda, washing soda, borax, and ammonia. Store-bought all-purpose cleaners like Fantastik, Formula 409, and Pine Sol contain potentially dangerous solvents. Here's Greenpeace's all-purpose cleaner recipe: 1 gallon hot water, ¼ cup sudsy ammonia, ¼ cup vinegar, 1 tablespoon baking soda. It's safe for all surfaces and can be rinsed with water. For stronger cleaner or wax stripper, double everything but the water. Use gloves.

2. The active ingredient in most oven cleaners is sodium hydroxide or lye, corrosives that eat through flesh as easily as they do through spilled spaghetti sauce. Try sprinkling salt on spilled food, then cleaning with a mixture of water, liquid soap, and borax in a spray bottle.

3. Drains can be kept open without drain cleaners. Never pour liquid grease down a drain; always use a drain sieve. Once a week dump a mix of 1 cup baking soda, 1 cup salt, and ¼ cup cream of tartar. Follow with a pot of boiling water.

4. Pass up scouring powders. Most contain chlorine bleach, which is especially dangerous if mixed with ammonia. (One chlorine-free scouring powder is Bon Ami.) Instead use baking soda, borax, or table salt.

5. For polishing metals, use:
copper: lemon juice and salt, or hot vinegar and salt
chrome: rubbing alcohol, or white flour on a dry rag
brass: salt and flour, a little vinegar
silver: a quart water, 1 tablespoon salt, 1 tablespoon soda, bring to a boil. Drop in silver, boil for 3 minutes. Polish with soft cloth.

6. Try to avoid any cleanser with an acid base. Most toilet bowl and drain cleaners are loaded with acids. Read the label. It may say "acid," but the ingredients may also be listed as hydroxide or hypochlorite. If you've got metal, wood polish, or wax that you want to get rid of, save them for collection, don't dump them in the trash. (Send $3.75 for a Household Hazardous Waste Wheel, Box 70, Durham, NH 03824.)

In the Bathroom

1. Use soap and water in a spray bottle to clean mirrors and glass.

2. Throw out air fresheners and grow house plants instead, which are a source of air purification. Putting baking soda in your refrigerator or garbage can helps. Most fresheners desensitize the nose by covering nasal passages with a thin film of oil, or simply mask one odor with another. In bathrooms use a herbal bouquet in an open dish.

3. Most commercial tub and tile cleaners contain chlorine. Instead, use a firm brush with either baking soda and hot water or mild all-purpose cleaner.

4. Toilet bowl cleaners are laden with acids, usually hydrochloric acid or sodium acid sulfate, which burn skin and can cause blindness if they get in your eyes. Instead, scrub with baking soda. To disinfect, use borax and boiling water. For stains, make a paste of borax and lemon juice.

5. The Greenpeace recipe for a simple, effective replacement for laundry detergent: Add ⅓ cup washing soda (sodium carbonate) to water as machine is filling. Add clothes. Add 1½ cup of soap. If water is hard, add ¼ cup soda or ¼ cup vinegar during first rinse. (Most detergents aren't bad, it's just that people use so much of them.) Use liquid laundry detergent, rather than powders, and non-chlorine bleaches like Borax.

6. Don't buy aerosol containers. If you've got them hanging around, save them for collection.

7. Avoid septic tank cleaner and drain open-ers, especially if they contain tetrachloroethylene, 1,1,1-trichloroethane, or dichlorobenzene.

8. Nail polish and remover usually contain phenol and petroleum distillates with a formaldehyde resin as basic ingredients. These are dangerous solvents. Don't use them.

In the Garage

1. Motor oil should either be collected or re-cycled. Do not dump it into the ground or sewers. (Just one quart of oil can contaminate up to 2 million gallons of drinking water. The 4 quarts in your car's crankcase can form an oil slick nearly 8 acres across.) Most states require service stations that change oil to accept up to five gallons of used motor oil free of charge from members of the public (unless their storage tanks are full). Service stations may also be able to accept transmission fluid, brake fluid, diesel oil, and kerosene.

2. The primary component in antifreeze is ethylene glycol, which is highly toxic. Pets and other animals find it very tasty, so be careful if you spill it. When you flush your car's radiator, anti-freeze can be captured and reused.

3. There are several pounds of lead in each car battery, and these are the predominant source of lead in the garbage we throw out. Batteries also contain sulfuric acid, which is highly toxic, so don't dump them in the trash. They should be collected or

recycled. Try to get the store or dealer that sells you a new one to take the old one. Put the burden of recycling on them—but ask if they are in fact going to recycle the battery, or throw it in the dumpster.

4. Cans of crusty car wax, half cans of brake fluid and diesel fuel, and gas and transmission fluid should be sent to a collection.

In the Workshop

1. Most paint these days is latex-based, which poses no serious environmental concern when properly disposed of. But oil-based paints including enamel, varnish, and lacquer contain solvents that can damage groundwater supplies. Older paints contain high levels of lead. Dry, hard paint can be thrown into the garbage.

2. Artists' paint should be handled carefully because it often contains much higher levels of toxic metals. These should be saved for collection.

3. All solvents, including paint strippers, spot removers and degreasers, are quite dangerous. Most are recyclable. Anything that contains chemicals with chloro- as a prefix should be handled most carefully. As with paint, if it's dried up, it can be tossed in the trash. (The Natural Choice, LIVOS Plantchemistry, 2641 Cerrillos Road, Santa Fe, N.M. 87501, 505-988-9111, publishes a list of paints, cleaners, stains, wood preservatives, and adhesives made from plant products.)

4. Paint thinner and turpentine can be re-cycled, given a proper collector in the community.

Miscellaneous

1. Swimming pool chemicals contain chlorine and strong acids and are corrosive, cause burns, and can also be a fire hazard. They should be collected.

2. Many old batteries (other than for the car) contain mercury, which can easily be absorbed into the skin and is highly toxic. Check with local universities, whose labs often save mercury for recycling. If the batteries are leaking, keep them in tightly sealed containers.

3. Photographic chemicals should be collected. Some contain silver, which can be reclaimed.

4. Fluorescent lights manufactured before 1978 contain polychlorinated biphenyls (PCBs). When broken, they are highly toxic and should be collected.

5. Mothballs (which are flammable and toxic), lighter fluid, and dry cleaning fluids should be collected.

Government Action

1. The most toxic chemicals should be taxed accordingly, as an incentive to industry to switch to less hazardous substances or to recycle.

2. Deposits on toxic chemicals should be required. Deposits would be refunded when those substances are returned to the proper facility for recycling or disposal. This would make proper disposal more attractive than illegal disposal.

3. The liability system should be strength- ened so that where government regulation fails to protect individuals from toxic chemicals, a compensation schedule is in place.

4. Incentives for toxic chemical exchange should be legislated, and the re-using and trading of chemicals from company to company encouraged.

5. Technologies and processes that minimize or eliminate hazardous waste should receive increased funding.

6. Labeling should be uniform, so that con- sumers and businesses know exactly what toxic chemicals are in the products they buy. This would hopefully discourage the purchase of products heavily laden with hazardous chemicals, and encourage producers to substitute safer substances.

7. Government, industry, and environmental groups should work together in an effort to encourage both source reduction and alternative waste management technology.

8. The mandatory excavation and proper stor- age or destruction of materials from industrial toxic waste landfill sites should be imposed.

Reading

Worldwatch Paper #79: "Defusing the Toxic Threat: Controlling Pesticides and Industrial Waste," by Sandra Postel. Worldwatch Institute, September 1987.

The Healthy Home: An Attic-to-Basement Guide to Toxin-Free Living, by Linda Mason Hunter. Rodale Press, 1989. (Mail-order: 33 E. Minor Street, Emmaus, PA 18049, 215-967-5171.)

"Hazardous Waste: Storing up Trouble," by Allen A. Boraiko. *National Geographic,* March 1985.

"Persistent and Poisonous. What does it take to get a toxic chemical off the market?" by Racquel Skolnick. *Greenpeace*, Volume 13, No. 1.

"Clamping down on international waste trade," by Judy Christup. *Greenpeace*, November/December 1988.

Laying Waste, The Poisoning of America by Toxic Chemicals, by Michael Brown. New York: Pocket Books, 1979.

Household Hazardous Waste Fact Sheet, October 1988, NYS Dept. of Environmental Conservation, 50 Wolf Road, Albany, NY 12233-7253.

"Stepping Lightly on the Earth: Everyone's Guide to Toxics in the Home," Greenpeace Action, 1436 U St., NW Suite 201-A, Washington, DC 20009, 202-462-1177.

Well Body, Well Earth: The Sierra Club Environmental Health Sourcebook, by Mike Samuels and Hal Zina Bennett. San Francisco: Sierra Club Books, 1983.

Nontoxic and Natural: How to Avoid Dangerous Everyday Products and Buy or Make Safe Ones, by Debra Lynn Dadd. Los Angeles: Jeremy P. Tarcher, 1984.

Hazardous Waste in America, by Samuel Epstein, MD, Lester Brown, Carl Pope. San Francisco: Sierra Club Books, 1982.

Waste Reduction: The Only Serious Waste Reduction Management Option, Citizens Clearinghouse for Hazardous Waste, Box 926, Arlington, VA 22216.

"From Pollution to Prevention: A Progress Report on Waste Reduction," U.S. Congress Office of Technology Assessment, Office of Public Affairs, Washington, DC 20510, 202-224-8996.

"Hazardous Waste from Homes," Enterprise for Education, 1320-A Santa Monica Mall, Suite 202, Santa Monica, CA 90401.

Everyday Chemicals: 101 Practical Tips for Home and Work, by Susan Hassol and Beth Richman. Snowmass, CO: The Windstar Foundation, 1989.

Organizations to Contact

Citizens Clearinghouse for Hazardous Wastes, PO Box 926, Arlington, VA 22216, 703-276-7070.

Greenpeace, 2007 R St. NW, Washington, DC 20009, 202-462-1177.

INFORM, 381 Park Ave. South, New York, NY 10017, 212-689-4040.

League of Conservation Voters Toxics Hotline, 1-800-922-5672.

National Campaign Against Toxic Hazards, 317 Pennsylvania Ave. SE, Washington, DC 20003.

National Response Center, 1-800-424-8802. (The U.S. Coast Guard and other military personnel are on hand 24 hours a day to take reports of anything harming the environment, from leaking oil drums to chemical spills.)

National Toxics Campaign, 37 Temple Pl., Fourth Fl., Boston, MA 02111, 617-482-1477.

8

Saltwater Pollution

Two environmental "incidents," each set against a pristine backdrop, capped the 1980s and perhaps marked a new era of public concern for the future of the planet. Both drew the world's attention to Alaska, both involved the open seas. The first was the tale of the whales, the trio (then pair) of grays trapped under inland ice near Point Barrow. Their plight became an international story, their rescue an international effort.

Less than a year later, and a thousand miles away around a jagged shoreline, the world's attention was drawn again to Alaska. This time the incident was more horrific, and focused attention not on the mysterious workings of nature, but on how man is trying his damnedest to spoil it.

The story of the *Exxon Valdez* began 20 miles southwest of the fishing village whose name, Valdez, would be indelibly stamped into the consciousness of a world audience. On March 24, 1989, the 978-foot tanker struck Bligh Reef, named for the notorious captain of the *H.M.S. Bounty,* who sailed those same waters in the eighteenth century. The reef tore into the ship's hull, and 11 million gallons of thick black crude spilled quickly into the calm night seas. If the captain had succeeded in rocking his ship off the reef, as he attempted, its entire cargo of more than 200 million gallons would have polluted Prince William Sound. The tragic spill required months of cleanup and cost billions of dollars and wrought public censure of Exxon and the oil industry at large. Six months later, a foot of black gunk still muddied the shoreline 135 miles south of Valdez.

The disaster focused attention on both the movement of oil through some of the world's most pristine passages, and on the globe's increasing demand for the precious black gold. That the accident occurred in an Alaskan harbor instead of a muddy Texas seaport or some industrial backwater near Tokyo made it seem glaringly worse. Set against the backdrop of snowcapped mountains and breathtaking vistas, the blackness of the spill received—and in many ways deserved—more attention than worse spills of the past.

In relative terms, the amount of oil spilled by the *Exxon Valdez* was small, especially compared to the *Amoco Cadiz* spill, which dumped more than 68 million gallons of oil off the coast of France in 1978. Small too, compared with the *Atlantic Empress,* which in 1979 spilled over 45 million gallons into roiling seas off Trinidad, or the *Torrey Canyon,* which ran aground off Sicily in 1967, spilling 37 million gallons.

The point of these comparisons is not to belittle the damage done by the wreck of the *Exxon Valdez,* but rather to illustrate just how short our "environmental mess" memory can be. Every week seems to bring a new environmental horror, and after months and years, all these spills, leaks, holes, dumps, and decimations tend to melt into an image of one big blotched world. We have developed a kind of environmental amnesia. During the summer of 1988, for example, miles of beaches in the United States, befouled by washed-up waste, were closed. But beach closings are not new. In fact, similar circumstances required the closing of many of the same beaches in the summer of 1976. (Oceanographers blame similar wind and current conditions in both years.) And as far back as 1931, New York was spending $10,000 a year per mile of beach for cleanup.

While ocean pollution is nothing new, the spill of the *Exxon Valdez* and the closing of beaches on the Eastern Seaboard received much attention, and led to congressional hearings, quickly enacted legislation, and newsmagazine covers. One can only hope that these events will serve as signposts to the world, warnings, reminders that we are slowly poisoning the oceans, too. For despite the appalling pictures planted in our global consciousness—vials of blood washed ashore, sea otters flopping around in an oily muck—the culprits are not just hospitals and oil companies. Condemning them is too easy. We the people should shoulder much of the blame.

We the people are responsible for the more than 14 billion pounds of sewage, sludge, and garbage that is dumped into the ocean each year. Nineteen *trillion* gallons of waste compared to the 11 *million* gallons lost by the *Exxon Valdez*. The stark contrasts between Alaska's blue waters and dark, gummy oil make for dramatic videotape on the nightly news. But the waste that runs daily from our streets, landfills, and sewers directly into the sea is a much more severe, and immediate, problem. The poignant pictures from Valdez will, one hopes, remind us daily of the damage we are perpetuating closer to home.

Like most of our environmental problems, ocean pollution is an international dilemma. The Mediterranean is clogged with sewage; so is the English Channel. The Baltic Sea and Persian Gulf and the waters off China and Japan are dumping grounds for growing populations. Toilet-bowl-cleanser containers from Italy, pop bottles from Australia, and shampoo bottles from Singapore wash up on beaches as far away as the French Riviera and the Puget Sound. Fishing vessels toss more than 340,000 tons of

garbage into the seas yearly, and cruise ships and navies add another million pounds of waste a day. There is so much Styrofoam floating in the heavily trafficked ocean passages that it sometimes appears to be a native marine animal. Even radioactive waste from nuclear reactors and platform drilling outfits is still dumped, almost nonchalantly, into the sea.

Governments have made some efforts to slow the most egregious ocean dumping. Before the Clean Water Act was passed by the U.S. Congress in 1972, industrial wastes were often flushed directly into the nation's waterways. Rivers, lakes, and coastal waters were literally used as toilets for factory waste. Since the Act was passed, progress has been made in cleaning up factory wastes, but we are still nowhere near its original goal of ending water pollution altogether. Roughly 1,300 factories and 600 municipalities in the United States continue to discharge wastes directly into coastal waters; together they dump about five trillion gallons of toxics annually. Some of the waste eventually washes ashore, some is carried thousands of miles by tidal currents, some sinks to the ocean bottom. Contamination in places is so bad that some watery sites have been designated for cleanup under Superfund.

In the industrialized world, three quarters of everything flushed down the toilet goes through just one stage of disinfecting treatment. The rest goes directly into the drink without any treatment at all. Throughout the Third World waste treatment is rare. But the problem is not just what is flushed down the toilet or pumped out industrial pipes. At least half of all water pollution comes from wastes that wash off city streets, farm fields, and building and mining sites and run directly into streams and rivers, headed for the ocean.

Much ocean pollution is simply the result of too much development at water's edge. From 1950 to 1984 the number of people living in coastal counties in the United States increased by over 30 million. Today 50 percent of the U.S. population lives within an hour of a coastline. Mile after mile of homes, roads, and storefronts snake down the coast-line, with a promise of more to come. Coastal states boast booming, multi-billion-dollar shoreline tourist industries. The accompanying swell of traffic and population taxes sewage treatment plants, encourages industrial development, and draws houses closer and closer to the seas.

As we choose to live more proximate to the ocean and all its natural beauties, it seems odd that we continue to contaminate the waters at an alarming rate. Annual consumption of fish and shellfish in the United States has reached 14.5 pounds per person, but much of what we eat is imported. More than 2.5 million acres of coastal shellfish beds nationwide are closed to fishermen because of toxic or bacterial contamination. Another 4.3 million acres can only be safely harvested during limited times of the year. Despite nature's own warnings—wastes thrown back up onto our shores, as if to say enough is enough—we keep on building, keep on consuming, keep on dumping.

Just how many "oceans" are there, and who has say over them? Pick up a globe. Spin it. Do you see any borders on all that blue? Any place where one ocean stops and another begins? Viewing the ocean from a global perspective, it is easier to see that there aren't *many* oceans—though we've given them individual names, like the Pacific, the Atlantic, the Indian—but just one.

Life began in the ocean more than 3.5 billion years ago; fossils of sea life predate those of land creatures. Salt water covers 71 percent of the globe, comprises 97 percent of all the water on Earth, and contains over 80 percent of all living matter. It warehouses and distributes the sun's energy, serving as a kind of global thermostat which helps regulate the world's climate. Water provides the cheapest form of transportation available, and supplies 60 billion tons of food each year. And how have we treated such an invaluable resource? We now put more trash into the ocean than the annual tonnage of fish we take out.

Lately, the global "thermostat" has been knocked off balance by all the garbage we've been putting in both the waters and air. As the atmosphere heats up, so does the ocean. Beneath the surface the ocean roils and churns, influenced by the heat of the sun, the Earth's rotation, and solar and lunar tides. Rivers as wide as states carve channels miles below and, propelled by fast-running currents, carry tons of water (and sludge and trash) over long distances. Their movement is as difficult to predict as that of the skies. Without this constant movement, northern Europe might feel more like the Arctic. Climate, ecosystems, and wildlife are all affected by the shifting moods of the globe's waters—and vice versa. Scientists worry that global warming may influence the ocean in ways we cannot yet predict.

The natural circulation of the ocean spreads the garbage we dump into it in unpredictable patterns. DDT dumped off the eastern coast of the United States has surfaced in the fat of Antarctic penguins. Sludge and chemicals blanket miles of sea floor with toxic ooze that takes years to dissipate. However, many pollutants tend to accumulate near their sources. River deltas, harbors around big cities, and heavily populated coastal areas suffer in proportion to their wastes.

As populations grow and consumption rises, people continue to test the limits of this giant goldfish bowl/garbage can. The ocean's ability to absorb this growing mess of sewage, toxic chemicals, radioactive wastes, and oil spills is unknown. The mocking motto of those who advocate continued ocean dumping, "Dilution is the solution to pollution," is under challenge. Unfortunately, we won't know if we have exceeded the ocean's limits until it is too late.

CAUSES

The great irony of ocean pollution is that much of the dumping is legal. Whether it's sewage or sludge, toxics or garbage, government permit, even government encouragement, allows much of the pollution—despite tens of thousands of pages of laws aimed at limiting its discharge.

Almost two decades after the Clean Water Act set a goal of returning all waters to "fishable and swimmable" conditions, the dumping of *sewage* is still one of the biggest environmental problems in the United States. The law's 1972 goal of chemically "treating" all raw sewage before it was released into the waterways that lead to the sea is today reached inconsistently. Most sewage passes through a first phase of treatment, which skims off grit and heavy material. Far less sewage ever sees the second (and highly recommended) phase of treatment, in which it is aerated, chlorinated, and further decomposed. Worst of all, more than a quarter of all sewage in the United States flows into waterways untouched by chemical disinfectants or filters. Globally, the percentage is more like half.

Most of this raw sewage is body waste, which is easy to treat. But the tons of feces are joined in the sewer systems by a horrid mixture of everything that is flushed down toilets or washed down sinks at every factory, home, apartment, business, and hospital, including but not limited to toilet paper, tampons, condoms, cigarettes, and household cleansers. All of this is united with toxic wastes flushed by a wide variety of industries: photo labs dump developer, dry cleaners discard dangerous solvents, gas stations deep-six oil and gasoline down sinks, plastic manufacturers junk reagents and by-products, gardeners and farmers dump pesticides and herbicides, and artists jettison solvents and paints. Once in the sewer system, this hazardous cocktail is topped off by roof, gutter, and curbside runoff.

What to do about this dirty drink is a dilemma shared by municipalities around the globe. In the United States, the example of its biggest city may serve to illustrate why cleansing the system has become such a bedeviling problem worldwide.

Most of New York's sewage pipes share their length with storm water drains. Every time it rains more than a quarter of an inch, the combination of sewage and rainwater overwhelms the treatment plants' capacity. This toxic mess overflows and heads for open water, not stopping for treatment along the way. Millions of gallons of raw sewage and everything from umbrella spokes to dead rats wash through the sewer system into the sea.

Treated sewage presents its own problems. A musty-smelling, watery black mud, it is aerated, baked, and decomposed. Dubbed *sludge,* it is shipped out to sea. In New York, barges laden with 2.5 million gallons of the odorific remnants leave Manhattan several times a week for a 15-hour-long, 106-mile voyage. Their destination is a 5-by-20-mile region known as the Deep Water Site 106.

This federally approved dumping ground is currently home to billions of gallons of sludge—as well as an abundance of sea life, including phytoplankton, fish, birds, and larger sea animals. Lobsters, crabs, and other crustaceans live near the bottom, and 200 species of fish breed close by. Whales, tuna, dolphins, and swordfish pass through seasonally. Similar dumping grounds can be found off coastlines around the globe—and some much closer to land than 106 miles. In fact, until the early 1980s, New York and New Jersey dumped their sludge just 12 miles off the coastline, in an area now virtually deprived of life due to the years of dumping. A new agreement with the EPA, signed by both New York and New Jersey, intends to end ocean dumping by 1991, but no easy solution to the area's waste problem is in sight. No matter how quickly New York builds and repairs treatment facilities, the demand grows. Each year more and more untreated raw sewage escapes into surrounding waterways, because of continued development and overflowing sewers. Yet for all New York's faults, compared to places like Bangladesh and Mexico City, its waterways are as clean as the Fountain of Youth.

Approximately one quarter of all wastewater is dumped directly into the ocean (above). Even when properly treated, sewage waste water (below) can contain enough pollutants—bacteria, nitrogen, and phosphorus—to reduce oxygen levels and suffocate life in coastal waters.

The array of discarded plastic toys here was piled up by this albatross to feed to its young.

Toxic chemicals dumped by both industries and government agencies are another major source of ocean pollution. More than 1,300 major industrial facilities still have federal permits to dump their waste directly into coastal waterways. Add all the household poisons, everything from crankcase oil to lawn fertilizers and window cleaners, which are dumped directly, filtered through runoff, or washed down the kitchen sink, and the problem worsens. Mix in the radioactive waste dumped from offshore oil platforms (the Louisiana Department of Natural Resources has measured such discharges as exceeding those of nuclear reactors), and the soup gets dangerous.

Of all the trash that ends up in the ocean, plastic is the worst. Every year almost 100 million tons of plastic finds a new home, floating somewhere in the ocean.

The $15-billion-a-year plastics industry isn't going to go away. More than one million workers are employed in plastics manufacture, producing $138 billion in finished goods. Today the United States produces twice as much plastic in a year as it does steel, copper, and aluminum combined. Since 1975, production has doubled and the industry's aim is to increase it by another 50 percent within the next decade. Unfortunately, the immensity and success of the plastics industry has produced a disastrous side effect. After years of experimentation and millions of dollars spent, the material does its job—it refuses to go away. A plastic six-pack holder has a life expectancy of 450 years.

How bad is plastic pollution? *Oceans* magazine reported this example. In September of 1987, a three-hour cleanup of 157 miles of Texas shoreline rounded up 31,773 plastic bags, 30,295 plastic bottles, 15,631 plastic six-pack rings, 38,540 plastic lids, 1,914 disposable diapers, 1,040 tampon applicators, and 7,460 plastic milk jugs. (Tampon applicators have become a standard if disgusting beach toy. Adults call them "Jersey seashells." Children,

who put them in their mouths and blow into them, refer to the pink, hollow tubes as "beach whistles.")

Oil, the main ingredient in the manufacture of plastics, is also one of the oceans' most dangerous enemies. But oil pollution is hardly new to the seas; oil has been spilled in the water since the Civil War. According to David Bulloch, whose book, *The Wasted Ocean*, details the history of saltwater pollution, in 1912 the New York Zoological Society reported that it could no longer use local harbor water for its tanks because oil contamination was killing specimens. In 1920, an East Coast researcher claimed that many of the mollusks once common to the Hudson River and Staten Island had disappeared, and he blamed spilled oil.

Today more than 70 percent of the world's oil exports travel by sea, almost 2 billion tons a year. In an average year between 1 and 10 million tons are spilled. But the major source of oil pollution is not accidents like that of the *Exxon Valdez*, but municipal and industrial runoff, the cleaning of ship bilges, and general sloppiness. The amount of oil lost worldwide at sea and on land through spillage, fire, and sinking has declined in the past decade, from 328 million gallons to between 24 and 55 million a year.

But in the summer of 1989, oil spills dominated the news. Within 12 hours on two days that summer—three months after the *Exxon Valdez* tragedy—three oil tankers wrecked, spilling their valuable but dirty cargo. A Greek tanker off Newport spilled 420,000 gallons of heating oil; a Uruguayan tanker ran aground off the coast of Delaware, dumping 800,000 gallons of heating oil; and a tug-driven barge collided with another ship in the Houston Ship Channel, and 240,000 gallons of heavy crude leaked out. These followed an earlier 230,000-gallon spill in Grays Harbor, Washington, and the grounding of an Argentine supply ship off Antarctica. It left behind a diesel oil slick 10 miles wide, and became Antarctica's first major environmental crisis. In each case, cleanup crews recovered no more than 10 percent of the spillage on average (an average which hasn't changed in the past 20 years). Once again, as it had been in the early 1970s, oil was back on the front pages. This time, though, scarcity was hardly the issue.

EFFECTS

Environmental messes have recently served not only as evocative magazine and television images, but also as provocative backdrops for politicians of all stripes. In 1988, George Bush stood in front of Boston Harbor, home to millions of gallons of raw sewage and sludge, and suggested that "somebody's got to take responsibility, somebody's got to clean this mess up." His opponent, the governor of Massachusetts, stumbled for a reply. It is interesting to note that cleanup monies were being stalled by the federal government; the problem was hardly all Michael Dukakis's fault. But the governor took the blame, and the fall, and an environmental mess was credited by default with helping Bush win the presidency. Now, of course, it's up to Bush to put money where his mouth was.

Politics aside, Boston Harbor does serve as a powerful example of just how badly we treat the coastal waters that surround us. The harbor *is* a filthy mix of sewage and toxic waste. When it rains, thousands of gallons of raw sewage and runoff routinely flow into it. More than a ton of toxic waste is dumped into the harbor each day. Sediment in the harbor has among the highest levels of toxic contaminants of any body of water in the United States. In some places along the harbor's bottom sludge lies two to three feet thick, in a mass divers call "black mayonnaise." Over the next 10 years, the state plans to spend more than $4.6 billion to build the nation's second-largest plant for wastewater treatment—and still the harbor won't be

clean, and many poisons will still be legally dumped into it.

Conditions reminiscent of Boston Harbor are found in waters hugging shores around the world, especially surrounding major urban centers with similarly antiquated sewer systems and greedy industry. Regions of the Adriatic and Aegean, the Mediterranean, the Baltic, and the Sea of Japan are murky with garbage, poisoned by industrial waste. The Irish Sea holds more than one ton of plutonium dumped there by a nuclear waste reprocessing plant in England.

Sewage and sludge remain the prime ocean pollutants, and overdevelopment is taxing waterways around the globe. Europe's coastline is fast becoming "cementified" by runaway development; the Florida Keys, now home to more than 1 million people, are overrun by buildings; more than 50 percent of California's wetlands and estuaries have been destroyed by dredging and filling; the Chesapeake Bay, the East Coast's largest estuary, has lost more than 90 percent of its marine vegetation because algae have choked the waters. Dead dolphins and fish, raw sewage, tar balls, and used syringes that wash up on beaches from the Long Island Sound to the Bay of Fundy serve as unsubtle reminders of our profligacy. Beaches close, newspapers run headlines . . . and kids decorate sand castles with tampon applicators.

Commercial and recreational fishing businesses worldwide (a $6-billion-a-year enterprise in the United States alone) are endangered. Ocean pollution has no preference, it affects shellfish and finfish alike. Pollution hits nature's food chain hard. Toxic chemicals and metals such as cadmium and lead are picked off the bottom of bays by small organisms eaten by fish and shellfish. Human illnesses—including hepatitis—caused by eating contaminated seafood have risen since 1980.

Once in the waters, the pollutants we dump are impossible to control. At Dump Site 106 off the

Some spent nuclear fuel is still being dumped at sea. The waste material will remain radioactive for hundreds or thousands of years. No one knows how long the containers will remain leakproof.

coast of New York and New Jersey, rivers 50 miles wide course a mile and a half below the surface, carrying sludge to points east and south. As a safeguard, a 150-square-mile region surrounding the dump site is closed to commercial shellfishing.

The estuaries that line the coasts around the world are hurt most by ocean pollution. They are being transformed by the population explosion along their edges. The influx of people and industry brings the excesses of what *Oceans* calls the "effluent society." The meeting place of rivers and the shallow salt water of coastal bays and inlets, estuaries are fertile grounds for fish breeding. In Third World countries they produce twice the amount of food proteins as are raised on nearby, often arid, lands. In the United States, two thirds of the annual commercial catch is drawn from such coastal areas, and they are home to most shellfish, including bay scallops, soft-shelled crabs, and hard-shelled clams.

A secondary result of estuarine pollution is the spawning of a natural killer. Red and brown algae thrive on many pollutants, especially the nitrates and phosphates found in runoff and effluents. As pollutants feed the algae, they soon cover wide swaths of bays and inlets, absorbing life-sustaining oxygen from the water, endangering plants and wildlife. When algae die, they continue suffocating other life forms, by settling to the bottom of the water like dead leaves from trees. Their decomposition blocks the sunlight that enables bottom vegetation to carry on photosynthesis. Windless days coupled with hot, cloudless weather provide perfect conditions for algae to bloom.

SOLUTIONS

In the summer of 1989, on a beach near Wildwood Crest, New Jersey, pollution drove five local businessmen to take matters into their own hands. Bacteria from overflowing storm water drains was running into the ocean, closing New Jersey beaches and drastically hurting shoreline profits. This quintet of middle-aged men got up early one morning and dumped 100 gallons of chlorine tablets into the Atlantic, near the spot where health inspectors would soon take readings to decide if the beaches were safe to reopen. Unfortunately for them, they were spotted in the act, arrested, and fined. (Unfortunately for the sea life in the area, chlorine is horribly toxic.)

Fortunately, calmer heads continue to search for ways to better control the amount of junk dumped into the seas, and to clean up the areas already fouled. Legislation is one path. Enforcement of laws already on the books is another. Reducing demand for plastics and other goods that generate waste should be the primary goal, worldwide.

The original aim of the Clean Water Act was to eliminate the discharge of *all* pollutants into the water by 1985. The law has been effective in some places, less so in most. (An interim goal of cleaning up water enough so that fish, shellfish, and wildlife could safely call it home by mid-1983 also proved impossible to achieve.)

Since the act was first passed, more laws have been enacted in attempts to purify the water. The abundance of regulations may, in fact, be part of the cleanup problem. Currently, according to David Bulloch's *The Wasted Ocean,* water quality is subject to 21 federal programs under eight major statutes administered by 11 different federal agencies. Responsibility under these laws is divided by territory, by function, and by administration. Though the bureaucracy and mechanics for trying to keep waters clean would seem to be in place, monitoring and implementation still lag. Untreated waste still spews into rivers and seas; industrial dischargers still dump dangerous materials. As the 1990s begin, the goal of making all waters safe is still far off.

Since 1972 more than $250 billion has been spent in the United States on attempts to clean the water and prevent more pollution. More than $44 billion has been spent since then to build or upgrade municipal treatment plants. The EPA estimates another $76 billion will be spent by 2008 on further efforts to live up to the original mandate of the 1972 law. But throwing money at the treatment side of the problem is only part of the solution.

(Eight years under the Reagan Administration helped little regarding both regulation and enforcement of water pollution laws. When Reagan took office, the EPA had nearly 15,000 employees, seven regional offices, and labs in 20 states. But with a string of anti-environmentalist appointments to his cabinet, including but not limited to James Watt, Anne Gorsuch, and David Stockman, morale, enforcement, and efficacy plummeted. By the time Reagan left office, the EPA staff had been reduced by 30 percent and its budget slashed.)

Cleaning the world's ocean is not a lost cause. Dozens of projects already underway are showing positive results. Industries are being pushed to recycle or reduce the amount of chemicals they use. Upgraded sewage treatment and bans on phosphates in household detergents are helping. Localities are pitching in. Maryland, Virginia, Pennsylvania, and Washington, D.C., have agreed to reduce by 40 percent the nitrogen and phosphorus flowing into the Chesapeake Bay by upgrading sewer plants and managing development and agricultural runoff more conscientiously. Florida, Maryland, and North Carolina have passed laws controlling coastline development. Volunteers are joining hands to clean up littered beaches.

In 1989 New York City and surrounding municipalities finally, after a ten-year fight with Congress, agreed to ban sludge dumping by the end of 1991. Unfortunately, officials say they will now pursue plans to incinerate the sludge, which burns down to dangerous toxic ash and residue. But environmentalists cite Chicago, Los Angeles, Miami, Milwaukee, and Philadelphia as cities successfully dealing with their mounting sludge. Some are recycling it to be used as compost, others use it as fertilizer, landfill cover, and even fuel. Austin, Texas, recently won the National Award for Beneficial Re-Use of Sludge award from the EPA. For 30 years the city had dumped its sludge in big lagoons on the outskirts of town. Today, through a complicated process, the city turns its 250 tons of sludge per month into fertilizer for city park grass and crops that feed cattle. The city also turns human waste into compost, which it sells to the public as "Dillo Dirt," named after the ubiquitous armadillo.

Many consider plastics the most devastating manmade threat facing the ocean. The U.S. Office of Technology Assessment concludes that plastic pollution is a greater threat to marine mammals and birds than are pesticides, oil spills, or contaminated runoff. It credits plastic with killing more than one million birds and tens of thousands of seals, sea lions, sea otters, whales, dolphins, porpoises and turtles annually. Because plastic is often transparent, it nets or entwines animals that cannot see it. It floats on the waves and can be easily mistaken for food. Animals surface stuck in six-pack holders or wash up on beaches, their stomachs swelled by garbage bags they've swallowed. Those pictures *are* dramatic, but unfortunately they're taken too late.

The amount of plastic dumped in the sea is slowly being regulated. Beginning January 1, 1989, it became illegal for ships registered in nations that had signed the International Convention for the Prevention of Pollution from Ships to discard plastics into the ocean. More than 29 countries signed the agreement (the United States did not) and violators can be fined up to $25,000.

Plastics manufacturers are trying to help. Several suppliers now offer degradable resins, and a few manufacturers in the United States, Italy, and Canada are already making degradable plastic bags. (The environmental consequences of both bio- and photodegradable plastics are not yet known. Some

Approximately 100,000 marine animals die each year from ingesting or becoming entangled in plastic discarded in the sea. Six-pack holders (above) are particularly destructive, as are lost drift nets that snag sea life, such as this blue shark (below).

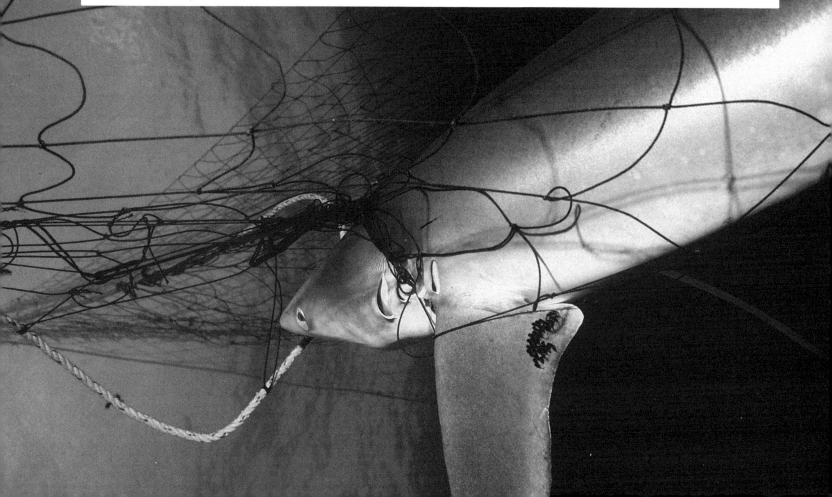

environmentalists are skeptical that these will help solve the problems of plastic disposal. In fact, if people get the impression that all plastics will eventually biodegrade, they may become even more nonchalant about how they dispose of plastic cups, disposable diapers, six-pack holders, etc.)

While the plastics industry may be more environmentally concerned, or at least cautious, plastic manufacturing continues at a furious pace. More than 20 million tons are produced each year in the United States alone, and not just for diaper linings and fast-food containers, but for car and computer parts, tank armor, and rocket engines. As plastic becomes more important in all aspects of life, it will inevitably become an even bigger pollution problem.

Organized, global protests have also proved helpful in trying to keep the ocean cleaner. Floating incinerators used to be scattered around the oceans, burning hazardous wastes for anyone willing to pay. They have largely disappeared as a result of international laws passed in the early 1980s. Seaborne incinerators were introduced in West Germany in 1969, and first tested in the United States in 1974, 110 miles off the coast of Texas. But these trials were followed by massive protest. The dangerous emissions and toxic ash that result from incineration were ultimately judged to be as big a threat to the ocean and marine life as dumping. Some burning at sea continues off the coast of Europe, but it is scheduled to end, through an agreement of the North Sea countries, by 1994.

After the most recent of beach closings, more efforts to police illegal ocean dumpers are being waged. Individuals like Michael Herz of San Francisco, whose Baykeeper program has enlisted over 100 volunteers, patrol area bays looking for polluters. Armed with binoculars and radios, they watch for illegal dumping and keep their eyes open for oil-slicked birds that suggest nearby spills. The Baykeeper hot-line receives calls daily, and its patrol has already led to the stoppage of an illegal dredging operation, after Herz notified the EPA. Other volunteer watches are cropping up along the world's coastlines. Herz insists such programs will succeed. "Tremendous faith is placed in us because we're just plain folks," he says. As more "just plain folks" get involved with monitoring the seas, industry and government will have to respond.

In reaction to the beach closings of recent years, Congress passed the Medical Waste Tracking Act, a two-year, ten-state demonstration program for handling, transporting, tracking, and disposing of medical waste. That was followed by the Ocean Dumping Ban Act, which mandated an end to sludge dumping by the end of 1991. Unfortunately, environmental hazards still seem to warrant legislative action only post-accident. Preventive regulations must become the focus of lawmakers and environmentalists.

Municipalities reacted differently to the medical waste and beach-closing scares. In New York, experiments were carried out with a variety of cleanup tools, from giant rakes to catamarans boasting skimmers that scoop up floating garbage. Helicopters and boats loaded with Coast Guard officials went out to search for garbage slicks (they found prime time for garbage-spotting to be during a full moon, when the tides run fastest). The city's sanitation department even put giant "hairnets" over the garbage barges that carry refuse from the boroughs to New York City's main landfill, Fresh Kills. But New Jersey officials may have come up with the most novel, and effective, way of policing their shores: con patrols. Inmates of local prisons collected 2,700 tons of debris along a 17-mile stretch of New Jersey shoreline in the late spring of 1989.

The beach closings have also created a new wave of anti-litter volunteerism. Beach cleanups sponsored by conservation groups and even local industries have become annual events on shorelines up and down the coasts. In April 1989, a cleanup effort swept 966 miles of Florida ocean, gulf, and river shorelines. Sponsored by the Center for Marine

The Exxon Valdez oil tanker struck a reef off the Alaskan coastline, spilling 11 million gallons of crude oil that spread over 135 miles of ocean (above and below), killing wildlife and closing many fishing lanes for at least a season. Even after cleanup, the spilled oil will persist in the sediment, continuing to harm marine life for several years.

Conservation, a Washington-based group, 12,041 volunteers picked up more than 307 tons of litter on one day. Similar efforts, with similar results, have been made from Maine to Hawaii, Egypt to Turkey.

Oil spills still provide the most vivid pictures of the devastation that can be wreaked by ocean pollution. Tens of thousands of oil-soaked birds, otters, and fish died as a result of the spill of the *Exxon Valdez*. Most of Prince William Sound's 5,000 bald eagles are threatened (at least 150 have been found dead) because their oil-coated intestines can't absorb nutrition. Zooplankton, the tiny animals that are the basis of the aquatic food chain, are being killed by the benzene they have ingested.

Biologists suggest the spill could cost the Prince William Sound fisheries more than $100 million in lost business into the early 1990s. But people beyond the sound will feel the effects, too. Fish populations may shrink and those that are caught and sold may very well contain unidentified levels of toxics and chemicals harmful to man.

Following the very public debacle of the *Exxon Valdez,* the U.S. Congress enacted a year-long ban on drilling off vast areas of the coasts of California and Florida, and created a 50-mile buffer zone stretching from Rhode Island to Virginia. Congress has never before urged so sweeping a ban on offshore exploration. They also voted in a year-long moratorium on oil and gas exploration in Alaska's Bristol Bay, an exceedingly rich fishing area. (Later in the year, the Senate passed a bill that would require cleanup monies to be set aside in a $1-billion fund financed by a new, three-cent-per-barrel tax on all domestic and imported oil.) In support, a Federal court ruled in mid-1989 that companies responsible for oil spills and other pollution should be forced to pay the *full costs* of restoring the environment to its original condition, not the more arbitrary *market value* of damaged natural resources that is currently assessed.

After the one-year ban on drilling, the future of oil exploration hinges on Congress's regard for the environment. Environmentalists contend that exploration in the Arctic National Wildlife Refuge in northern Alaska, for example, would disturb the breeding grounds of the continent's largest migrating caribou herd, disrupt other wildlife, and up the potential for more spills. Yet the Department of the Interior is still considering leasing millions of acres of oil and gas rights under both the Atlantic and Pacific Oceans, and oil companies are intent on expanding their domestic drilling operations.

The development of Congress's legislative strategy will be a tricky business. If the United States were to develop new domestic oil sources, the nation could reduce its dependence on foreign sources of oil, and by inviting fewer tankers into its harbors, reduce the risk of spills. Last year foreign producers provided the United States with 37 percent of its oil, up from 27 percent in 1985. If imports continue at that pace, by the end of the 1990s 90 percent of the oil consumed in the United States would arrive by tanker, up from 65 percent in 1989. Environmentalists cite this growing dependence, and the pollution risks that go with it, as another good reason to continue searching not for new oil wells, but for alternative energy sources.

State and federal officials must become stricter about enforcing the safety laws that now exist for oil tankers. And additional safety measures should be mandated, including double hulls for leakage protection, a ban to keep convicted drunk drivers from behind the wheels of tankers, and specified routes to keep ships out of sensitive areas. More oil must be transported by pipeline. Cleanup technology must be advanced, and monies set aside for accident prevention and emergency cleanup. (Currently the Coast Guard is the frontline emergency cleanup agency, with a total strike force of two teams, one on the Pacific and one in the Gulf. In the words of one expert on oil cleanup, "Current technology amounts to having a quarter-inch lawn mower working on a 40-acre field.")

After the spill of the *Exxon Valdez,* oil companies belatedly banded together and announced a program aimed at preventing, containing, and cleaning up major spills. They promised to provide workers and equipment at strategic locations along the nation's coastlines, at an anticipated cost of $250 million over five years. One Democratic senator said the plan was like calling for more lifeboats on ocean liners "three months after the *Titanic.*"

Oil spills draw attention to the continuing need for energy conservation and efficiency and stepped-up research in renewable sources. The less oil the world demands, the less chance of devastating spills. The first step toward reduction should be to raise the auto industry's fuel-economy requirements. Increasing the fuel efficiency to 40 miles per hour for cars and to 30 for trucks would save more than 13 billion barrels by 2008. The second obvious step is an immediate increase in the federal gasoline tax. Each one-cent rise would discourage unnecessary driving and add $1 billion to the U.S. treasury, part of which could be used to develop non-fossil energy sources. But it appears that as long as foreign crude remains relatively cheap, conservation will remain elusive.

Conservation efforts can be made in other areas, too. Improving the efficiency of existing oil and gas furnaces and water heaters would save the equivalent of 4.5 billion barrels of oil a year, roughly the same amount of oil that is believed to lie beneath the most sensitive geographic areas the oil industry still hopes to explore. Improved weatherization could save money and fuel in most homes.

The federal and state governments can adopt laws to try and slow pollution at the source. The number of permits granted to dump toxic waste directly into rivers and streams should be reduced. Landfills near waterways need extended "skirts" to keep their piles from blowing into the water. Secondary treatment for all wastewater must become law. Storm sewers and wastewater pipes must be separated. Oil companies and those who transport hazardous waste by sea must be charged higher registration fees, to help cover cleanup costs.

As for sludge, it's going to take close to $100 billion to overhaul the municipal waste-treatment plants in the United States to provide secondary treatment. Before that kind of money is spent, a more comprehensive plan—along the lines of the 1970s attacks on water and air pollution—needs to be adopted. It has been proven that water can be cleaned up. There are rivers and lakes across the United States that serve as testament. But the ocean is different, and more complex. It has no boundaries. It's too late to drop a shield down deep to contain the waste we've already dumped. If we continue to pollute the ocean at our current pace, the damage will be widespread, unpredictable, and irreparable.

SALTWATER POLLUTION

Each year over 100 million tons of plastic finds its way to the sea, plastic that may not decompose for up to 450 years. The floating, translucent material is often mistaken for prey by birds, turtles, sharks, and fish—they ingest it or get caught in it. More than two million birds and 100,000 sea animals die each year as a result.

It's not just plastic that is dumped in the ocean. In some parts of the world, the ocean has become a virtual garbage can for much human refuse. It is estimated that the garbage we dump into the ocean each year now outweighs the world's annual catch of fish.

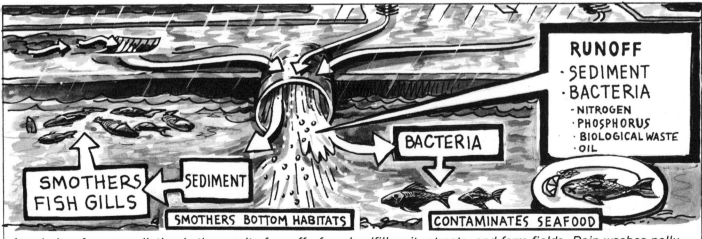

A majority of ocean pollution is the result of runoff—from landfills, city streets, and farm fields. Rain washes pollutants into waterways, then on to the ocean. This poisonous runoff is increasing as more and more people settle in coastal regions and the trees and plants whose root systems once hindered excess runoff are replaced by cement.

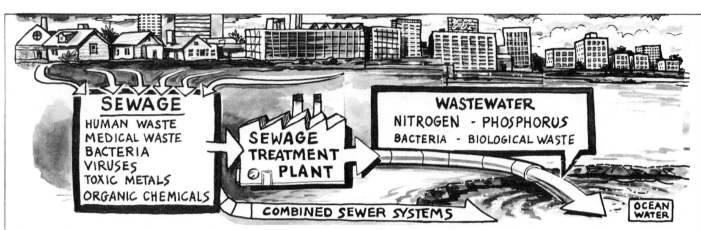

SEWAGE
HUMAN WASTE
MEDICAL WASTE
BACTERIA
VIRUSES
TOXIC METALS
ORGANIC CHEMICALS

SEWAGE TREATMENT PLANT

WASTEWATER
NITROGEN - PHOSPHORUS
BACTERIA - BIOLOGICAL WASTE

OCEAN WATER

COMBINED SEWER SYSTEMS

Sewage is another main source of ocean pollution. Treatment plants are far from perfect, hampered by chemicals from industry and phosphorus from household detergents. Twenty-five percent of treated sewage, containing substances harmful to ocean ecosystems, is dumped in the ocean. Also, thousands of sewer systems are linked to storm sewers—in heavy rain the overflow carries raw sewage directly into waterways.

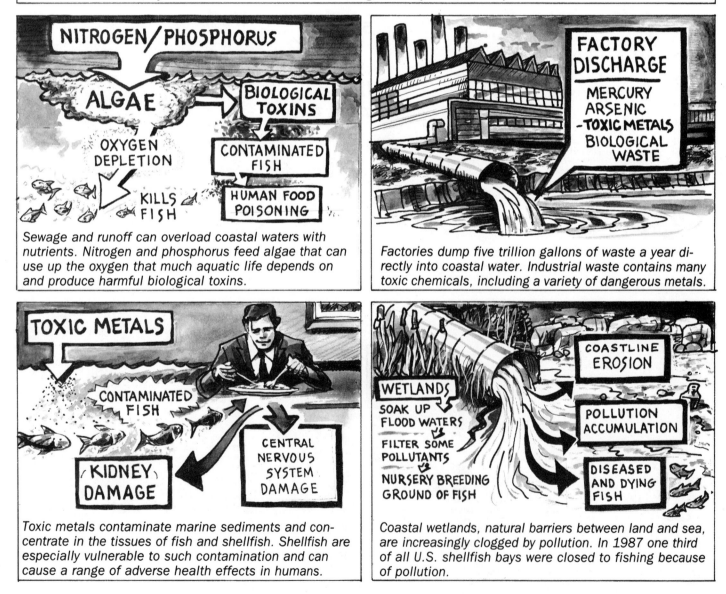

NITROGEN/PHOSPHORUS
ALGAE
OXYGEN DEPLETION
KILLS FISH
BIOLOGICAL TOXINS
CONTAMINATED FISH
HUMAN FOOD POISONING

Sewage and runoff can overload coastal waters with nutrients. Nitrogen and phosphorus feed algae that can use up the oxygen that much aquatic life depends on and produce harmful biological toxins.

FACTORY DISCHARGE
MERCURY
ARSENIC
-TOXIC METALS
BIOLOGICAL WASTE

Factories dump five trillion gallons of waste a year directly into coastal water. Industrial waste contains many toxic chemicals, including a variety of dangerous metals.

TOXIC METALS
CONTAMINATED FISH
KIDNEY DAMAGE
CENTRAL NERVOUS SYSTEM DAMAGE

Toxic metals contaminate marine sediments and concentrate in the tissues of fish and shellfish. Shellfish are especially vulnerable to such contamination and can cause a range of adverse health effects in humans.

WETLANDS
SOAK UP FLOOD WATERS
FILTER SOME POLLUTANTS
NURSERY BREEDING GROUND OF FISH
COASTLINE EROSION
POLLUTION ACCUMULATION
DISEASED AND DYING FISH

Coastal wetlands, natural barriers between land and sea, are increasingly clogged by pollution. In 1987 one third of all U.S. shellfish bays were closed to fishing because of pollution.

Coastal development brings ever more sewage, industrial waste, and garbage to the ocean. But development continues: Half of the U.S. population lives within 50 miles of a coastline; 90 percent of sewage generated along the rapidly "cementifying" Mediterranean coast is dumped raw into the ocean—stretches of the French Riviera are unsafe for swimmers.

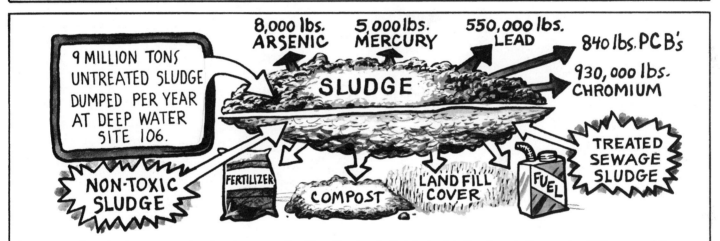

In a natural cycle, human and animal wastes fertilize the land. But industrialized societies make little use of these natural resources. After treatment, sludge is laden with dangerous chemicals. If sewage was properly treated it could be recycled and used for a variety of good purposes.

Reusable, nontoxic products must be the wave of the future. Also, conserving water lessens the amount of sewage that plants must process, reducing potential overflow (90 percent of water used for toilets could be saved by installing 1.5-gallon-flush toilets). Everyone must realize that what they dump in the washing machine, sink, and trashcan may contribute to ocean pollution.

Individual Action

1. The first thing to do is think about what you flush down your toilet and wash down your sink. Anything that can be used up or disposed of in a better fashion or even recycled should be.

2. In many cities, improperly disposing of sol-vents, grease, oil, paints, thinners, acids, and other chemicals is as harmful as tossing them directly into the ocean. Increasingly, there are recycling or recovery facilities for a wide variety of such chemicals. Check around your community to see if they exist. If they don't, encourage them.

3. To make sure that less plastic ends up in the ocean, try to buy as few plastic products as possible. Always opt for glass or aluminum, if possible, because they are recyclable. If your grocer insists on shrink-wrapping fruits and vegetables, gang up on him. Get a half-dozen neighbors and explain to him that you'd rather he cut down on his use of plastic goods, or you'll shop somewhere else.

4. Try to use cloth diapers. Discourage the use of Styrofoam. When shopping request paper bags.

5. Ask about plastic six-pack holders. Don't buy products that use them unless they are biodegradable. Even then, cut them up before disposal to safeguard against their becoming a noose for birds or fish.

6. If you garden, be careful about the chemi-cals you use. Remember that many of them will eventually end up in waterways and eventually in the ocean. The best bet is not to use pesticides or herbicides at all.

7. If you're a fisherman or boater, develop a system for containing waste and carting it back to land. Adopt one simple rule: Never dump anything into the ocean.

8. If you are a boater and you see others dump-ing trash overboard, notify the Coast Guard. Get the vessel's name, number, location, and type of trash.

9. If you live near a beach, join or organize beach cleanups, weekly, monthly, or annually. For information about such efforts, write Coastal States Organization, 444 N. Capitol St. NW, Suite 312, Washington, DC 20001.

10. If you live near a coastline, spend some time getting to know the trash that washes up on beaches nearby. Take notes on the debris. You may find it easy to identify the source of the waste once you take its total accumulation into account. If you want to join a national effort to track beach garbage, write the National Marine Debris Data Base, CMC, 1725 DeSales St. NW, Washington, DC 20036. They've already got more than 47,000 volunteers collecting both debris and information.

11. Contact your state's department of en-vironmental conservation, natural resources, or fish and game to see if they have programs for volunteers or need help publicizing their efforts to keep ocean coastlines clean. There is also a national beach cleanup week called COASTWEEKS, sponsored by a network of organizations. Every coastal state has a representative; contact the Coastal States Organization (444 N. Capitol St. NW, Suite 312, Washington, DC 20001) for details.

12. Cut back on oil use in your home, office, and car. Buy fuel-efficient appliances, tools, and automobiles. It's never too late to begin to walk, carpool, bicycle, or skateboard to work.

13. **Encourage your congresspeople to** strengthen existing sludge-dumping laws.

14. **Conserve water. Every time you flush or** wash things down the drain, you're contributing to the already flooded sewer system. Consider state-of-the-art toilets, which use only one gallon per flush, saving roughly 7,665 gallons a year per toilet.

15. **Efficient showerheads can save 75 per** cent of the shower's water use.

16. **Front-loading washing machines consume** one third less water (and two thirds less soap) than conventional top loaders, and are made by several leading manufacturers.

17. **Faucet aerators for kitchen and bathroom** sinks are designed with on/off switches, and can reduce the flow of water from your taps by 60 percent.

18. **Check faucets for leaks. A dripping fau-** cet can waste up to 20 gallons of water a day (a leaking toilet can waste 200 gallons a day).

19. **Run your dishwasher and washing ma-** chine only when you have full loads.

20. **Use phosphate-free, low-phosphate, or bio-** degradable dishwashing liquid, laundry detergent, and shampoo. Algae growth is stimulated by phosphate-rich water, causing fish and marine life to suffocate from lack of oxygen.

21. **Use natural fertilizers such as manure** or compost on your garden to limit the amount of dangerous pesticides that are swept into water-ways, and eventually oceans, by rain and snowmelt.

22. **Do not use water fresheners in your** toilet—the chemicals they contain are poisonous.

23. **Improve the drainage around your home** and yard. By landscaping your home with fore-thought, you can steer rainwater slowly across the yard so that it filters into the ground rather than running directly into the gutter. This keeps fewer fertilizers from reaching the ocean.

24. **If you are aware of water polluters in** your community, boycott their products if possible.

25. **Demand to know where the fish you buy** are from and avoid any that are caught in polluted coastal areas. Talk to your grocer and restaurant-owners about your decision.

26. **Consider forming a watchdog system in** your community to monitor coastal areas for pollut-ers. Familiarize yourself with local and federal wa-ter pollution laws and watch for violators.

27. **Encourage lawmakers to mandate tighter** regulation of ships that carry oil or hazardous waste, and to cut back on the number of industries legally allowed to dump hazardous waste into the water.

28. **Write letters to congresspeople, oil com-** panies, and plastic manufacturers to register your concern about ocean pollution. Encourage laws, com-plain when you think it might do some good, and don't hesitate to publicly support conservation.

Government Action

1. Nationwide pollution control requirements should be imposed for industries that currently pollute coastal waters, and should cover all industries and all dangerous pollutants. In places where technologies such as wastewater recycling are available, discharges should be prohibited altogether.

2. Businesses should be encouraged to find new ways of doing business without polluting: by producing factory goods using fewer toxic chemicals, making more efficient use of water and materials, and reducing the quantity of material entering municipal waste landfills through packaging reduction and materials recycling.

3. A nationwide program to collect and safely dispose of household hazardous wastes should be instituted.

4. All discharges of raw sewage from combined sewer outflows should be eliminated.

5. In order to reduce the flow to sewage treatment plants, and hence the danger of overflow, the use of water conservation devices in industry and the home should be promoted.

6. Farmers, developers, and other land users who cause poison runoff should be required to use buffer strips, runoff controls, integrated pest management, and other practices designed to prevent poison runoff.

7. A comprehensive national program should be instituted to protect coastal waters from oil spills by implementing national energy policies based on energy efficiency and renewable energy resources, thus reducing our dependence on oil, and by requiring those responsible for oil spills to pay the full costs of cleanup and restoration, and full damages to all injured parties, including damages for lost public resources. There should also be mandatory use of double-hulled and multi-compartment oil tankers for oil transport.

8. All ocean dumping of medical waste, both directly and through public sewers, should be banned.

9. The use of disposable plastics should be reduced.

10. Strict, new water quality standards that are designed to protect coastal habitats, fish, shellfish, and wildlife should be adopted. These should include standards setting pollutant limits in sediments, fish, and wildlife. All coastal dischargers and developers should be required to meet these standards.

11. Federal tax laws should be amended to prohibit all deductions or credits for the expenses of preparing wetlands for development. Tax benefits for wetlands conservation should be provided.

Reading

The Wasted Ocean, by David K. Bulloch. New York: Lyons and Burford, 1989.

"Plastic Reaps a Grim Harvest in Oceans of the World," by Michael Weisskopf. *Smithsonian,* March 1988.

"Oceans at Risk: Animals Face the Challenge of a Troubled Sea," edited by Joni Praded. *Animals,* January/February 1989.

"A Citizen's Handbook on Water Quality Standards," Natural Resources Defense Council Clean Water Project, 1350 New York Ave. NW, Suite 300, Washington, DC 20005.

"Ebb Tide for Pollution: Actions for Cleaning Up Coastal Waters," Natural Resources Defense Council, (see above).

"Troubled Waters: The World's Oceans Can't Take Much More Abuse," *Business Week,* October 12, 1987.

A Citizen's Guide to Plastics in the Ocean: More Than a Litter Problem, Center for Marine Conservation, 1725 DeSales St. NW, Suite 500, Washington, DC 20036.

Organizations to Contact

Center for Coastal Studies, Cetacean Research Program, 59 Commercial St., Box 826, Provincetown, MA 02657.

Center for Marine Conservation, 1725 DeSales St. NW, Suite 500, Washington, DC 20036, 202-429-5609.

Center for Plastics Recycling Research, Rutgers University, Busch Campus, Building 3529, Piscataway, NJ 08855.

Clean Water Action, 733 15th St. NW, Suite 1110, Washington, DC 20005, 202-547-1196.

The Cousteau Society, 930 W. 21st St., Norfolk, VA 23517, 804-627-1144.

Greenpeace USA, 1436 U St. NW, Washington, DC 20009, 202-462-1177.

National Association for Plastics Container Recovery, 5024 Parkway Plaza Blvd., Suite 200, Charlotte, NC 28217.

National Audubon Society, 801 Pennsylvania Ave. SE, Suite 301, Washington, DC 20003.

National Coalition for Marine Conservation, PO Box 23298, Savannah, GA 31403, 912-234-806.

Natural Resources Defense Council, 1350 New York Ave. NW, Washington, DC 20005.

NOAA/National Marine Fisheries Service, 7600 Sand Point Way NE, Bin C15700, Seattle, WA 98115, 206-526-4009.

The Oceanic Society, 1536 16th St. NW, Washington, DC 20036.

The Society of the Plastics Industry, 1275 K St. NW, 400, Washington, DC 20005, 202-371-5200.

THE WATER

9

Freshwater Pollution

Ninety-seven percent of the world's water is contained in the ocean. Snow, ice, bodies of fresh water, and groundwater comprise the rest. What they lack in volume, these freshwater sources make up in life-sustaining value. Humanity may depend on the ocean to regulate the climate and recycle oxygen and carbon dioxide, but our dependence on fresh water is more direct. Water is one of the most basic needs of life: many organisms can live without oxygen, but none can live without water.

Just as we take the air we breathe for granted, we seldom consider our dependence on fresh water. We worry far too infrequently about how its pollution will affect our lives, in part because water comes to us so cheaply and easily—at least in the industrialized world. With the twist of a knob, it gushes from kitchen taps and showerheads. Throughout much of the world, people use it as if there were a never-ending supply: on a typical day, each American uses more than 100 gallons. Less than 2 percent of that goes for essentials like drinking and cooking. The bulk of it is used for bathing, laundry, and dishwashing (32 gallons), and flushing (24 gallons). This kind of use—and abuse—of fresh water is hard to fathom in places like India, where less than six gallons is available per person, per day. In many Third World nations, rural villagers spend up to six hours a day retrieving water from distant, and often polluted, streams.

Fresh water's importance can't be minimized. Wars have been waged over its control and billions of dollars have been spent worldwide, in struggles to change its course, bend and shape its flow to irrigate fields and generate power. People have built millions of dams, irrigated hundreds of millions of acres, carved deep canals, created hundreds of thousands of public and private water utilities, drained a hundred million acres of wetlands, and drilled millions of wells—all with the goal of sustaining life, and accommodating the planet's sprawling population.

Bodies of fresh water can take hundreds of years to cleanse themselves of the pollutants we dump into them. However, many become overpolluted and "die" before they can "recycle" their waters. So far, no "dead" ocean has been reported, rendered lifeless from human abuse. But hundreds of lakes and rivers around the world have been read their last rites in just the past two decades. The challenge now is to resurrect them and keep others from a similar fate.

Freshwater pollution has a direct effect on man, through the drinking and cooking water we take for granted. Many people don't even know where the water that flows from their taps originates. Generally, tap water comes from two sources: surface water (springs, streams, rivers, lakes) and groundwater (underground aquifers).

Most of the globe's fresh water lies underground. Spread beneath the surface of the ground, these water systems range in volume from the Ogallala Aquifer, which lies beneath more than 98,000 square miles of farm country in Texas, Oklahoma, New Mexico, Kansas, Nebraska, and Colorado, to the thousands of pond-sized sources that supply a single town or neighborhood. Wells are tapped into these aquifers, which aren't really underground reservoirs, but vast systems of water-soaked, permeable rock. Springs that feed many lakes and rivers rise from aquifers, too. Yet these underground water sources remain largely unprotected—some contend that preserving them is the most important environmental job of all.

In the United States, aquifers provide half of the water needs. Every day, Americans consume 230 million gallons of groundwater. Like lakes, aquifers can cleanse and replenish themselves, but this process takes hundreds, maybe thousands of years. Given the toxics that are spreading into underground waters from a variety of sources, it's likely that our drinking water contains odorless, colorless—and potentially toxic—chemicals. But before it gushes from the kitchen tap it may have helped to irrigate farmland, and picked up herbicides, pesticides, and fertilizers along the way. It may also include remnants of the runoff from nearby streets that is laden with oil, grease, cadmium, and lead. While the water from your tap may have begun as an icy mountain spring, it may also have passed beneath a chemical company's discharge pipe. Hazardous waste injected deep into the ground may have spread to your groundwater source, or your water may be tainted by substances leaching from nearby landfills.

Water pollution dates back centuries. In the early 1700s, American rum-makers worried about using water that had been sitting in lead-lined stills. A December 1897 *National Geographic* story, "Pollution of the Potomac River," cautioned, "Until state or national legislation can be secured to regulate such matters, the Potomac . . . must serve as a sort of sewer into which towns and manufacturing establishments dump their refuse."

At first, dumping sewage into rivers and lakes did little harm. The refuse of a smaller population could be absorbed. Organic wastes were recycled into nutrients, which nourished plant life and fish. The river purified itself. But as villages grew into towns, and towns into cities, their refuse became pollution.

In the 1800s, rivers were considered inexhaustible resources. After filling them with topsoil and felled trees, humans proceeded to use them as both reservoirs and sewers. By the end of the century, most rivers in industrializing nations swam with raw sewage, slaughterhouse waste, and factory effluents. Town fathers dealt with such inconveniences irresponsibly. When pollution near a city became intolerable, they would simply draw drinking and bathing water from inlets farther upstream.

For years most lakes (like the ocean) were considered too big to be polluted by humans. But by the 1960s, one of the grandest lakes in North America, Lake Erie, was proclaimed "dead," a victim of eutrophication, the accelerated aging that results from the dumping of sewage, fertilizers, and chemical waste. Thick green algae floated on its surface, and breezes off the water carried the stink of dead fish and chemicals.

Today, in a reversal that has cheered environmentalists around the world, Lake Erie has risen from the dead, serving as an example of how pollution can be controlled. The lake's problems were lessened with the banning of phosphates in laundry products and tighter control of the toxic discharges from industries lining its banks. Since 1972, in a unique and successful joint venture, the United States and Canada have spent more than $9 billion on new and upgraded sewage treatment plants near the lake. The results are encouraging. Lake Erie is again used for recreation, its fish population is making a comeback, and the breezes that blow off it carry the scent of the lake, not the dump.

Though Lake Erie is much cleaner today, it is far from pure. More than 300 chemical compounds, many dangerous to man, still float in it. The success of its cleanup illustrates the challenge for the next decade for water cleanup programs. Better systems for the treatment of *organic* wastes have been installed, and proven successful. Cleaning up the *hazardous chemicals* in the water is an even bigger job.

If Lake Erie stood for years as an example of how people could ruin an "inland sea," the Cuyahoga River which flows nearby served as an example of our ruinous relationship with rivers. In 1969, the river caught on fire. Two-hundred-foot-high flames leaped from the river, burning bridges overhead and melting railroad tracks. Hot slag dumped into the river, whose surface layers were composed more of oil, chemicals, and debris than water, was pinpointed as the igniter. The Cuyahoga has not yet recovered quite as well as Lake Erie, but officials in towns along its length host tours of their waterfront, and brag about their cleanup efforts.

Successes such as Erie and the Cuyahoga are relative in a world still crisscrossed by polluted rivers, lakes, and underground aquifers. Despite international agreements and the passage of the Clean Water Act, enforcement officials are kept running just trying to monitor and stem the flow of sewage, toxics, and runoff into fresh water. Industries have been warned, fined, and warned again. Though sewage treatment plants have been renovated and upgraded, problems remain and in some places worsen. More than 65,000 permits still allow dumping of chemical waste into estuaries and rivers in all 50 states. But freshwater pollution hits so close to home that individuals are starting to pay attention. When *National Wildlife* asked 1,300 readers which environmental problem concerned them most, drinking-water contamination was at the top of their lists. Second was leaking hazardous waste sites, a major cause of groundwater pollution.

Today, three major stumbling blocks remain between people and clean water: we need to get rid of the toxics that already damage rivers and lakes; we need to clamp down harder on new discharges of such poisons; and we must continue to educate the world population about man's responsibility for the continuing pollution. Examples from around the globe illustrate the challenge.

• The bottom of New York's Hudson River is lined with toxic sludge, contaminated by years of chemical dumping. The sludge contains a high percentage of PCBs dumped by two General Electric plants over a 30-year period. State and federal environmentalists armed with a $40 million plan have been trying to clean up the Hudson since 1975. Dredging, burning, and burying have all been considered. So far, proper dumping grounds for the residue have not been found. It seems no one is anxious to have toxic sludge buried in their backyard.

• In the south of the Soviet Union, near the Aral Sea, two rivers, the Amu Darya and Syr Darya, have become little more than giant sewers, filled with the pesticide-laden or "nonpoint" runoff from nearby cotton fields. ("Point" pollutants are those that come straight from a source, like a sewage treatment plant or industrial discharge pipe. "Nonpoint" pollutants are those washed into waterways from streets, fields, building sites, landfills, or elsewhere.) The area has the highest infant mortality rate in the country, which is attributed primarily to the infection and disease spread by its contaminated water. The government has set up a commission to save the waters, but as yet, no specific plans have been made. In the meantime, reports of mother's milk contaminated by pesticides continue to crop up.

• Near Charles City, Iowa, a veterinary medicine manufacturer had, over 25 years, dumped more than a million cubic feet of arsenic-bearing wastes into an 80-acre sand and gravel pit. The dangerous chemicals seeped down into the aquifers and surfaced 50 miles away, contaminating the drinking water of more than 300,000 people. Groundwater poisoning is considered the most pressing hazardous waste problem today. Landfills, toxic waste dumps, and leaking underground gas storage tanks are the major contributors.

• The Vistula River that empties into the Baltic Sea at Gdansk, Poland, collects the garbage of 813 communities including the capital city of Warsaw along its way. Half of that sewage is not treated at all. The resulting stew has rendered more than 80 percent of the river's length unusable, even for industrial purposes.

• Pollution and its cleanup haunt underdeveloped countries, too. Dal Lake, in the center of Kashmir, India, is on the verge of an environmental disaster. Raw sewage and silt is poured into it, shrinking and choking the lake. More than 900 tourist houseboats and the city of nearly a million pump raw sewage into the lake, allowing weeds and waterborne diseases like viral hepatitis to thrive. The boats have no waste disposal system and thousands of toilets flush directly into the lake, from which bathing, drinking, and cooking water is drawn. This scenario is being played out in thousands of communities around the globe. For every success like Lake Erie, there remain hundreds of once-pristine rivers and lakes begging to be cleansed.

CAUSES

Examples of successful cleanups abound. Legislation has helped, as have citizen-initiated lawsuits, which have forced some industries despite their kicking and screaming, into near-compliance. Individual protests, pressure from environmental groups, community actions, and neighborhood meetings have all helped, too. The causes of most water pollution have been identified, but solutions remain a challenge.

• Toxic chemicals are fresh water's greatest threat. They find their way into rivers and lakes from both above and below the ground, are discharged directly

or leak from hundreds of thousands of toxic waste sites. They pour out of factory discharge pipes, leak from dump sites, disposal wells, corroded barrels, and holding tanks, belch from smokestacks, run off millions of acres of city streets and farmland, and blow in (in the form of acid rain) from as far away as South America. (Though banned in the United States, DDT pollutes North American waters by drifting in from Mexico and South America, where the chemical is still used prodigiously.)

Insidious and invisible, toxics are the most difficult pollutants to get rid of, because they don't float to the surface like garbage, or create slicks like oil. Most sink to the bottom of waterways, where they are eaten by plankton and passed up along the food chain, all the way to humans. In the United States, the EPA estimates that industries generate 150 million metric tons of chemical hazardous waste each year (a metric ton is about 2,200 pounds). The Congressional Office of Technology Assessment's estimate is higher, at 255 to 275 tons, or more than a ton of hazardous waste per person, each year.

The 4.5-square-mile Onondaga Lake in upstate New York is generally regarded as the most polluted body of inland water in the United States. Swimming has been banned there since 1940, and various cleanup battles have been waged almost as long. Currently, local residents and the state environmental department are suing Allied Signal, Inc., which they say dumped hundreds of thousands of pounds of toxic chemicals, including mercury, into the lake from its soda ash facility, which operated on the lake's shore until 1986. Despite the lake's official labelling as a hazardous waste site, legal hassles continue, preventing the lake's cleanup. Thousands of similar cases are being fought (and occasionally won) around the world.

• Sewage treatment, as discussed in the preceding chapter on ocean pollution, can do an increasingly good job of cleansing organic (human) waste, but most plants are not capable of ridding sewage of the toxic chemicals that are dumped, flushed, or washed down the drain. Industrial contributions are the most dangerous. A Shell Oil refinery near St. Louis, for example, recently agreed to pay a $380,000 fine for dumping ammonia, oil, grease, phenols, and hydrocarbons directly into the Mississippi River. The company also agreed to build a $50 million waste treatment facility on-site to help disinfect its dangerous residues.

• Some think that accidental or purposeful chemical spills of substances from DDT to Kepone, are an acceptable tradeoff for the business and transportation uses of the world's major waterways. This kind of attitude allows the continued pumping of oil, grease, and metal—legally and illegally—into ponds, lakes, and streams. Some of the worst spills are accidental, like the barge loaded with 500,000 gallons of industrial waste that buckled, split, and emptied its contents near New Orleans in April 1989, instantaneously killing fish in a nearby wildlife refuge. Other spills are more purposeful. That same month in 1989, near the Rocky Flat nuclear weapons plant 15 miles north of Denver, employees dumped toxic chemicals into creeks leading to local drinking water supplies, according to court documents. The dumping took place 10 days after the EPA refused a request from the plant's owner, Rockwell International, to dump in that location. The pollution was detected immediately, by nighttime infrared fly-overs.

(Ironically, in 1987 Rockwell had been awarded an $8.6 million bonus from the Department of Energy for "excellent management." The bonus was awarded despite Department findings that "some Rocky Flats waste facilities were 'patently illegal' and that Rockwell had significant problems in controlling radioactive contamination.")

• Toxic chemicals poured into rivers and lakes form poisonous sediment. Many lake and river bottoms are covered with several feet of poisonous muck. In heavily-trafficked industrial harbors, constant channel dredging, necessary to keep avenues open for shipping, stirs up the sediments and recontaminates the water.

The waters of the Indiana Harbor and Canal are poisoned by a bottom full of industrial sludge. In places, its floor is coated by sludge more than 10 feet thick. The highly toxic slime, laden with mercury, pesticides, and PCBs, has not been dredged for 17 years because no one can agree on how to dispose of the sediment safely. But a plan must be arrived at soon, because contaminants are so thick they are blocking ship traffic, and are spreading into nearby Lake Michigan.

The International Joint Commission, a U.S.–Canada agency that oversees management of the Great Lakes, reports there are 41 similarly contaminated areas around the lakes' shores. Most of the pollutants come from the steel mills, paper and pulp mills, and sewage treatment plants that line the lake's tributaries. The USC Corporation, for example, has been charged with dumping unauthorized amounts of cyanide and ammonia into the Grand Calumet River. But industry isn't the lone abuser. The EPA is also going after the city of Gary, Indiana, for dumping unauthorized waste.

Harbor bottoms outside Barcelona and Athens are similarly polluted. Shipping lanes outside Middle Eastern oil ports are clogged with contaminated sludge. Governments and local environmental agencies continue to search for ways to clean them up and are currently experimenting with both burying and burning options, with costs in the hundreds of millions of dollars.

• Recent federal studies have confirmed that paper mills are pumping dioxins and other chlorinated hydrocarbons directly into rivers, and they are accumulating at dangerous levels in fish. Dioxins are by-products generated when mills bleach paper pulp

Sixty-five thousand permits allow legal discharge of chemical waste (above) into estuaries and rivers throughout the United States. Heavy metals and toxic organic compounds accumulate at river bottoms to form toxic sludge, which, unless physically removed (below) contaminates ground-feeding organisms and fish.

WARNING
NO FISHING

TOXIC
POLLUTION

FOR MORE INFORMATION
CAMPAIGN FOR A CLEAN SWEEP RIVER
CONTACT:

GREENPEACE

with chlorine, and are known cancer-causing agents. Though scientists disagree over how much dioxin humans can safely absorb, the EPA is pressuring paper mills to get it out of their waste waters by 1992.

• Thermal pollution is a major yet little-talked-about problem. When power plants gulp in water to cool their steam generators, the liquid absorbs heat, and returns to its source warmer than when it came out. A rise in water temperature of just a few degrees can "cook" oxygen out of water, disrupting fish breeding habitats and killing off plant life.

• Leaching provides an insidious avenue for water pollutants to get into ground and surface waters. Pesticides and industrial toxics seep into the soil where they may remain for years, or they drip directly into wells, aquifers, or river and lake beds. Leaching is a growing problem and one that is hard to measure, especially in aquifers.

In the past, water drawn from beneath the surface of the earth was generally cleaner than that found in rivers and lakes. Most groundwater could be used for drinking, cooking, and bathing with only moderate treatment. Sometimes, water was consumed straight from the ground. Those days are past. Today, one quarter of all groundwater in the United States is contaminated, and in some regions around the globe, up to three quarters has been tainted with chemical residues.

The sources of leaching are known and multitudinous. Accidental spills, de-icing salts, pesticides and fertilizers, leaking septic tanks and sewers, landfills, leaking gas-station tanks, oil-well spills, coal- and strip-mining runoff, and industrial disposal sinks all contribute to groundwater contamination. According to the Association of State and Interstate Water Pollution Control Administrators, 41 percent of surveyed river miles, 53 percent of lake acres, and 28 percent of estuary acres are contaminated by runoff and leaching.

Two examples serve to illustrate the nefarious ways by which poisons leach into drinking water. During the 1970s, three New Jersey chrome refineries used two million tons of highly chemical waste as fill at demolition and construction sites surrounding Jersey City, a fast-growing community of 200,000. Today the refineries are closed, but 104 contaminated sites have been documented, most of them already hidden beneath housing and businesses. Both wells and surface water in the area are contaminated. Downstate, in Toms River, the Ciba-Geigy Corporation has created an underground lake of cancer-causing agents such as benzene, arsenic, and chloroform, which seeped from toxic waste burial pits and lagoons near a dye and plastics factory. The EPA estimates it will take 30 years to clean up, and will require about 3 million gallons of clean water a day to be pumped into the aquifer to flush the poisons out. Environmentalists fear that the process will take much longer.

More than 2,000 wells in the state have been closed due to similar toxic leaching. Twenty percent of the state's 300,000 wells do not meet standards of the Safe Drinking Water Act.

• Pesticides are one of the primary nonpoint pollutants poisoning rivers, lakes, and groundwater. They also remain the most difficult to police, and have proven exceedingly hard to legislate out of use. Since their introduction in the 1940s, pesticide use has proliferated. Today more than 4 billion pounds of harmful pesticides are sold worldwide.

Pesticides may be the most wily of all hazardous chemicals, because with the best of intentions they are sprayed over the world's food supply. As population growth continues and the demand for food increases, pesticide use escalates and their regulation becomes more difficult. Today, in many countries, the environmental hazards of widely unregulated pesticide use outweighs the pesticides' benefits.

Since 1945, 35,000 different pesticide formulas

have entered the global market. Worldwide sales have doubled since the mid-1970s, to nearly $18 billion a year, and much of that growth is in the Third World. For all the good they are designed to do, pesticides leave behind a trail of poisoned water, soil, air, and bodies. They are picked up by winds and carried across state and national borders. Their dangerous, persistent residue is found in the runoff from farm fields, in drinking water and breast milk, and on the plants and vegetables we buy at the grocer's. Today, the National Academy of Sciences lists more than a dozen foods in which pesticide residues present potentially significant risks, including tomatoes, potatoes, oranges, lettuce, apples, peaches, pork, wheat, soybeans, carrots, chicken, corn, and grapes.

The use of pesticides has intensified with the shift to one- or two-crop farms, which allows insects to thrive and grow stronger. Controlling these pests takes ever-stronger poisons. In the early 1960s, the industrialized countries began to recognize the disastrous long-term effects of many pesticides and began to ban the most dangerous. Today, more than a quarter of the pesticides we ship to the Third World are banned, restricted, or unregistered in industrialized countries. An ironic twist to this tale is that 70 percent of those pesticides is used on crops grown for export *back* to industrialized countries. Coffee imported by the United States from Latin America has been found to contain dangerous chemical residues, and beef shipments are sometimes stopped at international borders because they harbor several times more DDT than is permitted. In West Germany, tobacco grown in Thailand has been rejected because of high levels of pesticide residue, and Scandinavian countries have refused fruit and vegetables from Africa for the same reason.

The worst pesticide problems occur in underdeveloped countries. Third World countries use just one seventh of the world's pesticides, yet one half of pesticide-related poisonings and three quarters of

the estimated 20,000 deaths per year caused by pesticides take place in these countries, according to the World Health Organization. Brazil, now one of the largest producers and consumers of pesticides in the world, is the site of many of these poisonings. With a rural population that is almost 40 percent illiterate, Brazil's workers are ill-prepared to take the cautionary measures that all who work with poisons must. They handle toxic chemicals without masks, gloves, or any form of protection. Uninformed people store food and water in empty pesticide containers and wash their children's hair in lethal chemicals, thinking it will kill lice.

As an alternative to pesticide use and abuse, many encourage the practice of Integrated Pest Management (IPM), a system that combines biological controls (like natural predators of pests), cultural practices (planting patterns), and genetic manipulation (pest-resistant crop varieties) with a measured use of chemicals. The goal of IPM is not to totally eradicate insects and weeds but to keep them within safe, manageable limits.

Organic farming, which forbids the use of all synthetic chemicals, is seen as the wave of the future by many. Consumers hungry for fresh, organically grown vegetables, dairy products, and meats may help revive small farm business, especially near big cities.

So far, a mixture of different approaches has slowed pesticide use in some developing countries. In Brazil, pesticide applications to soybeans have decreased with the adoption of IPM; in Africa, parasitic wasps have been used to control pests on 160 million acres of cassava; in Sri Lanka, parasites have been found to control damage to coconuts.

While some pesticides can remain suspended in soil, when mixed with irrigation water or rain, added directly to the soil, or sprayed on foliage, most pesticides wash directly into aquifers or run into streams. Many have proven to be killers if ingested by man, but chemical pesticides and herbicides remain popular among farmers because they are easy to apply, effective, and long-lasting.

Laws that would allow governments to remove dangerous chemicals from the market more quickly have been proposed. Today, getting a pesticide off store shelves can take years. Even then, a pesticide banned in France may still be quite legal in Thailand. There is reason for optimism, though. Pesticide use has fallen around the globe since 1982, because of the growing international awareness of their potential harm to the environment, farm workers, and food consumers. The list of growers who use only safe, organic pest-killers is lengthening.

• Erosion is a subtle form of water pollution. Soil laden with chemical residue, fertilizers, or pesticides slides into lakes and rivers, adding more poisons to the water and contributes to the mounting pile of toxic sediment.

• Between 5 and 20 percent of gas and fuel tanks across the United States leak, creating a greater threat of oil spills on land than on the seas. They are potentially more dangerous than the spill of the *Exxon Valdez*, for example, because most of these leaks happen closer to home. Relatively few people live next door to a toxic waste dump; almost everyone lives in the vicinity of an underground gas storage tank.

In just a seven-county area along the Hudson River, over 1,300 oil spills were reported in 1988. Only 12 of those spills were classified as "major" (resulting from spills at facilities that store over 400,000 gallons) and only 11 were reported from vessels. The rest, anywhere from a couple of gallons to tens of thousands, occurred at gas stations or small industries, or were the result of underground tank failures.

• Keeping lead out of the food chain, air, and water is a challenge governments have been wrestling with for decades. Bans on leaded paints and leaded gas have been on the books for years. Now, as a result of corroded pipes, lead solder, and lead that has leached from the soil, the element has been found in high doses in drinking fountains and tap water. Even low levels of lead poisoning can cause irritability and aggravate high blood pressure. A recent EPA study estimates that nearly one in five Americans drinks excessively lead-rich tap water. In fact, drinking water is now thought to be the principal source of lead in the bloodstream (proving that environmental change can be legislated: the main cause of lead in human bodies used to be paint, but laws successfully mandated that lead not be added to paint). Plastic pipes are now being investigated for their potential to pass along plastic-heavy residues.

• As discussed in Chapter 4, acid rain is a major contributor to freshwater pollution. Fallout from fossil fuel emissions, waste incineration, and evaporation contribute volatile organic chemicals and heavy metals to our waters, and their dangerous effects are just beginning to be understood.

EFFECTS

Thousands of lakes worldwide are biologically dead because of the actions of man-made pollutants. Thousands more are threatened by the effects of acid rain. More than 70,000 different toxic chemicals are produced around the world, hundreds of millions of tons each year. Monitoring them is tough, assessing their damage even tougher. Most of them remain unregulated and unmonitored—the EPA has set drinking water standards for only about two dozen of the more than 300 toxics that have already been detected in the groundwater. The quality of most underground aquifers is questionable. More than 50 pesticides contaminate groundwater in 32 American states. The extent of toxic contamination

Oil and gasoline spills increasingly contaminate freshwater supplies. A leaking fuel tank beneath a gas station is excavated (above), and (below) rain will wash the toxic residue from these abandoned oil barrels into the soil and nearby river.

worldwide is unknown, simply because it is so hard to measure contamination.

In developed nations, 98 percent of all citizens have access to clean water. Most of the cities and towns of Europe, Canada, and the United States have good drinking water. But over half of all citizens in the developing world (China excepted) do not have access to clean water supplies. Where sanitation is below standard, an estimated 25 million people die each year, three fifths of them children, because of waterborne diseases. Dirty water is the cause of maladies ranging from hepatitis and blindness to malaria, elephantiasis, typhoid, cholera, leprosy, and yellow fever. The most serious disease is diarrhea, which kills more than 1,000 children in the world every hour. How do the diseases spread? In much of the Third World, water is used again and again and again, picking up additional pollutants with each use, and providing an ideal habitat for disease. Sadly, many people in the world live miles from "fresh" water, and spend hours each day retrieving and carting the polluted, disease-bearing fluid home by foot.

According to the United Nations Environmental Program, river pollution is most severe in Mexico, India, Colombia, and Brazil. An estimated 70 percent of India's total surface waters are polluted, and of the country's 3,119 towns and cities, only 217 have even partial sewage-treatment facilities, according to a 1986 study by the World Resources Institute. The Yamuna River, which flows through New Delhi, receives an estimated 50 million gallons of untreated sewage, plus another 5 million gallons of industrial effluents, including 125,000 gallons of DDT wastes—every day.

The problem is not confined to developing nations, either. More than a million residents of America's rural South depend on contaminated water for cooking and bathing. Yet despite the current and continued murkiness of many lakes and aquifers in the United States, water pollution has actually lessened over the past decade.

Pollution of drinking water in the United States is not a new concern. In 1900, 27,000 Americans died of typhoid fever, which was spread mainly through drinking water. Thirty years later, typhoid's annual death toll had dropped, even though the population had grown. As early as 1913, water from polluted rivers was being tapped and treated by filtration and chemicals to weed out sediment.

Today, virtually all public water supplies in developed countries undergo some kind of treatment. Most water is treated by filtration and disinfection—processes that are not much different from when sewage treatment was first introduced in 1908. But such simple procedures cannot possibly remove all the complex toxics found in drinking water today. Some substances, like radium, are the result of natural forces. Most are man-made.

Despite the best efforts of sanitation departments and environmental agencies worldwide, much human illness is caused simply by drinking dirty water. A 1983 EPA study of drinking water supplies in 945 towns and cities showed that 21 percent of the sample sites were contaminated by toxic chemicals.

The effects are as harmful to plants and wildlife as they are to man. Fish have developed cancers after being exposed to floating chemicals and refuse, and studies suggest there is an increased risk of cancer in people who eat a lot of fish. Pregnant women and nursing mothers are sometimes urged not to eat fish at all, because toxic chemicals that the fish may have absorbed are blamed for birth defects and damage to nervous and immune systems. Toxics accumulate in the tissues of fish and move through the food chain. But because so many of the fish and so much sea-life studied are steeped in chemical on top of chemical, it is exceedingly difficult to break out the effects of individual toxics.

And so, during the 1980s, sales of bottled water have soared. In the United States alone, sales have grown by nearly 500 percent in the last 10 years.

The market for home water purifiers has also skyrocketed. Sales of both are expected to continue to boom in coming years.

SOLUTIONS

In the United States, the 1972 Clean Water Act has helped. Many streams and lakes have improved since then. But the discharge of all pollutants did not stop in 1985, as had been hoped. The act regulated discharges, but was rarely enforced, primarily due to lack of manpower. To date, just a third of the 18,000 cities and towns in the United States that have been tested meet cleanup requirements. In 1974, the Safe Drinking Water Act was passed to expand federal responsibility for keeping drinking water clean. The latest amendment to the Clean Water Act, passed in 1987, provides $18 billion to help communities across the country build sewage treatment plants and promises $2 billion more to other water cleanup projects. While the building of new sewage plants and the upgrading of others did much to clean up sewage, little has been done about many of the hazardous chemicals which find their way into the water. In fact, the liberal use of chlorination in sewage treatment has added to the chemical pollution.

No cleanup law in the world has yet proved totally effective. Additional money is slated to be spent on cleanup, but there are still not enough deterrents in place to keep the most recalcitrant polluters from fouling the waters. Regulation and enforcement are difficult. But examples like Lake Erie's recovery suggest that environmental legislation and enforcement can work.

Many volunteers will be needed to enforce the laws already on the books. A shining example is the Hudson River Fishermen's Association and its watchboat, *The Riverkeeper*. The group was founded in 1966 by Robert Boyle, who can watch the Hudson twist and turn from his hilltop house in Westchester County, north of New York City. He started the watchdog effort before environmental protection was much of a concern, and did it for one simple reason. "Right before my eyes, the river began to turn the color of coffee grounds," he told an interviewer. "After that, everywhere I went, I saw pollution. Until then, I had never been a joiner. But at that moment, I became a founder."

Since its founding, the group has grown to include more than 250 members, who take turns patrolling the river watching for illegal dumpers and pollution. After winning several lawsuits against polluters, Boyle and the group built the 26-foot *Riverkeeper* and hired a full-time captain, John Cronin. Since then, they've mounted and won several more complaints, the most prominent of which was a $2 million settlement with Exxon. The oil company was rinsing containers of petrochemicals from its chartered tankers in the Hudson, and filling the tanks with fresh water to sell to businesses on the island of Aruba. A member of the Hudson River group brought back water samples from hotels and swimming pools for analysis, to prove that the water came from the Hudson. A suit was initiated, the fishermen's group was joined by the New York Department of Environmental Conservation, and Exxon settled out of court.

Robert Boyle has been called "the conscience of the river," by peers and foes alike. His example should inspire the consciousness of everyone who appreciates clean water.

In the next ten years, enforcement of existing laws and efforts to reduce industrial waste must become the focus of cleanup efforts. In many states, polluters caught dumping are given a year or more to clean up the contaminants before fines are even considered. Fines for dumping should be increased. (Though Exxon will spend over $1 billion cleaning up the spill of the *Valdez*, its federal fine will be around $50,000.) As contamination becomes more sophisticated—the chemicals more complex—cleaning

A regular inventory is required to assess pollution damage to surface water. At a water test site (above) on the Russian River, one of California's most polluted, water from the river's depth is pulled through filtering systems, so that scientists can sample for pollutants. Greenpeace environmentalists voluntarily monitor toxic discharge flowing into the St. Louis River in Missouri (below).

up our water in the twenty-first century should prove one of the more challenging environmental tasks.

The most specific challenge is to try and bring nonpoint pollutants under control. Today in the United States, just 9 percent of river pollution comes from industry. Roughly 65 percent comes from agriculture (pesticides) and other non-industrial sources. So far, world environmental lawmakers have evidenced little muscle against pesticides nor put much money behind education aimed at preventing toxic runoff pollution.

An international groundwater strategy has been proposed, which would be directed by consensus by federal, state, and local officials, with the goal of providing avenues for aquifer protection. Several such bills have been written, none yet adopted. Perhaps the best example of transboundary cooperation is the Great Lakes Water Quality Agreement, signed by the United States and Canada in 1986. Its goal is to eliminate toxic discharges from both shores within the next decade.

Keeping European rivers clean is a bigger problem because they often course through two or more countries on their way to open seas. Their cleanup involves international negotiation, teamwork, and a uniquely purposeful vision. Cooperation, unfortunately, isn't always easy. In November 1986, for example, a massive toxic chemical spill in the Rhine went unheeded for 24 hours because Switzerland, where the spill occurred, did not inform the nations downstream about the accident. An estimated 500,000 fish and eels died and potential human danger was immeasurable. Most large industrialized nations, including China, India, and Brazil, are so intent these days on using their rivers and lakes for increased hydroelectric power that freshwater pollution has become a secondary concern.

The United Nations is winding down a 10-year clean water education and development plan. Dubbed the "International Drinking Water Supply and Sani-

tation Decade 1981-1990," the plan had a goal of bringing clean water to 1.8 billion people, mostly in developing nations, by 1990. It's designers also hoped to provide access to sanitation to another 2.4 billion. While neither goal has been achieved totally, the plan's educational efforts have been a help. The plan fell short primarily because it cost $30 to $60 billion a year, which was to come from the governments involved and from worldwide development agencies. (That may sound like a lot of money, especially for already-strapped governments, but it works out to an expenditure of $80 million a day, less than a third of the $250 million the world population spends on cigarettes each day.) Too often, developing countries concentrate monies on hospitals and medicine to help solve the ills caused by waterborne diseases, when the key to stemming pollution is focusing not on more hospital beds, but on prevention.

Treatment facilities and governments are also looking into the possibility of burying contaminated sediment dredged from river bottoms in landfills, but no satisfactory system has yet been devised. The story of the Hudson River sludge that can't seem to find a home because of neighborhood complaints is one that has been repeated around the globe.

The battle over conventional pollutants, especially human waste, may have been won, at least in developed nations. But a tougher battle looms against toxics, involving much more subtle, insidious "warfare." The first step is to ban the discharge of toxic chemicals that have already been proven to be harmful. Unfortunately, no global consensus exists on which chemicals are safe, which unsafe. Although PCBs were outlawed in North America 10 years ago, they are still in wide use from South America to the Far East. And even though they are no longer manufactured in the United States, vast quantities of the chemical still exist in electrical transformers and other equipment and continue to make their way into the atmosphere and groundwater.

The recycling of chemicals by both industry and agriculture is an absolute necessity. Instead of flushing solvents and pesticides down sinks and into streams, there are ways for many of them to be safely recovered and reused. Recyling is the only way to keep toxics out of sewage treatment plants, where they can't be properly treated anyway. If recycling measures aren't adopted, the option may be banning a lot of chemicals altogether.

On the farm, experiments with biological pesticides are underway, and the pressure on farmers to use fewer inorganic chemicals is growing. In China, ducks are used to eat weeds in rice paddies. Egypt has been releasing 140 million sterilized male Mediterranean fruit flies each day to reduce the growing numbers of pests in vegetable gardens and fruit orchards. Similar experiments are being carried out with tsetse flies in Nigeria. In South Florida, vegetable growers are applying an insecticide made from crushed oyster shells. In Maine, Delaware, New Jersey, and on Long Island, potato farmers are using insecticides made from natural bacteria to battle crop-ravaging beetles. More government money steered towards experimentation with naturally-contrived pesticides and nontoxic plant care products would help.

Backed by a report by the National Academy of Sciences, which endorsed chemical-free farming as both productive and safe, many small growers are joining the organic foods bandwagon. Organic agriculture incorporates natural soil management practices that balance soil fertility, humus content, and biological life. Synthetic fertilizers, growth regulators, biocides, chemicals, pesticides, and herbicides are not used. Benjamin Wilcox, who farms in south-central Maine, grows 40 different kinds of vegetables without chemicals and boasts that not only is he providing good, safe food for his customers, but he's making a living at it, too. The trend has lured a variety of farmers, from apple growers in Massachusetts to lettuce producers in California, and estimates are that "pesticide-free" will be the farming success story of the 1990s.

In Oakland, California, Jim Knutzon, a one-time pesticide salesman who now advises farmers on pesticide alternatives, works for a company called NutriClean. Its goal is to get pesticides off the farm and out of the American diet. He promotes the use of insects that prey on other insects, and other types of biological controls to keep crops in bloom and dangerous chemicals out of groundwater and grocery stores. NutriClean is at the tip of a trend: in California, where 53 percent of America's vegetables and 42 percent of its fruits and nuts are grown, the number of organic farms using no man-made pesticides or fertilizers has doubled in the past year to about 1,500.

Farm states, like Iowa and Minnesota, have taken the lead in passing sweeping groundwater protection bills. The legislation is aimed directly at the heart of these states' agriculture. In Iowa, plastic pesticide containers, laden with dangerous remnants, were being burned, dumped, or buried; state law now requires higher fees on these non-recyclable containers. Higher taxes on dangerous herbicides like atrazine, which has been showing up in aquifers across the Midwest for the past 20 years, have also encouraged cleaner groundwater. Other states have passed higher taxes on oil and gas, and the increases are set aside to help pay for leaking underground fuel tanks. Iowa recently passed a $95 million bond issue to help small, independent gas stations repair or replace underground storage tanks. The bond is to be repaid through higher tank fees, cost-recovery revenues, and an environmental protection charge on gasoline.

Everyone—farmers, legislators, and even chemical manufacturers—agree that chemicals must be better tested, both before they are approved and at intervals afterwards. (The EPA has banned only 26 pesticides since it was created in 1970, even though the agency admits that at least 70 now on the market are carcinogenic in animals.)

Water Use

A tremendous amount of water is used daily, especially in western countries. Only a portion of it is consumed—incorporated physically into products, crops, our bodies. Much of it is returned, and it is this water that is increasingly polluted. However, the amount of water used affects its quality as well. Removing too much water from a stream or lake causes the temperature of the remaining water to rise (shallower water heats faster), harming fish and plants. A sewage treatment plant's effectiveness is impaired by excessive water return. Although water use has decreased slightly, according to the EPA 68 percent of the United States' streams and lakes are suffering the effects of overuse. Conservation improves water quality.

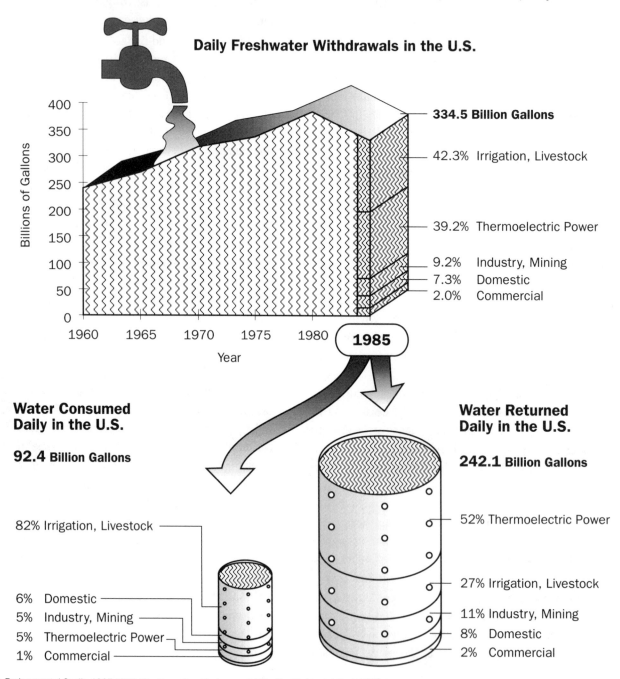

Daily Freshwater Withdrawals in the U.S.

334.5 Billion Gallons

42.3% Irrigation, Livestock

39.2% Thermoelectric Power

9.2% Industry, Mining

7.3% Domestic

2.0% Commercial

Billions of Gallons

Year

1985

Water Consumed Daily in the U.S.

92.4 Billion Gallons

82% Irrigation, Livestock

6% Domestic

5% Industry, Mining

5% Thermoelectric Power

1% Commercial

Water Returned Daily in the U.S.

242.1 Billion Gallons

52% Thermoelectric Power

27% Irrigation, Livestock

11% Industry, Mining

8% Domestic

2% Commercial

Sources: *Environmental Quality* 1987-1988. The Council on Environmental Quality; Worldwatch Paper #67: "Conserving Water: the Untapped Alternative" by Sandra Postel. The Worldwatch Institute, September 1985.

Not all nonpoint pollutants come from farm fields. Chemicals sprayed on city streets and others used to melt snow and ice all trickle into drinking water reservoirs. In all big cities, where leaking water mains and antiquated plumbing cause water waste and increase the risk of water contamination, more time and money needs to be spent on repair and replacement.

Groundwater monitoring is required by the EPA, and is supposed to detect leaks from landfills, but it is an often misleading science. Sampled wells may not pick up contamination, as fluid movement underground is hard to predict. Groundwater sampling is also hard to interpret; serious pollution may occur before the samples reach statistically dangerous levels.

Fines and education both play significant roles in preventing water pollution. In Connecticut, the state Department of Environmental Protection oversees a program that forces companies dumping dangerous chemicals into waterways to pay for the resulting damage. Since the program went into effect, three companies have been made to pay for every fish killed by their actions. So far the Abbott Ball Company of West Hartford has paid the highest penalty, $1,082 for nearly 5,000 crappies, sunfish, white suckers, brown bullheads, fallfish, and carp killed in a "relatively small" acid spill. While the fine and loss may seem insignificant, such actions help set a precedent for the next *Exxon Valdez*.

A key to environmental success stories is educating children about pollution problems early on. On Staten Island, ninth graders at Wagner High School, in cooperation with the National Park Service and Gateway Environmental Studies Center, organize beach cleanups and salt marsh plantings, and monitor area rivers and the coastline for pollution.

Some local water commissions have structured water rates to reward conservation. They have changed plumbing codes in an attempt to reduce flush and shower flows for new houses, and have distributed conservation add-ons to existing ones. Leaking or corroded plumbing decreases conservation and increases the potential for contaminated drinking water. National plumbing codes have been suggested, with both conservation and anti-pollution in mind.

In an age when gloom and doom seem to accompany every environmental problem, the Cuyahoga River today is a testament to what cooperation, legislation, and enforcement can do. The official stamp of approval came from the EPA, which has labeled the 40-mile section of the river from Akron to Cleveland a "recovering system." The cleanup is a result of tighter enforcement of regulations at steel, rubber, and chemical plants, which have all been working to reduce their discharges by building expensive treatment facilities.

The Cuyahoga is not yet pristine. The river, like many others, still faces overflows of raw sewage during heavy rains. But biologists are heartened by the reappearance in the river of several species of insects and fish that had all but disappeared. In past decades, the only thing that could survive in the Cuyahoga were the parasites of river life, like carp and bottom feeders. Today, upriver from Akron, people are actually swimming in the Cuyahoga—not a bad comeback for a body of water that 10 years ago was a fire hazard.

FRESHWATER POLLUTION

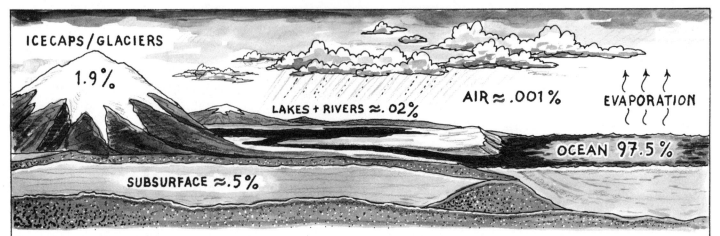

Less than 3 percent of the world's water is fresh. Of that, more than two thirds is locked up in the icecaps of Antarctica and the Arctic. The fresh water available to man is continually recycled through the land, rivers, lakes, seas, and air.

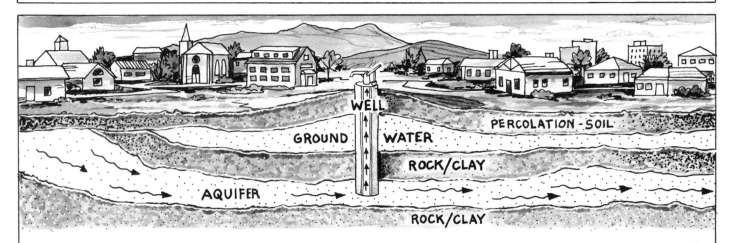

Most of the accessible fresh water is underground, in groundwater or aquifers—long stretches of porous rock, sand, or gravel. Groundwater and aquifers provide Europe and the U.S. with over half their drinking water.

Increasingly, the world's freshwater supply is being tainted by a variety of pollutants—acid rain, hazardous wastes, and poisonous runoff from streets and farmlands.

Underground fuel tanks are another source of water contamination. An estimated 100,000 fuel tanks in the U.S. leak tens of millions of gallons of gasoline each year—one gallon a day entering a groundwater source can foul the drinking water supply of 50,000 people.

Pesticides washed into streams and rivers by rain are a major pollutant. They can also seep through the soil into groundwater and foul aquifers.

FROM PESTICIDE PLANE TO GROUND

FROM GROUND TO WATER

MICROORGANISMS

PLANT-EATING FISH

PREDACEOUS FISH

Pesticides do not break down easily and are very soluble in fat. Once in the water they are absorbed or eaten by tiny microorganisms and then make their way up the food chain. At each step up the chain the concentration of the toxic chemical increases.

Thousands of dangerous chemicals have been found in the supposedly clear drinking water of industrialized nations.

In Third World countries, the same water is often used for the disposal of human waste, bathing, and laundering, spreading infectious diseases. Six million children die each year from diarrhea caused by dirty water.

As pollution grows, the amount of "safe" water available diminishes. Globally, 25 percent of our rivers are dangerously polluted, as are hundreds of thousands of lakes.

There are hundreds of ways in which water can be polluted—and cleaned. Enforcement of laws is a good place to start, as is tighter regulation of industry and agriculture. Individuals have to take responsibility, too, for what they throw in their garbage, on their lawn, or down the sink.

Individual Action

1. First things first: Never flush toxics of any kind down sinks or toilets. This includes disinfectants, most household cleansers, and solvents of any type. Keep in mind that anything you do flush away may come back out of your tap.

2. Have your tap water tested for lead and other contaminants. Most local utilities will do it for a small fee, or you can hire a private tester. Tested or untested, if a faucet hasn't been used for six hours or longer, let cold water run through the pipes for five seconds to two minutes to clear any potentially dangerous sediment sitting in the pipes.

3. Use only water from the cold water tap for drinking, cooking, and making baby formula. Hot water is likely to contain higher levels of lead.

4. Flush and clear sediment from your water heater every six months or so. If you go on vacation and it's not been used, run the hot water when you come back to flush any build-up.

5. For more information on drinking water contaminants, call the EPA's toll-free safe drinking-water hotline, 800-426-4791, to help with interpretations of the law and its enforcement.

6. The Safe Drinking Water Act requires mon-itoring of community water systems that have 14 or more service connections. If you have questions about your water, records of such monitoring should be available from your local environmental or health departments. For information about the quality of local water call your local village/city manager, or the state agency in charge of regulating public water supplies. If you are in a community water system, ask your supplier if the system contains lead piping. If the answer is yes, ask if it's being replaced.

Drinking water can be treated at the plant to make it less corrosive for an annual cost of less than one dollar per person.

7. We said it last chapter, but the same holds true for freshwater pollution: Conserve, conserve conserve. The less water used, the less demand worldwide, the less risk of contamination. Also make sure toilets and showerheads are the most efficient available.

8. The sale of bottled water continues to grow 15 to 20 percent a year. Worldwide, we consume 5.7 gallons of bottled water per person each year. For a rating of the dozens available, check out *Consumer Reports,* January 1987.

9. Water-purification systems for your tap are another option. But be careful. There are dozens on the market, each with a specific cleansing purpose. And there are as many hoodwinking purification systems salesmen as there are systems. They'll promise anything and deliver little. Careful investigation is an absolute. Try *Consumer Reports* for recommendations.

10. Buy organically grown fruits and vegeta-bles. As the demand for organic foods grows, pesticide use will eventually lessen—the better for both groundwater and consumers.

11. The U.S. Public Interest Research Group (USPIRG) publishes "Testing for Toxics: A Guide to Investigating Drinking Water Quality," which discusses relatively easy methods for communities or individuals to use to test their water for contamination. Write USPIRG, 215 Pennsylvania Ave. SE, Washington, DC 20003, for a copy.

12. **The Izaak Walton League of America operates** an extensive national volunteer program called "Save Our Streams." The league encourages community groups to adopt an area of a stream, remove debris, replant vegetation, and monitor water quality. (Address below, for information.)

13. **Use unbleached (non-white) and undyed** paper products whenever possible, for two reasons. First, the dioxins involved in the manufacture of bleached papers are primary polluters of rivers; second, dyed toilet paper and paper towels carry more pollutants into the water.

14. **Ask at your car wash if they recycle their** water. If they don't, find another washer. If you wash your car at home, be sure and turn the hose off when you're not rinsing.

15. **Many brands of toothpaste contain cadmium** (which becomes harmful as large quantities of it are released into the groundwater) but manufacturers are not required by the FDA to list it among the active ingredients. Write to the maker of your brand and ask whether it uses cadmium. If it does, pick a new brand.

16. **Use "gray water"** (i.e., water previously used, like dishwater or a pet's drinking water) or rain water for plants and garden, or use an underground drip irrigation system in the garden to send water directly to the roots without evaporation or wastage.

17. **If you have a small garden, use water-soluble** fertilizers. Available at most hardware and garden stores, they are absorbed almost immediately by roots and leaves. They don't dissolve in the soil and then leach into groundwater.

18. **Ask at your local nursery about which** plants will grow in your area with little or no watering.

19. **Don't hose down your sidewalk or driveway,** sweep it.

20. **If you live near contaminated water,** contact Clean Water Action (317 Pennsylvania Ave. SE, Washington, DC 20003, 202-547-1196). The group uses such reports to twist the arms of congresspeople into action. They are also a good source for information about how to get involved.

21. **Under the Clean Water Act, anyone who** discharges pollutants into a waterway must have a permit that spells out exactly what they are allowed to discharge. Every month, the company must report to the EPA or to the state on its compliance or non-compliance with the terms of that permit. The law also allows for citizens to take direct action against those companies. Several lawsuits have been originated, fought, and won against major companies based on citizen complaints. If you have a complaint, contact an office of the Natural Resources Defense Council, the local EPA, or another environmental group.

PESTICIDES

• Pesticides leaching into the world's waterways are among the Earth's most insidious and silent poisonings. The suffix "-cide" means "killer." Look for natural pesticides, available at most nurseries, greenhouses, or even hardware stores. It's not a bad idea to promote populations of beneficial animals such as ladybug beetles, bees, fly larvae, lace-wing larvae, praying mantises, dragonflies, spiders, toads, garter snakes, and birds, which all keep plant-killers away.

• Spraying tobacco water, hot pepper and water, garlic juice and rubbing alcohol, and diluted pure soap on foliage will keep most bugs away. Simply wash indoor plants with soap and water and rinse.

• To keep pests away from your house, first identify the pests. Monitor their populations and then choose the best weapons. Improve sanitation and maintenance (fix holes in screens, water and fertilize plants, trees, and shrubs); don't allow rainwater to sit in pools; mow the lawn with sharp blades, set high; fix holes and cracks in house to foil termites and wood borers; use fly swatters, fly paper, sticky traps for cockroaches. (Write Safer Gardens, PO Box 1665, New York, NY 10116, for a booklet on non-toxic gardens.)

• Always keep pesticides in their original containers. Empty containers should be rinsed well before they are thrown away. Even the rinse water should be saved and used as a pesticide. The empty container should be wrapped in newspaper and discarded in garbage.

• Any kind of bug spray for indoor or outdoor use, as well as flea products, insect repellents, and wood preservatives should be dropped at a collection.

• Be sure and contact your state environmental agency to find out which pesticides are banned in your area.

• Encourage your grocer to sell only safe, tested produce, free of pesticides. To be safe, wash fruits and vegetables well before use. For more information contact the National Coalition Against the Misuse of Pesticides, 530 7th St. SE, Washington, DC 20003, 202-543-5450.

• Children are exposed to more pesticides in their food than are adults, because they eat more fruit and vegetables, at a more vulnerable time in their bodies' development. Be particularly careful with the produce you give to kids. Wash and peel; try to find organically grown produce. Encourage the local supermarket manager to label imported produce. For more information write Mothers and Others for Pesticide Limits (Meryl Streep did their television ads), Box 96641, Washington, DC 20090.

Government Action

1. Strict nationwide pollution control requirements for industries that pollute water bodies, either directly or through public sewers, should be imposed.

2. New or increased discharges of factory pollution that would cause or contribute to violations of water quality standards should be prohibited.

3. A nationwide program to collect and safely dispose of household hazardous waste should be instituted.

4. All discharges of raw sewage from combined sewer overflows should be eliminated.

5. Pretreatment programs to reduce the discharge of toxic pollutants into sewage treatment plants should be strengthened.

6. The use of water conservation devices, to reduce the flow to sewage treatment plants, should be promoted.

7. Strict plans to reduce poison runoff (non-point source pollution) from existing development and to prevent runoff from new development should be required.

8. Each state or locality should implement comprehensive groundwater management laws that include the regulation of withdrawals from aquifers, the protection of groundwater against contamination, and a coordinated management of interstate aquifers.

9. Strict nationwide standards for toxic con-taminants of drinking water should be established.

10. The underground injection of industrial waste, the underground storage of toxic chemicals,

and the application of pesticides in areas above aquifers should be strictly regulated.

11. Local governments should implement strict urban water conservation plans.

12. Incentives and federal support should be provided for environmentally sound agricultural practices. The use of certain pesticides should be taxed.

Reading

But Not a Drop to Drink: The Lifesaving Guide to Good Water, by Steve Coffel, Rawson & Associates, New York: Macmillan Publishing, 1989.

" 'Taps' for Drinking Water? Efforts to Rid Our Nation's Tap Water of Pollutants Have Run Out of Steam," by Joanna Hoelscher and Amy Middleton. *Environmental Review,* Summer 1988, (Citizens for a Better Environment, 33 E. Congress, Suite 523, Chicago, IL 60605).

"Wastewater Treatment: Part of the Solution and Part of the Problem," by Eric Swanson. *Environmental Review,* Fall 1988. See above.)

"The Great Lakes' Troubled Waters," by Charles E. Cobb, Jr. *National Geographic,* July 1987.

"Water: Our Most Precious Resource," by Thomas Y. Canby, *National Geographic,* August 1980.

Laying Waste: The Poisoning of America by Toxic Chemicals (pp. 105–127), by Michael Brown. New York: Pocket Books, 1979.

"Water Quality Newsletter," Water Quality Association, 4151 Naperville Rd., Lisle, IL 60532, 312-369-1600.

"U.S. Water News" (monthly), U.S. Water News, Circulation Dept., 230 Main St., Halstead, KS 67056.

Drinking Water: A Community Action Guide, Concern, 1794 Columbia Rd. NW, Washington, DC 20009.

Water Rights: Scarce Resource, Allocation, Bureaucracy and the Environment, Pacific Institute for Public Policy Research, 177 Post St., San Francisco, CA 94108.

Groundwater Pollution: Environmental and Legal Problems, American Association for the Advancement of Science and Westview Press, Inc., 5500 Central Ave., Boulder, CO 80301.

The Late, Great Lakes, by William Ashworth. New York: Alfred A. Knopf, 1986.

Nor Any Drop to Drink, by William Ashworth. New York: Summit Books, 1982.

Not In Our Backyards!: Community Action for Health and the Environment, by Nicholas Freudenberg. New York: Monthly Review Press, 1984.

Endangered Rivers and the Conservation Movement, by Tim Palmer. Berkeley and Los Angeles: University of California Press, 1986.

Groundwater Contamination in the United States, by Veronica I. Pye. Philadelphia: University of Pennsylvania Press, 1983.

Drinking Water and Health, Safe Drinking Water Committee, Washington, DC: National Academy Press, vol. 1, 1977, vol. 2 & 3, 1980, vol. 4, 1982, vol. 5, 1983.

"Finding Safe Alternatives to Pesticides," by Thomas L. Oates and Kevin W. Thorpe, Ph.D., *Clean Water Action News,* Winter 1989.

"Intolerable Risk: Pesticides in Our Children's Food," report by the Natural Resources Defense Council, February 1989.

"The Pesticide Dilemma," by Allen A. Boraiko. *National Geographic,* February 1980.

Organizations to Contact

American Bass Association, 886 Trotters Trail, Wetumpka, AL 36092, 205-567-6035.

Center for a Better Environment, 59 E. Van Buren, Suite 1600, Chicago, IL 60605.

Clean Water Action Project, 733 15th St. NW, Suite 110, Washington, DC 20005, 202-547-1196.

Defenders of Wildlife, 1244 19th St. NW, Washington, DC 20036, 202-659-9510.

Environmental Action, 1346 Connecticut Ave. NW, Suite 731, Washington, DC 20036, 202-833-1845.

INFORM, 381 Park Ave. South, New York, NY 10016, 212-689-4040.

Izaak Walton League of America, 1401 Wilson Blvd., Level B, Arlington, VA 22209, 703-528-1818.

National Coalition Against the Misuse of Pesticides, 530 7th St. SE, Washington, DC 20003.

National Water Center, PO Box 548, Eureka Springs, AR 72632, 501-253-9755.

Natural Resources Defense Council, 40 W. 20th St., New York, NY 10011, 212-727-2700.

Save the Dunes Council, APO Box 114, Beverly Shores, IN 46301, 219-879-3937.

Sierra Club, 730 Polk St., San Francisco, CA 94109, 415-776-2211.

Soil and Water Conservation Society, 7515 NE Ankeny Rd., Ankeny, IA 50021, 515-289-2331.

Water Pollution Control Federation, 601 Wythe St., Alexandria, VA 22314-1994, 703-684-2400.

THE PEOPLE

10

Energy Consumption

These final chapters, on energy consumption and overpopulation, will break from the format of those preceding, for a simple reason. The cause and effects are self-evident: too many people are using far too much energy. Every one of the environmental problems we've already discussed is linked to energy consumption. Global warming is happening because too many people are using too much energy. Smog, acid rain, rain forest decimation, the mountains of garbage, and the pollution of our oceans, lakes, rivers, and streams all have roots in our excesses. These chapters will focus on solutions; ways by which the world can lessen its dependence on environmentally harmful energy practices and slow the booming birth rate.

"Energy is a slippery concept," scientist Thomas J. Wilbanks told a symposium of environmentalists in 1987. His reasoning was exact, if simple. Most people give little thought to the threads of various energy sources that connect the activities of daily life—to what powers their microwaves or fuels their cars. "Energy" is hard to define. It means different things to different people: to some, firewood is the ultimate power source, for others it is nuclear reactors. This indefinability, the "slipperiness" of the word and its manifestations, makes forecasting the world's energy needs so difficult. Such predictions usually involve equally hard-to-define words like "alternatives," "renewables," and "efficiency."

Unfortunately, energy is another of the facets of our existence that we have come to take for granted. Its sources, coal-powered electricity plants, nuclear

reactors, even firewood, are major contributors to the world's pollution problems. Without this mix of natural forces and fuels that power industry, transportation, and many of our everyday habits, the world would be a cold, dark, unproductive place. It would also be a cleaner place. In many instances, the "energy" that Wilbanks and his scientific peers study and theorize about is twinned with pollution.

The payoff for the staggering modernization the world has witnessed in the past 50 years is a monumental increase in energy-produced pollutions. Controlling energy's production (and pollution), whether through cleaner technologies, reduced dependence on fossil fuels, or more energy efficient lives, has become one of the most serious challenges of the coming decade.

Fossil fuels—coal, oil, natural gas—generate 90 percent of the world's electricity. Since the early 1970s, governments and industries have been tinkering with options including solar, wind, hydro-, and geothermal power. That such experimentation should continue is questioned by no one. But the reality is that alternatives, including renewable sources like wood and cow manure, will never completely replace fossil fuels. Our ability to locate oil reserves has become more technologically sophisticated, and its consumption is at levels unmatched since 1979. Coal reserves are up by 80 percent in the last three years. Natural gas reserves, once thought to be even more limited than oil, are doubling every ten years. Because of these newfound sources of fuel, the world's leading energy experts, at a Montreal conference late in 1989, predicted that carbon dioxide emissions may rise by 70 percent between 1985 and 2020. Even the most optimistic forecasters predict alternative energy sources will provide at most only 20 percent of the world's energy needs. If we are to reduce energy pollution there are three priorities: increased energy efficiency, continued refinement of the alternative sources that already exist, and further experimentation with new energy sources for the future.

Though most of the energy-related pollution is created by the industrialized nations, energy consumption is a global problem. In some Third World countries, power sources have not changed much in the past 2,000 years. More than 300 million people in China are still not reached by electricity. In Pakistan only 30 percent of all villages have electricity, only 8 percent in Sri Lanka, and less than 7 percent in Indonesia. Peasants in China and India still depend on animals, wind, water, sun, firewood, and foraging for most of their power. But as both economies and populations grow in developing nations, so does their energy use—and their pollution.

Promoting energy efficiency in the Third World presents a particularly severe challenge. Carbon emissions are growing at annual rates as high as 5 percent in some countries. China plans to more than double its use of coal by some time after the turn of the century, an "achievement" that might well push it past the United States and Soviet Union and into the lead in the "race" to overheat the atmosphere. In thinking about the monumental energy changes to come, it's illustrative to remember that as recently as 1850, the United States got 90 percent of its energy from firewood, just as Nepal does today. By the early 1900s, 75 percent of America's energy came from coal, just as China's does today.

Placing limits on how much energy developing nations can use seems unfair, especially to Third World business and governmental leaders. They are adamant that the industrialized world, which uses 80 percent of the globe's energy, must get its own energy and pollution controls in place first, and then preach global efficiency.

The United States is still the world's biggest energy consumer and worst polluter. While consumption by the average American household has slowed in the past decade, each still burns the equivalent of 1,253 gallons of oil per year. That's 330 times as much as the average Ethiopian, 90 times as much the typical Kenyan, 15 times the average Chinese or Brazilian, 2.25 times as much as the average Hungarian. Given our enormous consumption, Thomas Wilbanks encouraged his peers when thinking about energy not to visualize big dams, sprawling power plants, or oil rigs. The real symbols of our energy dependence, he insists, are the World Trade Center or the city of Houston; suburban malls, not coal mines; the all-electric home, not the boom town.

In 1973, the Arab oil embargo was declared, and the search for new energy sources took off. Saving energy became a global effort. Energy shortages and skyrocketing fuel prices did not last long, but energy consumption (in most industrialized nations) actually began dropping in the last years of the decade.

Most market-oriented industrial economies have improved their energy efficiency by between 20 and 30 percent since 1973, for a worldwide savings of more than $250 billion worth of oil, gas, coal, and nuclear power. But even if similar reductions and commensurate savings were to continue, even if industrialized countries managed to halve their carbon dioxide emissions, the population and economic growth in the developing nations would continue to drive up pollution. Though some countries like Taiwan, South Korea, and Brazil have begun to calculate energy efficiency into their growth, most Third World nations have not, and energy use rises unchecked.

In less-developed countries energy needs are often met by the use of renewable resources, such as the methane produced by composting animal dung (above). But as nations industrialize, ever greater sources of energy as well as methods for its transportation are needed (below).

ALTERNATIVE FUELS

Fuel	METHANOL	ETHANOL	
Source	• Natural Gas • Coal • Biomass	• Sugarcane, corn, and other crops • Lignocellulose plants (fast-growing plants)	
Impact on Global Warming	Tailpipe emissions produce less CO_2 than gasoline, but total CO_2 impact depends on source used. If coal used, CO_2 production will skyrocket to double the emissions of gasoline.	Produces less CO_2 in vehicle engines than gasoline, but total CO_2 impact depends on energy source used for distillation process and whether crop-growing is energy-intensive.	
Other Pollution and Hazards; Tailpipe Emissions	Produces fewer hydrocarbons and nitrogen oxide emissions, but also produces formaldehyde, a suspected carcinogen. Extremely toxic–as little as two teaspoons ingested can cause blindness.	Though not prevented, tailpipe emissions of hydrocarbons, carbon monoxide, nitrogen oxide, and carbon dioxide are all reduced.	
Pros	• good antiknock fuel • few engine modifications needed • biomass source is renewable	• better antiknock fuel • renewable energy source • few engine modifications needed • renewable source	
Cons	• produces less energy than gasoline-more frequent refueling and bigger fuel tanks needed • cheapest source is imported natural gas–increased U.S. reliance on imported energy • more corrosive than gasoline–embrittles rubber, corrodes some metals	• produces less energy per gallon than gasoline, requiring larger fuel tanks or more frequent fill-ups • production process is very expensive • requires large volumes of source crops • current distillation methods are energy-intensive	
Potential Annual Emissions of CO_2 (In Billions of Tons)	• Natural gas: 1.293 • Coal: 2.639 • Biomass: N/A	• Sugarcane and other: 0.868 • Lignocellulose: 0	
	Gasoline Use Produces 1.336 Billion Tons of CO_2 Annually		

Sources: *Powerline*, Environmental Action Foundation; *Environmental Action*, July/August 1989; "Motor Vehicle Fuel-Efficiency and Global Warming," The Union of Concerned Scientists.

COMPRESSED AND LIQUID NATURAL GAS	ELECTRICITY	HYDROGEN
• Natural Gas	• Current power sources • Non-fossil fuels	• Fossil fuels • Non-fossil fuels and electrolysis of water
With pipeline leaks of methane taken into consideration, the net greenhouse contribution from the use of natural gas could be higher than from gasoline use.	There would be a 100% decrease in CO_2 contributions if non-fossil fuels are used as a source.	If coal-fired electricity powers the electrolysis stage, total CO_2 could increase 25%. Otherwise, no carbon dioxide emissions.
Produces much higher emissions of nitrogen oxides as well as another greenhouse gas—methane.	Electric cars have no tailpipe emissions, but if an increased demand for electricity causes more fossil-fuel-burning power plants, this would create more pollution.	Virtually emission free.
• 6% to 15% more efficient than gasoline • requires few engine modifications • supplies of natural gas are more plentiful than those of oil	• very efficient • solar recharging a possible source • quiet • renewable sources	• 15% to 45% more efficient than gasoline • renewable sources
• requires cumbersome fuel tank, limiting use in small vehicles • high cost of retrofitting gas stations • non-renewable source • cheaper foreign sources could lead to increased U.S. reliance on imported energy	• presently, vehicles can only go for 50 to 100 miles before recharging is necessary–range must be increased • presently, vehicles only obtain speeds of 30 to 60 mph between recharges • could increase need for electric power plants	• expensive even under optimistic scenarios • full production is 20 years away
• Natural gas: 1.081	• Current power sources: N/A • Non-fossil fuels: 0	• Fossil fuels: 0 • Non-fossil fuels and electrolysis of water: 0

Pleas for conservation may seem tired, but thrift is still held as the most promising solution to both energy consumption and pollution problems. The goal is hardly controversial, but the means are. Government must encourage tougher regulations for the efficiency of houses and appliances, more tax incentives, and direct grants for activities like weatherization, some people say. Others feel that the market should decide. If people want more efficient refrigerators, for example, the market will provide them. The best argument for energy efficiency, though, is simple economics. It costs government, utilities, and individuals less to save energy than it does to look for new ways to create it.

Cheap oil, gas, and coal have not discouraged experimentation with alternative energy sources totally. But most alternatives are not yet cost effective, and some may eventually create as many pollution problems as they solve. While debates over their potential have dragged on, much of the monies for continued experimentation have dried up. Tax laws no longer encourage investment in alternative sources.

After a solid 10 years when it was a priority, conservation has once again been relegated to the back seat. Gas station lines dissipated and we're no longer asked to pay $2 a gallon for gas, so we've gotten cocky. Auto fuel-efficiency standards have been lowered, and we're driving more miles. The Reagan Administration favored nuclear power over alternatives and pumped billions into subsidies. Clean air legislation has been proposed but the bills are hard-fought. Alternative energy sources have been pushed to the back burner in part because at the height of interest in them, people assumed that oil would be selling for $40 to $50 a barrel by now. Instead it has stabilized at just under $20.

Japan is experiencing a similar crunch. Demand for oil has grown by 14 percent in the past three years, primarily because of the nation's booming industry and the strength of the economy.

In the United States, federal research and development money for alternative energy sources is down by 82 percent since its peak in 1980. According to David B. Goldstein, a senior staff scientist at the Natural Resources Defense Council, "There's lots of vocalizations about the importance of oil independence, the greenhouse effect, and acid rain. But when it comes down to a decision being made, not one penny is being spent to avoid these kinds of inevitabilities." A clue to U.S. priorities can be found in the federal budget. In 1989, the Bush Administration asked for $355 million for nuclear energy subsidies and $88 million for energy efficiency programs.

Yet renewable and alternative sources of energy are not completely dead. Renewable energy sources promise to be a bigger part of every country's energy strategy in the next century. Denmark is concentrating on wind turbines, the Japanese on a range of solar, geothermal, and ocean-powered technologies. Brazil, a leader in alternative energies, gets 59 percent of its power from renewable sources. Nuclear power research has fallen off everywhere. Solar and wind power have not grown to meet expectations, but their technologies have vastly improved in the last decade, and may someday prove a viable, mass-market replacement for fossil fuels. That the Big Three fuels—coal, oil, wood—will fall from grace permanently sometime in the next century is inevitable, whether because they become too scarce or too expensive, and the dominant energy source of the twenty-first century may not have yet been discovered.

Experimentation with alternatives must continue, but it is important to remember that the greatest energy savings will come from increased efficiency. Studies indicate that if conservation is left to consumers, they will take the minimal approach to saving energy—turning down thermostats and using the air conditioner less frequently. Too few will actually make investments in greater efficiency, such as weatherstripping, new storm doors, or increased insulation in floors, walls, and ceilings. Environmentalists are encouraged that energy use has dropped simply because so many have taken minimal measures, but it is now apparent that government will have to take a bigger role in promoting efficiency.

Too often in the past, energy policy has been made only during crisis, often under the influence of the self-interested—oil companies, automakers, utility owners. Bad pricing, subsidy of ineffective processes, and ineffective regulation resulted. Today, with fossil fuels cheap and available, government, not the marketplace, is going to have to provide the incentives necessary to encourage energy savings. As this decade concludes, let's hope such decision-making can be done with a focus always on the environment.

Energy Conservation

Scientists and visionaries of the 1890s could never have predicted the enormous growth of the world's energy demand in the coming century. Few could have imagined cars, planes, spaceships, electricity, nuclear power, computers, or television. Attempting to predict both the energy needs and the resources that will satisfy them a century from now, in 2090, is just as difficult.

An efficient, nonpolluting replacement for oil or gas will probably not be discovered anytime soon. The key to our energy future does not depend on the development of new technologies or resources. Using the resources we have better and more intelligently will be the true savior of the world's energy future. If efficiency isn't stressed now, global warming (the "show-stopper" as Thomas Wilbanks calls it) and energy-related pollutants will alter the future long before new technologies can be discovered, tested, and implemented.

One positive aspect of the 1970s oil-crunch was it proved energy conservation was possible and effective. But Dr. Arthur Rosenfeld, regarded by many

as the founding father of U.S. energy conservation, insists that "on the energy fat farm we've still got a long way to go." He represents a school of thought which holds that even vast investments in underused alternatives, like solar, wind, and hydro, will never replace conservation. No matter how often energy efficiency is stressed, he argues, its importance has yet to be fully understood, in part, because it is a straightforward solution, rather than a heartrending, headline-grabbing problem.

In the past, federal assistance helped create extraordinary, community-based energy-saving programs, from Buffalo to Seattle. Tax credits helped individuals make initial investments in efficiency measures like double-paned storm windows and weatherstripping. In 1983, the average American home used 20 percent less energy than in 1973. The Oak Ridge National Laboratory estimates that as a result of federal government conservation programs put in place during the late 1970s, the nation will save $41 billion in residential fuel costs by the end of the century.

Industry also cooperated in the energy-saving act. During the 1980s, the 3M Company reduced its energy consumption per unit of output by almost 24 percent, Dow Chemical by 40 percent. Since 1973, AT&T's business has grown 97 percent, while its energy use decreased 13 percent, a $2.3 billion savings. Overall, the U.S. economy consumes 19 percent less energy per dollar of GNP than it did in 1973.

To illustrate energy efficiency efforts at their best and worst, Dr. Rosenfeld cites the experience of the nation's two most populated states. "Look at California," he says, "then look at Texas. California has a tough, progressive public utilities commission that has encouraged things like zero-interest loans for improving home energy efficiency. It has the appliance standards and new office lighting standards that call for a watt and a half per square foot instead of two to four. It's giving its utilities big incentives to promote cogeneration and better load management, and this kind of basic, sensible stuff we should have done long ago. Texas, by comparison, is completely retrograde. It hardly does anything to encourage conservation.

"From 1980 to 1985, the population of both states grew by 2,100,000 people. But electricity demand growth in Texas went up 4.5 percent per year, while California's rate went up just 1.4 percent per year—a little over half the national average. Just to keep up with demand, in five years Texas had to build eleven 1,000-megawatt power plants; California had to build three and a half."

The key to saving energy is individual and community involvement. Localizing the problem, no matter if it's drug use, illiteracy, or wasteful energy practices, has proven successful worldwide. The Southface Energy Institute in Atlanta is a prime example. Situated in a Victorian house in an abandoned neighborhood near downtown Atlanta, Southface established a homebuilding school in the late 1970s for serious do-it-yourselfers, curious consumers, and seasoned building professionals. The school teaches people how to build energy-efficient homes, how to prevent the needless waste of heated and cooled air in leaky, poorly insulated houses, and how to increase those savings through passive solar techniques and natural cooling and venting systems. Students practiced what they learned on Southface's home. The result is a passive solar office and demonstration center that stands as a model for both individuals and government.

On the heels of the anti-environment Reagan years, George Bush's Department of Energy set up hearings aimed at creating a national energy "strategy" by December 1990. The strategists had their work cut out for them. From 1981 to 1989 the budget for research on renewable power sources like geothermal and solar energy was cut from $629.9 million to $108 million. In that same period, spending on improving energy efficiency and conservation fell from more than $800 million to just $88 million. The administration insists its objective is to plan now in order to avoid energy shortages in the twenty-first century. Such paper initiatives have been met with the usual mixed reaction by both environmentalists ("Totally inappropriate," says the Natural Resources Defense Council) and the energy industry ("Not enough money for us," say nuclear power advocates), but at least the administration tried to work on a plan.

Despite improved energy efficiency in some areas of the country, plenty of room remains for conservation. Dr. Rosenfeld calculates that of the 1982 U.S. energy bill of $400 billion, about $120 billion went for heating, cooling, and lighting buildings, and running equipment and appliances like pumps, fans, refrigerators, washers, dryers, and computers. Half that—$60 billion—was wasted, he estimates. "It could be saved, with no change in our lifestyle, if we simply made the optimum investments in lighting and daylighting, heating and cooling systems, controlling infiltration or supply of outside air, insulating, buying the most efficient appliances, reducing hot water waste and so on," he insists.

Surprisingly to some people, most utilities encourage conservation efforts. Energy savings keep their costs down, too. Pacific Power and Light in Hood River County, Oregon, outfitted some 3,000 homes with as much weatherization as was deemed cost effective, including fiberglass in the ceilings and basements, and triple-glazing on the windows. The cost to the utility was an average of $4,300 per home—which will translate into two or three cents for each kilowatt-hour it saves, less than it would cost to generate the power.

Florida Power and Light has also built energy savings into its future. Successful programs include rebates of up to $600 for replacing an old, inefficient air conditioner, and can also include a $75 rebate to the contractor who promotes the installation of a more

The "environmental costs" have not been figured into the pricing of coal. Coal-powered electric plants contribute vast amounts of CO_2 (above) to the atmosphere, and its mining degrades and pollutes valuable farmland (below).

efficient model. Similar incentives are provided for attic insulation, window film, and solar water heating.

Convincing utility companies that bigger isn't necessarily better is one key to saving energy; another is recycling. One fourth of the United States' energy is used to extract and process raw materials. When metal, glass, paper, and rubber are recycled, the energy that would be used to mine and process raw materials is saved. The potential energy savings from aggressive recycling are significant. Recycling one ton of steel requires only 14 percent of the energy needed to produce a ton of steel from raw materials; recycling aluminum saves 95 percent of the energy it takes to produce the same amount of aluminum from bauxite.

Amory Lovins is a leading proponent of energy efficiency, and has been promoting conservation for more than 20 years. About half of the global warming effects are due to the world's addiction to polluting energies, he argues, which pump carbon dioxide, chlorofluorocarbons, and other man-made gases into the air. His Rocky Mountain Institute in Snowmass, Colorado, figures that three fourths of that dirtying energy could be saved by simple efficiency measures. If American factories installed the latest motors and light fixtures, they could save three quarters of all the electricity they use, says Lovins. If commercially available, efficient light bulbs were in place, 92 percent of the energy spent on lighting could be saved. He envisions a day when enough electricity is saved that it can itself become a commodity. "Negawatts" he calls them, and hopes that some day they can be bought, sold, or traded by utilities, companies, even nations. While Lovins' critics admit his ideas are brilliant, they see them as impractical.

The world's energy future depends on such leaps of faith, on refining ideas, and on showing just how intertwined energy production, pollution, and efficiency are. The challenge for the next decade is translating theories like Lovins' into practical use and an internationally understood language.

Nuclear Power

Even before Chernobyl, nuclear power's status as the energy provider of the future was on shaky grounds. Plants were plagued by shoddy construction and cost overruns, government officials misrepresented the hazards, thousands of tons of nuclear waste are accumulating that cannot be safely transported or disposed of, malfunctions are all too frequent, and many people are adamant that nuclear reactors not be built in their midst.

As of mid-1989, 366 nuclear power plants were in operation worldwide, generating about 15 percent of the globe's electricity. Dependence ranged from 65 percent in France to 31 percent in West Germany, 23 percent in Japan, 16 percent in the United States, and 10 percent in the Soviet Union. Virtually none of the developing nations yet have nuclear power. High costs, slowing electricity demand, mismanagement, and political opposition have all taken their toll. A massive loss of public confidence may today be the nuclear industry's worst enemy.

In the United States, nuclear power has fallen on particularly bad times. The last new plant was ordered in 1974, and since then work on the 108 that were on the boards has been stopped. The rate of growth has slowed from 7 percent in the early 1970s to 1.8 percent since 1980. Ten years after the accident at Three Mile Island (March 28, 1979), nuclear plants in the United States had experienced nearly 30,000 mishaps, according to the Worldwatch Institute's energy expert Christopher Flavin, and fearful communities and environmental and political leaders had marshalled forces to stop their proliferation.

Only a handful of nuclear plants are still under construction and several of the older ones are slated for retirement. They have failed similar economic and political tests worldwide. In West Germany, activists and politicians have put up big fights to stop their construction. Planned plants in Italy, Spain,

Great Britain, Belgium, Finland, and Sweden have all been stymied since Chernobyl. Few are under construction, fewer still on the drawing boards. Many have been canceled. The Eastern bloc countries are cutting back on their nuclear plans, too. Even the Soviet Union, long a firm believer in the industry's potential, is reassessing its nuclear future. The most "successful" nuclear programs, in France and Japan, are healthy only when compared to their peers.

Among developing nations, the only countries likely to ever draw more than 10 percent of their electricity needs from nuclear power are South Korea and Taiwan, and only South Korea appears intent on expansion beyond the year 2000.

Why did nuclear fall so far, so fast? Over the past 40 years the industry benefited from an abundance of government support and made inroads. In theory it could replace coal-fired power plants and reduce carbon emissions. But since the beginning, nuclear power has raised more questions—about safety, expense, and radioactive waste—than it has answered, and the list of uncertainties keeps growing.

There are still some nuclear spokesmen *and* environmentalists who believe there is a future for so-called "inherently safe" nuclear energy. These designs promise to reduce or eliminate the possibility of a catastrophic meltdown. Brice LaLonde, founder of Friends of the Earth in France, and the country's environment minister, has said he is "reconsidering" nuclear power, based on such plans. The Climate Institute, whose board includes several respected environmentalists, recently called upon activists to "keep the door open" for safe nuclear energy. And members of the industry, as well as some utility companies that own nuclear power plants, continue to argue for expansion, and some even cite Three Mile Island as a defense. There were no deaths at TMI, they contend, and no major contamination as a result of the "accident." The amount of radioactivity released was insignificant and resulted in no long-term increases in cancer deaths (obvi-ously a premature conclusion). They blame the Chernobyl accident on bad design and poor management, and claim that those who are anti-nuclear are rushing to judgment.

Adding fuel to the expansionists' argument is that research on "safer" nuclear reactors continues. One such potentially "safe" reactor in the U.S. is still receiving federal funding. Called a High Temperature Gas-cooled Reactor, it is cooled by pressurized helium gas instead of water, and is designed not to get hot, even if the cooling system fails. The plants are small and produce much less power per unit volume of fuel than a conventional reactor. In 1971, such a plant in West Germany was purposefully subjected to the ultimate test: the flow of cooling helium was shut off and the control rods locked out of the core. There was no meltdown. The temperature of the core, after rising for five hours, began to drop. Other allegedly "safe" or "melt-down-free" designs in various stages of development give encouragement to nuclear's proponents. But even if they are as "safe" as designers say, there remains the question of radioactive waste disposal.

Nuclear power as we know it seems headed for extinction. In mid-1989, voters in Sacramento, California, shut down their utility's only nuclear power plant, despite a half-million-dollar campaign waged by the nuclear industry. The closing, a first by voters anywhere in the world, was based less on environmental and safety reasons than on economic ones. The long-troubled plant simply could not provide electricity at a competitive rate. Opponents of nuclear power had lost 14 similar referendums in 10 states during the previous 13 years. "This sends a message, a shot heard around the world," said Scott Denman, director of the Safe Energy Communications Council. The day after the vote, the plant closing began, and the community faced the next set of questions: what to do with the plant's spent fuel and how to safely dismantle the building.

Similar questions are being posed globally. Siting and constructing nuclear plants may have seemed like a nightmare to industry and opponents alike, and closing and burying them will hardly be a dream. The life of a nuclear plant is finite. In the United States, most licenses granted nuclear plants were for just 30 years. Five are already awaiting decommissioning. The question of how to dispose of the plants and their spent nuclear fuel safely and economically has no good answer.

The Shippingport Atomic Power Station on the Ohio River 25 miles northwest of Pittsburgh is currently being decommissioned. It was in operation for only 25 years, and was shut down in 1982. The painstaking decommissioning process began in August 1984 and has not yet been completed. The estimated cost: around $100 million. Similar challenges face the makers of nuclear weapons, who are sitting on tons of hazardous nuclear waste that has no final home. The U.S. Department of Energy has proposed spending $21.5 billion over the next five years to correct hazardous and unlawful conditions at its nuclear weapons plants and is asking for a total of $80 billion to clean up and modernize them.

The best argument against the continued subsidy of nuclear power is economic: The cost of building a nuclear power plant today, if you can find a region agreeable to having one in its backyard, is 8 to 15 cents per kilowatt-hour, more than double the cost of any other fuel, from oil to gas to solar. Polls today indicate Americans oppose construction of nuclear power plants two to one.

Solar

Sun Day, May 3, 1978, marked the dawn of the Solar Age, some people say. Over 20 million people in 31 nations attended rallies, workshops, and conferences to promote the sun's power that day. Within weeks, governments around the globe initiated pro-solar laws and created solar tax credits. In the United States, solar collectors were installed on the White House roof, and by 1981 the Carter Administration had budgeted $500 million for solar energy development. Optimistic predictions were that renewable sources including solar, wind, and hydroelectric plants would provide 20 percent of the United States' energy by the end of the century. Such optimism evaporated quickly in the 1980s. Oil prices dropped, and the nuclear-favoring Reagan Administration slashed funding for *all* renewable sources.

Solar energy dates back centuries. As early as the 1600s, northern Europeans experimented with solar "greenhouses" to protect the tropical plants brought home from distant lands by explorers. Two hundred years later, the first commercial solar water heater came on the market in the United States. Today they are sold at Sears.

Solar remains one of the simplest energy-producing processes available. Passive collectors can be built into most homes and offices. A simple collector consists of a glass-topped box with a dark bottom that traps the heat of sunlight. Solar's biggest advantage is self-sufficiency. Solar collectors can provide energy without being hooked up to the grids through which electricity and natural gas are distributed, and is also less vulnerable to political whims and upheavals. Oil embargos won't affect solar's availability.

Solar's enthusiasts are legion, despite the recent decrease in research funds. John Proctor bought a four-bedroom, south-facing tract house in Denver in 1980 and added a solar hot-water system. His heating bills have never been more than $100 a month, while his neighbors' often soared past $200. As a result, Proctor founded the Sun Power Consumer Association. Today the group has more than 500 members—mostly Proctor's neighbors—who each boast of saving up to 75 percent on heating bills.

Unfortunately, cost is still a problem. A typical residential solar water heater costs $4,000, com-

Solar power is an entirely clean, renewable energy source, both for solar vehicles—in limited use throughout the country—and for homes.

pared to a natural gas system which can be set up for $200. As a result of both the expense and the discontinuation of tax credits, the sales volume of solar heaters and collectors has dropped more than 70 percent from the 1984 level.

Worldwide, there are plenty of examples that encourage further investment and experimentation in solar energy. In Cyprus, the globe's largest solar energy user per capita, private industry has installed solar water heaters in 90 percent of the houses and in most apartment buildings and hotels. More than 4 million solar water heaters are in use in Japan. And in the remote corners of sunny Australia, 37 percent of households rely on solar collectors.

Israel may be the shining star of solar power. Roofs of homes and apartments across the country are covered with solar collectors. Hot water storage tanks line the roads that lead into Tel Aviv. More than 600,000 Israeli homes (65 percent) have solar water heaters. This proliferation was initially encouraged by government, via tax deductions for solar installation. Then in 1980, the Ministry of Housing required all new homes and apartments of four stories or less to heat their water with solar energy.

In the United States, Soldiers Grove, Wisconsin, is perhaps the best example of mass solar power. Townsfolk boast they "get their heat from 93 million miles away." The town of 600 turned to sun power in the early 1980s when its central business district was abandoned because of flooding, and consultants convinced Soldiers Grove to rebuild using solar power sources. Most of the existing collectors and water heaters were built between 1979 and 1983, and despite the occasional faulty compressor and leak, the community has become a powerful example of solar's potential. Today more than half the town's energy comes from alternative sources.

The town has changed street names to Passive Sun Drive and Sunshine Boulevard. Solar terms punctuate conversations in coffee shops—talk of "berms" and "r values" mixes easily with discussions of weather and farming. Savings have been felt around town. Rod Olson's Mobil station pays only $900 a year for backup heating, compared with $900 a month by a non-solar competitor. Perhaps the best testimonial is the new 7,000-square-foot IGA grocery store, which has collecting panels on the roof and fans that spread the collected heat into the ducts. The store's monthly heating bill? Zero. Managers insist the temperature inside never drops below 65 degrees. In a day and age when many small Midwestern towns are fighting to keep their populations steady, Soldiers Grove is growing. "People have reinvested in expansion out here themselves," retired physics teacher Gerald Schoville told a reporter. "Instead of building another nineteenth- or twentieth-century village, we decided to build for the twenty-first."

Photovoltaics

Direct solar energy is just one of the ways the sun can be used for energy. Sunlight can also generate electricity directly in two ways. One is by concentrating sunlight on water to generate steam, which is then used to drive an electrical generator—an expensive proposition. The other is the photovoltaic cell. These fuel cells generate electricity through chemical reactions. They are quiet, produce little pollution, and are more efficient than conventional power plants. Their appeal is heightened by their reliability, and because their fuel—sunlight—is absolutely free.

The cost of stringing transmission wires for conventional electrical sources into mountainous parts of the world is high, so photovoltaic cells already power many mountaintop telecommunications stations. In Phoenix, the nation's first solar electric suburban community is up and running. Twenty-four homes there get electricity solely from photovoltaic panels. The experiment has proven that roughly 10 acres of solar energy collectors could convert sunlight into electricity efficiently enough to keep lights burning and stereos blaring in a 300-home town with no change in utility bills—and with no pollution from smokestack or spigot.

The fuel cell concept dates back to 1839, but the first photovoltaics were not developed until 1954. Scientists at New Jersey's Bell Laboratories discovered that a silicon wafer could generate an electrical current when struck by sunlight. The first practical applications were in the U.S. space program in the early 1960s. Photovoltaic fuel cells provided power for both the Gemini and Apollo missions and today generate the on-board electricity for all the space shuttles.

As with many new sources of energy, economics rather than technology remains the barrier to expansion. The cost for adequate photovoltaic cells runs between $1,500 and $2,000 per kilowatt. (A 200-kilowatt station could supply enough power to serve a 30-unit apartment building or small factory.) Cell manufacturers think the cost must be cut to $800 to $1,000 for them to be competitive with local power companies. Makers are encouraged that prices have dropped by 90 percent in the past decade. (The first panels for spacecraft cost more than $10,000 per square yard. Today's off-the-shelf variety costs a twentieth as much.) Photovoltaics are already in use from rural communication systems to portable phones to more than 60 million pocket calculators. Cells could become a bigger energy source for both utility companies and individual homes and industries worldwide. Vijay Kapur, president of International Solar Electric Technology, envisions the day "you'll be able to go into your local hardware store and buy affordable photovoltaic panels for your roof." The newly revised Clean Air Act could encourage their adoption. Stringent air quality regulations proposed in southern California suggest that such fuel cells will soon be a necessity, primarily because of their nonpolluting capacity.

The spotlight is now on the leader in the photovoltaics, International Fuel Cells Corporation, a division of United Technologies Corporation. It has orders for 53,200-kilowatt generating stations to be delivered in the early 1990s. All of the orders are from gas companies. Other manufacturers in the United States, Europe, and Japan are starting to realize similar sales.

The biggest market for photovoltaics may be the still-unelectrified villages of the world. The first solar-electric village is in the United States, according to the Worldwatch Institute. Schuchuli (population 96), one of 53 villages on the Papago Indian reservation in southwestern Arizona, was electrified for the first time when an array of photovoltaics was turned on in 1986. Solar power replaced kerosene lamps and a diesel-powered pump and produces enough electricity for 47 fluorescent lights, a two-horsepower water pump, 15 small refrigerators, a sewing machine, and a communal washing machine. Similar electrification experiments are underway in western Africa and Asia.

Wind

Man's use of wind power goes way back. The first wind-powered water lift is believed to have been built in Persia, around 600 B.C. By A.D. 1100, windmills appeared across Europe and wind-powered sailing ships set out to explore the boundaries of the new world. Wind was first harnessed to produce electricity in the 1890s, and its use caught on quickly. In Denmark, industry was already getting one quarter of its energy from wind by the turn of the century. Farms across the United States were using windmills to pump water from deep wells for irrigation by the 1920s. But over the next few decades, as cheap oil and gas became more available and electricity spread, demand for wind power fell off. U.S. funding for wind-power experimentation peaked in 1981 at $86 million, and has dropped to less than $30 million in recent years.

The oil price jolts of the 1970s regenerated interest in wind and other alternative sources. During the decade that followed the 1973 oil embargo, over 10,000 wind machines were built worldwide. Most were small and used either to charge batteries or to produce minuscule amounts of electricity. The Danes again leaped to the forefront of wind-power technology, offering subsidies to encourage both industry and consumers. Today such technology is concentrated along the world's coastlines and mountain passes, primarily in the United States, Sweden, and Denmark. The industry appears to be undergoing a rebirth of sorts. During the 1970s, wind power was plagued by technical problems and high costs. But today, with technologies vastly improved and success stories mounting, thousands of windmills and wind farms—clusters of turbines—spin in 95 countries, from the tropics to the Arctic. Their potential would seem unlimited. It is estimated that sufficient wind energy is available in the United States to provide a quarter of the nation's projected electricity needs by the turn of the century. The future looks just as bright globally. According to Christopher Flavin, the Worldwatch Institute's energy specialist, "wind energy is capable ultimately of providing about 12 percent of the world's electricity-generating capacity."

In the United States, California has best mastered the winds. Wind-powered turbines that line the valleys of the Altamont, San Gorgonio, and Tehachapi mountain ranges produce more than 5 percent of the electricity that Pacific Gas and Electric Company sells its customers, and 15 percent of San Francisco's electrical power is drawn from wind. Just to the north, near the Washington-Oregon border, a project funded by the Department of Energy boasts three 2.5-megawatt wind turbines, each bearing 300-foot-long propeller blades made by Boeing. Standing on the windy gorge of the Columbia River, they feed electricity to a power plant in Bonneville, Oregon, and produce enough electricity for 2,500 homes.

The Chinese market for wind power continues to improve, because of a growing demand for nationwide television reception, and because 300 million people are still without electricity. According to a 1987 study of turbine shipments, five of the world's 10 largest manufacturers of small wind turbines are in China. But according to the Worldwatch Institute's Cynthia Pollock Shea, the most ambitious wind energy program is in India, where the Ministry of Energy is pushing to have both public and private developers install 5,000 megawatts of capacity by the year 2000, enough to provide electricity for five million people. But even wind farms have run into Not In My Backyard opposition. Some people who live near them complain about the constant noisy whir of machinery and increased traffic they attract. In 1985 the City of Palm Springs sued seven developers and the Bureau of Land Management, which had leased land to wind farm developers. The city was seeking to force them to dismantle, move, or camouflage existing machines and to stop them from erecting others.

Hydroelectricity

For at least 2,000 years people have been harnessing water to do work. In 85 B.C., the Greeks used it to power gristmills; by A.D. 610 the Japanese were using it for grinding flour, sawing wood, and producing textiles. It wasn't until the late nineteenth century that water was used to create electricity. The first hydrogenerating facility was built in Appleton, Wisconsin, in 1882, providing power for 350 local lightbulbs.

By the turn of the century hydropower met 60 percent of the United States' electric power demand. In 1932, the powerful triumvirate of President Franklin Delano Roosevelt, the federal Works Progress Administration, and the Army Corps of Engineers launched a massive dam-building effort. The results have been felt in the decades since. In 1933, the Columbia River watershed above Portland, Ore-

The Grand Coulee Dam (above) harnesses one of the Earth's most renewable energy resources—flowing water—as solar panels (below) "harness" another—the sun's rays. Both provide "clean" electricity.

gon, generated about 215 megawatts of power, most from a single source; by 1976 more than 20,000 megawatts were crackling out of 50-plus Columbia Basin dams.

Today hydropower generates 25 percent of the world's electricity, meeting about 5 percent of the total energy demand. Some visionaries see dams, small and large, as the oil fields of the future, supported by government, private business, and utility companies. A key to hydropower's appeal is that it produces no greenhouse-creating gases. In some regions, it remains an underexploited technology. Although tens of thousands of dams are already in place, most are not used for energy creation. But in other parts of the world hydropower has been an exploitive source of energy. In the rain forests of Brazil, across the United States, and elsewhere, massive dams have destroyed forests and wildlife habitats, wiped out small villages, increased erosion, polluted nearby water quality, and caused severe flooding.

Despite its potential for harm, hydropower is one of the few alternative energy sources that has met with acceptance in all regions of the world. A World Bank survey of 100 developing countries found that 31 had more than doubled their hydroelectric capacity between 1980 and 1985. As of 1980, 65 large dams more than 490 feet high were scattered around the globe—18 in the United States, 10 in the Third World. Since then, more than 40 more have been built—none in the United States, 29 in the Third World. The industry is growing especially fast in Brazil and China—some say too fast for the good of the surrounding environment. But in the United States, which has the largest installed hydroelectric capacity, not a single new dam was approved between 1976 and 1986. Environmental concerns have stopped some new construction, as has the feeling that the country has already dammed up plenty of waterways. The vast majority of the 60,000 dams in existence produce no power and

the move is on to harness them, rather than build new ones.

Concerns about overgrowth and destruction of natural habitats haven't slowed dam-building in most countries. In Brazil, where 4 out of 10 homes are still without electricity, 94 percent of the country's electric power comes from hydropower churned out by massive dams. In the next 20 years, the Amazon Basin is expected to supply Rio de Janeiro and São Paulo with 25 percent of their power, and to provide nearly half the electricity for the developing northeast. In 1986, Venezuela completed the Guri Dam, the largest in the world, at a cost of more than $10 billion. With a 10,000-megawatt generating capacity, it can produce as much electricity as 10 large nuclear power plants. Brazil is in the process of building a hydroelectric plant with 20 percent more capacity than the Guri, and China is contemplating an even larger one. Many countries, particularly in the Third World, are also installing generators thousands of times smaller on remote rivers and streams.

As hydroelectric plants become more common, drawbacks are emerging. Big dams have many parallels to nuclear power plants: they are expensive and boast new technologies with limited operating experience. The consequences of a catastrophe, losses in the billions of dollars and thousands of lives, would be devastating. They also pose potential environmental disaster, depending on how they are sited and managed. The tradeoffs for cheap, abundant electricity in many cases are the loss of surrounding forests, small towns, and farmland. Wildlife is uprooted or drowned. People must be moved. The temperature of downstream waters can be affected, harming fish and plants.

Yet the vast potential that flows through the world's streams and rivers holds much promise. Future developments appear to lie in smaller hydroelectric plants, so-called "micro-hydro" generators, which require dams only a few feet high.

Biomass

Nearly half the globe's population relies on the burning of wood, animal waste, and crops including sunflowers, soybeans, palm oil, sugarcane, water hyacinths, even kelp, algae, and peach pits, for their energy needs. Called biomass, such residues and remnants are the primary source of energy for heat and cooking in most developing countries.

In China, where almost one third of the total population still does not have electricity, more than eight million biogas digesters, which convert manure and other organic waste into methane, are used for cooking and lighting. This is a relatively easy and cheap form of energy. For an initial $20 investment, a unit can supply a family of five with energy. Only 10 minutes of work each week are required to transfer the manure of two to four pigs from the pens to the digester and to move the decomposed wastes from the digester to the fields for fertilizer. The process provides energy and soil management, *and* reduces waste production. In Delhi, biogas is widely used because India has 237 million cows that can't be slaughtered. Their waste provides a lot of fuel—more than 575 million tons of usable dung each year. Still, primarily due to lack of education, most Indians continue to gather twigs and sticks to burn rather than pay for a digester to produce methane gas.

In the United States, biomass provides 5 percent of the nation's energy needs. Six million residential homes are heated exclusively by wood, another 21 million supplement other power sources with wood. Since 1983, four utilities have built wood-burning power plants. In 1984, the Burlington Electric Company in Vermont invested $76 million in a 62-megawatt wood-burning electrical plant, which experts say is 20 percent cheaper to operate than a coal-fired plant. The Congressional Office of Technology Assessment has estimated that biomass could provide as much as 20 percent of U.S. energy by the end of the century.

Experimentation continues as more and more businesses test biomass as a potential energy-saver. The Union Camp Corporation in Franklin, Virginia, has been powered by peanut shells and pulping waste since 1937. The Farmers Rice Milling Company in Lake Charles, Louisiana, has used rice husks for power since 1984. And for several years a Procter and Gamble soap manufacturing plant on Staten Island has provided all of its own steam and electricity by burning up to 200,000 tons of waste wood a year. Scientists are looking into the potential for turning peanut shells and cow chips into fuel and electricity. In Modesto, California, the Tri/Valley Growers Cooperative already powers a 4.5 megawatt plant with peach and cherry pits and then sells the electricity to Pacific Gas and Electric.

While biomass is an infinitely renewable source in theory, in practice it is not. Forests are falling faster than they can replenish themselves or be replanted, and the resulting soil degradation threatens the forests' future. Smoke from wood-fired stoves and industrial furnaces contributes to the increased levels of greenhouse gases we're pumping into the atmosphere. Much of that pollution is unnecessary: The largely rural people who depend on biomass use, per task, between 3 and 10 times more energy (mostly from wood) than consumers of commercial fuels in developed countries, because of inefficient cooking and heating methods. Cooking over an open fire, for example, uses as much energy as running a car.

Geothermal, the Oceans, and Space

The roiling heat beneath the Earth may yet prove an energy savior. In fact, industries and utilities around the world are already tapping hot springs and geysers, and the molten rock that pours from erupting volcanoes.

The temperature of the Earth's core increases one degree Celsius every 100 feet below the surface. In geologically active regions it gets hotter faster. Energy is created naturally by the radioac-

There are approximately 150 geothermal-powered electric plants in the world, which harness the heat contained below the Earth's surface that is generated by hot water springs and steam geysers. The best sources of geothermal energy run along the Pacific Rim and the coastlines of New Zealand, New Guinea, western Siberia, the United States, Mexico, and Central and South America.

tive processes in the Earth's interior and is stored under the Earth's cooler crust. Geothermal power harnesses that energy by tapping into it and drawing heat to the surface, either directly (to produce hot water) or indirectly (to produce electricity). Today, more than 150 geothermal power plants worldwide produce electricity.

The richest sources for geothermal power line the Pacific Rim and the coastlines of New Zealand, New Guinea, western Siberia, the United States, Mexico, and Central and South America. Once extracted, the energy can be used to heat homes, greenhouses, or factories. Klamath Falls, Oregon, and Boise, Idaho, are already largely dependent on geothermal power for heating. A New Zealand paper company uses it to operate pulp and paper plants and timber-drying kilns. More than 2,000 megawatts of geothermal power have been tapped in Northern California. In the next several decades, low-temperature applications (for heating greenhouses and small buildings) could develop into significant markets. Some predict that by the end of the century, California could be drawing 25 percent of its electricity from powerful, below-ground sources.

Iceland is by far the leader in geothermal energy technology. Sixty-five percent of all Icelandic homes are heated by hot water drawn from underground, and most of Iceland's fresh tomatoes, lettuce, and cucumbers are produced in geothermally heated greenhouses. But Japan may soon edge Iceland out as the world's leader, as the Japanese continue experiments up and down their coast.

Geothermal's drawback is that the power cannot be easily transported. To take advantage of it, industries will have to move to a coastline where geothermal power is easily accessed. Such moves are already taking place. Geothermal sources are not close to being completely inventoried, nor are its uses fully explored. It's unlikely that we will fully understand its potential until sometime in the twenty-first century.

Japan also leads efforts to tap the power of the oceans. Wave power, tidal power, current power, and ocean thermal-energy conversion, which exploits temperature differences between the surface and depths, are all being tested. Oceans may seem like the ultimate energy source, but only a small fraction of their power is ever likely to be harnessed because of their uncontrollable nature.

Based on studies already underway, some scientists and government leaders envision space as a home for the energy-providers of the twenty-first century. Solar-powered satellites could be sent deep into space, and would be designed to capture and transmit solar energy back to earth. Such power sources, its backers contend, offer the ultimate ecological solution to energy creation: global warming would most likely not be a concern if the power source were operating tens of thousands of miles above the troposphere. But while those studies continue, there remains an abundance of non-polluting energy sources yet to be fully tapped here on Earth.

ENERGY CONSUMPTION

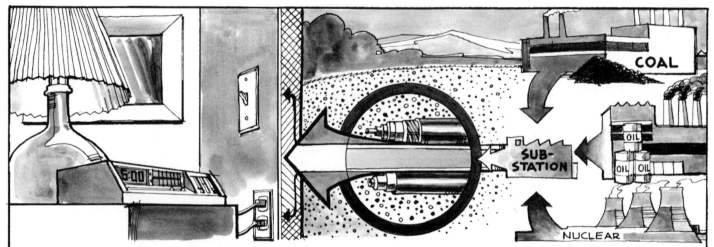

The simple task of flipping a light switch contributes to the world's pollution problems, whether your electricity is produced by coal, oil, or nuclear power sources.

Most electricity is generated by steam turbines. The hot water these turbines discharge usually ends up in rivers and lakes, threatening nearby animal and marine life.

If that steam heat was generated by burning coal, flipping your light switch also helps contribute to the creation of the greenhouse gas carbon dioxide.

If your local power plant is oil-heated, it also contributes to the greenhouse effect and acid rain. The transportation of that oil is also a pollution risk if it is accidentally spilled on land or in the sea.

If your electricity is provided by nuclear power you are contributing to the toxic waste such plants generate, for which there is not yet a satisfactory method of disposal.

The fossil fuels—coal, oil, and wood—that we most depend on for energy are the greatest contributors to the greenhouse effect. But energy is used—and pollution created—for virtually every man-made enterprise, including driving a car.

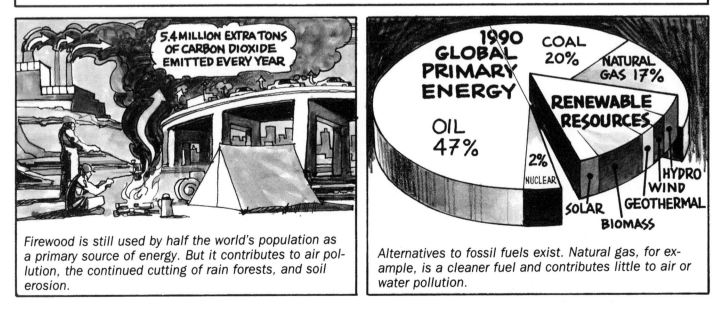

Firewood is still used by half the world's population as a primary source of energy. But it contributes to air pollution, the continued cutting of rain forests, and soil erosion.

Alternatives to fossil fuels exist. Natural gas, for example, is a cleaner fuel and contributes little to air or water pollution.

RENEWABLE

Experimentation with alternative energy sources continues worldwide. In Israel, for example, 65 percent of all homes have solar heated water.

In Brazil, 94 percent of all electricity comes from hydropower, although not without other costs to the environment.

RESOURCES

In Iceland, 65 percent of all homes are heated by geothermal energy.

Denmark has enough wind turbines to provide electricity for 30,000 people.

COOLING SHADE FROM TREES SHIELDING HOUSE FROM SUN · ENERGY EFFICIENT APPLIANCES · FLUORESCENT LIGHTING

INSULATION · TRIPLE INSULATED WINDOWS · ENERGY EFFICIENT CAR

Without a reduction in our consumption, it is unlikely that these non-fossil-fuel energy sources will ever completely satisfy the world's energy needs. Conservation remains the best alternative for reducing energy-related pollution. Studies have shown that up to 30 percent of our energy costs can be saved without drastically changing our lifestyles.

Individual Action

1. Be an informed consumer. Call your local utility and find out *exactly* where your electricity comes from. Many people will be surprised to learn what actually powers their stoves, VCRs, and typewriters. It will also give you an idea of what pollutions are being created when you flip a light switch or turn on the microwave.

2. Check with your local, state, and national government representatives to see what, if any, incentives remain to encourage investment in alternative or renewable energy sources. In the United States, some energy-efficiency rewards are still available through bills that provide help to individuals for improved weatherization of low-income homes, or through solar energy and energy conservation acts which may offer tax incentives or cheap loans. Also, a variety of grants for low- and moderate-income homeowners is still available for energy-efficiency improvements.

3. Some utilities offer free energy audits (of-ten mandated by state law). A representative will come into your house and advise you on what you can do to tighten up and save both money and energy, whether by improving insulation, installation of storm windows, or improving weatherstripping. Some can even suggest where to find low-interest loans if you want to make energy-related improvements to your house or apartment.

4. When it comes time, replace major appli-ances with more efficient ones. (In the United States, refrigerators consume about 7 percent of the nation's electricity, equivalent to the output of 25 big power plants. New refrigerators use considerably less.) According to John H. Morrille of the American Council for an Energy Efficient Economy, "If all the households in the United States had the most efficient refrigerators currently available, the electricity savings would eliminate the need for about 12 large nuclear power plants." There are also federally mandated energy efficiency standards for furnaces, central air conditioners, water heaters, freezers, window air conditioners, central heating systems, dishwashers, kitchen ranges, clothes dryers, furnaces, and pool heaters. Look for the required yellow tags on each that detail their energy efficiency, and comparison-shop for the most efficient.

5. There are similarly rated add-ons to show-ers, toilet bowls, and kitchen taps that are inexpensive, easily installed, and offer savings of up to 60 percent. Toilet flushing can account for 40 percent of a home's total water usage; showers and kitchen taps use lots of hot water. Making all three as efficient as possible will cut down on electricity bills.

6. If adding on or building a new home, use so-called "superinsulation," which doubles the normal insulation and includes an airtight liner within the wall. Costs increase by only 5 percent and are paid back in energy savings in five years. Some super-insulated homes in Minnesota require 68 percent less heat; others in Sweden have been measured to save as much as 89 percent of heat.

7. Install "superwindows," which have up to four times the insulating power of a conventional window. Amory Lovins, noted physicist and energy analyst, suggests that if everyone in the United States had such windows, the annual energy savings would be equivalent to all the oil passing through the Alaskan pipeline.

8. A third of the heat in homes escapes through closed windows. If it's not time to replace windows, try coating them with infrared reflectors, which keep heat inside.

9. Replacing all incandescent bulbs with com-pact fluorescent bulbs could cut electrical consumption by 6 percent. An 18-watt fluorescent provides the same amount of light as a 75-watt incandescent, and while they cost $15 apiece (versus less than a dollar for an incandescent), good ones last 10 to 15 times longer. Consider it this way: for every fluorescent lamp used, one fifth of a ton of coal is saved in a year, preventing that much air pollution, acid rain, and global warming. Homeowners should think about replacing the lights they use most—in the kitchen, hallway, or porch.

10. If you own a business, consider switch-ing to lighting with improved ballasts. During peak business hours, lighting uses up to 40 percent of the nation's electricity. Half of that is consumed by fluorescent lighting in commercial buildings. When one of those lights is turned on, a transformer-like device called a ballast provides an initial surge of current to get the gas inside to glow. Then it cuts the power back. All but a few million of the more than 900 million such ballasts are outdated. Replacing them with modern, more efficient ballasts could cut power use by 25 percent. Adding reflectors and sensors that would automatically adjust light levels could push savings to 80 percent or more.

11. Plant trees. You have already read how planting trees helps diminish global warming, but they also shade buildings and encourage cooling, especially in inner-city regions where asphalt and tar-roofs reign. Any shade helps cut down on air-conditioning needs and if planting is organized on a community-wide basis, the savings can be big.

12. In Los Angeles and elsewhere, legisla-tion proposes doing away with barbecue lighting fuels as a means of cutting down on air-polluting vapors. Here's an easy, environmentally sound option: solar box cookers. Already used in developing countries for stoves, they are simple to make from cardboard, aluminum foil, and a single glass plate, and they cost as little as $12. They cook more slowly than conventional ovens or open fires, and heat up to an average of 250 degrees. In tropical regions, they work year-round. For a manual (and recipes) send $5 to: Solar Box Cookers International, 1724 Eleventh Street, Sacramento, CA 95814.

13. Water conservation saves greatly on home heating bills, so use less.

14. Ask around your community to see if anyone is using solar collectors as an energy source. If so, find out what they cost, and what savings they have made. Ask who sells collectors nearby and investigate the possibility of installing one.

15. Save electricity whenever possible by us-ing candlelight or reading a book under a desk lamp instead of an overhead fixture. Open curtains and blinds to let daylight in, rather than turning on overhead lights during the day.

16. Wrap the hot-water heater in your base-ment in a blanket and lower the temperature to 120 degrees.

17. Use solar-powered calculators.

18. If you don't have a thermostat with a built-in clock, consider it. These control heat levels, so that when you're in bed at night, the furnace automatically shuts down, and then starts again in the morning. There is no reason to use (or pay for) electricity when you don't need it.

19. When you leave the house, make sure all lights, televisions, radios, etc. are turned off. Get a timer to turn lights on and off when you're away rather than leaving them on all the time.

20. Turn off your heat, water heater, and pilot lights when away on vacation.

21. Plug leaking windows and doors around the house with any of a variety of weatherstripping, from felt strips and flexible vinyl to rubber and metal strippings.

22. Caulking around windows and doors that have settled or around the holes where pipes and wires run into your house helps keep homes and apartments draft-free and warmer. This does not have to be done every winter season. A good caulking job can last up to 20 years.

23. Believe it or not, drafts can come through electric outlets, too. Test it yourself: hold a piece of tissue up by an outlet on an exterior wall and watch it flutter. You can buy fillers at the hardware store, or plug outlets yourself with simple pieces of foam-core or cardboard.

24. If your kitchen has an exhaust fan, it too can bring drafts in from outside. Most hardware stores should carry fan covers. If not, contact stove dealers in your area.

25. When you buy a new kitchen range, gas furnace, or broiler, be sure it has an energy-saving electronic ignition instead of a pilot light.

26. In the winter, wear an extra sweater instead of turning up the thermostat. In the summer, use fans instead of air conditioners.

27. Use a clothesline whenever possible, in the yard or basement, instead of a clothes dryer.

28. Close off and do not cool or heat unused rooms in your house. Use shades and curtains to insulate in both summer and winter.

29. Local self-reliance groups are organized in virtually every community. They instruct on getting by with less, and emphasize "sustainable" growth and lifestyles. Check with any environmental group, energy office, or utility for such a group to join in your area.

30. Find out where your congresspeople stand on nuclear power and make sure they know you would prefer seeing continued nuclear subsidies go to further exploration of alternative energy sources and energy efficiency programs.

31. Support national appliance efficiency standards. Every five years in the United States, the federal government reviews standards for major appliances, such as refrigerators, water heaters, and air conditioners. The public can participate in these reviews or make their feelings known by writing the Secretary of Energy or congresspeople.

Government Action

1. All increases in construction of mass transit should be supported.

2. Highway projects that have as their goal the reduction of traffic congestion by building more freeways should be opposed. Having more freeways simply encourages driving, which in turn encourages more fossil fuel use and pollution.

3. Local planning policies that encourage walking, bicycling, or using mass transit should be supported. These may include better pedestrian access to shopping, and higher density living near jobs, shopping, and mass transit.

4. Tough energy efficiency standards for buildings should be implemented.

5. **Local regulatory commissions should encourage** utilities to promote energy efficiency.

6. **Local governments should require the** weatherization of houses and the installation of cost-effective conservation measures prior to building or sale.

7. **Federal gasoline taxes should be raised.** Current low taxes encourage long commutes, resulting in urban sprawl and more pollution.

8. **Each nation should develop a consistent** national energy plan.

9. **Governments should increase their fund-**ing of research in alternatives to fossil fuels.

Reading

Worldwatch Papers:
#44, "Rivers of Energy: The Hydropower Potential," by Daniel Deudney, June 1981; #45, "Wind Power: A Turning Point," by Christopher Flavin, July 1981; #48, "Six Steps to a Sustainable Society," by Lester R. Brown and Pamela Shaw, 1982; #52, "Electricity from Sunlight: The Future of Photovoltaics," by Christopher Flavin, December 1982; #61, "Electricity's Future: The Shift to Efficiency and Small-Scale Power," by Christopher Flavin, November 1984; #75, "Reassessing Nuclear Power: The Fallout from Chernobyl," by Christopher Flavin, March 1987; all available from the Worldwatch Institute, 1776 Massachusetts Ave. NW, Washington, DC 20036, 202-452-1999.

Energy for a Sustainable World, the World Resources Institute, 1709 New York Ave. NW, Washington, DC 20006, 202-638-6300.

The Energy Saver's Handbook: For Town and City People, Massachusetts Audubon Society, Emmaus, PA: Rodale Press, 1982.

"The Impacts of Energy Development and Use," by Thomas J. Wilbanks.

Earth '88: Changing Geographic Perspectives, Washington, DC: National Geographic Society, 1988.

Audubon Energy Plan, by Jan Beyea. National Audubon Society, 950 Third Ave., New York, NY 10022.

Energy: 101 Practical Tips for Home and Work, by Susan Hassol and Beth Richman. Snowmass, CO.: The Windstar Foundation, 1989.

The Solar Home Book, by Bruce Anderson. Harrisville, NY: Cheshire Books, 1976.

The New Solar Electric Home/The Photovoltaics How-to Handbook, by Joel Davidson. Ann Arbor: AATEC Publications, 1987.

The Wind Power Book, by Jack Park. Palo Alto, CA: Cheshire Books, 1981.

Pedal Power, edited by James C. McCullagh. Emmaus, PA: Rodale Press, 1977.

Energy Efficiency: A New Agenda, by William Chandler, Howard Geller, and Mark Ledbetter. American Council for an Energy Efficient Economy, 1001 Connecticut Ave. NW, Suite 535, Washington, DC 20036.

Organizations to Contact

Alliance to Save Energy, 1925 K St. NW, Suite 206, Washington, DC 20036, 202-857-0666.

American Council for an Energy Efficient Economy, 1001 Connecticut Ave. NW, Suite 535, Washington, DC 20036.

American Wind Energy Association, 1730 N. Lynn St., Suite 610, Arlington, VA 22209, 703-276-8334.

Conservation and Renewable Energy Inquiry and Referral Service, US DOE, Box 8900, Silver Spring, MD 20907, 800-523-2929.

Energy Conservation Coalition, 1525 New Hampshire Ave. NW, Washington, DC 20036, 202-745-4874.

Energy Federation, Inc., 354 Waverly St., Framingham, MA 01701, 508-879-8572.

Fund for Renewable Energy and the Environment, 1001 Connecticut Ave., Suite 638, Washington, DC 20036.

League of Conservation Voters, 1150 Connecticut Ave., Suite 201, Washington, DC 20036, 202-785-8683.

Nuclear Information and Resource Service, 1424 16th St. NW, Suite 601, Washington, DC 20036, 202-328-0002.

Rocky Mountain Institute, 1739 Snowmass Creek Road, Old Snowmass, CO 81654-9199, 303-927-3128. (Information on efficiency in lighting, space cooling and heating, water heating and other applications.)

Safe Energy Communication Council, 1717 Massachusetts Ave. NW, Suite LL215, Washington, DC 20036.

U.S. Council for Energy Awareness, P.O. Box 66103, Dept. AY31, Washington, DC 20035.

THE PEOPLE

11
Overpopulation

In 1968, Paul Ehrlich, social scientist and environmentalist, published his first book about overpopulation. Called *The Population Bomb,* it was branded "alarmist" by some and "futuristic" by others, and it sold a million copies in two years. Ehrlich's argument that the prospect of an out-of-control sprawl of mankind was the world's most pressing problem was convincing, and his theories attracted a multitude of supporters.

The book set precedents in its pessimism. Ehrlich offered three scenarios for the future, all bleak. The first ended in nuclear war with 100 million dead Americans. Scenario two had Asia, Africa, and South America wracked by nationwide famines, the United States torn by civil conflict, and the superpowers igniting nuclear war. The third had 500 million dying of famine worldwide. (Ehrlich blamed the beginning of the population boom on the discovery of agriculture. When humans learned to grow their food the accompanying change in lifestyle encouraged a dramatic rise in birth: women were no longer wandering, which made child bearing easier, and food was better and more abundant, he contends.)

Over the past two decades, Ehrlich has watched his prophecies be either fulfilled or passed by. Some of his predictions were accurate. Since 1970, famine *has* dominated regions of the Third World, the population of the United States *has* doubled. Other prognostications were simply wrong. The population boom, for instance, has yet to bring on any outbreaks of nuclear war. Twenty years later, Ehrlich wrote a sequel to his bestseller, which bears an even more ominous title, *The Population Explosion.*

Things haven't changed for the better in the past two decades, he asserts. In fact, problems brought on by overpopulation have worsened. More important than the publication of his sequel, though, is that his once-novel warning about too many people on the planet is today mouthed by scientists, environmentalists, politicians, and the man on the street. Ehrlich's message is no longer "the sky is falling" rhetoric, but instead a harsh reality: our very numbers threaten nature, the future of the planet, and thus ourselves.

With hindsight, it hardly seems news that the Earth's population is booming, considering its dramatic rate of growth. According to the best estimates, about 5 million people inhabited the entire world 10,000 years ago; by the time of Christ that figure had grown to 130 million. The one billion mark was reached in the middle of the 19th century; two billion in 1930. In the spring of 1987 the world's population passed 5 billion, having doubled since 1950. If the current 1.7 percent annual growth rate keeps pace, the world's population is expected to reach 10 billion by 2027. The United Nations Population Fund's most recent projections are that the globe's population will stabilize near 14 billion in the second half of the twenty-first century.

Even that stabilization figure seems vastly optimistic. In 1989 almost 16,000 people were born every hour around the world, adding roughly 395,000 people to the planet every day, and 90 percent of them in developing nations that can ill afford to support them. (Roughly 140,000 deaths were recorded daily in 1989, worldwide.) Altogether almost

Rwanda is one of Africa's most densely populated and poverty-stricken countries (inset). Overpopulation and the demand for food have led to the complete cultivation of all available farming space.

93 million people were added to the world's population, more than in any previous year.

While some countries have been successful at slowing growth by introducing family planning, contraception, and even sterilization, the populations of most Third World nations are mushrooming. Pakistan's is expected to more than double over the next 30 years, from 110 million to more than 242 million; Nigeria's will reach 274 million, up from 115 million during the same period; Bangladesh's 115 million will grow to 230 million. The fastest-growing population in the world belongs to Kenya: today's 24 million is expected to nearly triple to 70 million in the next 30 years. If current trends continue, the world's population will have doubled in just 40 years and will continue to grow by approximately 1 billion people every ten years for decades to come.

This growth has had devastating effects on the millions of people who have been born into a world with not enough to eat and little hope for the future. It has also taken severe tolls on the Earth's environment. More people demand more energy, more energy creates more pollution, more pollution makes life more difficult, less certain. It is ironic that through most of human history, world population grew slowly due to epidemics, famine, and malnutrition. Our biological and technical advances—especially in health care—have extended life and thus the toll humankind takes on the planet.

In some spots on the map, penalties for overpopulation are already being paid. In Africa and Asia, the famine and starvation that Paul Ehrlich warned of are examples of the heavy fines that will undoubtedly continue to be meted out as populations burgeon. The United Nations estimates that almost 60 countries will experience critical food shortages by 2000. The World Bank suggests that 800 million human beings already live in "absolute poverty . . . a condition of life degraded by disease, illiteracy, malnutrition, and squalor." Around the world, lands are stripped by daily forages for food and fuel. Kenya's wildlife resources are being extinguished by poaching and habitat loss as population grows. In Indonesia, soil erosion is bringing on an "ecological emergency." In Ethiopia over 1 billion tons of topsoil are lost each year, because the population has ripped every growing thing from the ground in search of food.

The problems are only exacerbated when, to escape the poverty of the land, people move to the cities. There the air is dirty, the water undrinkable, sanitation unknown. Shantytowns and slums dominate most Third World cities, and their sprawl continues. In 1950, only seven urban centers were home to more than 5 million people: New York, London, Paris, Germany's Rhine-Ruhr, Tokyo-Yokohama, Shanghai, and Buenos Aires. Today, 34 cities boast more than 5 million, most of them in the Third World. The combination of massive traffic jams, chronic unemployment, stress on electric and water systems, lack of education and recreational facilities, and skyrocketing food expenses results in gloom and despair, poverty and hunger.

The solution to this "growing" dilemma seems simple. Slow down births. It is generally agreed that a fertility rate of about 2.1 births per woman would eventually lead to stabilization of the world's population. If that fertility rate were achieved globally, births and deaths would most likely level off. Such a balance has already been struck in many industrialized countries. In Europe, population growth has virtually ended and will likely slow to a halt in the next decade. Austria, Belgium, Denmark, Italy, and West Germany all have birth rates below 1.5. But stabilization cannot be achieved until fertility rates in places like Nigeria (6.6 births per married woman), Egypt (5.3), and Peru (4.4) are slowed.

Several stumbling blocks stand in the way of controlling population growth: cultural, social, and religious forces that no other environmental threat

Overpopulation and the ensuing overuse of the land and its overgrazing by cattle lead to soil erosion, which creates a dustbowl effect (top) and desertification of the land (bottom).

must reason with. Long entrenched, such attitudes make slowing growth in some ways more difficult than stopping acid rain or ozone depletion. Relief for all environmental problems depends on similar needs—money, commitment, and leadership.

Religious debate about the propriety of family planning makes all such efforts more difficult. Roman Catholics have fought against national family planning in Mexico, Kenya, and the Philippines, while Muslim fundamentalists have done the same in Iran, Egypt, and Pakistan. During the Reagan years, the United States contributed to the problem by drastically reducing funding for family planning programs around the globe, under pressure from fundamentalists and anti-abortionists. Since 1980, funds for both contraceptive research and domestic and international family planning have dried up. In 1989, $198 million was appropriated for "population assistance," a 50 percent reduction since 1972. A combination of political and moral battles and financial belt-tightening has left the United States, once a leading supporter of reproductive rights, a bystander in many ways.

Overpopulation problems are sometimes mistakenly attributed solely to developing nations. The United States and other industrialized nations contribute to the problem, too, even as their birth rates decline. In 1970, the United States' fertility rate was 2.5. Today it has dropped to 1.9. Population growth would seem to be under control, but those figures are misleading. In 1989, more babies were born in the United States than in any year since the mid-1950s.

The United States is still the fastest-growing industrialized nation, adding more than 2.3 million people each year. The Census Bureau projects that in just 11 years, the United States' population will reach 268 million, more than double that of the 1940s. The demand that population places on the world's resources continues to grow. According to Zero Population Growth, a lobbying and informa-tional group (founded by Paul Ehrlich in 1968), Americans, who constitute 5 percent of the world's population, use 28 percent of the world's energy. The birth of a baby in the United States imposes more than a hundred times the stress on the world's resources and environment as a birth in say, Bangladesh. Babies born in Bangladesh don't grow up to own automobiles and air conditioners or eat grain-fed beef. Their lifestyles do not require huge quantities of minerals and energy. The lesson to be learned is that only if lower birth rates are matched by less consumption will the environment ever really gain.

SOLUTIONS

The question of whether governments can or should attempt to control, or at least influence, population growth is a tricky one. It is a much tougher question to answer than "Can or should governments attempt to control carbon dioxide emissions?" The answer to the latter is "Of course." To the first? "Yes, maybe, and with great care."

Sex and childbearing have rightfully proven difficult for governments to regulate. No one should expect easy answers to slowing the planet's population growth. But today, with a growing list of options including fines and rewards, incentives and disincentives, contraception, and even sterilization, every country has the tools necessary to fashion a family planning program suited to their people, their culture, their religious mix. Unfortunately, in many places funding for such programs continues to be a stumbling block. But if governments or private sources don't make population growth a priority soon, many nations will find their infrastructures and environment crumbling under the weight of their own people. To date, only a few countries have put family planning at or near the top of their environmental priority lists. That number must grow as the twenty-first century approaches.

Family planning has already succeeded in much of the industrialized world. In the past 20 years, Europe's population has stabilized at a half billion and will most likely decline in the next few decades, according to the European Association for Population Studies. The rate of births per woman in all but a handful of European nations is well below 2.1. Austria, Denmark, Hungary, and West Germany have literally stopped growing. Belgium, Bulgaria, East Germany, Italy, Sweden, and the United Kingdom are expected to join them soon. Their stability is attributed to an almost generational shift in priorities, rather than concerns about the environment. Individualism, progressiveness, and "postmaterialism" are moving Europeans away from marriage and parenthood, says Dirk J. van de Kaa, of the Population Reference Bureau. He predicts that as few as 50 to 60 percent of European men and women in future generations will ever marry, and that having children will be much more a deliberate choice, rather than habit.

Some believe there are disadvantages to zero growth, though. In West Germany, if the population continues to decline from its 1973 peak of 63 million, by the year 2030 there will be one retired person for every person at work. The accompanying problems of an aging work force, slower economic growth, and the increased burden of supporting an elderly population could haunt the country. West Germany has actually begun encouraging births, with the goal of adding an extra 200,000 children a year to their population. But that example is rare. The advantages of slowing growth—producing a stable work force that allows able-bodied older people to work longer, fewer children to be educated, lower crime rates, and less pollution—are still worth it.

Gradually, even the most prolific nations are recognizing the importance of family planning. In Mexico, a family planning program was initiated in 1973 and the country's birth rate fell within four years from 45 per 1,000 to 38. (Today the country's birth rate is still too high but improving, at 31 per 1,000.) Colombia, Tunisia, Costa Rica, Sri Lanka, and Thailand have all recorded successes in slowing growth in the past decade. After the introduction of family planning in China and South Korea, birth rates have declined by as much as 60 percent. Breaking centuries-old traditions is a big challenge; increased frankness about sex has helped. Educating people about the changing demands and responsibilities of mankind as the twentieth century ends is the most important part of any family planning effort.

Such shifts have been slow, largely because as recently as the early 1970s, many governmental leaders felt population controls were racist, capitalist, or imperialist. Today, nearly two thirds of all developing nations have family planning programs of some kind. The choice should be obvious. Either adopt stringent smaller-family policies or the country's life support system will break down. Countries that have already made the shift to small families typically have four things in common: an active population education program, widely available family planning services, incentives for small families (and in some cases disincentives for large ones), and widespread improvements in economic and social conditions. It is difficult to succeed without some combination of all four.

The first goal is to make contraception available to everyone who wants it. Approximately 372 million of the globe's 860 million married couples of reproductive age use modern contraceptives, about 43 percent. Most studies indicate that more would use contraception if they knew about it or if it was readily available. Over half of the couples contacted in the 1980 All-India Family Planning Survey, for example, wished to limit family size, but only 28 percent were using modern methods of birth control. A similar 1985 survey in Egypt produced the same results: 56 percent of women said they wanted no more children, but only 30 percent were using contraceptives.

There is no one solution, no quick fix. But there are plenty of options. Where contraceptives have been successfully introduced into the culture, birth rates have dropped. Some countries pay people not to have babies. Such one-time payments made to individuals who are sterilized or use contraceptives, or to doctors and family planners who encourage either, are used in more than 20 nations, from Bangladesh to Vietnam.

Payment plans were first offered in India in the late 1950s, when men and women were offered two weeks' wages, six dollars, to be sterilized. (Sterilization is preferred by many governments for an obvious reason—it's permanent.) The plan continues today, and rates have climbed to $11 to $13. Cars with bullhorns and loudspeakers promote sterilization "camps," and clothing, food, and lottery tickets are used as incentives to lure participation. In Singapore, anyone undergoing sterilization receives full paid leave from work and their children receive priority admission to school.

Incentives may also take the form of governmental subsidies. In many nations, people continue to have big broods as a form of security for the aged, a kind of insurance. Others have large families to help bring income into the household. Still others have big families simply out of habit. If government steps in and provides more funding for the aged or helps insure income, the reasons for having big families are lessened.

Some governments make periodic payments to a savings account or retirement fund or life insurance for families who limit their offspring to two. In the 1970s in Taiwan, the government set up savings accounts in the township of Hua if families agreed to have no more than two or three children. Annual deposits of $15 were paid to families with two or less; smaller amounts if they had three kids. The money was to be used to send the town's children to school.

Similar community development "bribes" have been used with great success in Thailand. The coun-try's family planning guru, Mechai Viravaidya, encouraged villages promoting family planning to invest in a pair of water buffalo, which the village contraceptive distributors then managed. Participants in wise family planning could rent the animals at half the price charged to people not practicing family planning.

In other countries large families are actually penalized. Called "disincentives," fines are levied for breaking family planning "rules." In Singapore, the government withholds housing subsidies, employment benefits, or preferential school admission to families who insist on having more than three children. In other countries mothers receive maternity benefits for only their first four children and paid maternity leave is allowed only every three years. In South Korea and Pakistan income tax deductions are limited to families with two or fewer children.

As the debate over how far government should intercede in "helping" families make planning decisions continues, a number of examples of successful, and failed, efforts have been documented.

In Indonesia in 1972, 400,000 couples in the country practiced birth control. By 1989 that number had risen to more than 18.6 million. The nation's fertility rate had fallen from 5.6 to 3.4 children per woman. The massive shift is attributed to a combination of government and community education, as well as the distribution of free contraceptives to anyone who wanted them. The key to making free contraceptives work, especially in a rural environment, is to make them not just free but readily available, insists Judith Jacobsen of the Worldwatch Institute. In that respect, the pill and condoms are not widely promoted, because if you run out and have to walk two days to get them, they're of little use. IUDs have proven the best means of contraception in many areas that are off the beaten path.

China's efforts at limiting growth may be both the most successful and most debated. The most populous country in the world—one fifth of all people are Chinese—has been trying desperately to slow growth for decades. In 1971 the nation's leaders began to encourage late marriages, long intervals between births, and two-children families. But by 1979, the country's baby-boomers of the 1960s were maturing to childbearing age, threatening a baby boom of their own. Between 1949 and 1982, China's population had doubled, passing one billion, and was still growing. This inspired leaders to propose their "one-child" plan, with a goal of stabilizing population at 1.2 billion. They made it a "duty" for both mothers and fathers to practice family planning. Substantial pay increases, better housing, longer maternity leaves, and priority access to education were all offered as incentives to those who had just one child. Heavy fines and social ostracism were left for those who "disobeyed."

China's policies have gotten even more strict in recent years. Sterilization is compulsory for one of the parents in a two-child family. A mix of rewards (free or subsidized medical care for the children of small families) and fines (up to 10 percent of a couple's combined wages for the first 16 years of an unauthorized child's life) are levied for breaking the rule. While the plan has worked at slowing growth— China managed in just over a decade to reduce the average number of children per family from six to fewer than three—there have reportedly been some grisly aftereffects. In some rural regions, baby girls have been killed at birth. Not wanting to be penalized for having more than one child, some parents preferred that the one be a boy (more likely to be a wage-earner and carry on the family name), and often drowned unwanted girls before their births were registered. Chinese officials have condemned such killings, and have even written laws to help preclude them.

It is this kind of social engineering and coercion that breeds critics of government-mandated family planning. Yet, others maintain that policies like China's are necessary. Sociologist J. Mayone Stycos argues that education of both adults and adolescents, aimed at blending concerns about family behavior and natural welfare, have helped dramatically in China. He conducted a survey while touring the country, and found that of 5,000 high school students in Sichuan province, 85 percent correctly identified the size of the world population and 79 percent thought the world population was too large. Asking the same questions of high-schoolers in Costa Rica, Colombia, and Peru, he found that less than 5 percent in each country could identify world population size and less than half felt the world population was too large.

If China is succeeding in slowing growth, family planning efforts in the second-most-populous country on the planet, India, have so far proved failures. When the country's Ministry of Health submitted its annual report for the 1989–1990 budget it included a cry for help: "Population control can no longer be the responsibility of one ministry or department. The entire planning process must be geared toward controlling population."

India Today, the country's leading newsmagazine, predicts that within decades the country will have the world's largest number of illiterates and homeless and 400 million unemployed people. With a population of 810 million people already, it is estimated that India's population will pass 1 billion by the end of the century or soon after and overtake China as the most populous nation before the middle of the twenty-first century. For more than 20 years the nation's leaders have recognized the problem of overpopulation, but they have been unable to stop its growth.

Annual growth in the country is actually *down* to about 2.1 percent. But food is not evenly distributed, forests are being razed for firewood or furniture, and good drinking water is scarce. Large families are still spawned by a combination of low literacy and a lack of sustained information and follow-up services.

Growing populations in Third World countries have exacerbated the decimation of tropical rain forests—people flock to the rain forest land (above) for arable land, food and space for cattle grazing and habitation (below). Rain forest trees also supply these populations with their primary source of energy, firewood.

Using television, radio, and a myriad of other sources to get its message across, the government has attempted to sell a "small is beautiful" campaign, but it hasn't worked. The only real success is a massive sterilization program, sparked by cash rewards. As part of an Indira Gandhi-organized drive to revitalize the country's economy in 1975, compulsory-sterilization laws were authorized for anyone with three children. By the time the emergency ended in 1977, more than 8 million sterilizations had been performed, 90 percent of them on women. Many people reportedly stayed close to home during those 18 months for fear of being "rounded up." Today, contraceptive use is being emphasized, but without proper education, promotion, and availability its acceptance has been slow to take hold.

By comparison, family planning efforts in Brazil, a country not generally known for its environmental foresight, has had great success in slowing population growth. In one generation, the country's fertility rate has been cut almost in half. In 1970, married women in the country were having an average of 5.75 babies. Today that number has dropped to 3.2. The population of 145 million continues to grow, but best estimates are that it will stabilize near the year 2000 at 170 million, 50 million fewer than demographers had predicted ten years ago. (Though the 35 million more people than today will still stress the country's rain forests and other ecosystems.)

Brazil's decrease has been achieved without strong government policy and is attributed to a combination of factors: the rapid spread of contraceptives, economic stagnation over the last decade, and somewhat surprisingly, universal access to television. As recently as 1965, the ruling military encouraged big families and only 5 percent of fertile married women used contraceptives. Today, according to Bemfam, Brazil's largest private family-planning agency, two thirds of all married women use some form of contraception, and about 27 percent of married Brazilian

women are sterilized (well above the American level of about 17 percent).

The biggest change has been in the attitude toward family size, espoused by men and women in villages and cities. In an interview with *The New York Times*, Maria Izete Costa Marinha, a housewife and mother of three, explained that her mother had had 12 children. Maria's daughter wants just two. Economics are partially responsible for that shift. Many in the lower classes simply cannot afford to have babies.

Television's role in birth control has been to show the masses how others live. Heavily watched soap operas have introduced a modern world to Brazil's middle class, a world full of small families. "The soap operas very rarely show families with lots of children," says George Martine, a Canadian demographer who works in Brazil. "When they do, the families are poor and miserable."

In each of the countries that has made attempts to slow growth, no matter the path, one unifying thread has been identified as the best way to discourage women from having babies: Improve their economic status. By creating more jobs for women, educating girls about their opportunities, and introducing the idea of family planning to as many people as possible at a young age, overpopulation becomes a concern to more and more. Inevitably, women interviewed in developing nations say they would prefer smaller families, but most are unsure how or don't have the technology. When this has been corrected, when women in the developing nations have more control over their bodies, population growth should slow dramatically.

A shining example of efforts to upgrade the status of women exists in Bangladesh, a country with an enormous population problem. In 1975, the government began a project providing start-up loans to groups of rural village women interested in having their own businesses, such as making pottery, raising poultry, or running grocery stores. Over 120,000

How Many People Can the Earth Support?

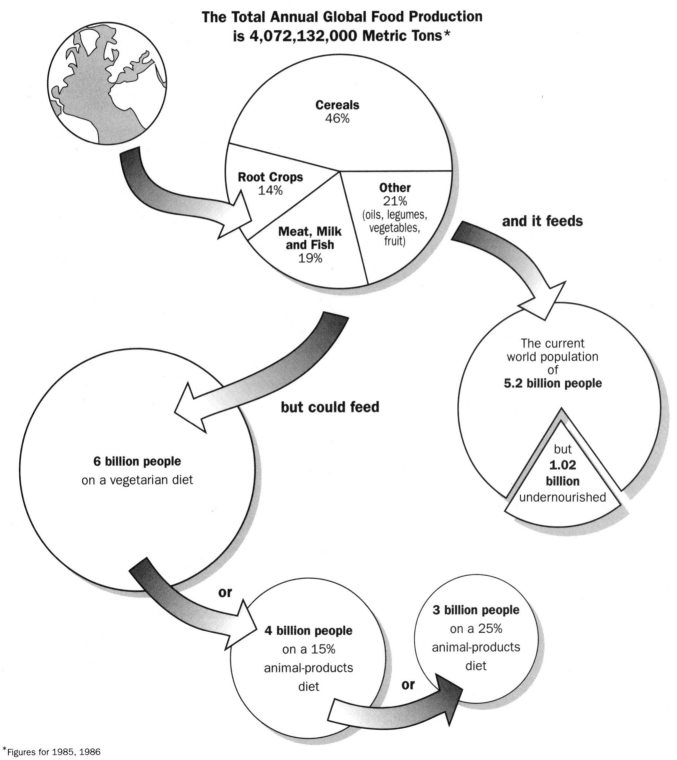

The Total Annual Global Food Production is 4,072,132,000 Metric Tons*

Cereals
46%

Root Crops
14%

Other
21%
(oils, legumes, vegetables, fruit)

Meat, Milk and Fish
19%

and it feeds

The current world population of **5.2 billion people**

but **1.02 billion** undernourished

but could feed

6 billion people
on a vegetarian diet

or

4 billion people
on a 15% animal-products diet

or

3 billion people
on a 25% animal-products diet

*Figures for 1985, 1986

Source: Zero Population Growth

women took advantage of the offer. They meet weekly in their communities to talk about business, health care, and their future. Information about contraception is available, and so are contraceptives. More than 75 percent of the co-op members use contraceptives—nationally the rate among married women is less than 35 percent.

Implementation of family planning efforts requires increased investment of time, energy, and money. Like any investment in the future, funds have to be laid out now if there is to be a return. Family planning is no different in that respect from any other environmental dilemma.

In recent years, funding for family planning has been curtailed globally, but particularly by the United States. The Reagan Administration backed off from supporting such efforts, citing societal and budgetary reasons. Private sources stepped in to fill some of the gap. (The MacArthur and Packard Foundations have provided $40 million in the past decade to programs aimed at stimulating "culturally appro-

priate" family-planning services.) But Dr. Joseph Speidel of the Population Crisis Committee in Washington, D.C. estimates that in order to achieve population stabilization by the end of this century, global expenditures must rise to $7 billion annually over the next decade. That's $5 billion more than is spent today, but relatively little compared, for example, to military expenditures.

The toll this booming mass of people is taking on the planet may well end life as we know it. Lester Brown of the Worldwatch Institute writes often about the need to focus on creating a "sustainable" relationship with the Earth. The keenest message he attempts to drum into public consciousness is that containing our population is key to sustainable development. "Time is not on our side," asserts Brown. "We have years, not decades, to turn the situation around. And even then there is no guarantee that we will be able to reverse the trends that are undermining the human prospect, but if we do it will be during the 1990s."

OVERPOPULATION

50%
LIVE WITHOUT
ADEQUATE FOOD
AND AMENITIES

16%
ARE AFFLUENT
WITH LIFESTYLES
LIKE AMERICANS

34% LIVE IN
EXTREME
POVERTY

5.2 BILLION
5 BILLION
2.5 BILLION
1.2 BILLION
0.6 BILLION
0.32 BILLION
0.15 BILLION
0.05 BILLION

1000BC 200BC 1100 1700 1850 1950 1985 1990

A combination of soaring birth rates (primarily in developing nations) and declining death rates has fueled an astronomical population growth. World population stands today at 5.2 billion, and isn't expected to stabilize until it passes 10 billion.

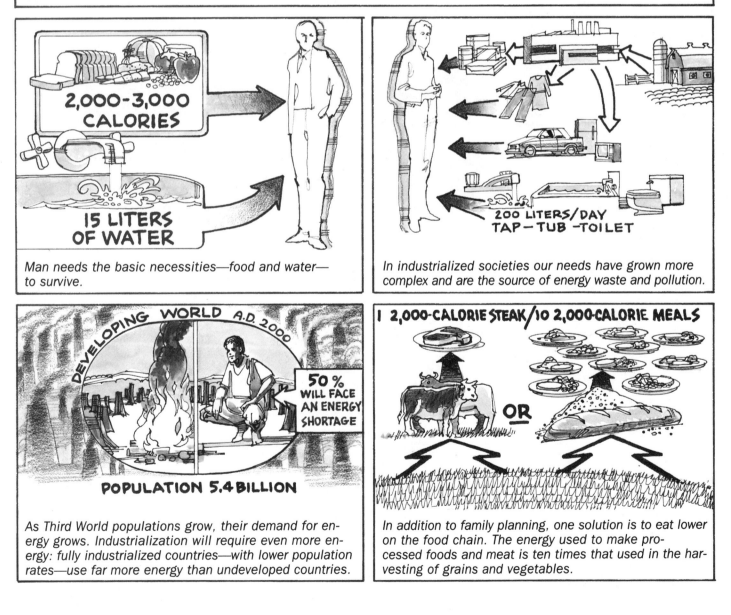

2,000–3,000 CALORIES

15 LITERS OF WATER

Man needs the basic necessities—food and water—to survive.

200 LITERS/DAY
TAP – TUB – TOILET

In industrialized societies our needs have grown more complex and are the source of energy waste and pollution.

DEVELOPING WORLD A.D. 2000

50% WILL FACE AN ENERGY SHORTAGE

POPULATION 5.4 BILLION

As Third World populations grow, their demand for energy grows. Industrialization will require even more energy: fully industrialized countries—with lower population rates—use far more energy than undeveloped countries.

1 2,000-CALORIE STEAK / 10 2,000-CALORIE MEALS

OR

In addition to family planning, one solution is to eat lower on the food chain. The energy used to make processed foods and meat is ten times that used in the harvesting of grains and vegetables.

Individual Action

1. **Becoming a parent means taking on major** responsibilities. Be sure to talk about family size with your spouse and plan your family accordingly. Postpone having children until you have been married or in a stable relationship for at least three years (exceptions will obviously be made by older couples, whose biological clocks are ticking). This makes sense for both family and population stability. (See Zero Population Growth's "Making a Difference.")

2. **It may seem antiquated, but abstaining** from heterosexual activity until you are ready to become involved in an intimate relationship helps limit pregnancies. When you are ready for such activities, consult your doctor, a clinic, or a school nurse about the different types of contraceptives, their effectiveness, and the method best suited for you.

3. **Sex and population education should be a** part of every school's curriculum. If it's not part of yours, talk to principals, teachers, and school board members.

4. **Support and respect the decisions of rela-** tives, friends and acquaintances who choose to have 0, 1, or 2 children, or who choose to adopt. In our society, there is still a great deal of pressure to have children, and those who opt for small families deserve support.

5. **As an option to having more children your-** self, consider working with a daycare center, summer camp, school, big brother/sister program, or abused children's program. Babysitting for friends may also fulfill some of the same needs.

6. **Urge legislators to support continued fund-** ing for research and development of new birth control methods. Science and technology may already have solutions to slowing population growth, but more money is needed to help focus and disseminate what is known. For example, a new "evening before" or "morning after" birth control pill (RU 486) is being readied for introduction in Europe. This would permit a woman to decide privately and inexpensively whether or not she wants to get pregnant, before or after intercourse. If the pill works and is widely disseminated, it could help do away with the need for abortions.

7. **Birth control information and devices** *should* be available to every man and woman. If they aren't in your community, lobby local or even national policy makers to insure their widespread availability.

8. **Anything that can be done to expand the** educational and employment opportunities for women has proven to help slow birth rates. Job opportunities and work place daycare should both be encouraged in every community.

9. **Children, especially girls, can be adversely** affected by young pregnancies. The more information and education provided about teenage pregnancy, the better. Social service groups in virtually every community can direct you to agencies in your area. The National Urban League, with branches in 34 states, provides counseling and emphasizes teenage-pregnancy prevention. (Headquarters: National Urban League, 500 E. 62nd St., New York, NY 10021, 212-310-9000.)

10. **National population policies in the United** States and elsewhere should be mandated. In the United States the Global Resources, Environment and Population Act can serve as a role model for others. It requires the federal government to consider a variety of economic, social, governmental, and environmental factors prior to passing legislation, and suggests another half-dozen cautions for legislators and voters alike.

Government Actions

1. National population policies should be established to help stabilize the population at a level that will allow for the sustainable management of resources as well as a reasonably high quality of life for all individuals.

2. Informational literature regarding the needs for and steps toward population stabilization should be funded and disseminated to the public.

3. All environmental education programs should provide information on the implications of population growth.

4. Governments should support and fund the work of the United Nations Fund for Population Activities.

5. Nations should work with other countries— by sharing technologies and manpower—to increase funding for population stabilization programs.

6. All economic assistance programs for individual countries should incorporate family planning.

7. Funds should be available for research on reliable demographic, natural-resource, and environmental information for use in federal planning and decision making, as well as for studies that evaluate national and global trends in population growth, natural resource availability, and environmental quality.

Reading

To Govern Evolution: Further Adventures of the Political Animal, by Walter Truett Anderson. New York: Harcourt Brace Jovanovich, 1987.

The Population Bomb, by Paul Ehrlich. New York: Ballantine, 1968. *The Population Explosion,* by Paul Ehrlich. New York: Ballantine, 1990.

Promoting Population Stabilization: Incentives for Small Families, by Judith Jacobsen. Worldwatch Paper #54, Worldwatch Institute.

"Trends in Global Population Resources and the Environment," by Rep. Buddy MacKay. *Congressional Record,* April 29, 1987, page E1640.

"The World's Urban Explosion," by Robert W. Fox. *National Geographic,* August 1984.

"Economic Consequences of Population Change in the Third World," by Allen Kelly. *Journal of Economic Literature,* Vol. 26, No. 4, December 1988.

The Birth Dearth: What Happens When People in Free Countries Don't Have Enough Babies, by Ben Wattenberg. Pharos Books, 1987.

Investing in Children, by William U. Chandler. Worldwatch Paper #64, Worldwatch Institute, 1986.

USA By Numbers (tracks trends from acid rain to zero population growth, for kids and adults). Zero Population Growth, 1400 16th St. NW, Suite 320, Washington, DC 20036.

"Country Rankings of the Status of Women: Poor, Powerless and Pregnant." Population Crisis Committee, Washington, DC, 1988.

"Population Handbook." Population Reference Bureau, Washington, DC, 1985.

The Crowded Earth: People and the Politics of Population, by Pranay Gupte. New York: W. W. Norton & Company, 1984.

Gaining People, Losing Ground: A Blueprint for Stabilizing World Population, by Werner Fornos. The Population Institute, Washington, DC, 1987.

The State of World Population 1989, by Dr. Nafis Sadik. UN Population Fund, New York, 1989.

World Population & U.S. Policy: The Choices Ahead, edited by Jane Menken. New York: W. W. Norton & Company, 1986.

Organizations to Contact

Center for Population Options, 1012 14th St. NW, Suite 1200, Washington, DC 20005, 202-347-5700.

Negative Population Growth, Inc., 16 E. 42nd St., Suite 1042 (F-2), New York, NY 10017.

Population Crisis Committee, 1120 19th St. NW #550, Washington, DC 20036.

The Population Institute, 100 Maryland Ave. NE, Washington, DC 20002.

Population Reference Bureau, Inc., 777 14th St. NW, Suite 800, Washington, DC 20005.

Sierra Club Population Growth Policy Program, 730 Polk St., San Francisco, CA 94109.

United Nations Population Fund, 220 E. 42nd St., New York, NY 10017.

Zero Population Growth, 1400 16th St. NW, Suite 320, Washington, DC 20036, 202-332-2200.

12

The Future

That time is running out is a sentiment echoed by a chorus of environmentalists, economists, scientists, politicians, and just plain ordinary folk worldwide. While attempting to keep an optimistic outlook, many are convinced that we've let this abundance of environmental threats paint us into a tight corner. We seem to spend more time patching over our mistakes than we do taking steps toward the future. Yet if we don't face up to every one of the globe's environmental problems today, their number will surely multiply.

What is done in the next 10 years will set the course for the century to come—this is a statement not of rhetoric but of fact. "I am utterly convinced that most of the great environmental struggles will be either won or lost in the 1990s," contends Thomas Lovejoy of the Smithsonian Institute. He is joined by a litany of voices that have been howling against environmental harms for decades. Fred Krupp, executive director of the Environmental Defense Fund, speaks for all these voices when he says, "It's *almost* too late for people to be waking up. We've got to make the 1990s an era where what was viewed as impossible becomes possible and we get a good head start at solving these problems. The next 10 years are absolutely critical." These people and others are too smart to cry wolf at this late stage. Those closest to the action are convinced that the next decade will serve as a test of how the world will take care of itself well into the next century.

Peoples' opinions have already been swayed by the mounting environmental problems in their own back-yards. Most people around the globe stand firmly behind cleanup efforts, whatever they may entail. Polls by Harris, Gallup, Roper, and *The New York Times* all report that upwards of 80 percent of us agree, in the words of one pollster, that "protecting the environment is so important that standards cannot be too high." The challenge now lies in balancing priorities as people attempt to take control of pollutants. If we are ever to get ahead of the curve and learn to control our harms, several shifts must occur simultaneously.

Climate change, ozone depletion, overpopulation, acid rain are all long-range fights. They need, and deserve, more than Band-Aids. Commitment and sacrifice will be required. Education, responsibility, and efficiency are the keys. One noted environmentalist suggests we must "tie the fate" of the environment to both government and individual, a sort of eco-handcuffs. Every action made, whether by government, industry, or individual, must take into consideration any harm to the environment that may result. Similar rules must be applied to corporations wrestling with their toxic waste, and to the suburban homeowner trying to figure out what to do with his lawn clippings.

A word of caution, though. We must guard against a tone that implies the end has already arrived when talking about our environmental mess. The problems may make us feel as though we have our backs against the wall today, but they are all solvable. The challenge of the 1990s is to apply technologies that already exist, come up with the appropriate solutions where needed, and then somehow wedge them into everyday life.

Redefining our attitudes toward waste is essential: horse manure compost proves fertile ground for growing mushrooms (inset); combinations of straw and horse manure are used in place of chemicals to fertilize farmlands.

Increased awareness of environmental problems has inspired a kind of "One World" theorem that is already flavoring international conferences, no matter their initial agenda. When energy, economic, or even social summits are convened, heads of state have made environmental concerns a lead item. This makes perfect sense, as no great leap is needed to recognize their importance. If environmental problems aren't addressed now by the *world's* leaders they will never get the attention they need back home. Senator Albert Gore, who has taken the lead in the United States Congress on environmental issues, told one gathering of world leaders ("Global Change and Our Common Future," May 1989) that environmental issues are already the highest priority on every nation's crowded plate. "In the not-distant future, there will be a new 'sacred agenda' in international affairs," he prophesied. "Policies that enable rescue of the global environment. This task will one day join, and even supplant, preventing the world's incineration through nuclear war as the principal test of statecraft."

His prediction was bolstered by Prime Minister Gro Harlem Brundtland of Norway, who proposed that all nations allocate one tenth of 1 percent of their gross domestic product to an "international fund for the atmosphere" to help developing countries industralize in ways that would not degrade the environment.

Similar themes were the focus of a later economic summit in Paris among leaders of the seven biggest democracies. The group, comprised of representatives from the United States, France, West Germany, Britain, Italy, Canada, and Japan, spent long hours debating their governments' role in leading the way in international environmental policy making. For the first time there was top-level recognition that development, debt reduction, and the environment are linked and must be addressed together. There was also a general agreement that environmental problems were invading matters of national and international security, by potentially creating serious threats to the political stability of some nations and looming as a potential source of conflict between neighboring countries. The final paper of the summit called for "all countries to combine their efforts in order to improve observation and monitoring on a global scale."

(Shortly after the summit, Japan, responding to criticism of its huge foreign trade surplus, announced that it would spend $43 billion on grants and loans to improve the global environment and spur economic growth in countries crushed by poverty and indebtedness. The plan included a three-year, $2.25 billion program of grants and credits for environmental needs, including tree planting and helping poor people find alternatives to wood for fuel and fodder.)

Government must lead the way in establishing the environment as a priority, but many environmental actions are a direct result of the prodding of an increasingly anxious electorate. As a result of both headline-making accidents and environmental dangers less publicized and closer to home, a "greening" of popular thought is stretching around the globe, flexing its muscles in both elections and economies. In the United States, electoral tickets are filled with candidates running on environmental platforms, motivated by dirty drinking water in their towns or a proposed toxic landfill in their county. Memberships in environmental groups have swollen worldwide. (The National Wildlife Federation averages 8,000 new members a month. After the disastrous spill at Valdez the group received 21,000 membership applications in the first nine days of May 1989.) Across Western Europe, politicians are championing environmental problems as small but powerful Green parties grow, and deliver votes. Green politicians are slowly making inroads into Eastern Europe, the Soviet Union, Mexico, even China.

Green parties in France and West Germany claim 10 percent of the national electorate. Active for two

Experiments with alternative ways of using waste: above, aquatic plant life is used to filter and purify sewage; below, methane from the landfill is used to heat this one-acre greenhouse.

decades, since 1983 they have won seats in national parliaments in Sweden, Austria, the Netherlands, Belgium, Switzerland, Finland, Portugal, and Italy. Chernobyl is given backhanded credit for helping to turn *their* concerns into *majority* concerns. Their success has been felt by politicians of all stripes. "Green thinking is a worldview, not just a set of issues," says Bart Kuyper, a longtime Netherlands Green. Their platform is simple: all forms of development must be judged not by "economic growth" but by how they affect the life of people and the Earth.

The greening has spread beyond western societies. In Taiwan, the most polluted country in the world, environmental groups are gaining a foothold. Here, where there is a dense and growing population and an industry base made up of heavy polluters like petrochemical and plastics manufacturers, the voices of environmentalists are now beginning to confront the long-vested power structure.

Since mid-1987, groups of 10 to 20 have been keeping a 24-hour vigil outside the government-owned China Petrochemical Corporation, a refinery in Houchin, to protest the firm's plans to build yet another large plant. Villagers who have lived for more than 40 years with the refinery as their neighbor are tired of the pollution. Black, smelly water from the plant pours into the Houchin River. Groundwater is saturated with oil, and 1,600 families, nearly half the town, draw their drinking water from local wells.

The government has tentatively agreed that now is the time for environmental protection, because the economy is strong and can afford a cleanup. The country's environmental protection agency has adopted tough measures including bans on certain toxic chemicals, reallocation of a portion of China Petrochemical's profits for river cleanup, and fining of plastics and food manufacturers for polluting. "They are really going after the big tigers, finally," reports a local environmentalist.

Environmental debate is growing in Eastern Europe and the Soviet Union as well. As Poland's government is reorganized, environmental concerns have moved a notch closer to the top of priority lists. And increasingly in the Soviet Union, experts can voice concern *before* projects are decided and criticize plans *before* they are implemented.

A kind of grass-roots greening is taking hold across Poland with the Polish Ecological Club as the acknowledged leader. Founded in 1980 in Krakow, it has 15 regional offices and 6,000 members across the country. Recognized by the state as a legal opposition group, it refuses official support. Government efforts to put the country's environmental movement under one state-sponsored umbrella have failed. In 1981, the club and its allies were successful in shutting down the Skawina Aluminum Works, a plant nine miles south of Krakow whose fluorine emissions had so altered the environment that cows in neighboring fields were no longer able to walk. Local schoolchildren were removed from the region at least once a year to get some fresh air.

These efforts are long overdue. Poland's air and water are filthy. An estimated 6,000 wastewater treatment plants are necessary. The country's industrial base is desperately in need of an upgrade, for both economic and environmental reasons.

In the Soviet Union, environmental problems are harder to pinpoint, in part because of the country's size. The world's largest nation (covering one sixth of the Earth's land surface and spanning 11 time zones), the USSR is unrivaled in natural resources. But for many years, Soviet scientists and officials found it difficult to believe these resources could ever be exhausted, and believed that socialism would eventually correct all ills. Today, dirty air and water, declining oil reserves, and the generally poor performance of the Soviet economy have forced reconsideration of the nation's wastefulness.

In the past two decades, the Soviet mass media have gradually begun to present diverse perceptions

Instead of being dumped in the ocean where it can harm aquatic life, treated sludge combined with woodchips (above), can be applied directly to farmlands as fertilizer (below).

of the natural environment. Green factions in the country are now speaking out more loudly and attracting a growing audience. Activists in the Baltic states of Lithuania and Latvia were the first to gain official recognition for their protests; Estonia was the first Soviet state to be allowed to join Friends of the Earth. In October 1987, the informal group Zemyna called for a public demonstration at the Ignalina Power Station. The station, which has the same kind of reactors as the Chernobyl power plant, was already experiencing fires when authorities announced their intent to add another reactor. The protest drew 30,000 people, who formed a "ring of life" around the station. A subsequent petition called for the complete shutdown of the plant until the International Atomic Energy Agency could inspect it. The plant was closed.

As more groups form, there's cause for optimism that environmental protest—and environmental solutions—may grow in other Eastern bloc nations. The Association for the Support of Ecology conducts public opinion polls on environmental issues and distributes its findings. The Social Ecological Union has launched a strong agriculture program aimed at problems of irrigation, soil erosion, and land reclamation. Perhaps the most ambitious environmental group in the Soviet Union is Ecology: 21st Century. The for-profit ecological cooperative offers everything from T-shirts to consulting for companies in need of pollution controls.

Similar greening has taken root in Mexico, where dozens of environmental groups have sprung up since 1980. Motivated by growing concern over nuclear power plants, tropical rain forest destruction, illegal traffic in wildlife, and the country's growing population, the two most visible groups are the Mexican Ecology Movement, with 52,000 members, and the Group of 100, a small collection of prominent artists and intellectuals formed in 1985. The Group has unusual leverage because of the

fame of its members, including writers Octavio Paz and Gabriel García Márquez.

All this public hue and cry may be taking place just in time. Pollster Lou Harris says his studies for the United Nations Environmental Programme show that growing concern over environmental issues may soon topple governments. In the first worldwide survey of people's attitudes about the environment, Harris reported that large majorities in 13 nations said their present environmental conditions were "negative." His concerns were borne out in mid-1989 when the government of the Netherlands became the first to collapse over arguments about the financing of a national environmental plan. The out-of-power Liberal party rejected the government's plan to charge car commuters in order to raise the funds to pay for part of a comprehensive national environmental plan. When the government refused to retreat from its position, it collapsed.

The Dutch case may serve as an example of what's to come as governments wrestle with who should pay for cleaning up and protecting the environment. The Netherlands' plan was the first proposed in the European Community and called for doubling spending on the environment to more than $6 billion a year by 1994 and ridding the country of all forms of pollution by 2010. The plan had 200 measures designed to tackle pollution in the soil, water, and air, increase public transportation, reduce waste disposal, and conserve energy. The government that proposed it collapsed, but the plan has been revived and is expected to be adopted in some form; it may still serve some day as an example.

In the United States, money has become a new weapon for environmentalists. Vermont's second largest bank now offers accounts that guarantee depositors their money will be lent only to ventures that meet certain social goals. The Socially Responsible Banking Fund permits customers of the Vermont National Bank to direct their money into a basket of

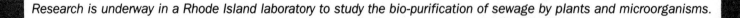

DEALING WITH POISONS

Remarkably, many microbes can even survive the toxins frequently dumped into sewers. Because the aquatic ecosystems in these tanks contain such a vast diversity of life forms, they are resilient and able to cope with the poisons which unfortunately are still common in the sewage of our industrial cities, such as Providence.

In the next few years, this facility will be used to study all these microbial processes in detail.

© 1989 Ocean Arks International

Research is underway in a Rhode Island laboratory to study the bio-purification of sewage by plants and microorganisms.

funds used for loans in affordable housing, agriculture, education, conservation, and small-business and nonprofit organizations. James Valliere, the fund's president, says "the real issue is whether depositors can make a deposit and know the money is not going into strip development or second-home condos." Deposits have grown so fast they are still awaiting borrowers.

Similarly, more than $40 billion has been invested in the United States by churches, universities, pension funds, and individuals in "socially correct" investment funds. Do you prefer that your stock market cash not go into companies with shaky environmental reputations, like Exxon or Dow? The Calvert Social Investment Fund, begun in 1982, today has more than 30,000 clients and manages $350 million. A product of Shearson-Lehman, the investment fund applies numerous tests to screen its investments, including bans on investments in manufacturers of plastic packaging and in companies that contribute to the destruction of rain forests abroad or old-growth forests in the United States. Similarly the $7.1 million New Alternatives Fund puts its cash into companies that are actively involved in conservation, alternative energy, and recycling. Its portfolio includes companies that produce energy-saving glass, cogenerate energy, and develop biomass technology.

The most sweeping effort to date to bring investors together with social action groups was organized in September 1989, taking the name the Valdez Principles. Modeled after the Sullivan Principles, introduced in 1977 to help govern conduct of American businesses in South Africa, Valdez is a coalition of environmental groups, religious organizations, and investors controlling more than $100 billion, including the pension funds of New York City and the state of California. Their innovative "code of conduct" is to be used in judging which corporations are environmentally responsible and deserve investment.

The 10-point code calls on companies to address the effect of both products and production processes on employees, communities, and the environment. Signatory members must protect the biosphere; use natural resources wisely; reduce and dispose of waste with care; use energy cautiously; reduce risk to employees and community; market only safe products and services; disclose accidents and hazards; compensate for damages; hire environmental directors and managers; and provide annual assessments and audits. The group also urges college students to consider which companies to work for, based on the code, and calls for annual environmental audits to identify potential liabilities like hazardous waste sites on property being sold or foreclosed. "This will represent the largest single tool for consumers to express their concern about environment that we have ever had," says coalition member Terry Gips, president of the International Alliance for Sustainable Agriculture.

For the individual who doesn't play the stock market or control a multi-million-dollar pension fund, there are still ways to direct money towards companies doing the right thing environmentally. The success of the "ecologically correct" mail-order catalogue Seventh Generation is a sign that individuals are ready to put their money where their conscience is. The catalogue sells compactors for aluminum cans; biodegradable trash bags, diapers, and sanitary napkins; solar battery chargers and fans; home radon test kits; lead-paint detectors; carbon monoxide alarms; and testing kits to detect chloroform, mercury, cadmium, or carbon tetrachloride in drinking water, as well as water-saving faucets and shower heads, a high-efficiency toilet, skin-care products that are not derived from petroleum, biodegradable cleansers, "low impact" stationery, and note pads and journals made from recycled newsprint.

The catalogue's name comes from a law of the Iroquois Confederation that instructed tribal leaders in any deliberation to weigh the impact of their actions on the next seven generations. Its founder, Alan Newman, says that kind of thinking will soon be forced on consumers and manufacturers by economic realities, as well as by new laws and regulations. He expects business to boom well into the next century. (Available for $2, from 10 Farrell St., South Burlington, Vermont, 05403.)

Similarly, the Council for Economic Priorities, CEP, publishes a handy little guide called *Shopping for a Better World*, which offers a rating scale of companies big and small based on their social and environmental conscience. The CEP's Corporate Conscience series also includes such titles as *Rating America's Corporate Conscience* and *Hazardous Waste Management* and, soon, *Ethical Investing Sourcebook*. (Council for Economic Priorities, 30 Irving Place, New York, NY 10003 212-420-1133.)

So far, the environmental problems we've addressed have been confined to Earth and its atmosphere. People are turning their gaze to the heavens, too, to see if there might be a way to use space to help better understand the way the Earth works. Soon after his inauguration, George Bush, along with NASA, announced a 25-year effort using a new network of satellites to better glimpse how the Earth's atmosphere, seas, and living creatures function as a global "team." Dubbed "Mission to Planet Earth," it is envisioned as one of the nation's most encompassing and urgent scientific programs. If it becomes reality, it will be undertaken in cooperation with the European Space Agency and Japan, which will each place in orbit a major piece of the system. The unmanned satellites, equipped with remote sensors, radar, lasers, spectrometers, and infrared beams, would observe and measure the actions of components of the global environment as they interact. Subject to congressional approval, the plan calls for the first platform to be launched in 1996; a second would follow in 1997.

The plan has critics, who are concerned there is only so much you can learn by observations from space. The core of the planet and its surface need to be investigated simultaneously, they argue, in order to measure the effects of changes to the oceans. Satellites may miss fluctuations in ocean currents, the amount of ice in the sea, the flow patterns of glaciers, deforestation, the spread of deserts, or the impact of living things, from plankton to human—all vital to forming a complete picture of how the Earth's systems work. Despite these concerns—and disregarding the $15 to $30 billion that some think might be better spent on the Earth—it is not too soon to look to ways man can better use space, and to look for his effects upon it.

Unfortunately, just as we have become particularly adept at despoiling the air, land, and sea around us, our forays into space have begun to take an environmental toll. That's right, space junk. The North American Air Defense System (NORAD) currently tracks more than 6,500 objects baseball-sized and larger in terrestrial and interplanetary orbit. Only 300 are operating satellites. Another 40,000 golfball-sized pieces are not tracked. The debris includes expended rocket stages, rocket panels, fragments from exploded satellites, nuts and bolts, and even tools that have slipped from the hands of space-walking astronauts.

The size of this floating landfill is expected to double during the 1990s from explosions, both accidental and purposeful. The concerns are real because even a postage-stamp-sized paint flake can crack the windows of space ships traveling at thousands of miles an hour. NASA and other agencies are devising plans to "scoop" the junk from space, employing a miles-wide net. An international agreement is in the works to resolve just who is responsible for cleaning up yet another of our messes.

Concluding such a long list of history, information, mild scoldings, and "things to do" neatly is

The Valdez Principles

In September 1989, a new coalition of environmentalists and investors, The Coalition for Environmentally Responsible Economies (CERES), proposed a code of conduct for businesses. The code calls on businesses to address their impact on the environment, communities, and their employees, and is named for the *Exxon Valdez* tanker that spilled 11 million gallons of oil in Alaskan coastal waters. Signatories to the code would agree to the following:

Pollution Prevention

- Eliminate pollutants from production processes
- Produce environmentally safe products
- Issue reports to the public on the impact of their products and processes
- Minimize production of hazardous waste
- Dispose of hazardous waste safely

Energy Efficiency

- Use energy-efficient processes
- Produce more energy-efficient products
- Use renewable resources
- Conserve non-renewable resources

Conservation

- Contribute to the preservation of biological diversity

Responsibility

- Report any environmental accidents
- Assume financial responsibility for restoration of damaged environment
- Financially compensate injured humans, employees
- Employ an environmental affairs senior executive
- Conduct an annual environmental audit of operations

Source: *The New York Times*

difficult. Perhaps the best conclusion is simply to hope that this book will serve as a small, daily reminder. A reminder that it is up to the individual to step in, now. As well as staying on top of the status of cleaning up the air over your city, or resolving the debate over the landfill coming to your town, you must invest time and energy every day in taking responsibility. Be conscious of how much plastic packaging you bring home from the grocery. Pick up just one piece of trash from the sidewalk each day. Spend 20 minutes a year getting your car's emission checked. Think about energy efficiency when you ready your home for winter. Leading a "cleaner" life is all anyone can ask.

A nugget drawn from a commencement speech delivered recently by naturalist Wendell Berry provides an eloquent articulation of the individual's responsibility. As well as personally serving as a fine example of how one man can make a difference, Berry has written more than 40 books and hundreds of essays that point the way to leading a simpler, cleaner, more responsible life. With a fresh decade looming on the horizon, the conclusion of his talk may serve as an apt motto for us all:

Beware the justice of Nature.

Understand that there can be no successful human economy apart from Nature or in defiance of Nature.

Understand that no amount of education can overcome the innate limits of human intelligence and responsibility. We are not smart enough or conscious enough or alert enough to work responsibly on a gigantic scale.

In making things always bigger and more centralized, we make them both more vulnerable in themselves and more dangerous to everything else. Learn, therefore, to prefer small-scale elegance and generosity to large-scale greed, crudity and glamour.

Make a home. Help to make a community. Be loyal to what you have.

Put the interest of your community first.

Love your neighbors—not the neighbors you pick out, but the ones you have.

Love this miraculous world that we did not make, that is a gift to us.

As far as you are able make your lives dependent upon your local place, neighborhood and household— which thrive by care and generosity—and independent of the industrial economy, which thrives by damage.

Find work, if you can, that does not damage. . . .

THE FUTURE

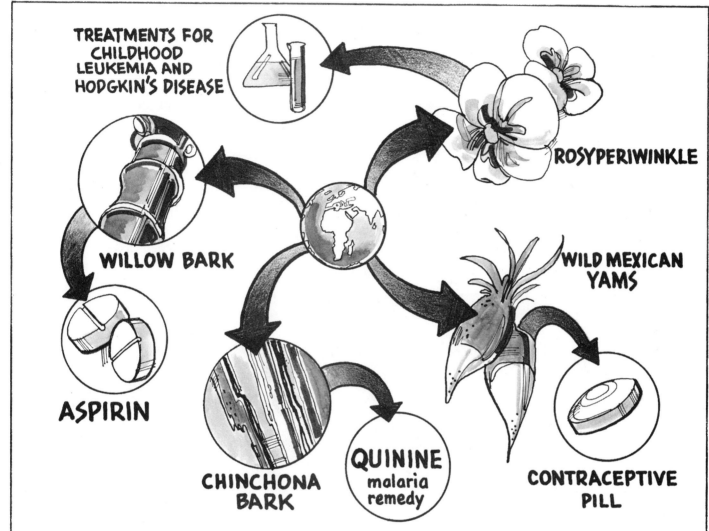

TREATMENTS FOR CHILDHOOD LEUKEMIA AND HODGKIN'S DISEASE

ROSYPERIWINKLE

WILLOW BARK

ASPIRIN

CHINCHONA BARK

QUININE malaria remedy

WILD MEXICAN YAMS

CONTRACEPTIVE PILL

Man depends on thousands of plant and animal species to provide life-sustaining food and medicine. Currently, the world's species are becoming extinct at the rate of 10,000 per year.

Much of the cause is habitat destruction: rain forests, for example, which hold 80 percent of the world's species, are being decimated rapidly, as are thousands of other habitats.

The small quilts of meadows and pastures between independently owned farms are being replaced by single-crop, pesticide-patrolled farmland.

UV-B RAYS **OZONE** **O₂** **PLANKTON** / **UV-B RAYS** **OZONE** **LESS O₂** **PLANKTON DECLINE**

While improved technology may help humans survive an increase in UV radiation that results from the thinning ozone shield, the phytoplankton that helps recycle the world's oxygen supply has no such defense.

6° RISE IN WORLD TEMPERATURES — RAIN FOREST, DESERT, PLAINS, BROADLEAF FOREST, CONIFEROUS FOREST, ALPINE MEADOWS

A sudden rise in global temperatures will affect man, but more importantly (and dangerously) it endangers the ecosystems that all life depends on.

Every individual can help reduce pollution by making small changes in his daily habits: recycling, walking, reducing electricity use, avoiding products containing toxic chemicals or that are overpackaged.

Individuals and communities can join the global and national programs that hope to reduce the global net carbon dioxide emissions by planting millions of trees.

PHOTOVOLTAIC CELLS — **WATER** — **HYDROGEN + OXYGEN** — **COMBUSTION** — **STEAM**

Alternative energy sources continue to hold hope for the future: researchers are now experimenting with using solar energy to produce hydrogen from water, for a safe, non-polluting, steam-producing fuel.

MONTREAL PROTOCOL — **CFC**

International cooperation is the key to the future. The best example of such cooperation is the treaty signed by 81 nations to end the production of ozone-depleting CFCs by A.D.. 2000. We all must cooperate in helping to protect the Earth.

ENVIRONMENTAL AND WORLD RELIEF ORGANIZATIONS

These listings should not be considered as endorsements.

AIR & WASTE MANAGEMENT ASSOCIATION
P.O. Box 2861
Pittsburgh, PA 15230
(412) 232-3444

Air & Waste Management Association is a nonprofit technical and educational organization that provides a neutral, objective ground for professionals to plan, develop, and present programs that can ultimately result in a safe environment. AWMA focuses on air pollution control, waste management, toxic air pollutants, ozone, indoor air quality, and acid rain, and promotes environmental responsibility while providing members with technical information.

AMERICAN CETACEAN SOCIETY
P.O. Box 2638
San Pedro, CA 90731
(213) 548-6279

A nonprofit volunteer organization that concentrates on the protection of marine animals, especially whales and dolphins, the American Cetacean Society is primarily an educational organization. Comprised of scientists, educators, and laypeople working to research and conserve marine life, ACS has nine offices across the nation and has both membership and volunteer programs.

AMERICAN FORESTRY ASSOCIATION
1516 P Street, NW
Washington, DC 20005
(202) 667-3300

This national citizens' organization is concerned with the management of trees and forests. Their current emphasis is on a "Global Releaf" campaign which stresses reforesting, better management and care of forests, and a halt to tropical deforestation. Membership programs are available.

AMERICAN LITTORAL SOCIETY
Sandy Hook
Highlands, NJ 07732
(201) 291-0055

ALS, a nonprofit public interest program comprised of professional and amateur naturalists, advocates the better understanding and protection of coastal environments. ALS is open to individuals, families, and those who wish the continued enjoyment of such activities as birdwatching, swimming, canoeing, and beachcombing. ALS is an active society devoting much of its energy to field experiments such as fish-tagging and dive and study trips.

AMERICAN RIVERS
801 Pennsylvania Avenue, SE, #303
Washington, DC 20003-2167
(202) 547-6900

AR is a nationwide charity whose mission is to preserve the nation's outstanding rivers and their landscapes. AR motivates Congress to add rivers to the National Wild and Scenic Rivers System and form legal protections for rivers and corridors by state and federal agencies. The American Rivers

Hydro Center is forging a new national policy that balances the need to develop some rivers and preserve others. Current emphasis is to protect 180,000 miles of free-running rivers by the twenty-first century.

AMERICAN WILDERNESS ALLIANCE

6700 East Arapahoe, Suite 114
Englewood, CO 80112
(303) 771-0380

A national, nonprofit conservation organization dedicated to the wise management of wilderness, preserves, fisheries, and recreation areas, AWA is currently involved in such issues as timber management, water laws, and the reintroduction of animals into their natural habitats. The Alliance has 5,000 members and has volunteer programs in their Colorado office.

AMERICANS FOR THE ENVIRONMENT

1400 16th Street, NW
Washington, DC 20036
(202) 797-6665

A nonprofit, nonpartisan tax-exempt organization that is working to provide a national resource for environmental education and training, AFE trains, educates, and involves the environmental community in issues and strategy and encourages activists to become involved in campaigns to elect environmentalists to office.

ARCTIC INSTITUTE OF NORTH AMERICA

University of Calgary
2500 University Drive
Calgary, Alberta
Canada T2N 1N4
(403) 220-7515

The AINA assists and cooperates in the orderly development of the Arctic region. The emphasis of the group is research in the areas of social science,

economics, and community-based curriculum development. AINA has a membership program and publishes the *Arctic Journal.*

ATLANTIC CENTER FOR THE ENVIRONMENT

39 South Main Street
Ipswich, ME 01938
(508) 356-0038

The Quebec–Labrador Foundation/Atlantic Center for the Environment (QLF) addresses the social and economic needs of rural communities within the context of building support for conservation. It is incorporated in both Canada and the United States and operates in northern New England and eastern Canada: the Atlantic Region. QLF is the principal sponsor of the Atlantic Region Stewardship Fund, a major initiative to create local capacity for resource protection and to promote sustainable development. QLF has a membership program.

CANADIAN COALITION ON ACID RAIN

112 St. Clair Avenue W., Suite 401
Toronto, Ontario
Canada M4V 2Y3
(416) 968-2135

The CCAR is a group composed of national environmental, conservation, business, and recreation groups who work to promote clean air in Canada and the United States. Their current emphasis is on the reduction in emissions of sulfur and nitrogen oxides.

CANADIAN NATURE FEDERATION

453 Sussex Drive
Ottawa, Ontario
Canada K1N 6Z4
(613) 238-6154

CNF, organized to promote the understanding, awareness, and enjoyment of nature, seeks to protect the natural environment so that ecosystems can be maintained. CNF has a membership of 20,000 and is composed of professionals and environmental groups as well as individuals.

CENTER FOR MARINE CONSERVATION
1235 DeSales Street, NW
Washington, DC 20036
(202) 429-5609

CMC is a nonprofit, nationwide organization dedicated to protecting marine wildlife and its habitats, and to conserving coastal and ocean resources. CMC has a membership of 110,000 comprised of government, private industry, and individuals working in the areas of research, public education, citizen involvement, program development, and lawmaking.

CITIZENS CLEARINGHOUSE FOR HAZARDOUS WASTE
P.O. Box 926
Arlington, VA 22216
(703) 276-7070

A community-oriented support group founded by Lois Gibbs, a former resident of Love Canal, CCHW is actively involved in dispensing information on hazardous waste and toxins and fighting polluters on the local level. Volunteer programs are available.

THE CONSERVATION FOUNDATION
1250 24th Street, NW
Washington, DC 20037
(202) 293-4800

The Conservation Foundation is a nonprofit, interdisciplinary, policy research institution which promotes the wise use of the Earth's resources. CF conducts research and educational programs that focus on land use, toxic substances, water resources, environmental dispute resolution, pollution control, and sustainable economic development in the Third World. It also reports on domestic and international environmental conditions and trends.

THE COUSTEAU SOCIETY
930 W. 21st Street
Norfolk, VA 23517
(804) 627-1144

An international, nonprofit organization dedicated to the protection and improvement of the quality of life for present and future generations. The thrust of the society is to inform the public—through film, research, lectures and publications—of man's interaction with ecosystems. The society is member supported and has over 300,000 members worldwide. Volunteer programs are available at the Norfolk office.

DEFENDERS OF WILDLIFE
1244 Nineteenth Street, NW
Washington, DC 20036
(202) 659-9510

This is a nonprofit national conservation organization dedicated to protecting wild animals in their natural communities, preserving biological diversity, and preventing endangerment. DW works through litigation, education, and advocacy to protect such species as the Florida panther, the grizzly bear, the desert tortoise, and their habitats. DW is a citizens' organization and open for membership.

EARTH ISLAND INSTITUTE
300 Broadway, Suite 28
San Francisco, CA 94133-3312
(415) 788-3666

This nonprofit organization develops projects for the conservation and restoration of the global environment, and provides organizational support for work on conservation issues. Involved in such projects as the International Marine Mammal Project and the International Rivers Network, EEI works to coordinate fundraising efforts and provide program outreach through their publication *Earth Is-*

land Journal and is a base through which projects can share resources and outreach efforts. EI has approximately 28,000 members.

ENVIRONMENTAL ACTION
1525 New Hampshire Avenue, NW
Washington, DC 20036
(202) 745-4870

An organization started by advocate Ralph Nader, EA concentrates on education, research, training, and political action in the areas of electric utilities, nuclear power, hazardous waste, and toxins. EA publishes the magazine *Environmental Action*. It is a nonmembership group.

ENVIRONMENTAL DEFENSE FUND
257 Park Avenue South
New York, NY 10010
(212) 505-2100

EDF, one of the oldest environmental action organizations, links science, economics, and the law to create economically viable solutions. EDF's key issues are: Greenhouse Effect, Ozone Depletion, Wildlife, Rain Forests, Water Pollution, Acid Rain, Toxic Chemicals, Antarctica, and Recycling. EDF membership is available at $10 for the first year.

FRIENDS OF THE EARTH
218 D Street, SE
Washington, DC 20003
(202) 544-2600

FOE is a nonprofit, global environmental advocacy group that has created a citizens' lobby to protect the planet. FOE has local chapters and an international network of 33 offices. The activist group takes steps through research and education to influence public policy and opinion to protect the future. Membership is available.

GLOBAL GREENHOUSE NETWORK
1130 17th Street, NW
Washington, DC 20036
(202) 466-2823

The Global Greenhouse Network is composed of national public interest organizations and legislators. The mission of the group is to raise awareness of and public interest in the greenhouse effect and global warming.

GREENPEACE, USA
1436 U Street, NW
Washington, DC 20009
(202) 462-1177

Greenpeace is an international environmental activist organization dedicated to protecting and preserving the natural world. It has offices in 22 nations and Antarctica. The primary focus of Greenpeace is toxic pollution, ocean ecology, nuclear issues, and energy and atmosphere issues. Those interested in becoming involved can join support memberships, a volunteer activist network, or regional volunteer programs and internships.

INFORM, INC.
381 Park Avenue South
New York, NY 10016
(212) 689-4040

INFORM is a nonprofit environmental research and education organization that identifies practical ways to protect our natural resources and public health. Their research, reports, and communications focus on four areas: hazardous waste reduction, solid waste management, urban air pollution, and land and water conservation. Their research is used by federal and state legislators, by national and local conservation groups, and by business leaders shaping environmental programs. INFORM is supported by individual and corporate donors and subscribers.

INTERNATIONAL RESEARCH EXPEDITIONS

140 University Drive
Menlo Park, CA 94025
(415) 323-4228

This nonprofit organization is involved in the research and study of marine biology, zoology, anthropology, archaeology, and botany. Composed mostly of professionals, IRE is membership supported. Volunteers join scientists in their field studies. A recent expedition took scientists and volunteers to the Peruvian rain forest to map territories, census populations, and record effects of human settlements in the area. After study, conservation projects are developed and implemented.

LAND STEWARDSHIP PROGRAM

14758 Ostlund Trail N.
Marine on St. Croix, MN 55047
(612) 433-2770

LSP is a research and educational group that promotes sustainable agricultural practices to farmers and the public. The thrust of the program is the research and development of new agricultural techniques. LSP has its own experimental farm in Minnesota.

LAND TRUST ALLIANCE

1017 Duke Street
Alexandria, VA 22314
(703) 683-7778

The Land Trust Alliance is a national organization of more than 800 land trusts. These private, nonprofit organizations work cooperatively with landowners and government agencies to buy or encourage donations of land and to permanently restrict the development on these parcels. Materials and advice on how to start a land trust or join a local or nationwide trust are available from the Land Trust Alliance.

LEAGUE OF CONSERVATION VOTERS

1150 Connecticut Avenue, NW, Suite 201
Washington, DC 20036
(202) 785-8683

This is a nonprofit organization dedicated solely to the election of pro-environment candidates to Congress. LCB supports these candidates with cash contributions, campaign staff, media events, and with volunteers. Current emphasis is on electing lawmakers who take a strong stance against polluters and are interested in reducing hazards of toxic waste sites, the threat of global warming, and garbage-strewn beaches. The League presently has 15,000 members.

MARINE EDUCATION AND RESEARCH LTD.

17 Hartington Park
Bristol, Great Britain BS6 7ES

Marine Education and Research Ltd. is dedicated to the preservation and research of whales and dolphins worldwide. The organization is comprised of professionals and members. Programs include boat-based studies which identify, monitor, photograph, and record whales, dolphins, and their activities. Those interested are encouraged to write for more information.

NATIONAL AUDUBON SOCIETY

950 Third Avenue
New York, New York 10022
(212) 832-3200

America's oldest conservation group, with 550 chapters nationwide and 580,000 members, their focus is to conserve native wildlife and its habitat; protect wildlife from pollution; further wise use of land and water; and seek solutions for global environmental problems. NAS has a network of wildlife sanctuaries and scientific research stations and a national elementary school program, and publishes several journals and magazines.

NATIONAL PARKS AND CONSERVATION ASSOCIATION

1015 31st Street, NW
Washington, DC 20007
(800) 362-3682
(202) 944-8530

NPCA has an active support organization within it called National Park Action Network. It is a watch group comprised mostly of volunteers and members who upkeep and protect parks and preserved lands. Volunteers receive monthly updates on current issues and developments in Washington and may participate in meetings on park issues.

NATIONAL TOXICS CAMPAIGN

37 Temple Place, 4th floor
Boston, MA 02111
(617) 482-1477

A nonprofit activist group concerned with education about the hazards of toxic waste, NTC has public education programs and plans campaigns to get environmentalists elected to public office. Volunteers are welcome and memberships are available.

NATIONAL WILDLIFE FEDERATION

1412 16th Street, NW
Washington, DC 20036-2266
(202) 797-6800

The largest U.S. environmental group, with more than 5.1 million members, the Federation offers effective conservation education promoting the wise use of natural resources and protection of the global environment. With affiliates in 50 states, the Federation helps litigate environmental disputes in an effort to conserve natural resources and wildlife. Its focus is on forests, energy, toxic pollution, fisheries and wildlife, wetlands, water resources, and public lands.

NATURAL RESOURCES DEFENSE COUNCIL

40 West 20th Street
New York, NY 10011
(212) 727-2700

NRDC is a nonprofit, membership organization dedicated to protecting the natural environment and improving the quality of the human environment. The staff is composed of professional lawyers, scientists, and environmental specialists. It has 4 offices within the United States and more than 130,000 members nationwide. The Council combines legal action with scientific research and citizen education in programs that concentrate on global warming, clean air, clean water, toxic substances, energy, public lands, urban environment, endangered species, coastal development, nuclear weapons, and the international environment.

NATURE CONSERVANCY

1815 N. Lynn Street
Arlington, VA 22209
1-800-628-6860

This is an international nonprofit organization committed to preserving the Earth's rare plants, animals and natural communities by protecting lands and habitats. The Nature Conservancy has offices throughout the United States, over 545,000 members, and manages the largest private system of nature sanctuaries in the world. Membership is available.

PACIFIC WHALE FOUNDATION

101 North Kihei Road, Suite 21
Kihei, Maui, HI 96753
1-800-942-5311

This nonprofit organization is dedicated to the scientific study of the ocean and its marine mammal inhabitants; the application of research findings to the preservation of the marine environment; and education and conservation programs to enhance ecological awareness. Their current emphasis is on field research of whale and dolphin populations; tropical reef studies; and the impact of marine debris. Membership and volunteer programs include Adopt-a-Whale and Ocean Outreach.

POLLUTION PROBE FOUNDATION

12 Madison Avenue
Toronto, Ontario
Canada M5R 2S1
(416) 926-1907

Pollution Probe is a nonprofit organization that works on a range of pollution issues. Their areas of emphasis include water quality, waste management, rain forest research, and the individual's role in the environment.

PUBLIC CITIZEN

Box 19404
Washington, DC 20036
(202) 293-9142

The emphasis of Public Citizen, an activist group associated with Ralph Nader, is to highlight the common concerns of environmentalists, consumer advocates, and progressives. The group does have membership and volunteer programs, and those interested are encouraged to call.

RAINFOREST ACTION NETWORK

301 Broadway, Suite A
San Francisco, CA 94133
(415) 398-4404

The Rainforest Action Network is a nonprofit organization that works nationally and internationally to protect the world's rain forests. RAN educates both the public and private sectors about the critical importance of the rain forests and how they can be preserved. Membership is available.

RAINFOREST ALLIANCE

270 Lafayette Street, Suite 5B
New York, NY 10012
(212) 941-1900

A nonprofit organization dedicated to the preservation of the rain forest, tropical animals, and human inhabitants, the Rainforest Alliance uses education and research to fund and operate projects in the numerous rain forests throughout the world. Membership and volunteer programs are available.

RENEW AMERICA

1400 16th Street, NW, Suite 710
Washington, DC 20036
(202) 232-2252

This nonprofit environmental education organization is dedicated to the development of a safe and sustainable environment. The group provides information and recommendations to local, state, and federal policy makers, the media, concerned citizens, and other environmental organizations. It develops programs to help communities identify and solve their environmental problems by offering examples of successful programs in place across the country. It is supported by a membership of individuals as well as charitable foundations.

SIERRA CLUB

730 Polk Street
San Francisco, CA 94109
(415) 776-2211

Established in 1892, the Sierra Club has influenced public policy decisions affecting the environment through a mix of legislative, administrative, legal, and electoral means. It is currently focusing on protecting the Arctic wildlife refuge, toxic waste regulations, and global warming. Volunteers are encouraged.

STUDENT CONSERVATION ASSOCIATION, INC.

P.O. Box 550
Charlestown, NH 03630
(603) 826-4301

Student Conservation Association, Inc., is a non-profit organization that provides youths with a chance to volunteer their services for the benefit of America's public lands. Volunteers engage in such activities as trail- and bridge-building, habitat restoration, endangered species research, land management projects, and researching at archaeological sites. SCA is a nationwide organization and many programs are available to high school, hearing impaired, and minority and low income students.

TRUST FOR PUBLIC LAND

116 New Montgomery, 4th Floor
San Francisco, CA 94105
(415) 495-4014

This is a nonprofit organization composed of a network of real estate, finance, and law experts dedicated to protecting land for the public's use and enjoyment. The Trust assists public agencies, landowners, and citizens' groups to protect land of recreational, historic, and scenic value. TPL has delivered half a million acres of urban, rural, and wilderness land—ranging from neighborhood garden plots to vast additions to forests and parks—from private to public use.

WATER POLLUTION CONTROL FEDERATION

601 Wythe Street
Alexandria, VA 22314
(703) 684-2400

WPCF is a nonprofit association composed of water quality specialists dedicated to enhancing and preserving water quality worldwide through education

tion and research. WPCF publishes several magazines, *Water Environment and Technology* and *Research Journal WPCF* and produces video tapes on the importance of clean water.

WILDLIFE CONSERVATION INTERNATIONAL

New York Zoological Society
Bronx, New York 10460-9973
(212) 220-5155

WCI is dedicated to saving wild animals and wild lands around the world through education, conservation, and community involvement, with the aid of their professional staff of biologists, conservationists, ecologists, economists, nutritionists, and veterinarians. WCI currently has 84 conservation projects in operation in 34 countries.

WORLD SOCIETY FOR THE PROTECTION OF ANIMALS

29 Perkins Street, P.O. Box 190
Boston, MA 02130
(617) 522-7000

WSPA is an international organization dedicated to the relief of animal suffering. Current campaigns are "Global Oceans," for the clean-up of oceans; "No Fur," the anti-fur campaign; the "Elefriends"—a campaign against the ivory trade. WSPA has education programs for children, membership and volunteer programs, and a quarterly magazine.

WORLDWATCH INSTITUTE

1776 Massachusetts Avenue, NW
Washington, DC 20036
(202) 452-1999

A nonprofit organization that takes a comprehensive look at global environmental, economic, and social issues by leading professionals in these fields. WWI publishes an annual report of its findings, *State of the World.* It does not have a member or volunteer program but those interested are encouraged to subscribe to their magazine, *World Watch.*

WORLD WILDLIFE FUND

1250 24th Street, NW
Washington, DC 20037
(202) 293-4800

World Wildlife Fund is a private organization with over 735,000 members. It is dedicated to the protection of wildlife and wildlands, particularly in Latin American, Asian, and African tropical rain forests. WWF promotes scientific research, monitors international trade, assists in conservation projects, and seeks to influence public opinion and the environmental policies of governments and private institutions.

ZERO POPULATION GROWTH

1400 16th Street, NW
Washington, DC 20036
(202) 332-2200

ZPG is a nonprofit membership organization working to achieve a balance between the Earth's population, its environment, and its resources. Their primary activity is educating the public in the areas of global warming, urbanization, and family planning through in-school programs, newsletters and publications, and action groups. Zero Population Growth has membership and volunteer programs.

PHOTO CREDITS

INDEX

Note: Names of organizations and
institutions are listed under the
heading "Organizations and institutions."

A Note on the Type

The text of this book was set in a typeface called Century Old Style. Designed by L. B. Benton for Century Magazine *in 1894, this typeface is especially readable in narrow double columns. His son, Morris Fuller Benton, is credited with the design of the display used here known as Franklyn Gothic. Both faces were recut by the Adobe Systems Corporation PostScript, a programming language used by the Macintosh computer, on which this book was designed.*

Composed by Jackson Typesetting, Inc.,
Jackson, Michigan
Printed & Bound by The Murray Printing Co.,
Westford, Massachussetts

Book Design by Eric Baker and Fearn Cutler

This book has been printed on acid-free recycled paper